CROOKED

CROOKED

*The Roaring Twenties Tale of a Corrupt
Attorney General, a Crusading Senator, and
the Birth of the American Political Scandal*

Nathan Masters

New York

Hachette Books
Hachette Book Group
1290 Avenue of the Americas
New York, NY 10104
HachetteBooks.com
Twitter.com/HachetteBooks
Instagram.com/HachetteBooks

First Edition: March 2023

Published by Hachette Books, an imprint of Perseus Books, LLC, a subsidiary of Hachette Book Group, Inc. The Hachette Books name and logo is a trademark of the Hachette Book Group.

The Hachette Speakers Bureau provides a wide range of authors for speaking events. To find out more, go to www.hachettespeakersbureau.com or call (866) 376-6591.

The publisher is not responsible for websites (or their content) that are not owned by the publisher.

Print book interior design by Jeff Williams

Library of Congress Control Number: 2022921822

ISBNs: 978-0-306-82613-9 (hardcover), 978-0-306-82615-3 (ebook)

Printed in the United States of America

LSC-C

Printing 1, 2023

To the memory of my parents,
Tom and Heidi Masters

Contents

PART III

Having been personal attorney for Warren G. Harding before he was Senator from Ohio and while he was Senator, and thereafter until his death.

And for Mrs. Harding for a period of several years, and before her husband was elected President and after his death,

And having been attorney for the Midland National Bank of Washington Court House, O., and for my brother, M. S. Daugherty,

And having been Attorney-General of the United States during the time that President Harding served as President,

And also for a time after President Harding's death under President Coolidge,

And with all of those named, as attorney, personal friend, and Attorney-General, my relations were of the most confidential character as well as professional,

I refuse to testify and answer questions put to me, because:

The answer I might give or make and the testimony I might give might tend to incriminate me.

> — *Harry M. Daugherty's handwritten statement*
> *to a federal grand jury, March 21, 1926*

A Note to Readers

This is a work of nonfiction, with no invented details or dialogue. Anything between quotation marks comes directly from historical sources, including FBI case files, Department of Justice records, newspaper reports, memoirs, archival collections, and the 3,338-page transcript of the Hearings Before the Select Committee on Investigation of the Attorney General.

CROOKED

Prologue

"I'll Get Daugherty"

O nly the president and a few trusted aides knew the attorney general's whereabouts on the morning of September 1, 1922. That he'd left the capital was public knowledge: there had been no hiding his departure the previous day as his westbound train steamed out of Washington's Union Station. His ultimate destination, however, wasn't quite clear, and in the midst of a nationwide railway strike that had crippled the economy and stoked fears of armed revolution, the attorney general's absence from the District of Columbia was conspicuous. To deter questions, the Justice Department announced that he was visiting his mother's family in Columbus, Ohio. This disinformation was credulously reported by the Washington press.

So, when Attorney General Harry Daugherty materialized in courtroom 627 of the Chicago Federal Building, striding through the side door with a thick legal document in hand, an audible tremor rattled the chamber's marble and mahogany walls. The nation's top lawyer rarely appeared in court and certainly never in district court proceedings such as these, so far from the capital. Now, here he was in a Windy City courtroom, interrupting a busy docket of Prohibition cases.

Spectators crowded to the front for a better look. While Daugherty's sixty-two years showed themselves in his thinning hair and drooping jowls, he was still in his prime. He was a large man, in both body and intellect, and his presence commanded the room. Reporters scampered for the telephones. Even Judge James H. Wilkerson seemed caught up in the moment, until he finally gaveled his courtroom back to order.

1

"The Court observes that the Attorney General of the United States is present," Wilkerson said. "Has he any business to bring to the attention of the Court?"

The attorney general did. As far as he was concerned, nothing less than the survival of the American republic had brought him on this secret mission to Chicago.

The nationwide strike by four hundred thousand railway shopmen, who were protesting two successive 12 percent cuts in pay, was now entering its third month. With only half the nation's trains running, the American economy had ground to a halt. Worse, sporadic violence was breaking out between picketers and strikebreakers, and the ongoing dispute threatened to plunge the country into all-out war between labor and capital. A revolution, Daugherty believed, was exactly the aim of the Red agitators behind the strike. Now he'd come all the way to Chicago, where the union was headquartered, to bring the full weight of the American justice system down upon the strikers. By arriving under cover of darkness and appearing in the courthouse unannounced, he'd caught his enemies off guard. Not a single lawyer for the unions was present—nor was one required for this *ex parte* proceeding.

In his hand were fifty-one typewritten pages, completed on the long train ride from Washington. With a judge's signature, these pages would become the most sweeping temporary restraining order ever imposed on American labor, enjoining the workers from peaceful picketing, newspaper interviews, meetings, soapbox speeches—essentially any words or actions promoting the strike, anywhere in the United States. The order would be enforced by special agents of the Bureau of Investigation, US marshals, and even army troops if necessary. It was probably unconstitutional. It was certainly unprecedented. But, Daugherty believed, it was necessary. President Warren G. Harding agreed and had given the maneuver his blessing.

"It is with great regret," Daugherty told the court, "that I am compelled to institute this proceeding on behalf of the government." As he presented his case, the attorney general made a great show of his reluctance, slowing upon certain words or phrases, suggesting that he wished their utterance unnecessary.

"The government of the United States," he said, "will never lift its hand against or touch a torch to the welfare of labor in its legitimate pursuit." But in his view, this strike was not a legitimate action—not when it stopped the trains from distributing the nation's agricultural output. "No labor leader," he continued, "will be permitted by the government of the United States to laugh in the frozen faces of a famishing people without prompt prosecution and proper punishment."

When he finished, all eyes turned to Judge Wilkerson. Even the face of Abraham Lincoln, painted on a frieze high above the dais, seemed to stare expectantly. Another judge might have waited to read the briefs or hear oral arguments before granting such a sweeping injunction—especially without opposing counsel present. But Daugherty had reason to be optimistic.

The fix was in.

At least, that's what critics would later charge. Only a few months before, Daugherty had plucked Wilkerson from the relative obscurity of the Illinois state prosecutor's office to replace Judge Kennesaw Mountain Landis, a titan of the federal judiciary who was resigning to become the first commissioner of major league baseball. With his reputation for absolute incorruptibility, Landis was thought by team owners to be the only man capable of cleaning up a sport still reeling from the Black Sox scandal, in which a gambling syndicate bought off eight members of the Chicago White Sox and fixed the 1919 World Series. Landis left big shoes to fill, but Daugherty assured President Harding that he'd found a suitable replacement.

At Daugherty's insistence, James H. Wilkerson was nominated for the vacant seat on the US District Court for the Northern District of Illinois. The Senate confirmed him, as it did most low-level judicial nominees, without debate. And when Wilkerson took his oath and donned the black robe of justice for the first time, Daugherty sent an emissary, Assistant Attorney General Rush Holland, to congratulate the judge on his lifetime appointment. It was a subtle reminder of a favor owed. Now, it seemed, the attorney general had traveled to Chicago in person to collect on his debt.

From the bar, Daugherty looked hopefully toward the bench. Wilkerson granted the injunction.

DAUGHERTY'S INJUNCTION HAD its intended effect. The striking workers, their voices muffled and willpower broken, returned to their jobs. Trains steamed across America once again. And yet, his shrewd legal maneuvering would incur great political costs. The American Federation of Labor pledged revenge. The House of Representatives entertained articles of impeachment against the attorney general. Even some of Daugherty's fellow cabinet members voiced outrage.

Like a political lightning storm, the injunction electrified the American Left. But amid the flashes and thunder over Washington and Chicago, Daugherty didn't notice the cyclone starting to spin under the big sky of Montana.

There, news of the injunction arrived just three days after Burton Kendall Wheeler's victory in the Democratic primary for US Senate. Wheeler was no friend to corporate interests. The forty-year-old frontier lawyer, a transplant from Massachusetts, had fearlessly battled Montana's entrenched corporations on behalf of the powerless. He'd taken on the railroads whose excessive freight rates were bankrupting the state's farmers. He'd fought the copper monopoly that exploited the state's miners. When he was campaigning for governor two years earlier, his brash, uncompromising style had sometimes gotten him in trouble. Once, he narrowly escaped a lynch mob by hiding overnight in a boxcar. His refusal to bend to pressure—even the threat of death—had won him the admiration of Montana's downtrodden. Now, running for federal office for the first time, Wheeler needed a new target for his populist ire, ideally one with a national profile. With his injunction, Harry Daugherty had stepped conveniently into Wheeler's sights.

Along a campaign trail that took him through pine mountains and windswept prairie, Wheeler raged against the attorney general in his Yankee accent, his wily blue eyes and tousled hair accentuating his anger. He savaged his Republican opponent, Rep. Carl Riddick, for supporting "Daughertyism," which he denounced as being "for the selfishness of Wall Street against the interests of the common people." He reminded Montana's working classes that he'd always been on their side. "This is your fight as well as mine," he told a packed house in the mining town of Anaconda, "and it is up to you to say at this time whether the big interests of this nation are to have another representative in the Senate, or whether you want to send me to fight for your interest there as I have fought in this state to protect the common people against the encroachments of special privilege."

BURTON WHEELER UNDERSTOOD his new adversary—and the potential depth of his villainy—better than most. As US attorney for the District of Montana from 1913 to 1918, Wheeler had always exercised restraint in summoning the judicial power of the United States. Amid the hysteria of the Great War, he refused to prosecute antiwar dissenters—a principled but unpopular stand that ultimately cost him his job. Prosecutors, he believed, should take great care in setting the machinery of justice into motion, especially when that machinery included jail cells and gallows trapdoors. Now, Wheeler was appalled that the nation's prosecutor-in-chief would mobilize the criminal justice system against the striking workers, who, after all, were only resisting a wage cut. That he would imprison anyone who dared resist was beyond appalling—it was antidemocratic.

Wheeler soon invented new ways to slash at Daugherty. After the war, Congress had tasked the attorney general with prosecuting the so-called wartime fraud cases in which defense contractors systematically overcharged Washington for weapons, aircraft, and munitions. In one notorious example, the Wright-Martin Aircraft Corporation had overcharged the War Department by $2,267,342, including $91,925 for employing detectives, $844 for dinners, and $995 for cigars—despite never delivering a single warplane to the European front. Under Daugherty, however, the Justice Department had taken little action against such politically connected companies. In a new stump speech, Wheeler scorched the attorney general for "protecting the profiteers who stabbed the soldiers in the back during the war." The veterans who packed Montana's union halls and town squares roared their approval.

As Wheeler sharpened his populist rhetoric, he had no idea how deep Daugherty's misbehavior might run. But he knew that the powers of an attorney general were truly awesome, constrained only by institutional norms and judicial independence. Now that the injunction had called the effectiveness of those checks into question, what was stopping Daugherty—if he really was as villainous as Wheeler imagined—from running the Justice Department as a personal vengeance machine? From weaponizing the department's Bureau of Investigation against his political opponents? From using his discretion to investigate and prosecute for political gain? Only Congress, channeling the righteous indignation of the people, exercising its subpoena power to compel testimony and produce documentary evidence, could expose the government's darkest secrets to sunlight.

In Washington, Daugherty was already swatting away one congress-man's feeble attempt at oversight. Rep. Oscar Keller, a prolabor Repub-lican from Minnesota, had introduced articles of impeachment against the attorney general, only to have the tables turned at the impeachment hearings, where Keller himself was made the subject of inquiry. The con-gressman suffered a nervous breakdown and fled the capital before the committee could even vote to dismiss the charges against the attorney general.

Wheeler assured voters he would do better. "Have patience and leave it to me," he promised. "I'll get Daugherty!"

Montanans liked what they heard. On November 7, 1922, they went to the polls and sent Wheeler to the Senate by a 12 percent margin. The stage was set for a showdown that would profoundly reshape the Justice Department, the Bureau of Investigation, and even the Senate—and for-ever change the way political scandal played out across America.

PART I

1

"Something Terrible Has Happened"

Most of Washington was still asleep on the morning of Memorial Day 1923 when a gunshot rang out from a sixth-floor apartment in the fashionable Wardman Park Inn.

The first law enforcement officer on the scene was none other than William J. "Billy" Burns, director of the Bureau of Investigation. Burns, who happened to live one floor down, was the nation's most famous detective, the twentieth century's Allan Pinkerton, instantly recognizable in his derby hat and bristled mustache. Before taking over the agency that would later be immortalized in three initials—FBI—he'd earned a reputation as a crafty sleuth for whom no secret was unobtainable. It wasn't a sterling reputation. It was true that he sometimes bent the rules or broke the law on a client's behalf. For the right price, his Burns International Detective Agency could fix a jury or frame the wrong man for a crime. Nevertheless, his career was marked by real triumph. As a US Secret Service agent, he tracked down the most accomplished counterfeiter in American history, a forger so good that even the Treasury thought his creations were genuine. As a private eye, he solved the infamous 1910 bombing of the Los Angeles Times building, which he proved to be an act of domestic terrorism by prounion extremists against a stoutly antiunion institution. Now, Burns took command of what was, politically speaking, an even more explosive crime scene.

Inside the bedroom of suite 600-E, Burns found the body of a man named Jess Smith, fifty, crumpled at the foot of one of two beds. In his right hand was a .32-caliber revolver. A single bullet had plowed through

Smith's right temple and lodged itself high in a doorjamb. Blood soaked Smith's purple silk pajamas, as well as the heavy carpets that must have deadened his fall. Most disturbingly, Smith's head had apparently fallen so that it was now stuffed, improbably, inside a metal wastebasket, atop the ashes of burned papers.

This was clearly a matter for the local authorities, but Burns knew better than to summon the police immediately. The situation called for discretion, for few in Washington had known as much as the man who now lay before him in a bloody heap.

IF JESS SMITH wasn't the only man to wield influence from the shadows of Prohibition-era Washington, at least he was the best connected. Smith dined regularly at the White House. He served as secretary of Warren Harding's inaugural committee. And he was most intimate friends with the attorney general of the United States—his roommate at the Wardman Park.

Daugherty was not home that fateful morning. The attorney general had been absent the past two nights and, at the moment, was still sound asleep in the Yellow Bedroom, the White House guest room named for its blond decor. Knowing that Smith couldn't sleep when they weren't sharing a room, Daugherty had dispatched his Justice Department assistant, Barney Martin, to stay in the adjacent bedroom. It was Martin who had fetched Burns after hearing a great crash in the other room.

Jesse Worley Smith and Harry Micajah Daugherty had grown up together in Washington Court House, Ohio, the county seat of rural Fayette County and a thriving business center on the road between Columbus and Cincinnati. Although Daugherty was eleven years Smith's senior, they formed a close bond. Both their fathers died when they were young, and the two boys filled the holes in their hearts with each other's company. Smith never strayed far from Daugherty's side. Townsfolk took to calling him "Jess Daugherty."

Brotherly, however, was too easy a label to affix to their relationship. Indeed, it only began to describe the intense bond. Though each man had married—Smith's marriage at age thirty-six to nineteen-year-old Roxie Stinson had lasted two short years, while Daugherty's invalid wife Lucie now rarely left her quarters at the Johns Hopkins Hospital in Baltimore—they clearly treasured each other above all else.

"THEY WERE THE most intimate friends," Stinson, Smith's ex-wife, later recalled, "and Jess adored him. He lived for him, he loved him."

"A word of praise or an expression of appreciation from the attorney general would cause Jess to 'purr' happily," an acquaintance once observed.

The affection was clearly mutual. When Smith once traveled back to Ohio without Daugherty, the attorney general sent a flurry of telegrams professing his loneliness and urging Smith's prompt return. Smith wired back, signing his cables "your little friend, Jesse."

That unusual intimacy inevitably spawned rumors of a sexual component to their relationship, and Smith only fanned the gossip with his sartorial choices. No matter what room he entered, Smith, tall and portly, with a close-cropped mustache, pink jowls, and round, owlish glasses, was always the best-dressed man. At one public appearance, he was described as a "symphony of gray and lavender," and he made a habit of matching the color of his handkerchief to his tie—which just so happened to be how gay men of the day signaled their availability to each other, safely and covertly. If Smith and Daugherty actually were lovers, no evidence survives, but those closest to them—the Hardings, for instance—always treated them as "a duo."

Whatever the exact nature of their relationship, Daugherty considered Smith indispensable, and not just because of their intimacy or because Smith carried his bags and opened his doors. What Smith lacked in intellectual refinement—his education stopped at high school, and he was a voracious reader of detective stories but little else—he made up for in jolly extroversion. He was never afraid to buttonhole a passerby on the courthouse square with a "whaddyaknow?" And despite his unfortunate habit of spraying listeners with saliva—"here comes Jess Smith," people would say, "get out your umbrella"—he excelled at making friends. As the less socially adept Daugherty grew in political stature and began venturing outside his native Ohio, Smith helped him navigate black-tie affairs, as well as the bawdier gatherings where the real political deal-making happened.

Likewise, what Smith lacked in political experience—before coming east he spent his entire career in retail as proprietor of Washington Court House's department store—he made up for in unwavering loyalty. Basking in his friend's reflected glory, Smith would never jeopardize Daugherty's career by spilling their secrets, lest he jeopardize his own sense of self-worth. He was an airtight receptacle for confidential musings, and the attorney general entrusted him with his most sensitive errands.

When in late 1919 fifty-nine-year-old Daugherty was named campaign manager for the long-shot presidential bid of Warren Harding, Smith made one of the first donations. By the time the long-shot candidate won the Republican nomination and then the White House, Smith had been admitted to Harding's inner circle. He abandoned his department store, his life's work, and relocated with Daugherty to the capital, where they took up temporary lodgings in a house at 1509 H Street owned by millionaire Ned McLean, publisher of the *Washington Post*. The president-elect considered appointing Smith commissioner of Indian Affairs or treasurer of the United States—two positions he was grossly unqualified for—but there was only one place he wanted to be. Shortly after Harry Daugherty was sworn in as the nation's fifty-first attorney general on March 5, 1921, Jess Smith followed him to the sixth floor of the Justice Department building and ensconced himself in an anteroom just outside the attorney general's private office.

Though he refused a place on the government payroll, he was a common sight inside Justice headquarters, dictating letters to department secretaries, flitting in and out of the Bureau of Investigation's offices on the third floor, and riding down the elevator with a bundle of official files under his arm. He could also be seen shuttling back and forth to the green limestone house on K Street where Daugherty's Ohio friends kept their political patronage files—a comprehensive record of who was owed what—and dispensed favors to friends of the administration.

That he enjoyed unparalleled access to the levers of power and political influence was widely known. Exactly what Jess Smith did with that access, however, remained a Washington mystery.

THAT MAY MORNING in the Wardman Park, Burns made a cursory search of the body. He removed the revolver from Smith's hand and then went through his pajama pockets. Inside one he found a last will, scribbled in pencil on Wardman Park stationery and dated two days prior. Burns then summoned the hotel manager, Elmer Dwyer. If he was to maintain control of the scene, he would need Dwyer's cooperation.

"Will you please come to Mr. Daugherty's apartment immediately?" Burns said over the phone. "Something terrible has happened."

Dwyer soon appeared outside the apartment in his dressing gown and slippers. Before the manager had a chance to press the buzzer, Burns opened the door and motioned Dwyer inside. Burns didn't need to explain anything—he simply led the manager to the crime scene.

The delicacy of the situation must not have immediately impressed itself upon Dwyer. "I'd better call Dr. Shoenfeld," he said, referring to the Wardman Park's house doctor.

"No," Burns snapped. "That can wait." Instead, Burns picked up the telephone and asked the operator for the White House. It was not yet seven in the morning, so there was some delay before the president finally came on the line.

"This is Burns of the Bureau of Investigation, Mr. President. I'm deeply sorry to bother you at such an hour, but there is dreadful news and I wanted you to be the first to hear it."

Harding demanded that Burns spit it out.

"Jesse Smith has committed suicide."

The line went silent. "That's terrible, Mr. Burns," Harding finally said. "Simply terrible."

As Dwyer listened on, the president urged secrecy until he had a chance to break the news to Daugherty personally. Harding also suggested that Lieutenant Commander Joel T. Boone, a navy physician seconded to the White House, be ordered to the scene.

And so it was that the president's personal doctor, rather than the District of Columbia coroner, made the first medical examination of Jess Smith's body. Boone immediately declared Smith dead (a self-evident conclusion) and just as quickly judged the cause to suicide (a less obvious one).

Only after Burns had searched the room and Boone had inspected the body were other investigators admitted to the crime scene. Dwyer summoned the Wardman Park's house detective (named, in an incredible coincidence, Harry J. Dougherty), who in turn alerted police at the local Tennallytown subprecinct.

When officers finally arrived, followed by Coroner J. Ramsay Nevitt, no one dared to remark that the revolver had gone missing. Burns had apparently "misplaced" it—but he was not a man to trifle with, even if he was tampering with a crime scene.

One detail could not escape notice, however. "How," Patrolman L. R. Keech asked, "could a man shoot himself and then get his head in the basket?"

The officer's question was never answered. Lording over the crime scene, the director of the Bureau of Investigation discouraged a thorough search of the forensic evidence. Instead, Burns offered up a compelling narrative of suicide for the DC authorities. He and Smith had been socially acquainted, and Smith, he reported, had suffered from chronic diabetes. Boone, who had treated Smith himself on occasion and knew that a wound from his recent appendectomy had never quite healed, backed up Burns's conclusion, ascribing the act to "brooding over his physical condition." Coroner Nevitt knelt down next to the body, noted the powder burns around the entry wound, and dutifully signed a certificate of suicide.

Later, all these details and unanswered questions would arouse much suspicion within Washington. Lawmakers would wonder aloud why the coroner failed to order an autopsy. Journalists would ask how Daugherty, who as a cabinet officer earned $12,000 a year, and Smith, who drew no government salary, could afford their lavish lifestyle at the Wardman Park, with annual household expenses exceeding $50,000. They would question how Smith, a man deathly afraid of firearms, could have ever handled a revolver, let alone held it to his right temple and pulled the trigger. And they would puzzle over how the federal government's top investigator, America's most famous detective, could somehow misplace the key to the crime scene—the suicide weapon.

Washington would soon discover that these questions, intriguing as they were, only scratched the surface.

2

"What a Bolshevist Really Looked Like"

E ven in the middle of the Atlantic Ocean, Burton Wheeler could not miss the news of Jess Smith's suspicious death.

Received as clipped prose by the SS *President Harding*'s Marconi operator, puffed into a proper story by the ship's editor, and set to type in the onboard printshop, it would have appeared in the *Oceanic Edition*, an eight-page daily tabloid recently debuted by United States Lines in partnership with the *Chicago Daily Tribune* and *New York Daily News*. And when Wheeler unfolded his copy and saw the article—"Daugherty's Chum Dies By Own Hand, Motive Not Known" was a typical headline— he would have become all the more impatient to assume his duties as the newest member of the US Senate.

After a resounding victory the previous November, Wheeler was hot to fulfill his fiery campaign promises. "Itching to try out my toga," he later recalled, "I departed Butte for Washington on March 1, 1923, with high hopes for legislative action." He arrived just in time to see the outgoing Senate gavel itself adjourned—and then learn that the newly elected Sixty-eighth Congress wasn't convening any time soon. Naively, he'd expected President Harding to call a special session of Congress to tackle the urgent issues facing the nation, from a deep agricultural depression to the ongoing conflict between railroads and their workers. Wheeler had a lot to learn. These were times he would come to deride as the "Warren G. Harding era of complacency," and the newly constituted Senate wouldn't gavel itself into session until its constitutionally prescribed deadline—the first Monday in December, more than a full year after his election. In the meantime, there would be little to do beyond watching the workers etch his name onto his fourth-floor door in the Senate Office Building, the Beaux Arts annex that had opened in 1909 across the street from the Capitol. No floor speeches, no committee meetings. No chance to "get Daugherty."

For a man constitutionally incapable of sitting still, the thirteen-month wait was impossible. And so Wheeler combatted his restlessness by booking transatlantic passage on the SS *President Roosevelt*. If he was powerless to investigate all that was rotten in the US government until December, then at least he could investigate conditions in the Old World while he waited.

"We're going to Europe," he informed his wife in a telegram, ordering her to proceed immediately from Montana to New York City. Lulu Wheeler, who had long since made peace with her husband's impulses, left their five children with a neighbor and caught the first train out of Butte. After a brief stay at the Waldorf Astoria and an afternoon of shopping on Fifth Avenue, the Wheelers steamed across the Atlantic toward a land many well-read Americans knew only through the works of Henry James.

Alas, the Europe of *The Portrait of a Lady* had been badly disfigured. The Great War had created more problems than it had solved, and the Continent was a cauldron of simmering resentments threatening to boil over into revolution. In Italy, the Wheelers were shocked by legions of black-shirted fascists. In Austria, they saw once-respectable women "driven into the streets to sell their virtue." Nothing disturbed them more, however, than the situation in Soviet Russia, where revolution actually had broken out.

"I have been called a Bolshevist so many times," Wheeler would quip, "that I really had a curiosity to see what a Bolshevist really looked like." Indeed, Montana's farmers were making noises about forming collectives, and Wheeler was eager to see that experiment in action. The reality he found in Russia gutted him. In the countryside, the newly collectivized farms had cut their output in half. In the cities, starving men and women formed long bread lines. The growing famine anguished Wheeler, but he was nearly as troubled by the prevailing atmosphere of illiberalism. The press was censored. Ordinary people were afraid to speak their minds. When Wheeler complained to the Soviet foreign minister about the restrictions on free expression, he was informed, matter-of-factly, that the Russian people would need another fifty years of "re-education" before they would "accept the communist way of life without question."

The threat of counterrevolution, it seemed, hung always on the horizon, and in response, the Bolshevik authorities had mobilized the Cheka, a secret police force with sweeping surveillance powers. Even Orthodox priests were being dragged into the Lubyanka and then executed merely for using the word *counterrevolution* in private correspondence.

At one point, the Wheelers themselves confronted this harrowing manifestation of state power when they were arrested for boarding a train without their passports. After questioning the senator and his wife at length, the Chekists went through a roll of film from Lulu Wheeler's camera. One of the photos turned out to be of an old fort—technically a military asset—which raised the specter of espionage charges. Finally, someone in charge realized the folly of antagonizing a visiting US senator, a guest of the Soviet state, and had the Wheelers released with an official apology.

The senator ultimately laughed off the incident. Nevertheless, for someone who had never left American shores, it was a sobering introduction to the realities of life in a police state.

THE BOLSHEVIKS' REVOLUTION might have gone off the rails, but Wheeler had no beef with their fundamental complaint—that the world was rigged in favor of money. It was a lesson he'd learned the hard way, navigating the contours of power in the Treasure State.

Montana was an unimaginable destiny for Burton Kendall Wheeler when he was born on February 27, 1882, in the small town of Hudson, Massachusetts. The tenth and youngest child of a shoemaker from a long line of Quakers who had called New England home since the 1630s, young Burt seemed all but preordained to live out his life in the Bay State. It wasn't to be. Even as a child, he dreamed of living in the "wild west." Upon graduating from Hudson High School, Wheeler departed for the University of Michigan law school. In 1905, as a newly minted LL.B., he moved west again, crisscrossing the Great Plains and Rocky Mountains in search of employment "anywhere," he wrote, "that was wide open with opportunity." Eventually, he landed in Butte, Montana, where, stranded after losing his shirt to a couple of card sharps in a game of poker, he settled down and launched his legal career.

Ann Arbor might have been where he'd studied torts, contracts, and civil procedure, but it was in the "rough, tough, and dirty" town of Butte where Wheeler learned how the law really worked. In his first criminal trial, a train robbery case, a judge conspired with the Northern Pacific Railway to send the innocent man he represented to prison. Another early client was railroaded by two police detectives, who lied on the witness stand to secure a conviction. In case after case, Wheeler discovered a web of manipulation emanating from the state's powerful business interests. A string was pulled in a wood-paneled boardroom, and in a distant courthouse, some poor soul lost his chance at justice. Wheeler became especially disgusted with the copper barons of the Anaconda Mining Company, who kept in their pocket the state's Republican Party and Democratic Party, all but three daily newspapers, most legislators, many judges and prosecutors, several county sheriffs, and, usually, the governor. It didn't matter what the statutes of Montana said, or even the Constitution of the United States. When public officials were in the pocket of powerful interests, the odds would always be stacked against the little guy.

And yet, when Wheeler had the good fortune to avoid corrupt courtrooms, his experience validated the most romantic notions of the law. His early legal practice came to specialize in personal injury suits against employers, and his cases often pitted him directly against Montana's entrenched interests. Representing the victim of one horrific industrial accident after another, Wheeler took on the corporations—and won. The statutes and case law governing employee accident claims weren't perfect (far from it), but they at least promised David a fair shot against Goliath. Where else but a courtroom would a soot-stained miner and the mighty Anaconda Company be treated as equals?

At its worst, the law could be a mere instrument of the powerful, which was certainly how men like Harry Daugherty saw things. But at its best, Wheeler believed, the law guaranteed civil liberties and cut down the privileges of class, race, and sex. After several years of private practice, Wheeler heard a higher calling. He rededicated his career to public service and in 1910 set out to remake the law into the servant of justice rather than power.

His one term in the state legislature as a Democrat accomplished little, and he soon found out, to his horror, that his election as a "reformer" had actually been engineered by the all-powerful Anaconda as a sop to disgruntled miners. But his appointment in 1913 as US attorney for the District of Montana at age thirty-one gave him a real chance to clean up the system. As chief federal law officer in the state, Wheeler prosecuted crooked business schemes. He put an end to dishonest investigative practices and confronted the widespread practice of jury tampering. And when nationalist hysteria overtook Montana during the world war and the mining company tried to harness those passions for its own political ends, he stood firm against popular sentiment, refusing to prosecute labor organizers and other so-called subversives for sedition.

Wheeler's principled public service earned him the admiration of Montana's downtrodden and exploited—but also the everlasting enmity of the Anaconda Company. Crusaders for public integrity, Wheeler soon learned, pursued justice at their own peril. When in 1920 he had the audacity to run for governor, the Anaconda tried to strangle his campaign. Across the state, company operatives whipped up angry mobs to intimidate Wheeler and shut down his events. At one scheduled appearance, he was nearly tarred and feathered. At another, he was driven away and forced to deliver a speech from atop a haystack. His most famous brush with mob violence came in the mining camp of Dillon, where a crowd of twelve or so paid agitators rushed his improvised stage—the bed of a Ford pickup—to cries of "get a rope!" Wheeler fled town, pursued by his attackers, and barricaded himself inside a boxcar. A local ranch hand sympathetic to his plight grabbed a shotgun and stood sentry outside the sliding door throughout the night. "I'll shoot anyone full of lead who opens that door!" he cried. By the time Wheeler emerged the next morning, unscathed, he'd earned a colorful epithet that would stick with him his entire life, a reminder that, in pursuing justice, he also courted danger. Burton Wheeler had become Boxcar Burt.

TIME PASSED SLOWLY aboard the SS *President Harding* as it cut across the gray Atlantic, taking the Wheelers home. At dinner, they were honored guests at Captain Paul Grenning's table. There they regaled their fellow passengers with tales of revolutionary Russia, as the ship's "milk steward"—a stray black cat adopted by the crew and advertised as one of the ocean liner's attractions—listened attentively. Sure, there were daily pogo stick races on the top deck and other activities designed to while away the time, but passage aboard the *Harding*, steaming toward the ordinariness of America with the spectacle of Europe in its wake, could be tedious.

News of Jess Smith's suicide came as a welcome if morbid diversion, especially for a man who had lobbed so many rhetorical fusillades at the dead man's bosom buddy. Already the papers were questioning why this "mystery man" had taken his own life. "His purpose and activities in Washington," the *New York Daily News* reported, "were always something of a mystery since the Harding Administration came into power, and this gave rise to much speculation regarding the cause of his suicide."

In an interesting coincidence, prominent suicides bookended Wheeler's trip to Europe. Five days before the senator set sail from New York, Charles F. Cramer had shot himself in the second-story bathroom of his Wyoming Avenue residence—a house that once belonged to President Harding. Cramer had recently resigned as general counsel of the Veterans' Bureau, where financial irregularities had lately forced the ouster of its director, too. On his dressing room table, Cramer left a news clipping about a pending congressional investigation and a handwritten letter to Warren G. Harding, which the president refused to open. Harding was still widely popular among Americans, but cracks in his administration's public image were starting to show. Many believed that Cramer, with his desperate final act, had avoided the shame of an unfolding scandal.

Smith's death now augured a similar reckoning within the Department of Justice, an organization with far more potential for mischief than the Veterans' Bureau. Founded in 1870 to more effectively enforce Reconstruction-era civil rights laws, the Justice Department consolidated federal law enforcement power, originally invested in US district attorneys across the country, into a single bureaucracy headed by the attorney general of the United States.

That office was as old as the republic itself, founded in 1789, but it originally wielded limited powers. Early attorneys general advised the president on legal matters, represented the United States before the US Supreme Court, and did little else. Since 1870, however, with an army of prosecutors, investigators, and US marshals at its command, and with solemn responsibilities in the areas of law enforcement and national security, the attorney generalship had become one of the cabinet's most important and most coveted offices. Given the great powers they wielded, it was a small miracle that attorneys general so rarely engaged in official mischief.

One notable exception was George H. Williams, the third attorney general to serve in the scandal-plagued Grant administration. Rumors

of impropriety began to dog Williams soon after President Grant nominated him for chief justice in 1873, when the Senate Judiciary Committee
learned that the attorney general and his socially ambitious wife, Kate,
were dipping into Department of Justice funds to maintain a lavish lifestyle. The most egregious example was the elegant carriage that whisked
Mrs. Williams through the capital, complete with a coachman and liveried
footman—all of it charged to a government account. Remarkably, while
that revelation sunk Williams's nomination to lead the high court, it was
not enough to force his resignation. He remained attorney general for
two more years, until 1875, when the Senate Judiciary Committee learned
that his wife had solicited and received a $30,000 bribe from a New York
merchant under criminal investigation, after which the Justice Department
had dropped its case. A senator on the committee quietly informed the
president, who demanded his attorney general's resignation at once. Not
even that was the end of it. In a desperate attempt to keep her husband
in office—and her financial lifeline intact—Kate Williams penned anonymous letters to President Grant, First Lady Julia Grant, and members
of the cabinet, threatening to explode secrets about the administration's
misuse of Secret Service funds. Ultimately, the blackmail failed. The Wil-
liamses left Washington quietly, and no charges were ever filed or even
publicly aired.

A half century later, Williams's malfeasance had proved to be an
aberration, even as his ambitious successors expanded the Justice Department's powers. Under Richard Olney, Grover Cleveland's attorney
general, the department first intervened in the struggle between capital
and labor, siding with the nation's railroads in the 1894 Pullman strike.
Under Charles Bonaparte, attorney general under Theodore Roosevelt, the
department laid siege to America's corporate monopolies. Under Thomas
Watt Gregory, wartime attorney general to President Wilson, it began po-
licing espionage and sedition. By 1923, the work of the Justice Department reached far beyond its original domain. It operated federal prisons,
enforced antitrust laws, prosecuted Prohibition violations, recommended
pardons and other acts of presidential clemency, and oversaw the eighty
US attorneys who represented the federal government in district courts
across the country.

Most ominously, it operated a growing secret police force: the Bureau
of Investigation. Created by executive action in 1908, the Justice Department's in-house detective agency had never been authorized by Congress,

and in recent years it seemed to have strayed from its original mission of gathering evidence for federal prosecutors. During the postwar Red Scare of 1919, Attorney General A. Mitchell Palmer mobilized the Bureau for sweeping raids that resulted in the deportation of at least five hundred suspected radicals and the arrest of another three thousand. Even after public cries of overreach put an end to the raids, the Bureau's undercover operatives continued to infiltrate labor unions, left-wing political parties, and even groups like the American Civil Liberties Union, snooping for any hint of disloyalty against the United States. Most recently, under the Bureau's shifty new director, William Burns, and his ambitious young deputy, John Edgar Hoover, there were discouraging reports that its special agents were spying on anyone who dared to criticize the Harding administration publicly, even members of Congress.

The Bureau was a ruthlessly effective intelligence-gathering operation, something Wheeler knew from personal experience. As US attorney in Montana, he had dispatched its detectives across sagebrush plains and into mountain camps in search of evidence in criminal cases pending before his office. Few secrets were safe from their prying eyes.

As Wheeler steamed across the Atlantic, memories of the Cheka fresh in his mind, a troubling thought would have been unavoidable. Under an unethical attorney general, the awesome power of the Justice Department could become something quite monstrous.

3

"Very Bad News"

Harry Daugherty was just finishing breakfast when President Harding barged into the White House's Yellow Bedroom. With him was Commander Boone, the navy physician who had come straight from the grisly scene at the Wardman Park.

"Harry, Boone has some news for you and it's very bad news, so get hold of yourself."

The attorney general was still in his pajamas. He looked at the handsome young doctor, who had risen well above his official station as medical officer aboard the presidential yacht to become a trusted member of Harding's entourage.

"General," Boone said quietly. He summoned all the calm he could muster. "Jess Smith has shot himself."

Daugherty's face went white. He said nothing, just stared, first at Boone and then at Harding, his eyes begging them to retract the report. A terrible silence filled the room. After some time, he dropped his head into his hands. Daugherty remained still, holding his head over his empty breakfast tray for so long that Boone felt compelled to check his pulse. The attorney general was still recovering from a stroke that, earlier that year, had put him out of commission for six weeks.

Eventually, Daugherty raised his head. "Why did he do it?" he cried. "My God, why did he do it? Why did he do it?"

The attorney general exchanged looks with his president. Despite Daugherty's anguished queries, both men knew exactly why Jess Smith had killed himself and who was responsible.

FOR HARRY DAUGHERTY, the presidency of Warren G. Harding was
a project more than twenty years in the making. It all began in 1899 with
a chance encounter at a shoeshine stand in Richmond, Ohio, where both
men happened to be in town for a Republican rally. Harding, already
in the bootblack's chair, was then the editor of the small-town *Marion
Star* and a candidate for the Ohio state senate. Daugherty, next in line
for a shine, was a lawyer and lobbyist seeking his party's nomination for
governor.

As he watched Harding interact with the bootblack, Daugherty sensed
the presence of a born politician. Harding's deep-set eyes and aquiline
nose gave the impression of a face chiseled, not grown, like the bust of a
Roman emperor. His bearing, however, was more democratic than impe-
rial, a fact underscored for Daugherty by the genuine courtesy Harding
showed the Black man attending to his feet. In fact, everything Daugherty
saw and heard—Harding's broad shoulders, his resonant voice, his generous good nature—convinced him that the man was destined for greatness.

"Gee," Daugherty thought to himself, "what a great-looking president
he'd make!"

Harding must have noticed the attention, and he promptly offered a
plug of tobacco to his new admirer. Daugherty took a bite and returned it
to Harding, who bit off his own chew. Upon that simple gesture of friendship, the two men built a formidable political marriage.

Even if Daugherty (who lost his bid that year for governor) never con-
ceded that his own electoral ambitions were unrealistic, early on he realized
that Harding (who won his state senate race) would be a more effective
avatar for his ambitions. Harding was younger, more eloquent, and more
handsome than Daugherty, whose fleshy jowls and mismatched eyes—
one brown and the other blue, a condition known as heterochromia—
could be unsettling at close quarters. Harding, moreover, offered voters
a clean reputation, whereas Daugherty would forever remain damaged
goods. During his one stint in elective office, as a state legislator in the
early 1890s, Daugherty had been accused of switching his vote in an important matter for "seven crisp $500 bills." The accusation was probably
false, but voters never forgot the image of those freshly printed banknotes
changing hands.

And so Daugherty wisely slipped behind the curtain. Eventually, he replaced Mark Hanna—the kingmaker who had guided his fellow Ohioan,
William McKinley, to the White House—as Ohio's unofficial Republican

political boss. All the while, with dreams of playing kingmaker himself, Daugherty kept a firm grip on the elbow of his protégé, who became lieutenant governor in 1903 and in 1910 captured his party's nomination for governor. Pitted against a popular incumbent, Harding lost that race, in which Daugherty served as his campaign manager. But by the time the candidate returned to his comfortable job as owner and editor of the *Marion Star*, Warren G. Harding was a household name across the state. Four years later, one of Ohio's US senators announced his retirement. It took some persuasion—"I found him sunning himself like a turtle on a log and pushed him off into the water," Daugherty recalled—but he eventually convinced Harding to run. This time, running for an open seat against an Irish American Democrat during an era of widespread anti-Catholic sentiment, Harding won handily.

As a senator and especially as an Ohioan, Daugherty's apprentice was now well positioned for an eventual White House bid. Six of the eight Republican presidents since the Civil War hailed from the Buckeye State, the so-called Mother of Presidents. Nevertheless, no one expected the inexperienced Harding, after only a few years in the Senate, to snatch his party's presidential nomination in 1920—no one but Harry Daugherty.

The death of one early frontrunner (former president Theodore Roosevelt) and the withdrawal of another (former Supreme Court justice Charles Evans Hughes) cracked the race wide open. Daugherty, who signed on once again as Harding's campaign manager, sensed that the Republican National Convention in Chicago would seize up in a series of inconclusive ballots. As political bosses brokered deals, candidates would drop out and delegates would switch votes. Working behind the scenes, Daugherty prepared for such a scenario. He cajoled, pressured, and persuaded hundreds of delegates into pledging themselves to Harding—not as their first choice but as their second. Several months before the convention, Daugherty revealed his strategy to the *New York Tribune*:

> I don't expect Senator Harding to be nominated on the first, second, or third ballots, but I think we can afford to take chances that, about eleven minutes after two, Friday morning of the convention, when ten or twenty weary men are sitting around a table, someone will say, "Who will we nominate?" At that decisive time the friends of Harding will suggest him and can well afford to abide by the result.

It was a bold prophesy, easily dismissed as wishful thinking. And when the delegates finally did gather and cast their inconclusive first ballot on July 16, Harding came in a distant fifth, winning only his home state of Ohio.

But just as Daugherty predicted, votes shifted ballot by ballot. Early leads eroded. By the seventh round, Harding had risen to fourth place, and then, after six hours of bickering in a backroom hazy with cigar smoke— the hotel suite of party chairman Will Hays—party bosses settled on the dark horse from Ohio as their nominee.

Just as Daugherty had foreseen, Harding's winning qualities shone through at this pivotal moment. A born campaigner with a magnetic personality and a mellifluous voice, he personified the values of small-town America in an age when Americans were moving in droves from the countryside to the village. His geniality was sincere, his tastes simple, his patriotism earnest. Moreover, while intraparty squabbles had soured friendships and fractured alliances, Harding's campaign trail mantra of "make no enemies" had kept him well above the fray, unsullied and acceptable to virtually everyone. His moderate conservatism even struck a credible compromise between the Republicans' progressive and hard-line factions. Finally, there were Ohio's twenty-four electoral votes; rumor had it that Democrats would nominate the state's governor, newspaper publisher James Cox, and Republicans hoped that by countering with one of its senators they would keep the perennial bellwether state (which had correctly predicted eleven of the past thirteen elections) in their column.

In hindsight, he appeared the natural choice—a fact that no one other than Harding's campaign manager had been able to grasp. Thus vindicated, Harry Daugherty became a legend of American politics overnight. Awe-struck newspaper reporters reprinted (and embellished) his months-old prediction about a backroom deal, coining a new cliché—the "smoke-filled room."

And yet the newly famous political operative had little time to revel in his triumph. During a well-earned vacation in Florida, Daugherty learned that one of Harding's former mistresses was blackmailing the nominee, and as leverage she possessed sexually explicit letters written in the senator's own hand. That much would not have shocked Daugherty, who knew Harding to be a relentless flirt and serial adulterer. But as Daugherty rushed back to manage the crisis, he learned just how sloppy Harding had been. At least three other women also possessed incriminating letters.

Another, a twenty-three-year-old who had fallen in love with Harding after seeing his face on a senatorial campaign poster as a teenager, was rais-
ing their love child.

If anyone could clean up this mess, it was Daugherty and his most
trusted lieutenant, Jess Smith. A web of strings ran from their den to offices of influence across the country, and now they played those strings like
a musical instrument. Daugherty's boyhood friend Billy Burns, hopeful for
a federal appointment in a Harding administration, offered the sleuths of
his detective agency, while fellow Ohioan Ned McLean (owner of the *Cincinnati Enquirer*, the *Washington Post*, and, for good measure, the Hope
Diamond) diverted some of his fabulous wealth into a blackmail fund.
Through burglary, intimidation, and outright coercion, this troubleshoot-
ing squad secured the women's silence. Public records that would corroborate the women's stories, like a 1918 District of Columbia police report
about a domestic violence call, went missing. So did love letters and other
private documents. When all else failed, Harding's lovers were paid hush
money. One was even sent (with her husband) on an all-expenses-paid
tour of China, her return trip scheduled for well after Election Day.

Daugherty's black magic ensured that voters weren't distracted from
Harding's winning message—that after eight years of crusading Wilsonian
progressivism, a two-year influenza pandemic that killed 675,000 Americans, a world war that upended daily life for most citizens, and widespread labor strife, what the country needed was "not heroics but healing;
not nostrums but normalcy; not revolution but restoration." Harding and
his running mate, Massachusetts governor Calvin Coolidge, pledged to
roll back some of the most significant reforms of the Roosevelt, Taft, and
Wilson administrations. In domestic affairs, they would pare down the recently enacted federal income tax (and its top marginal rate of 73 percent)
and partner with big business through regulatory agencies rather than
persecute it. On the global front, they would promote a slogan of "America first" and refuse entry into President Wilson's League of Nations. It
was exactly what American voters clamoring for a return to "normalcy"
wanted.

Democrats, meanwhile, saddled with defending Wilson's legacy, struggled to offer a viable alternative. With their party deeply divided—between
southern conservatives and northeastern liberals, western grain farmers
and southern cotton growers, anti-Prohibition wets and pro-Prohibition
dries—they nominated Gov. Cox of Ohio as anticipated, a dull, cautious

compromise choice. If Cox and his more charismatic running mate, Assistant Secretary of the Navy Franklin D. Roosevelt, ever had reasons to hope, they were dashed when a deep recession, blamed on the incumbent Democrats, swept across the US economy over the latter months of 1920.

The die was cast. On November 2, Harding cruised to victory, winning more than 60 percent of the popular vote and 404 electoral votes.

After this resounding triumph, Harding naturally retained the consigliere who had made it all possible. The president-elect duly offered Harry Daugherty the cabinet position of his choice. And there really was only one home for his talents, one office that would amplify his genius for weaponizing information and twisting arms.

Upon moving into the attorney general's sixth-floor suite at Justice Department headquarters, one of his first tasks—after planting Jess Smith in an adjoining office—was to install a dedicated telephone line that connected his desk with the Oval Office. It rang throughout the day.

THREE YEARS LATER, the heady optimism of those days had given way to something darker. June 2, 1923, was a good day for the cut-flower business of Fayette County, Ohio. Floral tributes from well-wishers near and far—high officials of Ohio's Benevolent and Protective Order of Elks, as well as senior functionaries of the Department of Justice—formed a multicolored mound next to the Smith family plot at the Washington Cemetery. Of these, two arrangements attracted the most notice. Standing graveside was a memorial wreath sent by the president of the United States, and draped over the casket of Jess Smith was a massive floral blanket from Attorney General Daugherty.

Neither man was present. Few questioned Harding's absence. He was the nation's chief executive, after all, and with First Lady Florence Harding in ill health, few expected him to make the trip to Ohio.

Daugherty's nonattendance, however, raised eyebrows. June 2 was an official day of mourning in Washington Court House, whose mayor ordered all businesses to shut their doors for one hour, and the attorney general—a native son of the city—was expected to lead the mourning. Instead, Daugherty remained forty miles away in Columbus, sending along the text of his eulogy. As a local judge recited the attorney general's tribute, the crowd of mourners could not avoid the question: How could Daugherty miss the funeral of his dearest friend?

In fact, he had traveled from Washington, DC, to attend, but on the day of the funeral found that he simply could not leave his house. The newspapers would report a "relapse in his physical condition" brought about by Smith's death, a reference to the stroke he'd suffered earlier that year. But what was the ultimate cause of this sudden decline, some wondered—grief or guilt?

AFTER THE BURIAL, two of Smith's pallbearers met for a secret conference. All the way from Washington, Assistant Attorney General Rush Holland had carefully guarded a sealed package containing some personal property of Jess Smith's, and he was eager to deliver it into the care of Mally S. Daugherty, Harry's younger brother and executor of Smith's last will and testament.

In the days to come, Mal Daugherty would wind down Smith's considerable estate, including an antique teakwood desk, a Cole sedan automobile, and more than $200,000 in cash. All these assets were carefully accounted for in Smith's will, along with his most prized possession: a box of diamonds acquired through mysterious means. According to the terms of his will, one jewel each would go to Harry Daugherty, Mal Daugherty, *Washington Post* publisher Ned McLean, and John T. King, a Washington power broker.

Thorough though it was, the will did not account for the parcel Holland brought with him from the capital. And yet its disposition was more urgent than any sparkling gemstone.

The day before his death, Jess Smith had gone into his Justice Department office and stuffed his briefcase full of official documents. Back at the Wardman Park, he gathered those papers, along with his financial accounts, his private correspondence, and some of the attorney general's private documents, and made a small bonfire in the metal wastebasket next to his bed. It was one final, selfless act of devotion to his idol—but he hadn't quite finished the job.

Holland now handed over the sealed package, which contained a sheaf of papers that had somehow escaped the flames. Mal Daugherty needed only one peek inside before burning its contents on the spot.

4

"Rumors of Irregularities"

For as long as Warren G. Harding occupied the White House, Harry Daugherty was secure in his position as attorney general. At least, that was the conventional wisdom. But as the two men discussed long-delayed Justice Department business in the Oval Office on the afternoon of June 19, 1923, a few weeks after Smith's funeral, there were hints of a growing rift between old friends.

Harding was scheduled to depart Washington in the morning for a 15,000-mile journey that would take him—along with the First Lady and a party of sixty-seven cabinet officers and aides, doctors and nurses, Secret Service operatives and journalists—across the full breadth of North America, up the coast of British Columbia, and into the vast untamed wilderness of the Alaska Territory. The trip was intended as a prelude to the president's 1924 reelection campaign, enabling Harding to bypass the biased journalists and self-interested politicians and speak directly to the American people. The president dubbed it his "Voyage of Understanding."

Between the trip's start on June 20 and its premature end on August 2, untold thousands would gather to hear Harding, then at the height of his presidential popularity, lay out his plans for battling joblessness and make the case for joining the World Court, an international tribunal set up in the Great War's aftermath to adjudicate disputes between nations. They would listen to him tout his first-term accomplishments, which included hosting the world's first disarmament conference and balancing the federal budget. One of his speeches would make history by being transmitted to both coasts by the new technology of radio broadcasting—the first time a president had addressed the entire nation with one breath.

Harry Daugherty would miss it all. When in early June the White House announced the president's traveling party, Washington was surprised to learn that Commerce Secretary Herbert Hoover, Interior Secretary Hubert Work, and Agriculture Secretary Henry Wallace (father of the future vice president) were all included, but not the attorney general. According to the official story, Daugherty's health was simply too fragile for such a marathon trip, and he would remain behind to recuperate.

Daugherty was indeed ailing—that much was true. Sixty-three, overweight, and plagued with chronic hypertension, he was still reeling from the mild stroke in January that had confined him to his apartment for several weeks. (At the time, the American people were told their attorney general had a "heavy cold.") Handing his day-to-day Justice Department duties over to an acting attorney general, he'd taken an extended vacation in Florida, where a doting Jess Smith nursed him back to health. By May he had regained most of his strength—only to suffer a crippling relapse upon Smith's sudden death. These days, he could barely make it out of his Wardman Park apartment. If a trip to his office on Vermont Avenue taxed his strength, Alaska might kill him.

Health, however, wasn't the only reason Daugherty was staying behind. The attorney general had been drifting out of Harding's inner circle for months. No longer was he the administration's shot caller, its patronage chief and mastermind of the president's reelection efforts. Postmaster General Harry New, a close friend of the president's from his days in the Senate, had succeeded Daugherty in those roles. On a personal level, genuine friendship still prevailed between the two men, who continued to swap bawdy jokes on the golf course and pass highballs across the poker table. But now, as their Oval Office meeting stretched into the evening, consumed by deliberations over railway mergers and presidential pardons, the president's face betrayed some unspoken trouble, as if distrust had wedged itself between them.

Anxiety washed over Daugherty. Had another dark secret bubbled up? As the administration's figurehead, its delegator-in-chief, the president smiled for the crowds and charmed the donors, but he trusted his subordinates to carry out the actual business of government. Trusted them too much, in fact. Not too long ago, some irregularities within the Justice Department had come to Harding's attention, a development that strained the professional relationship between the two men. There was always a chance that another disturbing rumor had found the president's ear.

Or perhaps, Daugherty thought hopefully, that look was a simple expression of weariness. Had the president's aides overdone it with the Alaska trip? Daugherty asked to see the itinerary and, after looking it over, commented that the nonstop schedule would have been too demanding even for a man half Harding's age. He suggested lightening the load.

That weary look remained on the president's face. Usually, Harding's private demeanor matched his public image—affable to a fault, intent on making those around him happy, eager to do a favor for a friend. In this moment, he was not his usual self. Daugherty fretted.

Harding must have noticed his friend's unease. "Now," he said, trying to lighten the mood, "I want to get some law business out of you for nothing."

Daugherty laughed. "Well, that's what you've been doing all day. What is it? Fire away."

Harding was selling his ownership stake in the *Marion Star*, the small-town newspaper that had launched his political career. He'd found two Ohio publishers who were willing to pay a half million for it, and he needed Daugherty to write the contract. Though it was highly irregular for an attorney general to act as a president's personal lawyer, the relationship between these two men was anything but typical. Even now, with their bond strained, there remained a loyalty stronger than any legal or ethical fetters. The attorney general agreed to represent Harding in the transaction.

With that matter settled, the president had one more request. It was an ominous one.

"I want you to draw a new will for me."

AT FOUR MINUTES past ten on the morning of June 29, just nine days into the "Voyage of Understanding," the presidential train steamed into the copper mining settlement of Butte, Montana, home to "the richest hill on earth." As the train backed into the depot of the Great Northern Railway, President Harding and First Lady Florence Harding appeared on the observation platform at the rear of their parlor car. A cheer went up from the assembled throng. Many waved miniature Stars and Stripes. A band struck up a tune, and the crowd sang along:

N

Tag:

*My country, 'tis of thee / Sweet land of
liberty / Of thee I sing . . .*

When the band finished, a group of local dignitaries joined the Hardings on their platform, and the president was greeted by the official chairman of the welcoming committee—Montana's newest US senator, Burton Wheeler.

There were questions that Wheeler, his suspicions stoked by Jess Smith's death, would have liked to ask the president. But this wasn't the moment, not with the adoring crowd straining for a glimpse of their handsome leader. Besides, Wheeler had a diplomatic role to play.

Instead they shook hands, meeting for the first time, and someone mentioned that Wheeler was a newly elected senator. A wry look crossed the president's face, who well remembered the indignity of freshman status in the seniority-obsessed Senate. "I don't know," he quipped, "whether to commiserate with you or congratulate you."

Though no speech was scheduled for the depot, the president stepped up to a microphone that was mounted to the back of his railcar. "We have witnessed a hospitality in the West that could not be excelled anywhere in the world," his amplified voice declared. "It is your wholesome life and your wholesome people, giving wholesome expression in the greetings extended us."

Wheeler must have set aside his political differences for a moment and watched with admiration as Harding, a far more seasoned politician, stroked the crowd's sense of self-worth. Harding excelled at delivering such sonorous and empty remarks. It was his trademark. He even had a name for it—*bloviating*.

"It has all been so happy and so delightful, that I have done nothing in my life that gave me such satisfaction as my determination to make the trip to Alaska and see the continent on the way."

The crowd roared its approval.

President Harding wasn't universally adored—a recent nationwide straw poll showed him narrowly trailing automaker Henry Ford in the following year's presidential election—but the crowd's reaction reflected the genuine affection much of the nation felt toward him. After so many years of war, plague, and economic hardship, Harding had seemingly delivered on his campaign pledge and shepherded the nation back to normalcy. Peace prevailed, the Spanish flu was a distant memory, and the economy was roaring out of its deep deflationary recession of 1920–1921. Even here in Montana, where downtrodden farmers and hard-working miners had sent Burton Wheeler to the Senate in protest of the president's business-friendly policies, Harding's affable nature made a strong impression.

Later, the president toured the Anaconda Company's famed copper mines and was afterward paraded through town. At Clark Park, the local baseball stadium, so many thousands showed up to hear him deliver a planned address on joblessness that the amplifying equipment, installed for a crowd of hundreds, was deemed insufficient. Instead of forcing his audience to strain their ears through a ten-minute speech, the president simply handed over his official script to the local press and bloviated some short, off-the-cuff remarks for the crowd. The Montanans loved it.

Back at the depot, the train, refueled and resupplied, was ready to depart for Helena. Harding resumed his place on the rear platform, and somewhere in the sea of humanity, Burton Wheeler watched the chief executive wave to an adoring crowd as the local band played "Till We Meet Again."

The song would prove an ironic choice. It was the last time Wheeler, or anyone in Butte, for that matter, would see the president alive.

TWO YEARS IN office had exacted their toll on Warren Harding's body. Like most presidents, Harding quickly discovered that whatever spring bubbles beneath the White House must have the opposite effect of the Fountain of Youth. The lines on his face deepened. His olive skin turned gray and sallow. The presidency was a singularly taxing job, to be sure. But recently, friends and aides had been noticing strange, unexplained symptoms that suggested something far more serious than premature aging. A recurring pain in his chest caused him to grimace. He tired easily and was often short of breath. On the golf course, where he once strutted through eighteen holes, he now struggled to make it past the ninth. Even public speaking left him dizzy and winded. Sometimes he'd stop midsentence just to catch his breath.

Most worrying was his insomnia. Before Harding left for Alaska, the White House butler had grown so concerned that he pulled aside Colonel Edmund Starling, head of the president's Secret Service detail.

"Colonel, something is going to happen to our boss."

"What's the matter?"

"He can't sleep at night," the butler said. "He can't lie down. He has to be propped up with pillows and he sits up that way all night. If he lies down he can't get his breath."

If something was indeed the matter with the president, his personal physician chose not to see it. Dr. Charles E. Sawyer, a goateed homeopath from Harding's hometown of Marion, had no business treating the chief executive. A stethoscope had been a basic instrument of medical care for decades, but Dr. Sawyer still preferred to place his ear directly on his patients' chests, and his prescriptions tended toward herbal remedies rather than evidence-based medicines. Yet Harding, himself the son of a homeopath, had appointed this country doctor as personal physician to the president and chairman of the Federal Hospitalization Board, with the rank of brigadier general in the Army Medical Corps.

Brigadier General Sawyer examined the president on the eve of his great trip and—in the face of mounting evidence to the contrary—declared Harding's health sound. The pain in his chest? Nothing more than indigestion. A systolic blood pressure that hovered around 180? Shortness of breath? Chronic fatigue? Just what you'd expect from a fifty-seven-year-old with the weight of the nation on his shoulders. There certainly was nothing wrong with his heart, Sawyer insisted.

Given a clean bill of health, Harding would proceed to deliver nearly eighty-five public speeches over his next six weeks of travel. If, as evidenced by his request for a new will, the president mistrusted his doctor's judgment, he certainly didn't act like it. He performed physical labor, driving the final, golden spike to complete the Alaska Railroad. He operated heavy machinery, steering a binder across a Kansan wheat field and operating a locomotive through Idaho's Bitterroot Mountains. He rode horseback through the sun-scorched, red-walled canyons of Zion National Park and hiked up 190 wooden stairs in Chickaloon, Alaska.

Harding put on a brave face, but his underlying health conditions sometimes showed through. In Missouri, he was forced to sit out a classic photo op—pinning medals on the chests of the local Boy Scouts—after his lips turned blue. It was a classic symptom of cardiac asthma, indicating that his heart was not circulating enough oxygenated blood. Dr. Sawyer diagnosed him with a sunburn and applied a cold compress to his lips.

If Warren Harding's body was failing, perhaps he was too distracted to notice. With every mile he put between himself and Washington, he became more aware of the malfeasance that had taken root under his watch.

The case of a rogue Bureau of Investigation agent named Gaston Means had unsettled him, as had an unfolding scandal in the Veterans' Bureau, the one that had pushed the Bureau's general counsel, Charles Cramer, to take his own life.

During a stop in Kansas City, Harding invited newspaper editor William Allen White, an old acquaintance from Republican circles, to join him in his parlor car. That night, as the presidential train rattled through the darkened Kansan landscape, White sensed that Harding desperately wanted to confide in him. But the president apparently never quite worked up the courage. The closest he came was a startling, mysterious admission: "I have no trouble with my enemies. I can take care of them. It is my friends, my friends that are giving me my trouble!" White tried to coax out more but could never get the president to elaborate.

Several days later, after boarding the USS *Henderson* for the voyage to Alaska, Harding summoned one of his trusted cabinet officers, Commerce Secretary Herbert Hoover, to his stateroom for advice.

"If you knew of a great scandal in our administration," he asked nervously, "would you for the good of the country and the party expose it publicly, or would you bury it?"

Hoover didn't bat an eye. "Publish it, and at least get credit for integrity on your side." Harding commented that such a tactic could prove dangerous, which naturally prompted the commerce secretary to ask for details.

The president explained that he'd heard "some rumors of irregularities" centering around Jess Smith, in connection with cases in the Department of Justice. Hoover asked the obvious follow-up: Was Daugherty involved? The president, Hoover recalled decades later, "abruptly dried up and never raised the question again."

Despite Harding's best efforts to leave his worries back East, troubling news followed him to the frontiers of American civilization. Just before he left Alaska, an airplane flew out to deliver a long, coded message from Washington. Some in his traveling party thought that the telegram pushed him to the brink of collapse. Its contents were never revealed, but for several days afterward, Harding could be heard muttering about "what a president was to do when his friends were false to him."

IN RETROSPECT, HARDING'S "Voyage of Understanding" seemed cursed from the beginning. In Denver, a streetcar nearly plowed full speed into the Hardings' automobile, stopping just four feet short after its inattentive operator belatedly pulled the brake. On a sightseeing trip in the Colorado Rockies, a motorcar went over a cliff, claiming the lives of its driver, an Associated Press reporter, and a representative of the Republican National Committee. And in Tacoma, Washington, a landslide wrecked the Union Pacific locomotive that, a few days earlier, had been pulling the presidential train, killing an engineer whom Harding had befriended.

One final omen came on July 27, when the presidential steamer *Henderson* was just thirty-eight nautical miles short of safely completing its return trip from Alaska. The *Henderson* was moving through the thick fog of Puget Sound, escorted by twelve US Navy destroyers and aided by the sound of foghorns and bell buoys. President Harding, who had been feeling unwell all morning, was in his stateroom when a sudden jolt rattled the ship. Screams of "All hands on deck!" echoed off the *Henderson*'s bulkheads, and before long Harding's valet burst into the presidential stateroom to check on the chief executive. He found the president supine on his bed, hands covering his face. Without removing his hands, Harding asked what happened, and the valet informed him that one of the ship's escorts, the USS *Zeilin*, had mistakenly turned in front of the *Henderson*. Despite quick action from the officers on the bridge, the *Henderson*'s bow had torn into the destroyer's hull at ten knots.

The president's troubling response: "I hope this boat sinks." (Neither ship did, although the *Zeilin* had to limp to shore after taking on considerable water.)

It was on this dark afternoon that Harry Daugherty chose to materialize, quite unexpectedly, in Seattle for an unscheduled conference with the president. His timing couldn't have been worse. Rattled by the collision and gripped by sharp abdominal pains, Harding was in no state to receive an attorney general who had become a thorn in his side. And yet the pair still snuck off for an hour, keeping the entire traveling party waiting. No record of their conversation survives, but the subject must have been important enough to bring Daugherty all the way to Seattle by way of Vancouver and the Canadian Pacific Railway (thus avoiding the American press).

Whatever they discussed, the president clearly wasn't himself when he arrived later that afternoon, almost an hour behind schedule, to address a crowd of forty thousand at the University of Washington's Husky Stadium. With the presidential standard flapping from the stadium's flagstaff, a hatless Harding stumbled through his speech under the unusually warm Seattle sun. The content of the address, which (correctly) predicted that Alaska would someday be admitted as the forty-ninth state and boldly called for restraint in exploiting the territory's natural bounty, elicited polite applause from the crowd. The delivery, on the other hand, won no plaudits. The president was downright "listless," according to observers, merely reading his manuscript and not doing even that well, garbling his words and praising the natural wonders of "Nebraska" instead of "Alaska."

Then, halfway through his speech, Harding halted. Wobbling on his feet, he clutched the desk in front of him and released the script from his hands. Its pages fluttered to the ground. Few in the stadium realized what was happening. Herbert Hoover, who had actually written the speech, sprang from his chair directly behind the president's lectern and gathered the mess of paper at Harding's feet. It took the commerce secretary a moment to put the pages back into the correct order, which was enough time for the president to regain his balance and decide, perhaps unwisely, to carry on. Years later, doctors would conclude that the president had suffered a mild heart attack, right there in front of forty thousand people.

That evening, Harding's aides wisely cleared his schedule and rerouted his train from Yosemite, its original destination, to San Francisco, where the chief executive could recuperate. As the train rattled south toward California, Harding's symptoms worsened. He developed a fever. He began vomiting whatever he ate. Dr. Sawyer examined his patient and, remarkably, still showed little concern. His diagnosis? Food poisoning, acquired from canned crabs he'd eaten several days before in Sitka, Alaska. The president's physician prescribed homeopathic purgatives to rid the body of its toxins and promised a speedy recovery.

On Sunday, July 29, President Harding mustered all his remaining strength, walked under his own power into San Francisco's Palace Hotel, and then collapsed on the bed of the presidential suite. Inside room 8064, two new physicians—Ray Lyman Wilbur, the president of both Stanford University and the American Medical Association, and Charles Cooper, a respected San Francisco cardiologist—began assisting Dr. Sawyer, and they quickly established how truly sick the president had become. His heart was severely dilated, his breathing shallow, his pulse irregular. The president finally had competent medical care, though it remained to be seen whether it was too late.

Amid this health crisis, Harry Daugherty appeared unannounced yet again to confer with the president. The medical team refused to admit him. "Everything troublesome was turned away," Dr. Wilbur later recalled—even an attorney general of the United States on what appeared to be an urgent mission. Daugherty reluctantly withdrew. On his way out of the hotel, he paused by a cluster of reporters and made a brief statement. He was giving the president some space, he said, but would return when his health improved.

WHATEVER IT WAS he wanted to tell the president, the chance never came. Twenty minutes past seven on the evening of Thursday, August 2, 1923, the president was propped up in bed as First Lady Florence Harding read aloud to him a *Saturday Evening Post* article titled "A Calm Review of a Calm Man," which praised Harding for quietly charting a steady course for the nation.

> The people have a fine type of American for President, a humble, understandable, modest, kindly man, with all the reserve force needed to govern capably.

"That's good," he told his wife. "Go on, read some more."

Suddenly, his face twitched and his mouth dropped open and then his body slumped. Warren G. Harding had suffered a final, fatal heart attack. Dr. Sawyer pronounced the official cause of death, incorrectly, as cerebral hemorrhage. None of his fellow physicians were bold enough to contradict him.

Daugherty soon returned to the Palace Hotel. This time, he gained entry to the presidential suite, where he stepped up to the president's lifeless body. He didn't utter a word. Tears coursed down his cheeks.

5

"The Hardest Blow of My Life"

"C alvin!"

The trembling voice of John Calvin Coolidge Sr. roused the vice president of the United States from his sleep.

"Calvin!"

It was half past two in the morning of August 3, 1923, and John Calvin Coolidge Jr.—better known simply as Calvin Coolidge—was at his father's farmhouse in the mountains of Vermont. As his father climbed the rickety stairs to the bedroom the vice president was sharing with his wife, Grace, Coolidge steeled himself for grave news. His father's stentorian voice never trembled, except in momentous occasions.

This was one of them. Bursting into the bedroom, his father announced that the president of the United States was dead.

Though drowsy, Coolidge immediately grasped the implications. He and his wife dressed hastily, knelt at their bedside for a word of prayer, and went downstairs to meet a small and eclectic group that had assembled around the dining table—his father, a stenographer, the vice presidential chauffeur, a news reporter, and Sen. Porter Dale of Vermont, who happened to be passing through town.

"Good morning, Mr. President," said the reporter. It was the first time he'd been so addressed.

The fifty-one-year-old politician, however, had plenty of experience adjusting to new titles. Over his twenty-plus years in Massachusetts politics, Coolidge had climbed the political ladder with a steady pace and sure footing that must have inspired a generation of political strivers. He rose from city councilman to state legislator, from mayor to state senator, from president of the state senate to lieutenant governor, and finally— after his decisive action in the 1919 Boston police strike restored order to the city and won him national fame—from governor of Massachusetts to vice president of the United States.

His measured conservatism—a staunch preference for limited government, tempered by support for such progressive measures as the abolition of child labor, women's suffrage, and workmen's compensation—won him broad appeal across the Bay State. So did his exceptionally high-minded approach to politics. As an undergraduate at Amherst College, he practically worshipped his philosophy professor, a mystical, Christian humanist named Charles E. Garman, who preached service to others as the ultimate ethical goal. Garman's teachings steered Coolidge first toward law and then politics and prodded him to seek more than mere earthly success. Of course, like any successful politician he weighed the pros and cons of his decisions, but Coolidge was far less calculating than most. His willingness to sacrifice his political welfare for the sake of a higher principle earned him the trust of voters and fellow officeholders alike. Friends, opponents, even enemies admired Calvin Coolidge for being that ultimate enigma— a politician who kept his word.

Even more puzzling than his adherence to principle, perhaps, given the demands of a politician's job, was his deep introversion. Coolidge hated small talk and, although he tolerated social events, favored his own company to that of others. He slept nine hours every night, napped two hours in the afternoon, and in his waking hours went long stretches of time without opening his mouth, even during official functions. Eventually he earned the nickname "Silent Cal," which he gamely adopted as his public persona—"the sly and laconic Yankee rustic," one observer wrote, "who was cleverer than he appeared."

If he was, however, Washington didn't yet know it. After more than two years as vice president, Coolidge remained a nonentity, with few allies and fewer friends. Despite his unprecedented attendance at cabinet meetings—he was the first vice president accorded that privilege—he rarely spoke up, and he contributed little to the Harding administration's signature policy achievements, including its income tax cuts, a balanced budget, and the international disarmament conference that resulted in the world's first arms control treaties. Coolidge was slightly more visible in his constitutional role as president of the Senate, where he presided over the chamber with some regularity, but during recesses the vice president could often be found eating alone in the Capitol cafeteria, in the complete silence he preferred.

Coolidge had so underwhelmed that, by the summer of 1923, conventional wisdom held that President Harding would not retain him as his running mate in the 1924 election—speculation that events now suddenly rendered moot.

By the light of a kerosene lamp—electricity had not yet made its way to this remote Vermont village—Coolidge examined a telegram from President Harding's private secretary in San Francisco:

> THE PRESIDENT DIED INSTANTLY WHILE
> CONVERSING WITH MEMBERS OF HIS FAMILY AT
> 730 PM. THE PHYSICIANS REPORT DEATH WAS
> APPARENTLY DUE TO SOME BRAIN EMBOLISM,
> PROBABLY APOPLEXY.
>
> GEORGE B. CHRISTIAN, SEC.

Coolidge then turned to the legal necessities. Was he required to swear a new oath of office, or would the vice presidential oath he'd taken on March 4, 1921, suffice? And if a new oath was required, who would administer it? Traditionally, the chief justice swore in new presidents. Should Coolidge wait until he could meet with Chief Justice Taft in Washington?

Another telegram soon arrived, unsolicited, with an answer. It was from Attorney General Daugherty:

> I RESPECTFULLY SUGGEST THAT IF YOU HAVE NOT
> ALREADY DONE SO, THAT YOU IMMEDIATELY TAKE
> THE OATH OF OFFICE.

There were still unanswered questions. What was the oath's proper wording, and who would administer it? Coolidge's father, a local justice of the peace and notary public, retrieved his copy of the Revised Statutes of Vermont, which included the text of the US Constitution. Article II, Section I, paragraph 8 prescribed the oath's wording but failed to indicate who was qualified to officiate. Coolidge made his first executive decision: his father, who had sworn in countless officials of the state of Vermont, would do it.

As kerosene light flickered on his face, and with the family Bible on the table next to him, Calvin Coolidge raised his right hand and repeated the words his father recited.

It was forty-seven minutes past 2 a.m.—an hour that for President Harding might have meant whiskey, poker, and showgirls. For a Massachusetts Puritan, it meant sleep. And so Calvin Coolidge went back upstairs, climbed into bed, and dozed away his first hours as the thirtieth president of the United States.

THE NEXT FEW days witnessed an outpouring of national grief not seen, perhaps, since the death of Abraham Lincoln. As President Harding's funeral train rattled by, some three million Americans lined the railroad tracks from San Francisco to Washington to glimpse, in somber silence, the late president's coffin through the windows of his parlor car. Men doffed their hats. Women threw flowers. Boys Scouts and war veterans dipped their flags. Harding had been popular, but what amplified Americans' collective grief was the sheer shock that it was the (outwardly) hale and hearty Warren Harding who had died rather than the obviously frail Woodrow Wilson. In cities from Reno to Omaha to Chicago, church bells tolled, and in some places so many mourners crowded the tracks that the locomotive could only inch forward. In Cheyenne, a thunderstorm coincided with the train's arrival, but not even sheets of rain and flashes of lightning could drive the crowd away or stop a chorus of children from singing "Nearer, My God, to Thee."

From inside the Washington-bound train, Harry Daugherty watched the tributes with admiration, grateful to know that Warren Harding was loved by his people. Moving as the scenes were, however, the grief of these ordinary Americans could never compare to what he was feeling. Harding had been more than a friend; he had been Daugherty's creature. Harding's political success was the product of his political cunning, and Harding's elevation to the presidency represented the culmination of his life's work. Just as Jess Smith had subsumed himself into Daugherty's identity, Daugherty had merged his own ambitions into Warren G. Harding's. In a very real sense, part of Daugherty also died in that San Francisco hotel room.

"I had received the hardest blow of my life," he would write in his memoirs. "I had felt the foundations of the world sink."

As grief consumed him, his enemies sensed weakness. From the moment of the president's death, speculation ran wild that the architect of the Harding presidency would have no role in the incoming Coolidge administration. On August 3, the Associated Press reported that Daugherty would resign as attorney general, citing anonymous "friends," while the *Boston Daily Globe* observed that, considering his influence "evaporates automatically into thin air with the death of his chief," he would surely resign to spare himself the humiliation. The following day, the *Akron Beacon Journal,* from Daugherty's home state, elaborated on the rumors, attributing its reporting to more anonymous "friends":

> [I]t is felt on all sides that Attorney General Harry M. Daugherty of Columbus will tender his resignation as soon as he can put the affairs of his office in shape. Harding's Damon [whose trust in his friend Pythias was legendary] is now regarded as having lost all interest in Washington and observers are taking his retirement in the near future as a matter of course. Daugherty, his own health in poor state, has been on the verge of resigning several times within the last year.
>
> Once he held off to fight the Keller impeachment proceedings. At other times his devotion to President Harding kept him on the job. Now he has no ties to hold him. He lost his pal, Jesse Smith of Washington C. H. several months ago, and now he has lost Warren Harding. With both gone his friends do not see how he could remain in Washington.

Such reports, Daugherty was convinced, were the work of his political foes. In truth, he had no intention of leaving office—not even for a lucrative partnership at a Washington law firm. "I would rather by a million-fold be attorney general of the United States than the richest man in America," he once said.

But these false rumors put him in a bind. Custom dictated that, in the event of a president's sudden death, all cabinet officers give the incoming president the option to build an entirely new administration, if he so chose. Sometime after the late president's funeral in Washington and his interment in Marion, Ohio, Daugherty and his colleagues would be expected to tender official letters of resignation. Coolidge wasn't likely to accept them, but if Daugherty denied the rumors now, it would seem that he was forcing the president's hand, and that was no way for a subordinate to start a relationship with his new boss. On the other hand, his continued silence in the face of these rumors would only lend them credibility and render his departure a fait accompli.

Daugherty was fighting mad about the spot he was in, but he also owed his enemies a grudging admiration. They'd struck when his grief was fresh and when, even if he possessed the strength, he was powerless to retaliate. It was cruel and calculating—and exactly the kind of play he would have made himself.

The knives were out.

OVER THE FOLLOWING days, the rumors grew louder and more emphatic, so that by the time the funeral train reached Washington on August 7 and President Harding's body returned to the White House one final time, reporters were expecting a resignation announcement at any moment. Harry Daugherty would correct the record as soon as possible. First, however, he would have to endure a long day of memorial services.

If Washington could do anything, it was mourn a president, and on this occasion the capital spared no pageantry. The funeral procession from the White House to the Capitol included thousands of uniformed troops and was led on horseback by General of the Armies John J. Pershing, the nation's highest-ranking military officer and the only American ever to hold that six-star rank. As the somber parade crept down Pennsylvania Avenue, military bands played dirges and children tossed flowers toward the flag-draped coffin, borne by a horse-drawn artillery caisson. Automobiles carried the three living presidents—Calvin Coolidge, William Howard Taft, and an ailing Woodrow Wilson, who rallied himself from his sickbed to mourn his successor—as well as the former First Lady, the Speaker of the House, governors of several states, and members of the cabinet, including the attorney general.

At the Capitol, Daugherty gulped and choked back tears as he entered the rotunda and saw the coffin placed atop the same catafalque that had borne Lincoln's body in 1865. But as he watched President Coolidge, that pinch-faced, moralistic little man, place an enormous wreath at the bier, his grief was tinged with a new and unsettling emotion: insecurity.

All his political capital—amassed over decades through fear and the strategic exchange of favors—had been converted into the presidency of his political protégé. With his friend at the apex of power, he had been able to suppress the social anxiety he felt as a small-town midwesterner among the eastern establishment, even if the office of attorney general never brought him the social respectability he thought it deserved. Moreover, his unique relationship with Harding had given him extraordinary freedom, and his role as top prosecutor had ensured that if he or his friends ever strayed from the bounds of the law, there would be no consequences. Now his grip on the office of attorney general was all that remained, and even that depended upon the good graces of a president who owed him nothing, personally or politically.

As the cabinet filed past the open casket, Daugherty could not bear to look at the face of his friend and political protector, now waxy and gray with death. Bent over in grief, he couldn't even glance in that direction. He was disconsolate, and he moved on without a final good-bye.

EVEN AS DAUGHERTY vainly tried to conceal his grief, Calvin Coolidge was feeling the pressure to dismiss his inherited attorney general. In the days leading up to the funeral, Sen. William Borah paid the president a visit at the New Willard Hotel, the Coolidges' temporary lodgings until former First Lady Harding vacated the White House. Borah advised the president to "get rid of Daugherty." A progressive from Idaho and an influential voice within the Republican Party, Borah was already looking ahead to 1924, when Coolidge would presumably stand for reelection. Presidential election years always stirred up rough waters, and Borah predicted that the attorney general would prove to be the administration's heaviest load. His management of the Justice Department had always been controversial, and who knew what revelations might surface during the campaign. Better to jettison him now, Borah counseled, before the ship started heaving.

The president listened to Borah's argument and, after careful thought, split it in half: he accepted the senator's premise but not his conclusion. Yes, Daugherty could prove a liability on the campaign trail. But he also knew that Daugherty didn't want to go and worried that dismissing him now could backfire. He was especially concerned that it would be perceived as a repudiation of Harding's presidency, which, after all, was what the American people had voted for in 1920, not a Coolidge presidency. In this last concern, Coolidge, a man of firm convictions, wasn't merely pandering to the electorate. As a caretaker president, Coolidge felt a moral obligation to continue his predecessor's policies and keep his appointees in place.

That reasoning wouldn't apply, however, if Daugherty left voluntarily. Of course, the trick would be to suggest the idea to the attorney general without revealing that it was Coolidge's wish.

By chance, Chief Justice Taft soon lumbered into Coolidge's office. The twenty-seventh president and a shrewd politician in his own right, Taft had come to offer his services as a sort of mentor to the thirtieth president, still a Washington novice. Coolidge received Taft's gesture with gratitude, and over the coming months he would lean on the portly chief justice as a confidential adviser. At the moment, however, the new president pegged him for a different role.

Taft knew Harry Daugherty well. From the Buckeye State to DC, the two men had maintained an amicable, mutually beneficial relationship. In fact, Taft, whose main aspiration had always been the nation's highest tribunal, owed his Supreme Court appointment to Daugherty, who lobbied President Harding on his behalf when the chief justice's chair became vacant in 1921. Now it occurred to Coolidge that if anyone could broach the subject of retirement with Daugherty, it was Taft.

As it happened, the chief justice and attorney general already had a meeting on the books for the very next day. The conference began with a discussion of the federal judiciary. Taft, somewhat ironically, disapproved of how the Harding administration's judicial appointments smacked of political favors. But the conversation remained cordial and productive—until the chief justice abruptly changed subjects to offer some unsolicited career advice. Privately, Taft felt that the office of attorney general was beyond Daugherty's limited ability as a lawyer and that his failure to appreciate his personal shortcomings would spell doom. Taft wisely kept these thoughts to himself; instead, he tactfully raised the issue of Daugherty's age and health. Perhaps, he suggested, it was time for the attorney general to return to their beloved Buckeye State and hand the reins of the Justice Department to a younger, healthier man?

His overture did not go over well, to say the least. Daugherty flatly told him that he had no intention of resigning. "Indeed," the chief justice noted in a letter, "he is very sensitive on the subject."

Simply refusing to resign, Daugherty had to know, would do little to strengthen his grip on his office. Nor could he rely on Coolidge's inclination to keep Harding's appointees in place; loyalty to a dead man was a slippery handhold. And so the attorney general approached Coolidge with an overture of his own. While Daugherty knew how to make an offer that couldn't be refused, this wasn't one of them. Nevertheless, it was a strong proposition, and the best he could muster from his weakened position: he promised to swing the Ohio delegation toward the president at the 1924 Republican National Convention.

Assuming he could deliver—and to be sure, he still held sway within the state's Republican Party—Daugherty's pledge was no small thing. As an unelected, accidental president, Coolidge was expected to face an intraparty challenge, especially within a Republican Party still riven between progressive and conservative factions. Ohio, furthermore, with its well-organized political machine and its status as a general-election swing state, played an outsize role in most Republican nominating contests. With Daugherty's support, Coolidge would surely beat back a challenge.

Embedded within the offer, of course, was an implicit threat: fire me, and you lose Ohio, and possibly the presidency. Coolidge had little choice but to accept. On August 17, Daugherty offered a pro forma resignation letter, as custom dictated, and the president refused it.

By then, the newspapers had been blithely repeating rumors of his resignation, which Daugherty attributed to his enemies, for two weeks. They now sheepishly corrected the record, reporting that Daugherty would remain part of the Coolidge cabinet after all—and at the president's request, no less. The *New York Tribune* quoted more anonymous "friends" who now confirmed that Daugherty considered it "his duty to stand by President Coolidge at this time and help 'carry on' with the affairs of the Administration."

In its report, Ohio's *Akron Beacon Journal* added that Daugherty was "vexed" by the erroneous reports of his imminent departure:

[Daugherty] was convinced that back of these reports was the same animus which led to last year's unsuccessful efforts in the house to impeach him and which had spread countless stories of his quitting the cabinet from time to time in Mr. Harding's term.

This reaction was characteristic of the Ohio cabinet officer. It was characteristic of the Daugherty who endured the bitterness of

Ohio campaigns; who underwent defeat with the philosophy with which he accepted victory; who never gave up in a campaign until the verdict was returned and then began planning the next; who has fought stubbornly through his own sickness, and returns to assure his friends of his recovery, and to notify his enemies that he has no intention of leaving the ring.

In Washington, Daugherty had finally regained his footing.

Far away, however, in the distant oil-producing lands of the Mountain West, a political scandal was brewing that would soon shake the foundations of the nation's capital. Anything connected to Harding might not be a safe bet for long.

6

"This Teapot Dome Thing"

Billings, Montana, in the early 1920s was poised to outgrow its modest origins as the western railhead of the Northern Pacific. Founded in 1882 where the tracks then dead-ended at the Yellowstone River, it had long been a mere transfer point, a place where freight moved from train to steamboat. Recently, however, vast oil fields had been discovered nearby in eastern Montana and northern Wyoming, and Billings was emerging as the headquarters of the region's booming energy industry. Banks were flush with deposits, new brick buildings dotted the streets, and the city's population had passed fifteen thousand, making it Montana's third-largest settlement.

Tom Arthur hoped Billings would grow even more. As the state's leading oil lobbyist, Arthur was committed to liberating the untold millions of barrels buried beneath the region's sagebrush flats and then circulating the resulting wealth through the local economy. His life's work was greasing the political wheels, making Montana a more inviting place for oil companies to operate. He was a dealmaker.

But there was one deal that stuck in his craw. Though he had no direct involvement in the transaction, even from a distance it reeked of official corruption and, worse, threatened to make a mockery of all the legitimate deals he brokered. And so, when Montana's next US senator—a man who would never tolerate an abuse of the law—stopped in Billings nearly a year before Harding's death on November 25, 1922, to attend a party thrown in his honor, Arthur seized the opportunity to report his suspicions.

Senator-elect Burton K. Wheeler, his election victory just two weeks old, was pressing the flesh, celebrating with the local Democratic elite, when Arthur pulled him aside.

"This Teapot Dome thing," Arthur told the senator, "is a scandal and ought to be investigated."

WHEELER WAS ONLY vaguely familiar with Teapot Dome. Located some 250 miles south of Billings, the Wyoming oil field took its name from a unique rock outcrop that featured both a handle and a spout. Formally known as Naval Petroleum Reserve #3, the land and its mineral contents had been set aside a decade earlier as an emergency supply of crude oil for the US Navy, a move cheered by military readiness advocates and conservationists alike. When word leaked out in April of 1922 that the Harding administration had leased Teapot Dome, along with the Elk Hills Naval Petroleum Reserve in California, to politically connected oilmen—in secret and without competitive bidding—conservationists cried foul. The land, they believed, ought to be saved for future generations, not turned into a quick buck.

Now Tom Arthur—nobody's idea of a conservationist—whispered to Wheeler that Teapot Dome was a "crooked deal." Arthur had no specifics to offer, only his oilman's intuition, but that was enough to cock the senator's ear. Arthur was a highly credible source. He wanted America's natural resources *exploited*, not conserved. He just wanted it done on the level. Arthur's suspicions, therefore, carried a lot of weight, and Wheeler knew he had to find someone who could act on them.

As it happened, immediately after departing Billings, Wheeler was scheduled to attend a conference in Washington of progressive-minded senators and congressmen, and its organizer was just the man who could put Arthur's tip to use. Aptly nicknamed "Fighting Bob," Sen. Robert La Follette—a Wisconsin Republican and staunch conservationist—had long been a thorn in the side of his party's conservative leadership, and the recent elections had only sharpened his sting. Angry farmers, struggling to recover from a deep agricultural depression and joined by railroad workers under the banner of the newly formed Conference for Progressive Political Action, had gone to the polls en masse and sent a class of insurgent freshmen to Congress—Republican senators like Iowa's Smith Brookhart and North Dakota's Lynn Frazier, as well as Democrats like Wheeler and

Washington's Clarence Dill. To them, the "normalcy" promised by the Harding administration and delivered in the form of tax cuts for the rich, tariff hikes that cost American farmers $300 million, and a Justice Department openly hostile to the labor movement represented a step backward.

Now La Follette was organizing these "yahoos of the west" into an informal caucus that could challenge the Senate's two-party system. "The time has come," he announced, "for the organization of a well-defined group, cooperating in support of accepted progressive principles and policies." Ultimately, twelve senators and twenty-eight representatives attended; another three senators and fifteen representatives endorsed the proceedings *in absentia*. Given the Republicans' slim margins in both the House (where they held a six-vote majority) and Senate (where it was only four), La Follette's caucus could, if it banded together, potentially control the Sixty-eighth Congress of the United States. And if there was one issue that could unite these insurgents from separate parties, it was protecting America's natural resources from grafters and corporate raiders.

When they were first revealed in early 1922, the secret oil leases had stoked progressives' anger at the Harding administration. Wagging his finger on the Senate floor, his pompadour mane of white hair bobbing above him as if to accentuate his anger, La Follette recounted all the irregularities surrounding the deals. First, there was President Harding's executive order transferring the petroleum reserves from the Navy Department, where they'd been for a decade, to the Interior Department. Then there were the contracts between the Interior Department and the oil companies, executed in secret and without competitive bids. Lastly, there was the fact that both leases went to companies controlled by friends of Interior Secretary Albert Fall: Harry Sinclair of Sinclair Oil, who gained control of the Teapot Dome field in Wyoming, and Edward L. Doheny of Pan American Petroleum, who obtained the rights to the Elk Hills reserve in California.

It had all been suspicious enough to persuade a unanimous Senate, by a fifty-eight to zero vote, to authorize an inquiry by the Committee on Public Lands and Surveys. Unfortunately for La Follette and his conservationist allies, like so many Senate votes, this one, too, turned out to be symbolic. Senators had gone on record in support of an inquiry, just in case something rotten turned up, but there was no real sentiment for action. By November, more than seven months had passed, and the committee still hadn't convened a single hearing on the matter. Worse, no one had yet come forward with solid evidence of foul play.

Wheeler's source had none of that to offer, but as the young Montana senator recounted Tom Arthur's statement to La Follette, the progressive leader got an idea. Properly deployed, the oil lobbyist's word might be just the nudge the committee—or, to be more precise, a key member of the committee—needed to fulfill its charge.

It was time, La Follette insisted, for Wheeler to have a talk with the other half of Montana's Senate delegation, who happened to be a member of the Public Lands committee: Thomas J. Walsh.

TWENTY-THREE YEARS HIS senior by age and ten years by Senate service time, Walsh was the closest thing Wheeler had to a mentor within the US Senate (with the possible exception of La Follette). When they first met in the bustling mining town of Butte, Montana, Wheeler had been a fledgling labor lawyer and Walsh one of the state's most respected attorneys. Late one night, Wheeler was burning the midnight oil inside his office when Walsh passed by and introduced himself to the young lawyer. "Young man," Walsh offered as a greeting, "that's the way I got my gray hairs." His warning had no effect. Both were compulsive workers, both stubbornly principled, both Democrats, and soon they bonded in the trenches of legal and political combat against Montana's all-powerful Anaconda copper monopoly. As a member of the state legislature, which in those days (before the soon-to-be-enacted Seventeenth Amendment) elected members of the US Senate, Wheeler championed Walsh's candidacy. After prevailing in 1913, Senator Walsh, in turn, orchestrated Wheeler's appointment as US attorney for Montana, the post that launched the upstart lawyer to statewide prominence.

Now, a decade later, they were colleagues in what was widely billed as "the world's greatest deliberative body." Both men pursued justice with a bulldog's determination—but in style they could not have been more different. Where Wheeler was bombastic, Walsh was austere. Where Wheeler embellished, Walsh was meticulous with the facts. Wheeler walked around with a thin cigar clamped in his mouth and enjoyed the occasional shot of whiskey, Prohibition be damned. Walsh neither drank nor smoked. Even in appearance they struck quite the contrast: Wheeler with his wily eyes and clean-shaven, youthful face, and Walsh with his pitilessly cold gaze and a gray, bushy handlebar mustache straight out of the nineteenth century.

Someone once described Tom Walsh as "an Irishman without a sense of humor, a lawyer who will not appeal to the emotions of a jury, a senator who cannot sob or scintillate." Wheeler concurred. "He was not what people would call a good politician," he later recalled. "He was not the back-slapping, baby-kissing kind." In his public speeches, Walsh had the unfortunate tendency of droning on about the facts or explaining legal points that sailed straight over the heads of Montana's farmers and miners.

His virtues as a lawyer, however, outshone his shortcomings as a politician. "People voted for him," Wheeler remembered, "because they respected his honesty, integrity, and his great ability." He was never afraid to challenge Montana's entrenched mining interests on behalf of the common man, to dig into the arcana of mineral rights law and mining leases in pursuit of justice. In fact, he relished it. If anyone could take on the oil lease controversy—if anyone could be counted on to immerse himself in the law surrounding mineral rights and public lands—it was Tom Walsh.

The two men were close friends—each summer their families retreated to neighboring lakefront homes in Glacier National Park—and Wheeler felt comfortable approaching him with almost any request. But when Wheeler first broached the subject of Teapot Dome, suggesting that Walsh should take an active role, Walsh demurred. "Well, I can't do everything," he said.

Walsh was referring to his status as the Senate's hardest-working member. He had accepted more committee assignments than any other senator. (In addition to Public Lands, he served on the committees on Indian Affairs, Interoceanic Canals, Irrigation and Reclamation, Judiciary, Mines and Mining, Naval Affairs, Pensions, and Privileges and Elections.) But there were deeper reasons behind his reluctance. As was typical of western senators, Walsh mirrored his constituents' feelings toward the conservation movement—he worried that it would slow the region's economic development—and in principle had no objection to drilling on public lands. He didn't get along with La Follette, either, and saw no reason to aid his cause. Quite the opposite, in fact. Walsh was on good terms with Interior Secretary Fall, an old Senate colleague. He was even better friends with Edward L. Doheny. The oilman, who generally enjoyed a reputation as an upstanding citizen, had hosted Walsh at his Los Angeles mansion after his wife's sudden death in 1917, allowing the senator to grieve in private.

Wheeler couldn't have been surprised by his friend's reaction. But he held an ace in his hand, and now he laid it down: "Walsh, I don't know anything about this except that when I passed through Billings, Tom Arthur said he thought Teapot Dome was a scandal and ought to be exposed."

La Follette's instincts were on target. At the mention of the oil lobbyist's name, Walsh's hesitation dissolved. Arthur was an old friend, and Walsh knew his job—rather, his life's work—was promoting the energy industry. Tom Arthur wouldn't denigrate an oil deal without good reason.

Walsh's dark, bushy eyebrows arched with interest. "Tom Arthur said that?"

"He certainly did."

CHAIRMAN REED SMOOT may have gaveled the Senate Committee on Public Lands and Surveys to order on October 22, 1923, a few months after Harding's death, but there never was any doubt who would act as its prosecuting attorney. Spurred on by his conversation with Wheeler, Tom Walsh had pored over reams of geology reports, legal briefs, and Interior Department records. He had been single-handedly carrying the burden of prep work for the hearings, and now his colleagues were content to saddle him with the equally demanding job of examining witnesses and introducing evidence. For the committee's Republican leadership, who in their self-interested partisanship prayed the investigation would lead nowhere, it was a gamble, but no one was willing to share the labor with the industrious Democrat.

At first, the Republicans' hope seemed well placed. During its first day of hearings, the committee heard from two consulting geologists, who reported that private wells on land adjacent to the naval reserves were slowly sucking Teapot Dome dry. That bolstered the administration's main rationale for the leases: that the reserves would eventually become worthless if the government didn't open the land to drilling.

The next day, Walsh suffered another setback with his first major witness. Garrulous yet evasive in a western drawl that perfectly complemented his drooping mustache, former interior secretary Albert Fall held the party line. He insisted that the leases were a good business deal for the federal government, which would receive handsome royalties, and that he had felt compelled to turn a profit on the reserves before they were drained completely. When Walsh questioned him about the secrecy surrounding the deals, Fall invoked national security, explaining that the leases were part of a broader administration strategy to prepare for possible war with Japan (a common worry among US military strategists), and as interior secretary, it hadn't been his place to advertise the details of America's military readiness.

Most crucially, Fall asserted that no benefit had accrued to him personally as a result of the deals. Fall had resigned the previous spring, supposedly to return to New Mexico and resuscitate his struggling cattle ranching business, but since then he'd found other ways to keep busy. He'd traveled to Russia on behalf of one of the oilmen involved in the deals, Harry Sinclair, and public filings now listed him as an adviser to the other, Edward L. Doheny. Walsh grilled him about these activities—it wasn't unheard of for companies that dealt with the government to reward public officials with cushy jobs after some important decision was made in their favor—but Fall flatly denied that he'd received compensation from either Sinclair or Doheny. It was all unpaid work for friends, he claimed, and all he ever asked for was repayment of his expenses.

The next two witnesses, Sinclair and Doheny, also revealed little of value, although Walsh did elicit some startling estimates of the leases' value. "I would say that we will be in bad luck if we do not get a hundred million dollar profit," Doheny said of the Elk Hills reserve. Sinclair guessed that Teapot Dome was worth roughly the same amount to him. Both also admitted to longtime friendships with the former interior secretary. Sinclair and Fall, for instance, had traveled to the Kentucky Derby in the oilman's private railcar. Doheny's bond was even tighter. The two men had known each other since the 1880s, when they were young fortune seekers in the silver mines of New Mexico.

By the time the committee adjourned for a four-week break on November 2, 1923, having heard testimony from the three principals involved in the oil transactions, Walsh still had nothing to hang his suspicions on. Republicans like Smoot, well aware that scandal could disrupt his party's chances in the 1924 election, were hopeful that the hearings would soon conclude with a complete exoneration for Fall. Even Walsh had to wonder: Had Tom Arthur been off the mark?

But Tom Walsh was an experienced courtroom attorney and knew the virtue of patience. In many cases, a prosecutor (or a newspaper publisher or a congressional investigator) could air charges against some notable person without a key piece of evidence in hand and then let the scent of accusation waft over the public. Newspaper headlines would reach someone with a grudge. Word of mouth would find that key witness with an acute sense of justice. Inevitably, evidence would trickle in against the accused.

In the case of Teapot Dome, it was more of a deluge. Walsh's office was flooded with so many tips that he could only follow up on the most promising. Among these was a telegram from Sidney Whipple, editor of the *Denver Express*. Whipple told Walsh of a reporter at the rival *Denver Post*, Diedrich F. Stackelbeck, who had investigated Albert Fall's financial situation until his editors abruptly killed the story after coming to a private understanding with Harry Sinclair. (There were rumors of a $1 million transaction between Sinclair and the *Post*'s owners that essentially amounted to a blackmail payoff.)

At Walsh's behest, Whipple met with Stackelbeck and wired back his findings:

```
HE TELLS ME FALL WAS BROKE BEFORE TEAPOT
DOME AND THAT AFTER THE DEAL HE CAN SHOW
FALL HAD SEVERAL HUNDRED THOUSAND DOLLARS
DEEDS TO LAND ETC OF WHICH HE HAS RECORD
WILL BEAR OUT CONTENTION STOP HE HAS DATES
RECORDS AND NAMES TO CORROBORATE STOP
DENVER POST APPARENTLY SUPPRESSED HIS
REPORT AFTER IT WAS MADE BUT HE SAYS THAT IF
PUT ON WITNESS STAND HE WOULD DIVULGE WHOLE
DEAL WHICH HE CHARACTERIZES AS ROTTEN STOP
STACKELBECK SEEMS AFRAID OF HIS JOB UNLESS
CONFIRMATION IS FORCED FROM HIM STOP FULLY
BELIEVE HE HAS VALUABLE STUFF AND NAMES OF
WITNESSES AND FACTS PERTINENT TO PRESENT
INQUIRY AND HES WILLING COME TO WASHINGTON
IF YOU WANT HIM PLEASE ADVISE
```

Walsh knew he was on to something. He immediately summoned Stackelbeck to Washington for a private conference, where the reporter related what he knew and turned over his list of sources. A flurry of Senate subpoenas followed.

When the committee reconvened four weeks later on November 30, Walsh called one witness after another with strange tales of a sudden turn in Fall's financial fortunes. In 1920, Fall—then a member of the Senate—had been in dire financial straits. He wasn't paying his taxes, and his ranch in Three Rivers, New Mexico, was on the verge of bankruptcy. To stave off financial ruin, he agreed to sell off his interest in the *Albuquerque Journal* to a rival newspaper publisher, who visited Fall's ranch to close the deal. The publisher recalled for the committee how Fall had been desperate for the $25,000 the transaction would net him—and how he needed the proceeds in cash. At the time, Fall drove a broken-down Franklin, and the "road" running to his ranch house was little more than a pair of ruts in the earth.

Three years later, after Fall had signed over the oil reserves, the publisher returned to Three Rivers and barely recognized Fall's ranch. "There had been pillars built up to this road," he told the committee, "and beautiful woven wire fence put along, and trees planted, and beautifully concreted gutters, and a very expensive road up to the ranch house."

Other testimony confirmed that Fall was no longer acting like a bankrupted rancher. At a cost of $40,000, he had installed a new electric lighting system on his ranch, complete with its own hydroelectric power plant. At a cost of $91,500, he had purchased the ranch adjoining his own. At a cost of $33,000, he had bought still more land—and had made other, smaller expenditures for new fencing, new construction, and repairs to existing buildings. The total outlay, the committee was told, approximated $175,000.

Walsh then buttressed the testimony with more damning evidence. Local tax records revealed that Fall had been in arrears on his property taxes for nearly a decade—until June 1922, when, about two months after signing the lease to Teapot Dome, he suddenly paid nine years of back taxes. Even for the committee's most partisan-minded Republicans, that was a hefty coincidence to swallow.

Walsh now circled back to the former interior secretary. Could Fall return to Washington, he asked, not so politely now, and explain his apparent windfall? As the committee waited for a response, some still hoped for an innocent explanation, but that stretched the limits of wishful thinking. A pauper in 1920, the prince of Three Rivers in 1923, and in the meantime all he'd done was sign away petroleum rights worth $200 million. Any senator could do the math.

TOM WALSH WASN'T alone in peeling back layers of Washington mystery in the fall of 1923. As the Public Lands committee investigated the suspicious oil deals, two floors down in the Senate Office Building another panel uncovered evidence of staggering corruption at the Veterans' Bureau—fraudulent hospital contracts, kickbacks, and some $200 million unaccounted for. The graft might have seemed petty if it hadn't been so grand in scale. The bureau, for example, bought floor wax and cleaner from a federal contractor at 98 cents a gallon when a fair price would have been 4 cents—and purchased $70,000 worth of it. It later offloaded surplus goods with the same casual disregard for price, selling, for instance, 84,000 brand-new bedsheets at 26 or 27 cents each when they had cost $1.37 apiece. In total, it sold $7 million worth of surplus supplies for only $600,000, all while disabled veterans struggled to obtain basic medical care.

But the Select Committee on Investigation of Veterans' Bureau probed far beyond the walls of that embattled agency, whose director had already been forced to resign and whose chief counsel had committed suicide. Its hearings also cast light onto a shadowy world of fixers, bribe brokers, and other so-called mystery men who had infested the nation's capital since President Harding's inauguration, selling political favors to industrial titans, bootleggers, organized crime bosses, and anyone with enough cash. "These men drop quietly into the swirling pool of inside politics here," the *Dayton Daily News* reported, "and soon acquire prominence through their ability to reach men in high places by means unknown."

These tandem Senate probes became the talk of the town—and not just in the capital but across the country. Americans followed each day's new development from the Teapot Dome or Veterans' Bureau hearings in the same way they tracked Babe Ruth's pursuit of a home run record. In this they were aided by a scandal-happy press. Indeed, Washington correspondents wrote of little else, and their editors back home translated each new revelation into a banner headline: The *Atlanta Constitution*'s double-decker "INTRIGUE, DEBAUCHERY, CORRUPTION ARE CHARGED AGAINST FORMER DIRECTOR OF VETERANS' BUREAU" was typical of the matter-of-fact sensationalism that graced nearly every morning and evening edition.

Before long, a dark cloud of suspicion hung over Washington. Just three years earlier, Americans had embraced Warren Harding's "return to normalcy." Enticed by all the thrills of the Roaring Twenties—the runaway stock market, the manic hedonism—they had willingly overlooked the dark undercurrents swirling beneath the good times. Now the two Senate probes pried their eyes open. Politicians could no longer evade suspicion with beaming-smile promises of prosperity. "No one above ground or below," the *New York Herald-Tribune* editorialized, "is beyond the reach of innuendo." So many millions who had mourned Warren Harding just months before now reevaluated his legacy, wondering how the late president, who had signed the executive order transferring the reserves from the US Navy to the Interior Department, could have allowed himself to be manipulated by his cronies.

And Harry Daugherty was perhaps the most manipulative of those cronies. He had done nothing as attorney general to aid either Senate investigation, even after the committees produced evidence that crimes had probably been committed. As the revelations from Capitol Hill became more scandalous, his refusal to refer the cases to a prosecutor or mobilize the Bureau of Investigation became all the more glaring. Even within the Justice Department, some of Daugherty's subordinates voiced frustration. On November 21, Assistant Attorney General John W. H. Crim, a widely respected, apolitical lawyer who headed the department's criminal division and rarely saw eye to eye with his boss, wrote to Daugherty that the Veterans' Bureau matter was one that "somebody ought to be handling with a view to a very speedy prosecution." The attorney general promptly shot down Crim's suggestion, falsely claiming that the Senate committee chairman had asked him to stay on the sidelines. "This is the situation," was Daugherty's curt response. "Thank you for your memorandum notwithstanding."

In the face of this inexplicable inaction, lawmakers and journalists were beginning to wonder, out loud and in print, whether Daugherty had something to hide. In particular, they speculated about what role the attorney general's deceased roommate had played in that shadowy network of Washington mystery men. "Among their acquaintances," reported the November 22, 1923, *Miami Times*, for instance, "was the late Jess W. Smith, the intimate friend and agent of Attorney General Daugherty, whose suicide . . . has never been explained."

The sober mind of Tom Walsh harbored suspicions, too. "Harry Daugherty has a hand in every dirty piece of business which has come out of the Harding administration," he once whispered in private. "There is every reason to believe, at the very least, Daugherty is one of the men who knows the whole sordid story of the oil leases—and there is enough evidence to warrant the suspicion that he himself might have profited from them."

For Burton Wheeler, whose campaign pledge to "get Daugherty" had grown a year old, these surfacing suspicions made him all the more impatient to join his mentor in shaking the foundations of Washington. Soon he would get his chance. On December 3, the Sixty-eighth Congress was scheduled to convene its first session, at which point Wheeler would finally be invested with the powers of a US senator.

Eager as he was, however, some disquieting reports from Walsh gave him pause. In recent weeks, Montana's senior senator discovered that his own phone lines had been tapped, his mail opened, and his office ransacked at least twice. Out West, a detective was snooping around Walsh's past for dirt. Not even the senator's family was sacrosanct. As his daughter and three-year-old granddaughter were strolling down a DC street, a strange man accosted them and warned that they must persuade Walsh to drop the investigation—or else. Walsh had no doubt who was behind these intimidation tactics, and he shared his thoughts with Wheeler.

"The Department of Justice and its Bureau of Investigation are hand-picked by Daugherty and rotten to the core," Walsh said. "It is my conviction that the man would go to any lengths to protect himself and his friends—and, make no mistake about it, the people we are after are friends of the attorney general."

7

"I Object!"

Freshmen senators were expected to behave like well-bred children, seen but not heard. As Burton Wheeler later explained it, a first-year senator would typically "take his seat in the last row, silently learn proper senatorial decorum from the veterans, and in time perhaps come to be accepted as a member of the 'club' within the club that is the heart of the Senate." Wheeler, however, had never been one to bow to tradition.

Soon after the Senate convened for a new session on December 3, 1923, and Montana's junior senator finally took his oath of office, majority leader Henry Cabot Lodge of Massachusetts was going through a series of routine motions to organize the Senate's thirty-four committees. Technically, the rules required separate roll-call votes for each of the chairmanships, but that could easily consume several days of business. Instead, in the spirit of comity, the majority and minority leaders usually dispensed with a vote entirely by agreeing on committee assignments in advance and combining them into a single resolution. Lodge had already hammered out all the details with his Democratic counterpart, Joseph Robinson of Arkansas, so he expected no dissent when he requested his colleagues' unanimous consent to adopt the organizing resolution.

"Is there objection?" the presiding officer asked. It was the most perfunctory of questions, all but assuming an answer in the negative.

A time-honored tradition of the famously collegial Senate, unanimous consent was the lubricant that kept its parliamentary engine from seizing up. Several times a day, senators would ask their colleagues to set aside the formal rules in the name of expediency and proceed with

some uncontroversial action—to dispense with the reading of the previous day's journal, to forgo a roll-call vote and pass legislation of little
consequence, or even to ratify a complex backroom deal agreed to by the
floor leaders of each party. The presiding officer would then pause for the
shortest of moments before announcing that "without objection, it is so
ordered." Any senator had a right, technically speaking, to object, but to
do so in response to a routine request was considered a grave breach of
etiquette.

As far as some were concerned, however, far more than etiquette had
been breached in Washington in recent years. In response to Lodge, a voice
bellowed from the back row.

"I object!"

Heads swiveled in search of the voice's source and found Burton K.
Wheeler standing behind his mahogany desk. Stunned silence gave way to
frantic chatter as the Senate tried to process what had happened. Minority
Leader Robinson spoke up and reminded the Senate that unanimous consent requests required, well, unanimity.

"Who objected?" asked a senator who hadn't been paying attention.

The presiding officer apparently hadn't paid attention, either. He incorrectly identified Robinson as the objector: "The senator from Arkansas."

"I have not objected," Robinson said. "I merely stated that any senator has the right to object."

Someone whispered something into the ear of the presiding officer, who now corrected the record: "The junior senator from Montana
objected."

"Did the senator from Montana object to the resolution?" another
senator asked, seemingly incredulous that anyone would begin his senatorial career this way.

"I objected," Wheeler answered.

"Very well."

A senior Democrat, concerned that this young man from Montana
might not understand how things worked in the Senate, hurried over to
Wheeler's desk and whispered: "This is the time to follow the leader."

Wheeler flashed his blue eyes at his older colleague. "Leader, hell!" he
said. "I have a duty to perform here."

He soon made it clear that he wasn't merely being impertinent. He had
a substantive objection to the resolution. It was unfinished business from
the 1922 railway strike—namely, the nomination of Republican Albert

Cummins as chair of the Interstate Commerce Committee, which oversaw transportation policy.

Although Harry Daugherty had authored the sweeping injunction that ended the strike, he hadn't done it alone. When the attorney general strode into that Chicago courtroom to secure a court order, he invoked a statute that had hamstrung the railway unions, one that lopsidedly favored the railroad corporations in labor disputes—the Esch-Cummins Act of 1920. It was Senator Cummins's signature piece of legislation, and it had done more than anger the labor movement. It had also lifted restrictions on freight rates, a move that enriched the railroads and brought the nation's farmers to their knees.

By reshaping federal railroad policy into something that favored the rich and powerful at the expense of the poor and marginalized, the law offended Wheeler's sense of economic justice. Moreover, Wheeler knew that, among Montana's farmers and workers—his political base—the law's coauthor had come to represent all that was wrong with Washington's subservience to Wall Street. A principled as well as shrewd politician, he was willing to use any and every parliamentary trick to block Cummins's appointment.

For the moment, his objection had that effect. Although Republicans enjoyed a 51 to 45 majority on the Senate's official party rolls, seven of them were progressives who, it now turned out, shared Wheeler's misgivings about the reactionary Cummins. Although they'd initially lacked the audacity to object themselves, when Wheeler forced the issue and the Senate proceeded to a roll-call election, these progressive Republicans defected and voted for one of their own, Robert La Follette. On the first ballot, no candidate achieved a majority—Cummins received 41 votes, Democrat Ellison "Cotton Ed" Smith 39, and La Follette 7. A second ballot and then a third ended the same way. The Senate was deadlocked. For now, the chairmanship remained vacant.

Just one week into his freshman term, the Senate's second-youngest member had upended the well-laid plans of party leaders who boasted decades of experience. It was a debut unprecedented in the annals of the seniority-obsessed Senate. A senator's term lasted six years, however, and Wheeler knew quite well that he'd need more than parliamentary games to sustain his success.

Over the ensuing weeks, as Lodge, Robinson, and other leaders tried to cobble together a majority for chairman of the Committee on Interstate

Commerce, the young senator quietly sponged up whatever wisdom he could from the masters of the Senate.

As a Republican party elder with progressive sympathies, Sen. William Borah of Idaho was a natural match for Wheeler, and he was especially generous with his advice.

"Wheeler," Borah told him over lunch, "there's a chance for you to make a reputation for yourself."

"How?"

Although Borah was affectionately known as the Lion of Idaho for his thick mane of brown hair and his fierce independence, his exceptional features were a deep, resonant voice and a natural stage presence. Perhaps he was about to give Wheeler some pointers in oratory.

"If you're honest," he said, "and you've got ordinary intelligence, and you're willing to work."

Wheeler didn't follow: "How do you figure that?"

"So damn few want to work."

TOM WALSH WAS one of the damn few. Despite its awesome constitutional responsibilities, the Senate of the 1920s was sorely undermanned. Individual senators were entitled only to a small personal staff, consisting of a clerk, an assistant clerk, a stenographer, and a messenger. Making matters worse, standing committees had no dedicated personnel of their own; their clerks doubled as the chairmen's office assistants. And so the Senate's essential legislative work—drafting legislation, planning committee hearings, poring over official reports, researching the law—often fell to the senators themselves. Where his colleagues shrank from such demanding labor, however, Walsh knew that late nights and long hours eventually bore fruit, as his work on behalf of the Teapot Dome investigation had begun to prove.

Yet despite his dogged search for the truth, as the new year approached Walsh and the Public Lands committee were still awaiting an explanation from former interior secretary Albert Fall for his sudden reversal of fortune. When Walsh invited him to return to the Capitol Hill hearing room, Fall had respectfully declined, citing doctor's orders. He was confined to his bed at the Waldorf Astoria in Manhattan "with an exceedingly bad and threatening cold," he complained in a letter, and could not travel to

Washington. Letters were exchanged, entreaties made, but Fall would not appear in person.

On December 26, the committee finally received an explanation from Fall, albeit in the form of a long, rambling letter. The story was hard to follow, but Fall seemed to suggest that an acquaintance had wanted to get into the New Mexico cattle ranching business. As it happened, the ranch adjoining his own was for sale at the time. As a personal favor to this acquaintance, Fall offered to snatch it up before anyone else could and then later transfer the deed. He just needed some quick cash to take it off the market. That acquaintance, apparently a trusting soul, then loaned him $100,000. It was a convoluted explanation, but at least the punchline was plausible: "The gentleman from whom I obtained it and who furnished me the cash," Fall wrote, "was the Hon. Edward B. McLean, of Washington, D.C."

If anyone could gamble a hundred grand on an unsecured personal loan to a bankrupt rancher, it was Ned McLean, the millionaire playboy who happened to be good friends with Attorney General Daugherty as well as the late president Harding. McLean certainly had the cash, but would he confirm the details?

Now it was McLean's turn to feign illness. When Walsh invited him to share his side of the story with the Senate committee, he promptly received a letter from McLean's lawyer, former attorney general A. Mitchell Palmer, informing them that the publisher could not appear in person, struggling as he was with a nasty sinus infection at his winter home in Palm Beach, Florida. The train journey would simply be too hard on his fragile nasal cavities. McLean's lawyer did, however, confirm that his client had loaned Fall $100,000 in 1921 and, to satisfy the committee's curiosity, offered a sworn, written affidavit. That pleased no one—particularly not Walsh, who doubted that McLean's story would hold up under cross-examination, nor the Republicans who desperately wanted something more definitive that would put the matter behind them.

The telegraph wires between Washington and Palm Beach hummed as all parties searched for a solution. Walsh advised that he'd undergone treatment for sinusitis himself and that if McLean saw the right doctor he could be fit to travel to DC within days. That advice was ignored; the publisher was clearly determined not to testify in person. Instead, McLean leaned on several Democratic friends, who approached Walsh

concerned for "poor Ned's health." When Walsh showed no sign of re-
lenting, McLean started bargaining for immunity, using the editor of the
Washington Post as a go-between, but the committee was reluctant to
grant any favors before it heard McLean's story.

Ultimately, Walsh hit upon a simple solution. He had himself appointed a subcommittee of one. If McLean wouldn't travel north, Walsh
would instead go south and take the publisher's deposition, in person and
on the record. And so he boarded a Florida-bound train and on January
11, 1924, the special "subcommittee" of the Committee of Public Lands
and Surveys convened inside Ned McLean's Palm Beach home.

With a stenographer transcribing the proceedings, Walsh recited Fall's
letter and then asked his witness directly: "Mr. McLean, did you loan a
hundred thousand dollars to Mr. Fall?"

At first, McLean seemed to confirm the story. "I did, yes, sir, in checks."

"Whose checks?"

"My own checks."

This might have been the death of Walsh's case—if the senator had
stopped here. But he pressed on: "Have you got the checks?"

"I do not think so—I am not positive."

"What became of them?"

"Senator Fall returned them to me."

"They never did go through the bank?"

"No, sir."

McLean, it seemed, had been willing to confirm Fall's fabrication to
the Senate committee in writing and had even been willing to mislead
Walsh in person, but when it came time to lie on the record, he couldn't
bring himself to do it. And so he told the truth. He had indeed cut checks
totaling $100,000—that was no lie—but Fall had returned them, unde-
posited, after coming across a new source of funds.

"So that so far as you are concerned you did not give him any cash?"

"Cash? No, sir."

With that admission, the investigation turned back to Fall, who had
gone into hiding. Walsh persuaded McLean, who knew how to get in
touch with the former interior secretary, to pass along a letter. Its central
question was blunt: "If you did not get $100,000 from Edward B. McLean
of Washington to help finance the purchase of a ranch at Three Rivers,
NM, where did you get it?"

AS WALSH AND the country awaited an answer, Wheeler's objection continued to work its chaos in the US Senate. One roll-call vote after another ended in deadlock as the various factions failed to unite behind a choice for Interstate Commerce chair. Pressing business was held up. Party lines broke down.

At one point, a conservative Democrat, aghast at Wheeler's insurgency, crossed party lines to vote for Cummins, a Republican. More Democrats were poised to follow suit—until Wheeler cowed them into submission with a fiery threat.

"You can say for me," he told a newspaper reporter, "that if any such plunderbund is organized it will result in the disruption of the Democratic party in the Senate. There are several Democratic senators, of whom I happen to be one, who won't stand for any such conspiracy, and I am ready to carry my own objections to the point of leaving the party."

One potential solution to the stalemate proved elusive. If only the insurgent bloc of progressive Republicans would cross party lines and vote for a Democrat, someone less reactionary than Cummins, the Senate could move on. But that was a bridge too far for the progressives, and the one man who could coax them across, Robert La Follette, was stuck in Wisconsin, recovering from the flu.

Inaction gripped the Senate for weeks until, finally, after thirty-one deadlocked ballots, a deal was brokered. On January 3, La Follette returned to Washington and rallied his supporters from both sides of the aisle, Wheeler included, to support a compromise candidate. Voting as a bloc on January 9, progressives handed the committee's gavel to a man who, despite his vile, white supremacist politics, would at least give the railway unions a fair shake: the Interstate Commerce Committee's ranking Democrat, "Cotton Ed" Smith of South Carolina.

No senator could remember the last time a member of the minority party had won a major committee chairmanship. But then again, it was a long time since anyone had seriously challenged the Senate's two-party system. With both parties torn between conservative and progressive wings and organized along sectional lines as much as political affinity, there hadn't been any such thing as ideological cohesion. But whereas Senate Republicans had long struggled with rebels like La Follette, Senate Democrats had always maintained functional party unity—until now. A freshman from Montana was leading an insurgency within the Democratic caucus, and he was winning adherents. Senators Dill of Washington, Adams of Colorado, Ferris of Michigan, Copeland of New York, and Ashurst of Arizona, Democrats all, had joined Wheeler in bucking their party's leadership. And in following him, these progressives learned an important lesson: if only they were willing to ignore party lines, they could punch above their weight and realize their goals.

Wheeler had triumphed, and against overwhelming odds. With his two obstinate words and his disdain for the old rules, the forty-one-year-old had outfoxed the white-haired masters of the parliamentary chessboard, handed a defeat to the railroad corporations, and won a small victory for labor.

It was the first time most of the nation had heard of Wheeler, and the press heralded his arrival as a Washington player. Some newspapers vainly tried to paint him as a frontier bumpkin, unschooled in the more refined ways of the nation's capital, but they were only avoiding an unsettling truth. The *Philadelphia Evening Public Ledger* hit upon the real significance of Wheeler's victory. "If I were to pick the best fighter in the U.S. Senate," wrote the paper's Washington correspondent, "I should lay my money on Burt Wheeler."

For Washington potentates like Harry Daugherty, the message was alarming. Hitched to Boxcar Burt, the US Senate was off the rails—and who knew where it would go careening.

8

"Mere Bagatelle"

As the Teapot Dome probe closed in on his old cabinet colleague in the middle of January 1924, Harry Daugherty still refused to lift a finger.

In theory, Walsh and the Senate committee had done the Justice Department a great favor. Up on Capitol Hill, they'd heard nearly 1,700 pages of sworn testimony, gathered financial records, and developed investigative leads that, in the hands of professional detectives, might produce evidence of criminal conspiracy. And yet, down at Justice's Vermont Avenue headquarters, there was no team of federal prosecutors building a criminal case and not a single special agent tracking down the committee's leads. The Bureau of Investigation, in fact, still had yet to open a case file on the matter.

The attorney general's inaction did not go unnoticed. "I have been both detective and prosecutor," said Tom Walsh, "and up to this moment I have received absolutely no assistance from any investigating arm of the federal government. There is the Bureau of Investigation of the Department of Justice, at the head of which is that greatest of detectives—the greatest, they say, since Sherlock Holmes. Yet that bureau has not uncovered one particle of evidence, it has not suggested a single witness, nor has it in any other way aided the committee in its efforts to get to the bottom of this Teapot Dome affair."

Other critics howled that Daugherty was protecting his political cronies, or maybe the legacy of the late president, or perhaps even himself. "I rather imagine," declared Sen. Thaddeus Caraway of Arkansas,

Daugherty's longtime antagonist, in a blistering Senate speech, "that if it were not for my distinguished 'friend,' the present attorney general, all these men would be indicted, but I am conscious that as long as he sits at the helm of the Department of Justice they may sell the White House and be absolutely immune from any prosecutions."

The White House wasn't actually for sale, but its occupant was keeping just as quiet as the attorney general about the mushrooming scandal. Back in the fall of 1923, Calvin Coolidge had asked Chief Justice Taft what to do.

"Do nothing," the politician-cum-jurist counseled. Taft cited an improving economy, which was still climbing out of the recession of 1920–1921. "In the returning prosperity," he said, "people are glad to have a rest from watching Washington, and your wisest course is to be quiet for a while."

That was fitting advice for a man nicknamed Silent Cal, and for a while it worked. The economy boomed, and with it the president's popularity, all while Coolidge kept mum about misdeeds that, after all, had happened under his predecessor's watch. As the revelations on Capitol Hill mounted, however, Coolidge realized that his predecessor's scandal, if left alone, might consume his own presidency. Thanks to Attorney General Daugherty's stubborn inaction, an inquiry into the Harding administration's sins of commission was turning into a question of the Coolidge administration's sins of omission.

That was the last thing Coolidge needed—especially with a stiff intraparty challenge looming at that summer's convention. Although as a sitting president he was the odds-on favorite to lead the Republican ticket in November, he didn't necessarily have a lock on his party's nomination. Already automaker Henry Ford and Pennsylvania governor Gifford Pinchot—an old friend of Theodore Roosevelt's and thus a darling of the progressives—had thrown their hats into the ring.

So had California senator Hiram Johnson, another progressive who was making an effective campaign issue out of Teapot Dome. By January 19, Johnson declared that the oil scandal had effectively knocked Coolidge out of the race.

"I have visited six states in the last two weeks," Johnson said, "and in every one of them numerous men voluntarily expressed their opinion that the Teapot Dome scandal has absolutely put an end to President Coolidge's possibilities as a Republican nominee. It has damaged Mr. Coolidge's administration from one end of the country to the other that he has made no move to assist the investigators."

The statement apparently struck a nerve. Although presidents usually granted their attorneys general complete autonomy in matters of investigation and prosecution, lest politics intrude on matters of criminal justice, Coolidge felt this situation warranted his direct intervention. The very day after his challenger's remarks, Coolidge summoned his attorney general.

Daugherty appeared at the White House on a rainy January day to suffer a private humiliation. Coolidge ordered him to send a representative to the Senate hearings and monitor the proceedings for evidence of criminal conduct. If any was produced, the president directed, then the attorney general would enforce the relevant criminal statutes, as his oath of office required.

No one told Harry Daugherty how to manage his own department, but open defiance of a direct presidential order would cross a line, even for him. And so the Justice Department finally leapt into action.

For Walsh and the Senate, the timing couldn't have been more fortuitous. Rumors had just reached both the committee and the Justice Department that Albert Fall was in New Orleans, where he was preparing to flee the country by steamship.

Within hours, a newly helpful Director Burns ordered special agents of his Bureau of Investigation to track down the former interior secretary and prevent him, by force if necessary, from boarding any ship. "Ascertain immediately whether he has booked passage," Burns instructed. "Under no condition is he to be permitted to leave the country." Agents caught up with Fall at the Roosevelt Hotel in New Orleans and placed him under surveillance.

Meanwhile, another agent of the Justice Department was entrusted with a Senate subpoena that would finally compel Fall to testify again before Walsh's committee. As the Bureau detectives looked on, a deputy US marshal intercepted Fall in the hotel lobby and served him with the summons. Fall immediately realized he had no chance of escape. Within twenty-four hours, he was on an eastbound train, resigned to appearing before the committee.

All told, it was extraordinary presidential intervention in Justice Department affairs, and for once Coolidge was not bashful before the press. "I don't suppose it needs to be stated that if any irregularities are disclosed," he told the White House press corps, off the record, "or any misdeeds on the part of anyone, they will be subject to investigation by the Department of Justice, and such action taken as the laws of the country require."

Publicly shamed, the attorney general managed to swallow his embarrassment and offer the White House his support. He still had some leverage over the president—with a primary challenge from the Republican Party's left flank, Coolidge would need Daugherty and his Ohio delegation more than ever—but his grip was slipping. On January 24, he sent the president a letter that struck an uncharacteristically servile tone. "All phases of this matter are under observation, investigation, and consideration by the Department," it read, "and I can with great pleasure assure you that your instructions and desires meet with my hearty and cordial support."

AS THE CLOCK struck two in the afternoon of January 24, Tom Walsh settled in on one side of a big conference table, just to the left of the Public Lands committee's new chairman, Republican Irvine Lenroot. (Senator Smoot had handed over the gavel to become chairman of the powerful Committee on Finance.) In front of Walsh sat piles of legal files and transcripts. Across the table, an empty chair awaited the man of the hour.

It was the only unoccupied seat. Word had spread that a surprise star witness—not Albert Fall, who was still in transit from New Orleans, but someone else connected to the case—had arrived at the Capitol to tell his story. Senators soon deserted the legislative chamber and packed themselves into the stuffy hearing room. Reporters crowded the exit, jockeying to be the first to the telephones when news broke. Perhaps the most conspicuous sight was an assistant attorney general, Rush Holland, who, at the president's personal direction, sat behind the chairman, pencil and notebook in hand.

"I asked the committee to meet this afternoon," Walsh announced, "because I was informed that Mr. Doheny desired to come before the committee to make a statement. If he is present we would like to have him now."

A face in the crowd, wearing gold-rimmed glasses and a white walrus mustache, stood up.

"All right," said Edward L. Doheny, who moved into the empty chair opposite Walsh. His lawyer, Gavin McNab, was a prominent film-industry fixer who had represented Fatty Arbuckle, Charlie Chaplin, and Mary Pickford, among other movie stars, squeezed in next to him.

Doheny, in contrast to his slick Hollywood lawyer, struck a folksy appearance. But Walsh knew that the affable, rosy-cheeked oilman could be just as conniving. That past December, during a break in the hearings, Walsh had received Christmas greetings from his old friend—along with an invitation to invest in a surefire oil proposition. Although framed as a neighborly gesture, the kind of thing any good millionaire oil tycoon did for his friends, it was a clever trap, a scheme to compromise the senator before his investigation could strike pay dirt. Walsh wisely and politely declined. "This may be squeamishness on my part," he wrote in response, "but I prefer rather to be thought oversensitive than to be under suspicion of having utilized the position to which my people have elevated me for my own profit." Even after Walsh refused the bait, Doheny kept trying to reel him in, invoking their friendship and explicitly urging the senator to drop his investigation. Walsh simply stopped responding.

Now Doheny peered through his spectacles at his friend-turned-adversary and read from his prepared statement. "I wish to state to the committee and to the public the full facts," he said, his voice soft and contrite. "I regret that when I was before your committee I did not tell you what I am telling you now. When asked by your chairman whether Mr. Fall had profited by the contract, directly or indirectly, I answered in the negative. That answer I now reiterate."

Everyone in the room sensed the "but" coming. Doheny delivered. "I wish first to inform the committee," he continued, "that on the thirtieth of November, nineteen twenty-one, I loaned to Albert B. Fall a hundred thousand dollars upon his promissory note to enable him to purchase a ranch in New Mexico. This sum was loaned to Mr. Fall by me personally. It was my own money and did not belong in whole or in part to any oil company with which I am connected."

His pending business before the Interior Department, he stressed, in no way influenced his generosity: "In connection with this loan there was no discussion between Mr. Fall and myself as to any contract whatever. It was a personal loan to a lifelong friend."

Crafted by his lawyer, Doheny's statement strained to make the transaction sound aboveboard. Walsh's cross examination homed in on the story's absurdities.

"How did you transmit the money to him?" Walsh asked.

"In cash."

"How did you transport the cash?"

"In a satchel. The cash was put up in a regular bank bundle, and taken over and delivered to him."

With each question, Walsh handed Doheny a chisel: "Who acted as your messenger in that matter?"

And with each answer, Doheny chipped away at his story's plausibility: "My son."

When Walsh asked why cash and not a more conventional method for a transaction of that size—check, for instance—the oilman offered no answer. Instead, he emphasized how trivial that bundle of banknotes, a mere hundred grand, was to a man like himself.

"I realized that the amount of money I was loaning him was bagatelle to me; that it was no more than twenty-five or fifty dollars to the ordinary individual. Certainly a loan of twenty-five or fifty dollars from one individual would not be considered at all extraordinary, and a loan of a hundred thousand dollars from me to Mr. Fall is no more extraordinary."

A hush fell over the crowded room.

When Walsh finally broke the silence, his rejoinder was acid: "I can appreciate that on your side, but looking at it from Senator Fall's side it was quite a loan."

ACUTELY AWARE OF his own criminal liability, Doheny stuck to his story, even as it became laughably obvious that the $100,000 "loan" must have had some connection to the $100 million transaction executed between the two men around the same time.

And then, when Albert Fall finally appeared in the hearing room a week later on February 2, under subpoena and shadowed by Bureau agents who were ready to block any escape overseas, he would act exactly as a guilty man would, declaring that the committee had no legal authority to investigate the matter and then, for good measure, invoking his Fifth Amendment rights.

Even before that, though, a newly emboldened Calvin Coolidge had intervened again. On Saturday, January 26—just two days after Doheny's startling admission—Coolidge was cruising down the Potomac on his presidential yacht when he learned that the Senate Public Lands committee was about to recommend the appointment of special counsel who would be empowered to cancel the leases through civil litigation and, if the evidence warranted, bring criminal charges against the guilty parties.

Senator Walsh had already written the necessary joint resolution, and the committee's Republicans felt compelled to support it. Coolidge, for once, was determined to get ahead of events.

That evening, the president huddled with his advisers and drafted an announcement that presented the appointment of special counsel as his own idea. In fairness, he did put his own twist on Walsh's proposal, mandating a team of two special counsel, one Republican and one Democrat. Furthermore, these prosecutors would operate independently of the Justice Department, reporting directly to the White House. The case would effectively be walled off from Harry Daugherty's influence.

News of the president's decision reached the vacationing Daugherty in Miami mere hours before the White House was set to hand it over to the press, and it caught him off guard. Coolidge's action was a daring (if not unprecedented) insertion of presidential power into the professional domain of lawyers and a direct challenge to the attorney general's authority. Daugherty scrambled to get ahead of the news by dashing off a telegram to President Coolidge. Carefully crafted to give the impression that the special counsel was not Walsh's, not Coolidge's, but *his own* idea, the cable feigned ignorance of the imminent announcement. He immediately leaked it to the press.

"May I again urge," it read, "the desirability you immediately appoint two outstanding lawyers, who as such shall at once take up all phases of the oil leases under investigation." A suddenly statesmanlike Daugherty assured the president that he did "not desire to evade any responsibility in this or other matters, but considering Mr. Fall and I served in the cabinet together, this would be fair to you, to Mr. Fall, and the American people."

Clearly designed to spare himself outright humiliation, Daugherty's ploy couldn't keep eyebrows from arching all over Washington. To anyone but the most credulous observer, it was clear that Coolidge was sidelining his attorney general. But why? Maybe it was simply that Daugherty had waited too long to aid the Senate investigation and only then under direct presidential order. Or perhaps the president sensed that Daugherty, a political animal to his bones, would inevitably taint an investigation that ought to rise above politics.

Whatever his reason, Coolidge declined to state it. But the implication was both clear and astounding. The president couldn't trust his own attorney general to pursue impartial justice. For Daugherty's enemies—Wheeler included—it was like throwing meat to the sharks.

9

"Resolved"

On Tuesday, January 29, the Senate was concluding its business for the
day when Burton Wheeler rose from his desk to offer a resolution.
He asked that it be read aloud. It was short, he promised. Nevertheless, given his reputation, it surely made some of his colleagues nervous.

A sheet of paper made its way to the rostrum, where the clerk read the
text of Senate Resolution 137:

> Whereas several weeks have transpired since the evidence was
> presented and disclosures were made before the Public Lands Com-
> mittee of the Senate charging past and present public officials of the
> Government and others with conspiracies to defraud the Govern-
> ment, violations of law, and corrupt practices, and no prosecutions
> have been undertaken; and . . .
>
> Whereas it appears that Harry M. Daugherty has lost the con-
> fidence of the President of the United States as exemplified by the
> President's statement that he intends to employ at great expense to
> the Government special attorneys not connected officially with the
> Department of Justice, indicating that this department can not be
> trusted with the prosecution of the cases which have arisen by rea-
> son of the disclosures before the Senate Committee on Public Lands
> and Surveys; and
>
> Whereas said Harry M. Daugherty has lost the confidence of the
> Congress of the United States and of the people of the country and
> the Department of Justice has fallen into disrepute: Therefore be it

> *Resolved*, That it is the sense of the United States Senate that the President of the United States request the immediate resignation of Harry M. Daugherty as Attorney General of the United States.

For Wheeler, the moment was a long time coming. Some fifteen months had passed since the former federal prosecutor, his sense of legal righteousness offended by an unfair and probably unconstitutional injunction, pledged revenge against the attorney general. And yet his promise had lost no urgency. To the contrary, with scandal swirling and criminals running free, the legal bureaucracy of the United States needed a trustworthy officer at the helm more than ever.

On this Tuesday in January 1924, however, S. Res. 137 was too bold a measure for immediate action by the upper house of Congress—the "saucer," to use George Washington's analogy, that cooled a hot cup of tea. Burton Wheeler might have been ready to declare war on the attorney general of the United States, but the Senate was not. The resolution was laid on the table for further consideration.

Nevertheless, it served one immediate purpose. In the uproar over Teapot Dome, administration critics were making specific demands for justice—canceling the leases; prosecuting Albert Fall; dismissing the navy secretary, Edwin Denby, who had transferred the petroleum reserves to the Interior Department. Only then, these critics declared, could the Coolidge administration put the scandal behind it.

Wheeler's resolution added one more demand. Not until Attorney General Daugherty was sacked and replaced by a law officer who would pursue impartial justice could the nation move on.

The press, which had been speculating for well over a year about when the often-ailing and clearly out-of-favor Daugherty would leave office, wondered if this cannonball from Capitol Hill might finally be the one to dislodge him. "Republican leaders were predicting Tuesday," the *Kansas City Star* reported, "that the oil lease exposure would lead to changes in the cabinet. Secretary [of the Navy] Denby and Attorney General Daugherty were slated to resign in these predictions."

But when reporters caught up to Daugherty—still vacationing in Florida—the attorney general shrugged off the resolution as nothing more than an empty partisan gesture. As 1924 was an election year, a senior Republican figure like Daugherty could expect abuse from an ambitious young Democrat trying to make a name for himself.

"I am here to play," he told the reporters. "I'm not worried about the situation in Washington, and I don't consider it necessary to make a reply to the attacks which have been made against me."

That was his public position, at any rate. Privately, the attorney general was already sharpening his axe. This young western senator, clearly unschooled in the ways of Washington, needed to learn that no one could take a shot at Harry Micajah Daugherty and walk away unscathed.

ALTHOUGH ITS LANGUAGE was forceful and its tone indignant, Wheeler's resolution hewed close to publicly known facts. Few could dispute that the Justice Department had ignored Teapot Dome long after reasonable suspicion was aroused, or that President Coolidge had betrayed a loss of faith in his attorney general by appointing special counsel. There was no need to embellish with gossip or innuendo. The public facts were damning enough.

And yet, in the days that followed, Burton Wheeler found himself flooded with private suspicions. Any rumor circulating about Harry Daugherty drew itself to Wheeler's ear with the force of gravity. Anyone with a grudge against the attorney general (and that was half of Washington) knew that the road to revenge now ran through the senator's office. Letters poured in from Ohio, telegrams from Pittsburgh. Some of Wheeler's best sources came from within the federal government. There was even a whistleblower at the Federal Trade Commission who reported that the Justice Department had failed to act on more than fifty antitrust cases referred for prosecution. They were dropped, the whistleblower claimed, in return for donations to the Republican National Committee.

Surprisingly, Wheeler heard little connecting the attorney general to Teapot Dome, aside from a tip that he owned stock in Sinclair Oil. Wheeler, along with Tom Walsh, had initially guessed that Daugherty was complicit in the suspicious oil deals—but maybe he'd simply been too busy with other schemes to get involved. Indeed, all the available evidence now suggested that Daugherty had spent the past three years twisting his powers as attorney general to his own advantage.

"Tips came to me in bunches," Wheeler later recalled, "that Daugherty was up to his neck in massive graft." And many of those tips mentioned the man found dead in the attorney general's bedroom some eight months earlier. Because the attorney general could never be seen with a member of the criminal underworld or with an executive of a corporation under investigation, he had allegedly dispatched Jess Smith as an intermediary to collect bribes in return for protection from prosecution or other under-the-table favors.

The accusations were both shocking and unsurprising. They revealed a grave breach of public trust. But as Wheeler knew firsthand, public justice ultimately came down to nothing more than the private integrity of individuals. As a US attorney, Wheeler had routinely made decisions that meant life or death, imprisonment or freedom, millions of dollars or none at all—and that was as the chief federal law officer of Montana, a state of half a million. Imagine the weighty issues placed in the hands of the nation's chief law officer—and how much his discretion might be worth to interested parties. A Justice Department true to its name hinged on the honesty of one man.

ON FEBRUARY 11, just as a truly crooked picture of the nation's fifty-first attorney general was crystallizing in Wheeler's mind, Harry Daugherty played his first countermove. It took the form of a letter, written on Justice Department stationery, to Frank B. Willis of Ohio, his closest ally in the Senate and the man who occupied Warren Harding's old seat:

> My Dear Senator: Upon my return to Washington yesterday my attention was called to Senate Resolution 137, introduced by Senator Wheeler, of Montana, on January 29, 1924.
>
> I believe the purpose of this resolution is to give the President of the United States and, I think, the country some information relative to my administration of the office of Attorney General of the United States . . .
>
> I think full authorization should be granted a committee to proceed with a hearing so that Senator Wheeler and those interested with him in the subject matter of this resolution may be fully heard and the President and the country fully informed and the matter disposed of on its merits . . .
>
> I suggest as a matter of courtesy to Senator Wheeler, with whom I have no acquaintance, that you request him bring

about this action on the resolution, and if, for any reason, he should not care or be willing to do so, then I respectfully request that you yourself institute in the Senate such action as may be necessary . . . This is fair to everybody.

RESPECTFULLY YOURS,
H.M. DAUGHERTY, ATTORNEY GENERAL

On its face, the letter made little sense. Daugherty was essentially demanding a Senate investigation of himself, daring Wheeler to participate. What could Daugherty possibly gain by escalating the situation? But from the very moment Senator Willis made the letter public, Wheeler recognized it for what it was—a move out of the attorney general's old playbook.

He recalled what had happened the last time a legislator had challenged Daugherty before a committee. When Rep. Oscar Keller, a prolabor Republican from Minnesota who was furious about the attorney general's railway injunction, introduced fourteen articles of impeachment in September 1922, strange things started happening to the congressman. In Washington his House of Representatives office was ransacked, and in Minnesota an investigator went around asking questions about where Keller got the money for his house. By the time the Minnesota Republican Party endorsed his Democratic opponent in the fall election, Keller realized what he was up against. Behind the scenes, Daugherty was pulling wires, twisting arms, and calling in favors—all in an orchestrated campaign to ruin the congressman's career.

Sure enough, when the House Judiciary Committee convened its impeachment hearings, it was Keller himself and not Daugherty who was put on trial. None of the congressman's charges—that the attorney general had failed to enforce the antitrust laws against monopolies, that he had violated his pledged impartiality by favoring the railroad corporations over the labor unions, that he had appointed untrustworthy people to the Bureau of Investigation—was taken seriously. Instead, under Daugherty's influence, the committee badgered Keller about his sources, implying that the congressman had broken the law in obtaining his information. Keller refused to betray confidences, and the committee responded by threatening to have him arrested by the sergeant at arms and locked in the Capitol jail. At this, Keller denounced the hearings as a "comic opera proceeding" and a "barefaced attempt to whitewash Harry M. Daugherty." A shouting match ensued. The chairman banged his gavel. Keller stormed out of the hearing room—and promptly collapsed from a nervous breakdown. By the time the committee later voted twelve to two to dismiss the charges against Daugherty, it had become a mere afterthought.

Now Daugherty was luring his latest challenger into a similar ambush. It would prove to be a rare blunder for the master political strategist.

Unlike Oscar Keller, Burton Wheeler was no newcomer to political combat, not after a decade-plus in Montana's rough-and-tumble arena. In standing up to wartime hysteria as US attorney, he'd nearly lost his legal career. In challenging the state's political machine as a candidate for governor, he'd nearly lost his life. His courage was hard-earned, and he hadn't left it behind in the Treasure State. With right on his side, he could steel himself for battle with any Washington foe.

Wheeler got to work on a revised resolution. If Daugherty was demanding an investigation, Wheeler was not about to disappoint.

MEANWHILE, EVEN AS a new Senate probe took shape, another was winding down.

After exposing one of the greatest corruption scandals in American history, Tom Walsh and the Senate Committee on Public Lands and Surveys had pursued the Teapot Dome affair as far as they could. The time had come, Walsh believed, for President Coolidge's bipartisan special counsel to take up the matter.

Two days after Coolidge announced that he would appoint two independent prosecutors to void the oil leases in federal court, follow up on investigative leads developed by the committee, and prosecute the guilty parties, Walsh introduced a joint resolution codifying the plan. Both houses of Congress swiftly adopted the legislation, and Coolidge signed it into law. After an embarrassing false start—his first two picks, it turned out, had ties to the oil industry—the president decided on two accomplished and undeniably impartial lawyers: former US senator Atlee Pomerene, a Democrat, and Pennsylvania lawyer Owen Roberts, a Republican.

Coolidge was adamant that he wanted their investigation to serve the public interest. "If you are confirmed," he told Roberts in a White House meeting, "there is one thing you must bear in mind. You will be working for the government of the United States—not for the Republican party, and not for me. Let this fact guide you, no matter what ugly matters come to light."

Although the path to justice would be a long one—months of confidential investigations and years of dragged-out litigation, conducted
not in the congressional spotlight but in the relatively sedate setting of
a federal courtroom—Walsh was satisfied that Teapot Dome was finally
in the hands of competent and independent prosecutors. As they worked
diligently behind the scenes, Walsh would offer his confidential advice but
otherwise take a back seat. The hearings would conclude. The scandal that
had captivated the American people for the past months, eroding their
trust in the national government, would disappear from the headlines.

As Tom Walsh stood down, Burton Wheeler prepared to step up.

After months of watching his friend and mentor shake the foundations
of American politics, Wheeler had learned a thing or two about how to
stage a public investigation. With any luck, he could hope, Teapot Dome
would prove to be only the first domino to fall—a prelude to an even more
troubling scandal that would expose threats to impartial justice, congressional independence, and the rule of law itself.

10

"The Least Embarrassed Person Here"

As Burton Wheeler sharpened his resolution from one simply censuring the attorney general into one authorizing a full congressional inquiry, Republicans fretted. The fact that Harry Daugherty himself had invited the investigation gave little comfort. With the November 1924 elections less than nine months away and the Harding administration's once-sterling image already tarnished by the Teapot Dome and Veterans' Bureau revelations, the last thing GOP leaders needed was a public inquiry into the record of their controversial attorney general. One by one, senior Republicans—Secretary of State Charles Evans Hughes, Secretary of Commerce Herbert Hoover, Sen. Henry Cabot Lodge, Sen. George Wharton Pepper—began lobbying President Coolidge for Daugherty's swift dismissal, hoping it would forestall any such investigation.

Coolidge was torn. Facing reelection, he was not blind to the risk of keeping on his embattled attorney general. But the stubbornly idealistic president also saw higher principles at stake.

"First, it is a sound rule," he explained to one Republican advocating for Daugherty's ouster, "that when the president dies in office it is the duty of his successor for the remainder of that term to maintain the counsellors and policies of the deceased president."

As an unelected, accidental president, he owed that not just to his predecessor, he believed, but also to the sixteen million Americans who had cast their ballots for Warren G. Harding.

"Second," he continued, "I ask you if there is any man in the cabinet for whom—were he still living—President Harding would more surely demand his day in court, would more surely not dismiss because of public clamor than the man who was his closest personal and political friend?"

Still, even Coolidge understood that high-minded principles alone could not guide him through the swamplands of national politics. If there was a conflict between his moral obligations and cold political calculations, that at least deserved an airing. To that end, on the evening of February 18, one of Daugherty's most vocal Republican critics received an urgent summons to the White House.

WHEN SEN. WILLIAM Borah arrived in the president's second-floor study a little past eight o'clock, Coolidge skipped past the dreaded small talk and got right to the point. He demanded to know the senator's current thinking on Harry Daugherty and the Department of Justice.

Months earlier, in the dark days after President Harding's death, and long before the oil scandal broke, Borah had counseled the president to "get rid of Daugherty" before the controversial attorney general could become a political liability on the campaign trail. Now Borah repeated his advice and in more emphatic terms. Daugherty had lost the confidence of the American people, who deserved for attorney general a man they could trust to pursue impartial justice.

He was in the middle of making his case when a White House usher announced the arrival of a visitor—the attorney general of the United States. A moment later, in walked Harry Daugherty with "his jaw set and his eyes like flint," one observer recalled.

Borah glanced at the president, whose face revealed that it had been his plan all along to bring the two men together. "Now senator," said Coolidge, "I wish you would state your position again."

Irritated, angry even, the great orator fell uncharacteristically silent.

"Well," Daugherty said, "don't let my presence embarrass you."

At that jab, Borah regained his poise and shot back: "I think I should be the least embarrassed person here."

"Let's lay all our cards on the table," Daugherty said. "The president is the one man who should know the facts." He continued: "I know there are some who want me to resign. There is Pepper who wants me to resign because I would not recommend one of his men for judge. Then there are others whose desires I have thwarted who want me to resign. I don't know why you should want me to resign. I have never had to turn you down. You have never asked me for anything."

Daugherty evidently believed that all politics was transactional. Principle could play no role.

An exasperated Borah simply said that it was not his place, nor even the Senate's, to demand the attorney general's resignation. That was the president's duty. But he did believe the president would be warranted in doing so. A shouting match ensued for nearly an hour, with Daugherty issuing his denials at the top of his lungs, protesting that his political enemies were ganging up on him.

All the while, Silent Cal remained true to his nickname, puffing on a cigar as his two guests thundered.

"The country's against you!"

"Because deceived by liars—"

"The press is against you."

"The press has been deceived and I have never been heard in my own defense."

"Then put it another way," Borah said, decisively. "It makes no difference. The whole thing has been planned on the Hill. It can't be stopped. They have decided that you must go."

Daugherty stepped close to the senator and huffed: "Well, if the whole thing has been framed, you may go back to the Senate and tell them to build their scaffold before the presiding officer's desk and I will walk up on it tomorrow at twelve o'clock. But I will never resign under fire unless the president himself requests it."

Daugherty stormed out, white with rage, leaving Borah alone with the president. Only then did Coolidge open his mouth.

"Senator," the president said, "I reckon you are right."

AND YET, DESPITE this private concession, Calvin Coolidge continued to stand by Daugherty in the days to come, even as calls for his dismissal mounted. However he claimed to reckon things, the president was determined to let his attorney general leave on his own terms. His moral obligation to President Harding's voters stayed his hand, yes, but he also had reason to doubt whether firing Daugherty was the politically safe decision.

Indeed, Daugherty had recently threatened, in a letter to a Republican senator, to "carry the issue to the country and in public addresses denounce the action of the administration" if he were forced to resign before he could mount a proper defense.

One of Daugherty's colleagues in the cabinet proposed a novel solution to the president's dilemma.

"If it would be of any help to you," Secretary of State Charles Evans Hughes offered, "I think I could arrange to have all members of the Cabinet place their resignations in your hands. You could then reappoint those you wish to retain."

Coolidge considered the suggestion for a moment and then quipped: "No, don't do that. It might leave me alone with Daugherty!"

11

"A Bigger Fool"

At five in the afternoon of February 19, Burton Wheeler rose from his desk in the back row to deliver his first full speech as a US senator. By the time he obtained recognition from the presiding officer so late in the day, most of his colleagues had trickled out of the chamber. The few who remained now slouched in their chairs, lulled into a kind of parliamentary stupor by the day's proceedings: a seemingly endless debate over adjusting compensation for veterans of the Great War, followed by a lengthy report on economic conditions in Scandinavia. No one was prepared for the fury Wheeler was about to unleash. Like a bank robber in the moment before he pulls a gun, Wheeler enjoyed his private knowledge that he was about to shatter the calm.

He glanced at Henry Cabot Lodge. Reclining in his chair, the majority leader faced forward, unwilling even to turn his head for the maiden speech of Montana's junior senator.

"I want to be frank with the Senate and with the members of the Senate and to say that in this instance I want a real investigation," Wheeler began in a courteous, low-pitched voice. "I want to know that the Department of Justice will be thoroughly investigated."

In response to Daugherty's letter, Wheeler had introduced new legislation. Unlike his earlier resolution, which merely demanded the attorney general's resignation, S. Res. 157 proposed a select committee to investigate Harry M. Daugherty and his maladministration of the Justice Department.

Such an investigation by the Senate of a sitting cabinet officer would be without precedent. Throughout most of its history, and with the notable exception of Teapot Dome, the Senate had taken a back seat to the House of Representatives in probing executive branch misbehavior. That made sense, given the way impeachment worked under the Constitution: the lower chamber acted as prosecutor, the upper as judge and jury.

Wheeler's proposal essentially cut the prosecutor out of the process. As he explained to his colleagues, the House had already proved it wasn't up to the task: "Let me say to the members of the Senate that I do not intend to fall into the same trap that was set for the member of Congress who introduced an impeachment proceeding in the House." Wheeler was referring, of course, to the hapless Oscar Keller, who was forced to flee the very Judiciary Committee hearings he'd initiated back in 1922.

What warranted this unprecedented Senate inquiry? His colleagues deserved an explanation, and here he had to bluff. In his heart he knew Harry Daugherty was guilty. At this point, however, all he had were anonymous tips, not sworn statements; rumor, not fact. So, in the absence of actual evidence, he launched into a monologue on what "everybody" knew—that the attorney general was friends with Doheny and Sinclair, that he had consulted with McLean on the eve of the publisher's deposition, that his former law partner was collecting money for the dismissal of whiskey cases in New York. Was any of it true? He was sure. Could he prove it? Not yet.

And then he invoked the name that was on the lips of all his confidential sources.

"Everybody knows," Wheeler bellowed, his voice reverberating off the chamber's glass and iron ceiling, "that Jess Smith, who was brought from the State of Ohio and had an office in the Department of Justice, and who was not on the payroll, was accepting money in connection with various cases that arose in the Department of Justice."

By now, Lodge was upright in his chair. The name of the man found inside the attorney general's bedroom with a hole in his head was often whispered around Washington but never shouted in such a public forum.

Wheeler continued: "Everybody who knows anything about the history of the matter knows that other friends and confidential advisors of the attorney general of the United States were collecting money and giving as their reason for collecting it that they could use influence with the attorney general. Of course it is very difficult to trace these matters and to show by his close personal friends that he accepted this money.

"It recalls to my mind distinctly how a good many years ago, when I was a young attorney starting out to practice in the city of Butte, Montana, an individual came to me and said that he had been paying the county attorney for protection. He said there had been a man collecting money for the county attorney. I went to see the county attorney and he said to me, 'I have not accepted anything from those men.' I said to him, 'If you have not received the money you are a bigger fool than the people think you are, because it is being collected for you.'"

Having set it up, Wheeler now delivered the caustic punch line: "So I say that if the attorney general has not actually got the money that has been collected in these various cases from one end of the country to the other he is a bigger fool than the people of the United States give him credit for being."

At this point, Lodge's eyes were fixed on Wheeler, his hands posed in concentration.

"I say to you, senators on the other side of the chamber, that this is not a question of Democratic or Republican politics. A veiled threat was held out over me to the effect that if a certain man testified, it would involve some Democrats as well as Republicans. I say to the senators here tonight that it makes no difference to me whether there are Democrats involved or whether there are Republicans involved."

With righteous indignation welling up inside him, Wheeler began biting off the ends of his words and stabbing the air with a pointed forefinger.

"The greatest duty that we can perform is to show up the crooks, whether they are Republicans or whether they are Democrats."

As he drew to a close, Wheeler promised testimony "showing, beyond any question of doubt to my mind, that the attorney general of the United States, the highest law officer in the nation, instead of prosecuting crime has been protecting crime and criminals."

When Wheeler finally settled back down behind his mahogany desk, he could tell that his maiden speech to the Senate had rattled that august body. The *New York Times* hailed it as "the most sensational speech of the present Congress," and the *St. Louis Post-Dispatch* described it as "an attack so savage that even the Senate flinched."

For Wheeler, there was a lesson in the headlines. With little more than gossip and innuendo as supporting evidence, he'd aired half-baked charges against one of the government's most powerful officers. If as a federal prosecutor he'd said the same things in a courtroom, he'd have been summarily dismissed and rightfully so. In this case, however, he uttered them on the floor of the US Senate, protected by congressional immunity—and won the news cycle.

WHEELER'S COLLEAGUES, MEANWHILE, simply weren't accustomed to hearing such naked accusations against a sitting cabinet officer. Some of them sensed trouble.

In an evening conference at the attorney general's Wardman Park apartment, a delegation of Republican senators shared their concerns. Unlike Daugherty's earlier challengers, this young, idealistic senator gave no sign that he would yield and no indication that he could be silenced. Its appetite whetted by Teapot Dome, the public now craved more scandal, and unless Daugherty retracted his earlier demand for an investigation (Wheeler was only delivering the investigation Daugherty had asked for), the Senate would have no choice but to approve the resolution. The senators wanted to know: Was the attorney general prepared for war?

The site of this meeting was steeped with significance. This was the same suite Daugherty had shared with his indispensable friend, his closest companion, a sweet if flawed man whose name this insolent muckraker had dragged through the mud of the Senate floor.

The attorney general reassured the senators. Burton Wheeler was hardly the first to take him on. He wouldn't be the last. In due time and in his own fashion, Harry Daugherty would "take care of this upstart from the sagebrush."

THREE DAYS AFTER Wheeler's scorching speech, the Senate convened for what was supposed to be a more sedate oration. Every year on February 22, in a tradition stretching back to the dark days of the Civil War, a senator would recite Washington's Farewell Address while his colleagues solemnly reflected on the founding father's appeal for national unity. This year, Sen. Frank Willis was chosen for the honor, and, as the chaplain approached the dais for the morning prayer, there was no indication that this 7,641-word recitation by the Ohio Republican would be anything but mundane.

Until, that is, Harry Daugherty strode onto the Senate floor and casually sank himself into a sofa behind the Republican senators. In an instant, the atmosphere inside the chamber became electric. Even the spectators in the gallery above stirred, grasping the significance.

It wasn't that Daugherty was trespassing. He wasn't. Attorneys general, like all cabinet officers, technically enjoyed Senate floor privileges, although they rarely used them.

No, what electrified the Senate chamber was Daugherty's shamelessness in entering the very place where, days earlier, Burton Wheeler had all but hung him in rhetorical effigy. Now here he was in the flesh, communicating a simple but audacious message: he wasn't scared, and he wasn't about to back down.

As Senator Willis launched into the Farewell Address, Daugherty made a show of following along with a printed copy of the text, making a note here or there.

> The alternate domination of one faction over another, sharpened by the spirit of revenge natural to party dissension, which in different ages and countries has perpetrated the most horrid enormities, is itself a frightful despotism.

During the reading, several Republican senators came up to shake his hand. The attorney general smiled. The message was implicit but clear: Harry Daugherty was no pariah here.

And then, in the midst of the reading, running a little late, Burton Wheeler strolled in. Almost immediately, someone pointed out the Senate's unexpected guest, and from across the chamber, Wheeler gaped at the balding man in the back seat.

> [Parties] are likely, in the course of time and things, to become potent engines by which cunning, ambitious, and unprincipled men will be enabled to subvert the power of the people and to usurp for themselves the reins of government.

It was the first time Wheeler had ever set eyes on the man who was quickly becoming his archnemesis. Daugherty's presence in the Senate chamber, Wheeler knew, was a classic power play and made his investigation all the more necessary.

The attorney general glanced up from his copy of the speech and met Wheeler's gaze. An icy tension gripped the room. Both men understood that now was not the time for battle.

At the moment, all they could do was glare.

12

"How Secure I Am"

What started with a bang, to paraphrase a poet of the age, ended with a whimper. Burton Wheeler had been prepared to go all twelve rounds to ram through his proposed investigation of the attorney general. Diminished though his influence may have been, Harry Daugherty still counted some friends in the US Senate, and Wheeler had every reason to expect that they'd fight long and dirty.

It was nothing short of remarkable, then, when no one appeared in the opposing corner. Wheeler's resolution was debated and amended, and Daugherty's allies took every opportunity to denounce the young senator's rhetoric. But the resolution cruised past the usual Senate roadblocks.

On March 1, 1924, less than two weeks after Wheeler had introduced it, S. Res. 157, "Directing a Committee to Investigate the Failure of the Attorney General to Prosecute or Defend Certain Criminal and Civil Actions, Wherein the Government Is Interested," passed by a vote of sixty-six to one, with twenty-nine senators abstaining.

While the lopsided vote may have surprised Wheeler, there were reasons to expect it. One interpretation was that, after the revelations of Teapot Dome, the public's appetite for investigating credible allegations of corruption was simply too strong for the Senate to deny. But the *New York Journal of Commerce* cautioned against reading too much into the outcome, offering an alternative explanation. "Naive observers exclaim at the easy victory of the progressives in the Senate," it editorialized. "The truth of the matter is that the old line group has come to the conclusion that there is little use in trying further to control the machinery of the investigation and that it may well be worth their while to let the extremists make the most of it in the belief that with enough rope allowed them, the senators who are given to making unfounded charges will render themselves ridiculous."

In other words, Daugherty's aiders and abettors were hoping that Burton Wheeler would soon be swinging from a noose of his own making. That was a risk Wheeler was more than willing to take.

MEANWHILE, AMID THE greatest crisis of his political career, Harry Daugherty vanished.

On the afternoon of February 27, the attorney general was once again at the White House, boldly informing President Coolidge that he would not resign unless the chief executive demanded it in writing—a step the famously indecisive president, Daugherty must have reasoned, would never take. Reporters then saw him hurry from the West Wing to a waiting car, which whisked him away to Union Station. There, a Baltimore & Ohio train was idling, half an hour late for its scheduled departure, held up by the railroad authorities for one distinguished passenger. The attorney general stepped aboard, and the train steamed away.

Secrecy shrouded the destination and purpose of Daugherty's trip. The Justice Department refused comment. Even the White House was apparently kept in the dark. The president, it was reported, was "surprised and displeased" at his attorney general's sudden flight from the capital.

It was not until nine the next morning that Daugherty turned up in Chicago's Federal Building of all places, where in 1922, after a similarly secret journey, he'd secured his notorious railway injunction. When the newspapermen caught up to him, Daugherty refused to say what brought him to the courthouse this time.

"I am here on government business," he said, "and therefore cannot disclose it." The inevitable follow-up question failed to extract a better answer. "Gentlemen," he snapped, "there is no use cross-examining me. I shall say what I have to say later."

In the absence of a real answer, speculation turned to a grand jury that had been meeting inside the building for more than three weeks. Under the personal direction of the incorruptible John W. H. Crim, who had resigned as assistant attorney general to become a special prosecutor for the Justice Department, jurors were hearing testimony about waste, graft, and fraudulent contracts worth a staggering $225 million in connection with the Veterans' Bureau scandal. Maybe Daugherty had come to resolve some procedural issue. Or perhaps, mindful of his beleaguered reputation, he was simply there to draw attention to his department's prosecution of the case, belated though it was.

The truth was neither. As the jury foreman would report a couple days later, the grand jury had learned new facts, which prompted it to widen its investigation beyond the Veterans' Bureau to include other irregularities across the executive branch. The Justice Department was one target. There the jurors uncovered evidence, the foreman wrote, "that money was accepted by certain individuals (not attorneys) for the purpose of obtaining clemency for prisoners through their intimacy with officials," and that "money was collected by certain individuals (not attorneys) for obtaining through such intimacy permits for intoxicating liquor." In other words, friends of department officials were taking bribes and using their influence to secure legal favors.

Crim and the grand jury apparently believed that the attorney general of the United States could offer insight.

The upshot instantly conferred credibility on Wheeler's wild claims: Harry Daugherty had appeared before the grand jury not in his capacity as the nation's top legal officer but as a witness to criminal acts.

AROUND THE SAME time, an envelope arrived at the White House by special delivery, marked "personal" and addressed directly to President Calvin Coolidge. Inside was a four-page letter, written in Harry Daugherty's slanted cursive. Although it remained silent on the grand jury matter, the letter addressed his looming battle with Sen. Burton Wheeler. It assured the president that—despite all appearances to the contrary—the attorney general maintained the upper hand.

Senator Wheeler was expecting a "one-sided, unfair, pretended investigation," Daugherty wrote. But the Montanan was in for a surprise. "There will be a *real* investigation," he reassured Coolidge. "We have our plans. The hands behind the scenes will not easily give up."

Daugherty's missive—a plea for patience and for his job—hinted that the gears of his redemption were already in motion. "All things will come out all right," he promised. "You will not be injured but helped. I see the way. The straight path."

He ended the letter on a cryptic note.

"I haven't told you how secure I am."

PART II

13

"Pull Wheeler off Daugherty"

T he man from Washington insisted that he was in Nashville on a strictly personal mission.

Middle-aged and egg-bald with a well-trimmed moustache, Charles Furness Hately of Washington, DC, was waiting in room 505 of the fashionable Maxwell House hotel when John S. Glenn, a local certified public accountant, arrived. Glenn had been summoned to the hotel by telephone, told that an important visitor needed to speak with him.

Glenn was a retired federal agent, and he immediately pegged this mysterious out-of-towner as a fellow detective. Hately seemed to sense this, but he declined to identify which agency he was with. Instead, he emphatically stated that he was traveling on personal business.

Only then did he ask his first question: Did Glenn know Senator Wheeler?

Glenn hadn't seen him since 1917, but yes, he knew the senator, who'd been in the news lately with his bold call for an investigation of the attorney general. "As a matter of fact," Glenn told the visitor, "I know him exceedingly well."

Throughout the 1910s, Glenn had roamed the Mountain West on behalf of the Department of Interior, enforcing a longstanding federal law against selling liquor to Native Americans. Glenn's work frequently brought him into contact with Wheeler, who at the time was US attorney in Montana and personally tried the cases that Glenn submitted for prosecution. Often the two men conferred in Wheeler's home, where Glenn became well acquainted with Lulu Wheeler and the couple's five children.

"What kind of a fellow is Wheeler?"

"He's as square a man as anyone I ever met," Glenn answered. "Square as a die."

The detective clearly wanted more, so Glenn offered some mild criticism. If Wheeler had a fault, he said, it was that he tended to "push his convictions to the finish."

Hately volunteered, apropos of nothing, that he'd come from Washington by way of the Ohio burgh of Washington Court House, which happened to be Harry Daugherty's hometown. And then the detective rephrased his earlier question, asking Glenn directly about Wheeler's morals.

That put Glenn on guard: "Senator Wheeler's morals are beyond reproach."

When Hately pressed him about the senator's private life, Glenn told him he was "barking up the wrong tree," adding that "Mr. Wheeler's life is clean and his domestic relations of the happiest character."

By now, Glenn was beginning to put together what had happened. Days earlier, shortly after Wheeler skewered Attorney General Daugherty in his Senate speech, Glenn had accompanied a fellow accountant on a business trip to Memphis. This colleague happened to be a former resident of Washington Court House and an acquaintance of the attorney general's, and naturally, over the course of their travels, the subject of Wheeler's fiery speech came up. Glenn mentioned that he knew the senator and wondered where he was getting the information for his bold claims. Evidently, his offhand comment found its way to Harry Daugherty's ear and, as in a game of telephone, morphed in its retelling into an offer of help, maybe even a hint that he was willing to divulge private knowledge about the senator. Daugherty must have dispatched this detective to collect.

Glenn now flatly demanded to know what Hately wanted. He would never betray Burt Wheeler, whom he considered a friend, and his patience was growing thin.

The detective responded that he wanted Glenn to "try to pull Wheeler off Daugherty"—and then again insisted that his mission was "absolutely personal."

His suspicions confirmed, Glenn changed tack. Instead of shutting down Hately's questions, he would play detective himself and try to learn what he could about this strange man and his mysterious mission. Soon he had Hately hooked on the idea of a secret summit between the senator and the attorney general, who still had never actually met, their glaring encounter in the Senate chamber notwithstanding. Glenn suggested that he could help arrange for a private conference, and perhaps the two men would work out their differences through conversation. "That might clear up the whole matter," Glenn suggested.

This seemed to satisfy Hately, who must have been happy to have something—anything—to report to his superiors. He urged Glenn to accompany him immediately back to Washington, but the accountant protested that business demanded his presence in Nashville for another week and a half. However, Glenn, friendly and ever helpful now, did offer to escort Hately to the local telegraph office. There he watched the detective produce a red, leather-bound memorandum book from his baggage and compose a coded telegram to Washington. "I have seen party at Nashville," the original, unencoded version read. "Returning to Washington tomorrow."

Glenn took special care to note the recipient of the cable. It was William J. Burns, director of the Bureau of Investigation at the Department of Justice.

By the time Glenn saw Hately off at the train station, where the detective paid for his Louisville & Nashville ticket with a government requisition, alarm bells were ringing. He knew Wheeler as a man of great courage, someone who could never be bullied away from his duty. But as tough as his enemies in Montana had been, the senator had never gone toe-to-toe against anyone like the attorney general of the United States, who evidently had no scruples about tasking his department's secret police with political assassination.

There was no time to waste. Glenn rushed back ten blocks to his office in the Stahlman Building and jotted down a full account of the encounter while it was fresh in his mind. And then he composed a letter to his old friend Senator Wheeler. It bore a chilling warning: Harry Daugherty had unleashed his hounds.

FOUNDED IN THE waning days of Theodore Roosevelt's trust-busting presidency, the Bureau of Investigation was originally meant to be a small in-house crime detection force for the Justice Department, no more.

Before the Bureau's creation, the department, when in need of men trained in the art of detection, had been forced to borrow agents from the US Secret Service, who, though competent, ultimately owed their loyalty to the secretary of the Treasury. Roosevelt believed his attorney general, a fellow reformer, could more ruthlessly pursue land-grabbers, monopolists, and other plutocratic criminals if he had his own detectives, and in 1908, Roosevelt directed him to "create an investigative service within the Department of Justice subject to no other department or bureau, which would report to no one except the Attorney General."

On July 26, 1908, Charles Joseph Bonaparte, who held the unique distinction of being both Napoleon I's grandnephew and Theodore Roosevelt's attorney general, complied. He quietly hired away nine agents from the Secret Service and, along with twenty-five other detectives, appointed them special agents of the Department of Justice.

This new Bureau of Investigation, created by fiat of a Bonaparte rather than an act of Congress, immediately elicited howls of outrage from Capitol Hill. Some raised the specter of the Okhrana, the tsar's notorious secret police force. Others more pointedly invoked "Foucheism"—a reference to Napoleon's ruthlessly effective police chief, Joseph Fouché, who, one critic recalled, "grew so powerful that he intimidated the emperor himself by reasons of the state secrets he held." To these critics, nothing less than the independence of Congress was at stake. What would stop these government sleuths, they asked, from gathering compromising information on congressmen who refused to do the president's bidding? Or from framing senators who pried too indelicately into executive branch affairs? They warned that the Bureau would inevitably devolve into a tool of political surveillance and repression. Government by blackmail seemed assured.

Roosevelt shot back at the critics, claiming they were only trying to protect their own indiscretions from public exposure. Bonaparte was equally dismissive. "Anybody can shadow me as much as they please," he said. "They can watch my coming in and my going out. I do not care whether there is somebody standing at the corner and watching where I go or where I do not go."

In spite of this glib response, the critics' voices faded soon after Roosevelt and Bonaparte left office and were replaced by the new (and less combative) administration of President William Howard Taft. Within a year, Congress retroactively approved Bonaparte's action through the annual appropriations process, officially acknowledging and funding the new agency.

The Bureau, in return, seemed determined to prove its critics wrong. Its special agents, armed with badges (but not yet firearms), came from

accounting or legal backgrounds, and their investigations rarely strayed
into controversial territory. There were also, in those days, relatively few
federal criminal statues on the books, so nothing more than a modest
detective force was needed. The Bureau of Investigation hardly seemed a
threat to America's constitutional order. As late as the spring of 1917—
only four years before Daugherty was to assume command of the Justice
Department—the Bureau employed only 265 agents and operated with a
lean annual budget of $617,534.

And then America waded into Europe's Great War. Called on by the
Wilson administration to help defend the nation against enemies, foreign
and domestic, the Bureau bulked up. Its detective force doubled virtually
overnight, its budget ballooned to nearly $2 million, and a newly muscular
Bureau strayed from a strictly crime-solving role. Its agents hunted German spies. They rounded up tens of thousands of draft-dodging "slack-
ers." They drew up a list of suspected German sympathizers, a group
that, among many examples of overreach, somehow included publisher
William Randolph Hearst and Wilson's former secretary of state, William
Jennings Bryan. Most controversially, they used the recent Espionage Act
to stifle antiwar opinions, labor organizing, and any political dissent they
deemed unpatriotic—a campaign of repression that birthed the American
Civil Liberties Union. By the end of the war, anxieties about a secret police
force had returned.

Subsequent events did nothing to quell them. In the Red Scare that
followed the armistice, the Bureau asserted itself more than ever as a full-
fledged domestic intelligence agency. That transformation was largely the
work of a fresh-faced Justice Department lawyer and former Library of
Congress cataloguer named John Edgar Hoover. Soon after an Italian an-
archist bombed the house of Attorney General A. Mitchell Palmer (who
survived), Hoover, ambitious well beyond his twenty-four years, was
placed in charge of the newly created General Intelligence Division with
access to all of the Bureau's investigative resources. Charged with keeping
tabs on threats to the American way of life, the former Library of Congress clerk started cataloging those threats as if they were books. Drawing
upon field reports, case summaries, and other Bureau records, Hoover
developed a card index to the nation's radical activists and organizations,
its hundreds of thousands of entries cross-referenced and governed by a
Dewey-like decimal system. With Hoover's card catalogue at his fingertips,
Attorney General Palmer then orchestrated sweeping and controversial

raids—many of them carried out by Bureau agents—on union organizers, socialists, and dissenters of all stripes. Thousands were arrested and
hundreds deported, many guilty of nothing more than leftist political
sympathies.

By 1920, the year Warren Harding was elected president, the Bureau had evolved far beyond the modest trust-busting, crime-detecting
force envisioned by Bonaparte and Roosevelt. It now boasted a veritable
army of 579 sworn field agents (who still did not carry guns), assigned to
headquarters as well as field offices across the nation, all vacuuming up
information to supply the Bureau's secret files in Washington. This was
the Bureau of Investigation that Harry Daugherty inherited when he was
sworn in as the nation's fifty-first attorney general on March 5, 1921.

A seasoned political fixer with a keen appreciation for the power of
secrets, Daugherty wasted little time in asserting control over the agency.
Never mind that an accomplished detective, William J. Flynn, already
served as the Bureau's director or that the post was considered an apolitical appointment, above the fray of partisan loyalties and presidential
elections. Some five months after taking office, Daugherty announced a
shake-up at the Bureau of Investigation. The politically independent Flynn
was out, replaced by two men starkly different in temperament but both
committed to the dark art of sleuthing. In the newly created office of assistant director, he placed John Edgar Hoover, sorcerer of the Justice Department's secret files. And as director, he installed an old friend from Ohio,
William John Burns.

Burns was a particularly brilliant appointment, for few could question
the new director's qualifications. He was already the most famous detective in all the United States, a man dubbed "America's Sherlock Holmes"
by no less an authority than Arthur Conan Doyle. A longtime Secret Service agent who later founded his own private detective agency, Burns was
renowned for cracking big criminal conspiracies that had baffled other
detectives. In one celebrated case involving forged Central American cur-
rency, he started with nothing more than a cryptic marking on a scrap
of burlap: "2 XX / 64." Before long, he'd nabbed the counterfeiters and
foiled a plot to overthrow Costa Rica's government.

Some ascribed such triumphs to supernatural abilities, but in truth his
most potent weapon was a gift for plain logic. When confronted with a
seemingly impenetrable mystery, Burns broke it into smaller pieces. Complex crimes, he realized, almost always required a team of conspirators

chosen for their unique talents. By focusing on one particularly rare skill—safecracking, for instance—Burns could build a relatively short list of potential suspects, zero in on one, and from there unravel the entire conspiracy. That was how Burns captured William "Long Bill" Brockway, the greatest counterfeiter in American history. Rather than directly targeting the master forger, whose identity had been a complete mystery for a quarter century, Burns canvassed the entire nation for plate engravers who used a certain photomechanical process, which led him to two accomplices in Philadelphia and ultimately to Brockway himself.

By 1903, when someone asked the Secret Service for its "best man," the agency sent Burns. On a personal assignment from President Roosevelt, the detective untangled a web of graft that controlled San Francisco politics, ultimately bringing down the city's mayor, its board of supervisors, and the political boss who controlled them all. On loan to the Interior Department, he identified a multimillion-dollar land-fraud conspiracy in Oregon that led to indictments against one of the state's senators and both of its congressmen.

Burns, in short, brought an impressive résumé to his new post. But that was hardly the only reason Daugherty hired him or even the most important.

There was also, for instance, Burns's pragmatic concern with ends rather than means. As head of the William J. Burns International Detective Agency, founded in 1909, Burns employed shady characters who knew the criminal underworld through personal experience, as well as detectives who wouldn't balk at committing one crime to solve another. Burns agency operatives broke into offices, bribed, and blackmailed, all without batting an eye. (They also often functioned as ruthless strikebreakers.) Even Burns himself, back in his Secret Service days, was credibly accused of fixing a jury—an action that invited denunciations from President Taft and his attorney general but nevertheless cemented Burns's reputation as a detective who would deliver results, ethical principles be damned.

What most attracted Daugherty to Burns, however, must have been their forty-year friendship. The two men had met in Columbus, Ohio, when Daugherty was an aspiring politician and Burns a novice gumshoe, and they'd remained chummy ever since, as both rose to the top of their respective professions. Decades later, they still traded favors as freely as they did bawdy jokes around the poker table, and they shared not a few secrets, including details of the 1920 blackmail campaign against Warren

Harding, which Burns had helped crush. After four decades of friendship, Daugherty trusted Burns implicitly—to watch his back, to carry out the most sensitive assignments, even to mobilize a secret police force in service of the attorney general's own personal and political interests. With Billy Burns at the helm, Daugherty could expect absolute loyalty from the Bureau of Investigation. And now, in 1924, that was exactly what he required.

SPECIAL AGENT CHARLES Furness Hately might have returned from his fishing expedition in Nashville empty-handed, but his wasn't the only hook in the water. In late February of 1924, as Wheeler's investigation awaited its vote and Harry Daugherty girded for the fight of his political life, Billy Burns swarmed the Capitol complex with Bureau agents in search of any information that would give the attorney general leverage over Senator Wheeler or insight into his planned investigation.

Some of these undercover operatives took a rather direct approach, tapping into the Capitol phone lines and eavesdropping on what were presumed to be private conversations. (It was a legal gray area to be sure, but at the time there was no explicit prohibition against warrantless wiretapping.) Others simply haunted the hallways of the Senate Office Building, watching who came and went through Wheeler's door, or lurked in common gathering spaces, hoping to pick up stray gossip. One of the Bureau's few female detectives took up residence in the building's ladies' room, where stenographers and typists often chatted about their work.

Perhaps Burns's best Capitol Hill source was a supposed reporter for the *New Haven Union*, Connecticut's leading Democratic broadsheet. Ever since Congress reconvened in December of 1923, this journalist had been shuttling between Capitol offices for interviews, usually with Democratic members of Congress, which made sense given his paper's partisan tilt. What didn't quite add up was how this particular reporter's questions always circled back to the Department of Justice, no matter what was in the news at the moment. His single-minded focus might have raised eyebrows, but journalists were often idiosyncratic in their nosiness, and this one, moreover, made himself useful. He was well informed about the business of the Congress and the executive branch, and he was eager to divulge the odd secret he'd picked up here or there—provided another was given in return. So senators dished, congressmen confided, and by the time

Senator Wheeler declared war on Daugherty, this roving reporter knew more than anyone about the state of relations between Congress and the Justice Department—who in the Senate would back Wheeler's investigation, who was secretly in Daugherty's pocket, and, most crucially, where the senator was getting his information.

Readers of the *New Haven Union* never learned his insights, however. This intrepid "journalist" was no reporter at all but one Thomas M. Smith, a special agent of the Bureau of Investigation, dispatched to the Capitol by Director Burns himself. Smith's findings landed not in a newspaper but on Burns's desk in the form of confidential memos. They numbered as many as five a day, as Smith had a lot to share. In addition to his "interviews" with unwitting assets, he had confidential informants everywhere—a secretary in Senator Frazier's office, an assistant clerk in the Supreme Court, the clerk of the Senate Judiciary Committee. Smith even ingratiated himself with Senator Wheeler's harried secretary by performing free legislative research on his behalf and was repaid with advance copies of the senator's resolutions.

With all these undercover operatives roaming the halls of the Capitol, the Bureau of Investigation—and, by extension, Attorney General Daugherty—hoped to stay one step ahead of the Senate's budding investigation. Even if they failed to turn up any dirt that could potentially be used to blackmail Senator Wheeler (a still ongoing hunt), knowing the senator's moves before they were announced gave Daugherty an edge.

That advantage would crumble, however, if Wheeler actually hit pay dirt and uncovered evidence of truly damning misbehavior within the Justice Department.

AND SO, AS both sides prepared for battle, Burns must have been unnerved by one particular memo from yet another undercover agent. Allen Olds Myers was one of Burns's most dependable lieutenants, which meant his reports warranted careful consideration. In fact, Myers was only moonlighting as a special agent. In his day job, he served as assistant general manager of the Burns International Detective Agency, where he headed up investigations of left-wing radicals (and where Burns, despite having nominally turned control over to his sons, remained in charge).

Myers worked for the Bureau as one of its so-called dollar-a-year men, a group of politically connected cronies that included a Republican

National Committee chairman, several former senators, Ned McLean, a Vanderbilt, and even the attorney general's alcoholic son, Draper Daugherty. Although he received only a nominal government salary, Myers, like the other dollar-a-year men, carried a government badge and credential card and was fully empowered to carry out the most sensitive assignments, including the one Burns had recently given him—shadowing Senator Wheeler himself.

Almost immediately, Myers's surveillance produced a harrowing revelation. In the days following his speech on the Senate floor, Wheeler had welcomed into his office and home numerous lawyers and businessmen with an ax to grind against the attorney general. One visitor, however, demanded special notice—former Bureau of Investigation special agent Gaston Bullock Means. A devilishly clever detective with a checkered past, Means had carried out special tasks for Director Burns, Jess Smith, and even the White House—until, that is, his Justice Department career came to an ignominious end in the summer of 1923.

If Means and Wheeler were huddling up, it couldn't be good news for Harry Daugherty.

"It is reported," Myers cautioned Burns, "that this combination are doing all they can to destroy the Attorney General."

As it would turn out, Means was not the greatest of their concerns— not by a long shot.

14

"If She Can Be Kept Quiet"

Roxie Rebecca Stinson knew she was under surveillance. For weeks now, strange, hatted men had been lurking outside her Columbus, Ohio, apartment at 445 East Gay Street. They had followed her every move as she ran errands in the central business district or called on friends in the neighborhood. They were also, presumably, the source of those strange noises she heard during her telephone conversations.

These government detectives—as she presumed them to be—were monitoring her calls and movements not because of anything she'd done. She was suspected of no crime. Instead, she was being watched because of what she *knew*.

It was all enough, she later recalled, to make her "nervous and jumpy and annoyed."

Around this time, an old flame named Alexander Louis Fink offered Stinson a vacation from her troubles. Calling long-distance from Buffalo, New York, Fink invited her to Cleveland, where he would be traveling on business and would have plenty of free time on his hands. Although Stinson, thirty-eight, would always remember Fink, twenty-nine, as the "irresponsible boy" she'd met some twelve years earlier, a professional gambler and racetrack man, she knew that he'd since grown into an irresponsible *man*—a conniving, enterprising stock promoter who operated in the gray areas of the law. Now that she was in a jam, someone of Fink's flexible ethics and dubious acquaintances might be just her way out of it.

Stinson agreed to join him in the lakeside city.

MUSIC WAS WAFTING in from the adjacent dining room when Stinson and Fink, an elegant redhead and a woolly stripling, strolled into the lobby of the Hollenden Hotel. It was Monday, February 18, the eve of Burton Wheeler's maiden Senate speech declaring war on Harry Daugherty, but the acrimonious politics of Washington seemed, at the moment, a world away. Crystal chandeliers hung from the ceiling, and mahogany wainscoting adorned the walls. Fink, thoughtfully, had booked her a room in one of Cleveland's finest hotels.

Unbeknownst to her, however, he had gone one step further and reserved it under a fictitious name—and not that of a single woman but of a man traveling with his wife. And so, when Fink stepped up to the reception counter around 8:30 p.m. and announced the arrival not of a Miss Roxie Stinson of Columbus, Ohio, but instead a "Mr. and Mrs. A.L. French" of Pittsburgh, Pennsylvania, she was mortified.

Stinson wasn't worried so much about the law, although it was true that, in many jurisdictions, including the state of Ohio, it was a crime for an unmarried couple to falsely register at a hotel as man and wife. What troubled her was the potential embarrassment if anyone discovered the ruse. There could be any number of reasons for a man to emerge from a single woman's hotel room, some more plausible than others, even in the wee hours of the morning. Why that man and woman had registered under assumed names was much harder to explain away. As a respectable divorcée, Stinson had a reputation to guard, and so for that matter did Fink, who had a wife and two sons back home in Buffalo.

Maybe Fink was still an irresponsible boy, after all.

Soon after a bellboy escorted the "Frenches" to room 456 and then departed with his tip, Stinson let Fink have it. She demanded to know what he had meant by his prank and why he had placed her good name in jeopardy. In response, Fink pleaded that he had meant "nothing disparaging." He recalled how Stinson had intimated that she had something confidential to discuss and argued that the assumed names would guarantee them maximum secrecy, shielding their true identities from the local detectives who were known to scan hotel registries.

Stinson might have stormed out of the room. Instead, she managed to overcome her fury and give Fink, who had somehow intuited that she was under surveillance, the benefit of the doubt. It was true, after all, that privacy would be welcome.

Anger abating, she told him all about her unhappy predicament. It had to do, she explained, with an inheritance she'd recently received from her ex-husband. Despite a generous $25,000 bequest, she was locked in a legal dispute with his estate's executors, two powerful brothers, over a brokerage account containing $11,400 in Liberty bonds. Although her ex-husband had been the one to open the account, he had done so on her behalf and had registered it anonymously because the firm refused to issue accounts in the name of unmarried women. Stinson had documentation to prove that the account rightfully belonged to her. She'd even hired a lawyer to plead her case, but the executors refused to budge.

Only one thing could explain their obstinance: they were holding the Liberty bonds hostage for her silence.

Until his recent and untimely death, Stinson explained, her ex-husband had operated in the shadows of Washington, DC, as an influential fixer, dealing in favors, loopholes, bribes, and discretion. In the opinion of those who worked in the gray areas, he had known far too much, and many breathed a sigh of relief when he was found dead in a hotel room. As it turned out, however, his secrets were not buried with his body. Despite their divorce, Stinson and her ex-husband had remained the closest of friends, and he often confided in her the most explosive secrets about how the Harding administration operated behind the scenes—medicinal liquor permits as end runs around Prohibition, blank stock certificates as bribes, thousand-dollar bills in money belts. Even Teapot Dome was discussed. Not only that, she possessed letters, telegrams, and even bank deposit statements corroborating the stories she'd heard. It was damning material—and especially threatening to a senior Republican official who happened to be one of the estate's executors. If made public, it would surely destroy his political career.

Fink took this all in before telling Stinson that he knew "a way out."

She could, of course, turn the tables on the executors and extract the Liberty bonds as her ransom. Her sensational story was easily worth more than the $11,400 they were keeping from her. The thought had already occurred to Stinson: a simple threat to go public might swiftly resolve the dispute in her favor.

But what if they thought bigger? At some point during their rendezvous, Stinson and Fink raised the possibility of instead selling her story to "some strong Democrat" who could weaponize it, particularly in a presidential election year. There certainly would be no shortage of potential buyers. Newspaper reporters were already knocking on her front door, promising cash rewards. She had brushed them all off and not only because of their paltry offers. At the time, she was reluctant to sully the memory of her dear ex-husband by spilling her secrets. But the bad faith shown by the executors, on top of years of mutual resentment, was beginning to change her mind. And Fink, who had spent his adult life working at racetracks and in the notorious "bucket shops" that fleeced aspiring investors by taking bets on stocks rather than trading any actual securities, was at ease in high-stakes negotiations. With him acting as a broker, the pair surmised, Stinson's secrets might fetch a small fortune, a figure that would dwarf the disputed $11,400. Maybe as much as $150,000—a tidy sum in an era when the president made only half that.

Were "Mr. and Mrs. A.L. French" forging a criminal conspiracy? Or were the old lovebirds merely indulging in a flight of fantastical speculation? Precisely what transpired in room 456 that evening would forever remain a mystery. Stinson later claimed that they only *discussed* the possibility of extortion, and no documentation survives proving that she ever came to a criminal understanding with "Mr. French." What is clear is that by the time Alexander Fink emerged from Stinson's room around one in the morning—well past the hour of respectability—he had lost all interest in peddling shares of the Ideal Tire & Rubber Co., the local firm whose stock offering had initially brought him to Cleveland. Instead, he set out from the Hollenden Hotel intent on a new mission.

He would blackmail the attorney general of the United States.

IT MIGHT HAVE been said that Roxie Stinson's marriage to Jess Smith, solemnized on November 10, 1908, at the First Presbyterian Church in Washington Court House, Ohio, was doomed from the start. Smith was the most eligible bachelor in the town of eight thousand, proprietor of the local department store, wealthy, genial, and always marvelously dressed with a flair for pattern and color that easily surpassed the average man's fashion sense. It was a small miracle that he was still on the market at the age of thirty-six, and when he asked for the hand of Roxie Stinson after having turned down so many socially acceptable matches, the townsfolk clucked their disapproval. Even Smith's mother objected. Roxie, twenty-three, was pretty, to be sure. In fact, she was considered the most beautiful woman in all of Washington Court House—tall, red-haired, and always clad in the latest style. She also gave off an air of refinement, honed over three years of musical schooling in France and Germany. None of that, however, made up for the fact that she came from the "wrong" family. Even before Roxie lost her father at an early age, forcing her widowed mother into the workforce as a piano teacher, the Stinsons were absent from the society pages and country club membership rolls. Underscoring her class deficiency was her status as Jess Smith's tenant; she lived in a rented apartment, which doubled as her mother's music studio, above the Smith department store.

In the end, the union lasted eighteen months and was dissolved for reasons other than provincial snobbery. Officially, Stinson's divorce filing cited "extreme cruelty and gross neglect of duty," but townsfolk scoffed at the notion that sweet Jess could be cruel to anyone, least of all the woman he so clearly adored. The real explanation was likely a simple one and understandably kept private. Perhaps condemned by the prejudices of the age to either eternal bachelorhood or a marriage of convenience, Smith opted for the latter and then found it wanting. Regardless, his affection for Roxie had always been genuine. That much became clear once the law restored his bachelorhood and her maiden name, and yet they remained an item. Before long they once again became inseparable, attending dances and concerts together, strolling down Main Street as if they were still husband and wife—all while he advised her on her gentlemen suitors. Jess doted on the former Mrs. Smith, showering her with flowers, chocolates, show tickets, hundred-dollar bills, and his dearest secrets. The town of Washington Court House was shocked all over again. "Never," commented one mutual friend, "was there a queerer aftermath to divorce."

Only one thing could come between Jess Smith and his ex-wife, and that was his boyhood idol, Harry Daugherty. As the ruling clan of Washington Court House, the Daughertys had always looked down on Stinson. Harry and his brother Mally, the town banker, once went so far as to block her admission to the local country club. Harry, in particular, resented the time Jess spent with her and seemed perpetually embarrassed to be in her presence. That feeling was reinforced by an incident in late 1920, when President-elect Harding and his wife, Florence, invited her to Christmas dinner as Smith's guest. There, Harding gave Stinson the seat reserved for the First Lady to be and proceeded to flirt with his young dinner companion all evening long. A minor scandal ensued, and Daugherty vowed that Roxie Stinson would never again be a source of consternation to him or his political project. When Daugherty, with Jess Smith in tow, moved to Washington in 1921 to assume command of the Justice Department, he forbade Smith to invite her to the capital. Jess obeyed. During the twenty-eight months of the Harding presidency, Roxie Stinson never once set foot in the District of Columbia.

Despite the distance between them, however, the divorcées remained in close touch. Rare was the day when Jess failed to write or wire her, and every three weeks or so he returned home, trailed by a stream of telegrams from an annoyed attorney general professing his loneliness. In Ohio, he lavished Roxie with insider gossip. Their hushed conversations revealed that Jess had undergone a profound transformation. The sensitive, small-town retailer who once dispensed fashion advice to housewives now complained of being hounded by office seekers and spoke of "deals" he had brokered for the attorney general of the United States. He boasted of fishing trips with the president and dinners at the White House.

Maybe the greatest change was his financial standing. "We," he once told her, referring to himself and Harry Daugherty, "are all very much better off than we ever have been before." Smith and the attorney general certainly lived like it. Rent on their Wardman Park suite exceeded the attorney general's $11,000 annual salary, and their total household expenses, which they split evenly between themselves, easily surpassed $50,000 a year. Smith had become even more generous to his ex-wife, as well. Sometimes, she recalled, pieces of mail arrived with five-hundred-dollar bills "just loose in an envelope." Once, a letter came bearing twenty-two shares of stock in the Pure Oil Company. Another time, Smith hand-delivered twenty-five shares of White Motor Company stock, freshly issued by the corporation and registered to no one.

After moving to Washington, DC, Jess Smith suddenly had more money than he'd been accustomed to. How that could be possible, given that he'd turned down a paid job within the Harding administration, was a mystery that she and Harry Daugherty alone could explain.

Daugherty's continued silence was a given. Hers would come with a cost.

FOR REASONS THAT she kept to herself, Roxie Stinson decided to remain in Cleveland—but not at the Hollenden. Although she had forgiven Fink for the ruse—she even had breakfast with him the following morning—she was too embarrassed to remain at a hotel under the name of Mrs. A. L. French. Too embarrassed, even, to face the receptionist.

Fink, ever helpful, offered to check out of room 456 on her behalf.

As Stinson, two blocks away, registered at the Hotel Statler under her real name, Fink informed the Hollenden's front desk that the Frenches were checking out. He arranged to have Mrs. French's luggage sent to the Statler, paid the bill for $7.50, and carefully tucked away the receipt for safe keeping.

Fink, it would turn out, was not the only man to walk away with a paper record of the Frenches' stay. Later, another man stopped by the Hollenden's front desk. Upon showing his credentials, he was handed the page from the hotel register for February 18, 1924—the date of the Frenches' arrival. That document promptly made its way to the office of Director William J. Burns at the Bureau of Investigation in Washington. Fink's ruse was not quite so good as it seemed.

IT TOOK SOME time, but on the third day following his rendezvous at the Hollenden with Roxie Stinson, Alexander Fink strolled into the offices of Samuel Ungerleider & Co. inside Cleveland's Leader News Building, confident he'd found the perfect middleman for this delicate transaction.

From the moment Stinson told him all about Jess Smith, Harry Daugherty, and how the two men used the power of the Justice Department for their own personal gain, Fink knew he had "a young fortune staring me in the face," as he confided to a business associate. The only question was which side to sell her story to. Republicans were reeling from Teapot Dome, and some rich Democrat would surely open his pocketbook for another explosive scandal that might derail President Coolidge's reelection chances. On the other hand, Harry Daugherty himself, whose own political life hung in the balance, could be an even more motivated buyer—though extortion would put Fink squarely on the wrong side of the law.

Of course, he'd tread there before. In 1921, Fink was indicted for grand larceny after hoodwinking an oil executive into granting him a large block of shares at steeply discounted prices. (In a lucky break, the charges were dropped after the executive suddenly dropped dead at the age of forty-four.) In 1923, Fink was again charged with grand larceny for diverting an elderly woman's $60,000 nest egg into a bogus stock he was promoting. (Those charges were still pending.)

But never had Fink actively courted the law's attention as he now would have to—and not just the ire of a local prosecutor or city detective but the man who sat atop the pinnacle of American law enforcement, the attorney general of the United States. This called for great care.

In approaching Samuel Ungerleider, Fink attempted to thread the needle. A former distiller who had transformed himself into Cleveland's leading stockbroker upon the dawn of Prohibition, Ungerleider was a well-connected Ohio Democrat, which meant that Fink could plausibly approach him under the pretext of selling political dirt to Daugherty's political opponents. And indeed, when Fink initially asked for a referral to a Democratic power broker, Ungerleider promised to connect him to "a man big enough to expose Daugherty." That gave Fink some measure of legal cover. At the same time, Fink suspected that Ungerleider, who happened to manage the attorney general's personal brokerage accounts, would duly report the inquiry back to his client. It was a clever twist on blackmail—indirect, veiled, and plausibly deniable.

It worked. On February 21, Fink was escorted into Ungerleider's private office, where he found not Democratic national committee member John O'Dyer, as promised, but Mal Daugherty, younger brother of Harry, and James Holcomb, a prominent Cleveland lawyer who, in introducing himself, deceitfully gave the impression that he worked for the Justice Department. Evidently, Ungerleider had passed along word that Stinson's story was for sale, and the attorney general found the matter so urgent and so sensitive that he dispatched his own brother to clean it up.

Inside the office, Mal Daugherty sat finishing his lunch. He was the spitting image of his more famous older brother, with the notable exception of his gaunt cheeks and his horn-rimmed, Harold Lloyd–style eyeglasses, which added a hint of levity to the dour Daugherty countenance. At the moment, however, Mal Daugherty was not in a humorous mood.

He let Holcomb do all the talking, and the lawyer started by issuing a threat. The Justice Department, or the Daughertys, or both—Holcomb wasn't clear here—"had the goods" on Fink and would not hesitate to slam shut the jail door. This might have been a reference to the blackmail attempt itself, or perhaps to his outstanding grand larceny charges, or to any number of his past schemes.

"On the other hand," the lawyer continued, all parties were prepared to make a deal if Fink "behaved" himself. What would it take, he asked, to keep Stinson quiet?

Fink, eager to negotiate, insisted that he found the idea of blackmail personally repugnant but complained that he was at the mercy of a strong-willed woman. "I cannot convince this woman," he said, "and I'm frank to tell you I'm stumped."

Holcomb opened with a modest offer. Roxie Stinson owed the Midland National Bank, of which Mal Daugherty was president, nearly $10,000. "You can tell Miss Stinson," Holcomb said, "that Mal Daugherty says if she'll keep her mouth shut, she needn't worry about the money she owes his bank."

Stinson's silence was worth more than the forgiveness of a $10,000 debt, and everyone in the room knew it. Fink countered aggressively. He announced that $150,000 would do the trick, and for that price both he and Stinson would be willing to leave the country and remain far beyond the reach of a congressional subpoena until after the November elections.

It was a ransom the Daughertys might have been willing to pay—although it would have been hard for even a banker to scare up that much cash—but the attorney general's representatives had come prepared with another strategy. Even if they bought Stinson's silence, they must have realized that there was no guarantee she would honor their deal. And so instead of simply paying off Stinson and her middleman, they'd cleave the blackmail conspiracy in two. If Fink could be flipped to their side, if he could find some way to engineer leverage over the woman with all the secrets, then he would be rewarded handsomely.

"We worked out a plan," Holcomb explained. "If she can be kept quiet, that will mean a lot of money to you." Fink was intrigued.

The plan was to grant Fink a lucrative permit to operate a liquor concentration warehouse, a special facility guarded by agents of the Treasury Department where legal, pre-Prohibition spirits were stashed. Inside these warehouses, millions of bottles awaited the day America would change its mind about its "noble experiment." But bootleggers schemed to liberate the liquor much sooner—meaning that anyone who operated these facilities was the potential beneficiary of graft. There were only twenty-eight such warehouses in all of the United States, and the Daughertys had already identified one in Pittsburgh that Fink would run.

"Mr. Mellon has the only other one there," Ungerleider chimed in, repeating a rumor that was not grounded in fact, "and he's been cleaning up millions of dollars from it."

Dollar signs flashed before Fink's eyes. Under his agreement with Stinson, he would have received a 20 percent commission, meaning a $150,000 deal would have netted him only $30,000. Now the Daughertys were dangling something far bigger before him. Fink assured Holcomb that he could prevent Stinson from telling her story.

"Why," Holcomb asked, "do you think this woman will not go through with her proposed plan?"

Fink produced a slip of paper from his pocket and tossed it on the table.

"I know this will prevent her from attempting to do this," he said, "because she is afraid of publicity."

It was the bill from the Hollenden. The Mr. and Mrs. A. L. French who occupied room 456 for one night, Fink explained, could easily be identified by hotel staff or other guests as himself and Roxie Stinson—and here was physical proof they'd registered under a fictitious name. It was evidence of a crime against the state of Ohio, yes, but more importantly it was also evidence of a crime against the social customs of the day. Roxie Stinson would never want it made public.

Daugherty's men were impressed. One act of blackmail would enable the other.

Ungerleider and Stinson happened to be old acquaintances. "I will go with you to the Statler," Ungerleider said, "and convince this woman that she's got to keep quiet."

IT WAS TIME for errands, and Roxie Stinson already had on her hat and was nearly out her hotel room door when she heard a knock.

"*Entree.*"

Fink burst in. "We are under arrest!"

"Who is under arrest?" Stinson asked.

"You and I." Fink was all nervous energy, a stark contrast to the muted browns, grays, and blues of the hotel decor.

"What for?"

"For being under a fictitious name."

"Is that the cause for arrest? I am not under arrest."

"Yes, you are, and the bars are staring you in the face." Fink went on to explain that registering under assumed names might be the least of their worries. At that very moment, he claimed, a warrant was being issued for their arrest "for conspiring against Harry Daugherty." He got to the point: "Unless you promise not to tell anything about Harry Daugherty, we will have to go behind the bars."

Never had Stinson seen someone so excited. "You make me laugh," she told him and giggled to prove it.

Fink threw up his hands. "It's no use. I am going and I know it. I have heard about the third degree, but I never saw it before. Why, they even put shackles on my wrist."

Something didn't add up. Before plying his trade in Buffalo, Fink had learned the art of persuasion from some of Chicago's most talented swindlers. He should have been able to collect himself under pressure, but here he was behaving as if he'd never before been threatened with handcuffs. Was he softer than she'd imagined? Or was something else going on?

Soon, there was another knock on the door. At Stinson's second "*entree*," in walked Samuel Ungerleider.

"Will you tell me what this is all about?" she asked.

"I don't know much about it myself," Ungerleider said, "only it seems there has been a conspiracy of some kind against Harry Daugherty." He explained that Fink had been peddling a story about corruption in the attorney general's office, backed up with damaging letters from Harry Daugherty to Jess Smith, and had named Stinson as the source of his information. A warrant had been issued for their arrest, Ungerleider said, and she was to be held under a $100,000 bond.

Fink was now pacing up and down the Axminster carpet.

"Why don't you sit down?" she told him, but he kept pacing with the dramatic flair of a Broadway castoff. What could explain the show he was putting on? His anxiety struck her as more than inauthentic, yet it was edged with real emotion. Was it guilt? Greed? Both? Something was at stake, gnawing at his nerves, but she didn't believe it was the threat of jail time. Quite suddenly, the truth dawned on her: she had been betrayed. Her erstwhile lover was now in league with the Daughertys, and who knew what he'd told them. Certainly that they'd shared a hotel room under a fictitious name and perhaps more.

Stinson turned to Ungerleider. Now she was indignant. "Take me behind the bars," she said. "Take me just the same. Wouldn't it look pretty, Jess Smith's widow behind the bars?"

Ungerleider sighed. "You are all too much for me."

"If you have a warrant for me," Stinson continued, "where is it? I know this is a frame up, pure and simple. Why doesn't Mal or Harry, or whoever is engineering this affair, come to me?"

"They don't want to talk to you," Ungerleider answered. "They just want your promise not to say anything or conspire against Harry Daugherty."

Stinson didn't believe this talk about outstanding warrants and $100,000 bonds. At the same time, she knew that if she remained non-compliant, the entire world would learn that she'd shared a hotel room with Alexander Fink, and it was clear that whatever scheme they'd cooked up at the Hollenden was going nowhere.

So she offered Ungerleider a vague promise: "I have been asked for months to talk about Harry Daugherty. I have not done so to anyone whatsoever." Just recently, she explained, an Associated Press reporter had appeared at her front door, notebook and pencil in hand. But she had brushed him off, just as she'd continue to decline every opportunity to tell her story for profit or publicity.

"But you may go back to your friends," she continued, "and tell them also, and with my compliments, that if I am subpoenaed at Washington I shall tell everything I know. It is a frame up, and I am going to tell them so."

"I wouldn't do that," Ungerleider said coldly. "You know Harry Daugherty is a pretty stubborn man."

"So am I, and he is not going to strong arm me." And then she saw fit to effectively end the conversation by adding: "I am not Jess Smith, and there is not going to be a convenient bullet in my head."

AFTER THAT EXCHANGE, Stinson heard no more from Fink or Ungerleider, who, despite her threat, told her that he considered the matter as "absolutely closed."

As she checked out of her room on the afternoon of February 21, however, the presence of a detective on her tail suggested that Harry Daugherty thought otherwise.

This strange man, who shared all the habits of the investigators who had shadowed her back home in Columbus, followed her into the elevator and down to the lobby, where he watched her pay her hotel bill of $10.80. He must have tailed her taxi, too, for she soon saw him again at the rail station, where he followed her aboard her Columbus-bound train.

When later asked to describe this man, the best she could come up with was "plain" and "a nice looking gentleman"—exactly how Bureau of Investigation agents, who took pride in blending into crowds, wanted to be remembered. In fact, her tail was none other than the special agent in charge of the Bureau's Cleveland office, John V. Ryan, a former military intelligence officer, the same man who had confiscated the registration sheet from the Hollenden Hotel and who was now reporting all the details of Stinson's visit to his superiors in Washington, DC.

There, deep inside the Justice Department's Vermont Avenue headquarters, in the locked file room of the Bureau of Investigation, Ryan's report joined a thickening file on Harry Daugherty's political enemies.

15

"The Peculiar Nature of This Inquiry"

The Select Committee on Investigation of the Attorney General convened for its first executive session on Monday, March 3. With at least a week to go before the first public hearings, this initial meeting promised little in the way of blockbuster revelations. What made it newsworthy, rather, was what it revealed about the five-member panel's internal dynamics.

On paper, the committee broke toward the Republicans, three to two:

Smith Brookhart (R) of Iowa, Chairman
George Moses (R) of New Hampshire
Wesley Jones (R) of Washington
Henry Ashurst (D) of Arizona
Burton Wheeler (D) of Montana

Because of the Republicans' Senate majority, the committee was always going to tilt three to two in their favor, but Wheeler had found a way to even the score. In drafting his resolution, he took the unusual step of nominating the committee's membership himself—a task usually reserved for the Senate's president pro tempore. Two of his chosen Republicans, the moderate Senator Jones and the old-line conservative Senator Moses, could be expected to back Daugherty, but his inspired choice for the panel's third Republican and its chairman was Senator Brookhart, a solid progressive swept into office by disaffected Iowa farmers.

Almost immediately, a three-to-two anti-Daugherty majority asserted itself as the independent-minded Brookhart sided with the two Democrats in one decision after another—most significantly, denying the attorney general the privilege of calling his own witnesses and placing sharp limits on his lawyers' ability to cross-examine. Exactly as Wheeler had hoped, the chairman's fellow Republicans appeared powerless to steer the proceedings in Daugherty's favor.

Instead, Wheeler himself would hold the tiller. In its inaugural meeting, the committee effectively named the young Montana senator its chief counsel, appointing him a "subcommittee of one" with authority to gather all relevant evidence, call the first witnesses, and even fix the time and date for the hearings. Brookhart technically chaired the committee, but everyone knew who was really in charge. It was the man who had brought the panel into existence, whom the press was now describing as "prosecutor" of the "Brookhart-Wheeler committee," which, for concision as well as accuracy, was often rendered simply as the "Wheeler committee."

Before Chairman Brookhart could gavel this inaugural meeting to a close, Wheeler asked to address his colleagues.

"One must see the peculiar nature of this inquiry," he cautioned them. "We have the terrific job of investigating the investigating department of the government."

For all its august pretensions, the US Senate was badly equipped to probe any executive department, let alone the Department of Justice. It had no detectives on staff, and whereas Wheeler would be allowed to hire just a single law clerk to review evidence and pre-interview witnesses, the attorney general commanded a veritable army of lawyers. Worse, unlike the Justice Department, which could drag uncooperative witnesses before a grand jury, Congress's power to compel testimony was untested in the courts. In a legal dispute with the Justice Department, the Senate was badly outmatched.

Moreover, Wheeler continued, they should expect nothing less than active obstruction from the attorney general. "Because of the vast power of the department," he said, "we fear the intimidation of our witnesses. We know that an effort has already been made to hush up certain witnesses. And if we should permit the names of others to become known, we are fearful there would be the same effort to keep them silent that there was in the oil case."

Victory, he declared, could be achieved only with outside help: "We will therefore have to depend entirely upon the voluntary assistance of individuals anxious to see an important branch of the federal government cleaned up."

He was referring, in part, to Frank A. Vanderlip, the retired president of the National City Bank of New York and cofounder of the Federal Reserve system. Though a lifelong Republican and a former McKinley administration official, Vanderlip had recently turned on his own party in a much-publicized speech that called for a "moral crusade against corruption," denouncing Attorney General Daugherty's "sinister inactivity." The banker's rhetoric mostly aligned with public sentiment—until he unwisely repeated baseless rumors about Warren G. Harding, alleging that the late president had laundered Teapot Dome kickbacks through his sale of the *Marion Star*. Vanderlip underestimated how much the late president's honor still meant to friends like Daugherty, and the backlash was swift and severe. Republican newspapers accused him of murdering the ghost of President Harding. The *Star*'s new owners sued him for libel. And—stinging most of all—one corporation after another forced him off its board of directors, first the American Can Company, then United States Rubber, and so on, until his name had been all but erased from the world of American business. Vanderlip was sure that Harry Daugherty had orchestrated it all and vowed to strike back.

Thus Senator Wheeler had found himself on the receiving end of a multimillionaire's generosity.

Over lunch at the house of a *New York World* correspondent who brokered the meeting, Vanderlip informed Wheeler that he was setting up a private investigative agency, the Citizens' Federal Research Bureau, to "ferret out corruption in Washington." Vanderlip wanted to put this new organization at Wheeler's disposal.

"I want to serve you in your work of investigation," Vanderlip told him, "in any way I can, spending my money as you may direct to assist the investigation, and even being your office boy if I can help in that way."

VANDERLIP'S RESOURCES WERE already proving indispensable. But someone else was providing "voluntary assistance" behind the scenes—a man Wheeler could hardly trust, could hardly even stand to share a room with, but who nevertheless offered his best hope at piercing the veil of secrecy around Harry Daugherty and his illicit activities.

The man Daugherty had been warned Wheeler was meeting with, Gaston Bullock Means, claimed to have all the "dope" on the attorney general, and recently this notorious detective from North Carolina, dismissed from the Bureau of Investigation the previous fall and then indicted on four federal charges, including mail fraud and violation of the National Prohibition Act, had become a regular visitor to Wheeler's three-story house in the leafy Washington, DC, neighborhood of Chevy Chase. Means intimated that he could give sensational testimony about how the Department of Justice actually operated—how the attorney general had sharpened it into a tool for political warfare and how Bureau operatives routinely spied on Daugherty's congressional critics. All the documentary evidence, he claimed, was inside the bulging accordion-style case he always carried with him—eleven black binders containing "minute-by-minute diaries" of his confidential work for the Bureau. These books, he insisted, would remain closed until he was duly subpoenaed and testifying before the committee.

In the meantime, he spun fantastic stories that lay well outside the scope of the Senate's investigation. He told Wheeler, matter-of-factly, that President Harding hadn't died of natural causes but had been poisoned in Alaska. He spoke casually about the president's girlfriend, Nan Britton, and claimed that First Lady Florence Harding had once hired him to spy on the young woman. Indeed, Means seemed determined to bait Wheeler away from his investigation's primary target, insisting that Secretary of the Treasury Andrew Mellon would be the bigger catch. "Go after Mellon on whiskey," Means advised, tempting the senator with arcane details of Prohibition graft and how the treasury chief, a multimillionaire many times over, not to mention Daugherty's chief rival within the cabinet, was supposedly involved.

Wheeler was sure he saw through what had to be misdirection. Moreover, he suspected worse of his informant. Although Means was currently awaiting trial in federal court and claimed to have completely severed ties with his former employer, a hunch told Wheeler that this wily detective had, nonetheless, been sent by the attorney general to spy on the Senate investigation.

It was such an obvious possibility that, when they were first introduced, Means evidently arrived with a plan to combat the senator's skepticism. Wheeler had often been dubbed a "radical"—a label he always resisted because he believed his bold, left-wing views merely reflected America's founding values.

In their first meeting, Means invoked that label in a transparent attempt to get in the senator's good graces. "You know," he said, "I'm a radical. I'm a radical."

Wheeler wasn't impressed. "Well, Means, you know I am a conservative. I'm not a radical."

Means launched into a passionate diatribe against child labor, anyway, attempting to prove, in his molasses drawl, that he and Wheeler were cut from the same cloth. When he finished, the detective creased his face into a cherubic grin. Behind that dimpled smile, Wheeler sensed, lurked something sinister. Wheeler's misgivings lingered even as Means proved genuinely helpful in understanding how Daugherty's Justice Department operated and where the opportunities for mischief had been.

"He gave me some really good tips," Wheeler later recalled—but suspected they all could have been part of his elaborate cover as a double agent. Wheeler was accordingly cautious with his informant, aware that every question he asked revealed something about the shape of his investigation. Over time, Wheeler sensed a growing respect from Means, who had probably underestimated the young senator at first.

For his part, Wheeler grew in awe of the detective's evil genius. "Means had a brilliant mind and could have distinguished himself if he had used it in constructive channels," he later recalled, "but you never knew when he was lying."

At this stage—and until Means revealed the contents of his accordion case to all the world—his greatest service might have been illustrating just how far men like Daugherty were willing to go. In one of their private conferences at the Wheeler residence, Means thoughtfully offered to gin up some publicity for the investigation by dynamiting the sun porch. Imagine the headlines, the detective purred—"Daugherty's Prosecutor a Victim of Bomb Plot."

The suggestion sent a shiver down Wheeler's spine. His investigation had just barely set sail, and already he was in uncharted waters.

16

"A Three-Ring Circus"

As he plotted his opening moves over the first week of March, perhaps stepping more gingerly than usual over his porch floorboards, Wheeler pursued several promising leads. He chased rumors that Bureau of Investigation agents had encouraged a 1921 rebellion in Baja California against government forces hostile to American oil interests. He looked into accusations that Daugherty, through his influence with the president, had installed questionable characters on the federal bench, including one attorney who'd escaped disbarment on a technicality. He followed up with the Federal Trade Commission whistleblower who claimed that the Justice Department had ignored fifty-five antitrust cases referred by the commission for prosecution. These were serious allegations, and any one of them might have provided grounds for Daugherty's dismissal. (At this point, despite his earlier suspicions, Wheeler reluctantly accepted that the attorney general wasn't involved in Teapot Dome; the evidence just wasn't there.)

Despite his need for something concrete, though, Wheeler found himself drawn to the even more salacious gossip swirling around the attorney general—rumors of self-dealing and crooked friendships that were ready-made for the tabloids, complete with a mysterious suicide.

For more than a month now, one tipster after another had advised him to look into the "Ohio crowd" that rode Daugherty's coattails to Washington and capitalized on their intimacy with the architect of the Harding administration. From the moment Daugherty took his oath on March 5, 1921, word had apparently spread through the realms of business and

126

organized crime that certain persons could "fix" things at the Justice Department, for the right price—men like Jess Smith, for instance. If Wheeler probed Smith's activities and followed the money, he was told, he just might connect Harry Daugherty with a corruption scandal rivaling Teapot Dome in scale and audacity.

Now news came from Chicago that the federal grand jury investigating the Veterans' Bureau scandal had not only looked into those very rumors but uncovered evidence substantiating them. "The hurried visit of the attorney general to Chicago," the Brookhart-Wheeler committee was informed, "was occasioned by the desire of the jury to question him concerning *charges involving his friends* and his administration of the Department of Justice." And yet the grand jury, sensing it was straying from its legal mandate, had dropped the line of inquiry. Wheeler gladly picked it up. He pumped Gaston Means for information about Jess Smith—the two men had been well acquainted—and searched for witnesses who could shed light on Smith's alleged shady dealings.

Inevitably, word leaked that Wheeler was planning to hear testimony from "ex-convicts, men under indictment, discharged government employees," and the like. Inevitably, Daugherty's allies cried foul. They denounced Wheeler as a "Montana scandalmonger" and an "assassin of character." To anyone who complained about the character of his prospective witnesses, though, he had a ready retort: "Daugherty didn't associate with preachers."

And yet those verbal barbs stung more than Wheeler let on. He had once pledged himself to the federal prosecutor's code, which counseled great restraint before airing accusations, at least until an indictment and then trial provided the accused with a proper forum for defending himself—the courtroom. Strict adherence to legal process, he had been taught, led to justice. Now he was shouting sensational charges from the Senate floor, unbound by evidence, reveling in the publicity he could garner with a single obnoxious utterance.

However, as much as he embraced the title of select committee "prosecutor," Wheeler was no longer operating, strictly speaking, within the legal arena. And thank goodness. One needed to look no further than the railroad injunction to see how the powerful had hijacked the law. The legal process that produced the court's restraining order appeared regular in form; the government made a request in open court, and a judge granted it. But it was hardly justice.

In President Harding's America, and now President Coolidge's, men like Harry Daugherty exploited the legal process. To have a chance of defeating him, Wheeler would have to play by different rules.

AS A YOUNG lawyer in Montana's frontier courts, the grandiloquent oratory that often passed for legal argument turned Burton Wheeler's stomach. The local district attorney at the time, a transplanted southerner, was famous for his "hearts-and-flowers style" of addressing the court. "It seemed to me that many criminal lawyers wasted emotional flamboyance on a jury," Wheeler explained. "What I strove for was a repetition of the basic facts in various ways." *Let the evidence speak for itself* was his mantra. Respect the legal wisdom of the judge, the common sense of the jurors. Courtroom theatrics were an insult to the law.

No longer was Wheeler that naive litigator. His formal training at the University of Michigan law school notwithstanding, it was in the courthouse that he learned how the law really worked. He saw wobbly cases propped up by stagecraft, juries swayed by emotion, and courtrooms overtaken by spectacle.

He also learned from his mistakes. In 1917, then US attorney Wheeler prosecuted his first major corruption case, a mail-fraud scheme that implicated Montana's political and economic elite. The eleven defendants, members of a real estate syndicate, included the Democratic state treasurer and secretary of state alongside several Republican heavyweights, and they were represented by a legal dream team that included two former state attorneys general (both Republicans) and a former governor of Idaho (a Democrat).

Not to be intimidated, Wheeler marshaled overwhelming evidence showing that the syndicate, which was purportedly in the mortgage loan business, had effectively functioned as a Ponzi scheme. It had issued stock and redirected the proceeds to the company directors who'd lent their prestigious names. Little of the $300,000 the syndicate took in from investors, the evidence showed, actually financed the purchase of farms or the construction of new homes and apartments.

On paper, Wheeler had a strong case—but his courtroom performance left much to be desired. Somehow he forgot that he was pleading his case not to some inhuman, unfeeling arbiter but to a jury, twelve laymen who wanted the evidence presented as a compelling narrative of guilt or innocence. Sticking to his "repetition of the basic facts," he overwhelmed the poor jurors with detail, questioned too many witnesses for too many hours, and introduced more than two hundred exhibits in the first week alone. He even managed to bore the judge, who at one point snapped: "If you have not shown enough letters already to show that the company used the mails, why you never will." In the end, the jury convicted just two of the eleven defendants and not a single one of the corrupt officeholders who had monetized their political status.

Now given a chance to pursue corruption at the highest levels, Wheeler would not make the same mistake. Instead, he would design his case against the attorney general to pique the curiosity and ignite the imagination of his audience—not just a jury of twelve this time but some one hundred million Americans who would follow the investigation as it played out on the front page of their newspapers. There would be facts, yes, but there would also be showmanship, spectacle, and more than a little headline-worthy scandal.

AS WHEELER KNEW full well, the Roaring Twenties were transforming the news media in ways that would forever change how Americans consumed political scandal.

Journalist Frederick Allen was a popular chronicler of the age, both as the editor of *Harper's* magazine and as author of the 1931 classic *Only Yesterday: An Informal History of the 1920's*. "It was now possible in the United States," he wrote, "for more people to enjoy the same good show at the same time than in any other land on earth or at any previous time in history. Mass production was not confined to automobiles; there was mass production in news as well."

Newspapers were consolidating. Press barons imposed consistent messaging across their big-city newspaper empires. Even in smaller cities and towns, wire services like the Associated Press, United Press Associations, and International News Service ensured that readers from Long Beach, California, to Miami, Florida, would find the same reports from Washington folded inside their broadsheets.

Tastes were changing, too. Heavily illustrated tabloids like the *New York Daily News*, launched in 1919, presented American life, to use Allen's words, "as a three-ring circus of sport, crime, and sex," bombarding their readers over and over, through text and photographs, with the one big story of the day or week—until the next story broke. It was called "jazz journalism," and Americans couldn't get enough of it. Within a couple years, the *Daily News* became the country's best-selling paper, spawning copycats like New York's *Daily Mirror* and *Evening Graphic*. The success of these tabloids, meanwhile, nudged the older, full-sized dailies, which had yet to drop the wartime habit of big, screaming headlines, further toward sensationalism. By 1924, gossip had become news, and journalism, entertainment—something the ten million Americans huddling around their living room radio sets for the evening news, much of it recycled from the newly captivating print media, could not deny.

"The result," wrote Allen, "was that when something happened which promised to appeal to the popular mind, one had it hurled at one in huge headlines, waded through page after page of syndicated discussion of it, heard about it on the radio, was reminded of it again and again in the outpourings of publicity-seeking orators and preachers, saw pictures of it in the Sunday papers and in the movies, and (unless one was a perverse individualist) enjoyed the sensation of vibrating to the same chord which thrilled a vast populace."

Those chords rang in several tones, all orchestrated by the emerging national news media. There was coast-to-coast adulation of celebrities like silver screen heartthrob Rudolph Valentino. There was revelry of the criminal masterwork of gangsters like Al Capone. There was the triumph of athletes like Jack Dempsey. And there was the nationwide smirking (or sneering) at the true-crime scandals of the day—the rape and manslaughter trial of comedian Fatty Arbuckle, for instance, or the supposedly "perfect crime" of Leopold and Loeb.

In the Roaring Twenties, the possibilities for a legislator on an investigative crusade had never been so grand.

BY THE SECOND full week of March, Wheeler had sifted through nearly all the available evidence, assisted by the committee's one staff attorney as well as a larger complement of private investigators on Frank Vanderlip's payroll. Solid information about Jess Smith was still scarce, but at least one prospective witness could offer tantalizing details about the dry goods salesman's role within the Department of Justice—Gaston Means. And so, on Monday, March 10, the Brookhart-Wheeler committee announced that hearings would begin the following Thursday and formally subpoenaed the former Bureau of Investigation agent. Wheeler still mistrusted Means, but at the moment he represented the best source of information about the "Ohio crowd's" influence within the Justice Department. If Wheeler wanted to expose wrongdoing in the attorney general's inner circle—if he wanted to solve the riddle of Jess Smith—then Gaston Means, for all his faults, seemed the witness to do it.

That plan suddenly changed when, shortly after announcing the subpoena, Wheeler walked into the committee's office and found two strangers chatting with Chairman Brookhart. He didn't recognize the men's faces, one young with a full head of curly hair, the other creased with wrinkles and balding, but he would soon come to know them well.

These men, he learned, had rushed down from Buffalo to offer the committee a witness even more sensational than Gaston Bullock Means—a woman who knew the principals of the investigation quite well. Although she would never testify voluntarily, a simple subpoena could persuade her to appear in Washington.

And if the witness did testify, Wheeler was assured, she would blow the lid off.

17

"You Are Hereby Commanded"

Train wheels click-clacked on a moonless night. Wheeler was half-way between Washington, DC, and Columbus, Ohio, crossing the Alleghenies under the cover of darkness.

He could trust no one else to carry out this sensitive task. Not those two strangers from Buffalo. Not the Senate's sergeant at arms. And certainly not the local US marshals, who technically worked for the Department of Justice. No, if he wanted to ensure that his star witness appeared before his committee, untainted by any outside influence, he had no choice but to present himself at Roxie Stinson's front door and serve the subpoena himself.

It had almost played out differently. When Wheeler arrived at the committee's office to find Alexander Fink talking with Senator Brookhart, claiming that an old flame had valuable information about Jess Smith and Harry Daugherty, he was mortified to learn that the well-intentioned but often careless committee chairman was prepared to send Fink and his lawyer, Henry Stern, off to Ohio to subpoena her themselves.

He pulled Brookhart aside. "You mustn't do that. Do you know these people?"

"No, but Wadsworth and Colonel Donovan sent them down, and Wadsworth brought them over here—"

"Listen, it doesn't make any difference who sent them down."

Actually, it did, but Wheeler spared Brookhart the long explanation—US Attorney William J. "Wild Bill" Donovan was an employee of the Department of Justice, and his political mentor, Sen. James Wadsworth of

New York, had been a staunch ally of President Harding. There was every reason to be skeptical of anyone dispatched by Donovan and Wadsworth.

"You can't let someone else go out and subpoena your witnesses," he told Brookhart. "You give the me subpoena, and I will go out there."

And so Wheeler, despite the pressing business awaiting him in Washington, found himself on a Baltimore & Ohio overnighter the evening of Monday, March 10, a mere three days before the scheduled start of the hearings. He'd allowed the two fellows from Buffalo to tag along, partly for their potential usefulness—Fink knew where Roxie Stinson lived and what she looked like—and also to keep an eye on them.

Otherwise, he guarded his overnight mission with extreme secrecy. He purchased the train tickets with a borrowed hundred-dollar bill rather than with a government requisition, which might have alerted the Senate paymaster to his plan. He also ripped the identifying tags off his luggage before boarding so that no one would glimpse his suddenly famous name.

The nation's capital, he knew, was crawling with spies. There were also disturbing reports that the woman he was going to see had been threatened with arrest and even deportation to some faraway place, beyond the reach of a congressional subpoena. He could not allow Harry Daugherty to get to her first.

IT WAS NO small relief, then, when Wheeler arrived at the threshold of 445 East Gay Street, Columbus, Ohio, to find Roxie Stinson unharmed, unthreatened, and apparently unaware that her name would soon be printed on the front page of every American newspaper.

At once he knew she'd make a compelling witness. Stinson was glamorous, witty, and undeniably attractive—"a statuesque redhead," Wheeler later recalled, "with the figure of a showgirl." Better yet, a strong jaw complemented her delicate eyes, the former projecting confidence and the latter eliciting sympathy. Her face bore a striking resemblance to the version of Lady Liberty then circulating on the silver dollar, which cultivated a sense of faint recognition wherever she went. Her presence, Wheeler was convinced, would command the hearing room. Just as importantly, given the growing influence of mass media, her appearance would capture the attention of newspaper readers across the country.

There was only one catch: she didn't want to testify. Fink had warned Wheeler that she would make a reluctant witness. It wasn't in her nature to court publicity, and she dearly wanted to protect the reputation of her late ex-husband. (What Fink likely did not tell Wheeler, but which only reinforced her unwillingness, was that Harry Daugherty was in possession of the Hollenden Hotel bill and could quite easily smear her reputation in retaliation.)

Stinson was also skeptical of the man standing on her doorstep, claiming to be a US senator, hundreds of miles from the national capital, his arrival unannounced. She demanded to see Wheeler's credentials. Her caution in these times was understandable, admirable even, and Wheeler produced his Senate identification card.

Stinson's mood softened—but only a little. She shifted her approach, attempting to talk him out of calling her as a witness.

"Probably if you discuss this matter with me," she said, "you might not want me to come."

"No. You will have to come anyway."

"Don't you want to talk to me first? Maybe it isn't of any consequence."

"Yes, I will talk with you."

"Do I have to go anyway?"

"Yes."

"I won't talk to you."

Wheeler unfolded a one-page document. Printed under the heading of "Congress of the United States," its language made it abundantly clear that this was no request.

He handed her the subpoena. "Pursuant to lawful authority," it read, "You Are Hereby Commanded to appear before the Select Committee on Investigation of Department of Justice of the Senate of the United States to testify what you may know relative to the subject matters under consideration by said Committee."

"Hereof fail not," it continued, "as you will answer your default under the pains and penalties in such cases made and provided." It was signed by Smith Brookhart, chairman.

Stinson finally relented: "When do I have to come?"

In truth, nothing in the subpoena required Stinson to accompany Wheeler back to the capital immediately—she wasn't under arrest—but the senator wasn't taking any chances. "Right now."

Outside, Fink and Stern were waiting near an idling taxi. Wheeler stepped out to make an announcement: "I have persuaded the little lady to return to Washington with us."

They departed Columbus immediately—stopping only to drop off her dog, Nose Bud, at the kennel—and Wheeler used the long train journey to probe his witness.

At first he found Stinson if not evasive then guarded. Although she could barely conceal her contempt for Harry Daugherty, she was especially protective of Jess Smith and refused to divulge anything that might reflect poorly on her late ex-husband.

At one point, Wheeler excused himself and found Fink and Stern in the smoking compartment. "My God," he told them, "I can't get her to loosen up." If only the parlor car served liquor—but they were four years into Prohibition.

An idea occurred to him. They had a four-hour layover in Pittsburgh, and Wheeler would use the downtime to his advantage. That evening, as the four travelers strolled into the William Penn Hotel for dinner, Wheeler handed Fink a ten-dollar bill.

"If you know anyone around here," Wheeler said, "for God's sake get a pint of whiskey."

Fink, who had been to Pittsburgh on business in the past, dutifully sought out a particular bellboy and returned with a jug of bootleg liquor.

At dinner, Wheeler ordered a bottle of ginger ale and glasses of ice for the table and discreetly topped off his companions' fizzing glasses with the whiskey—taking care to reserve most of the jug for Stinson. As the evening wore on and the jug emptied, Stinson lowered her guard. Her worries about what testifying in Washington might do to Jess's reputation, as well as her own, apparently melted away. Under the influence of the bootleg liquor, she even grew affectionate toward the senator.

Wheeler's witness was ready to spill her secrets.

IF THEIR DINNERTIME conversation suggested anything, it was that Roxie Stinson was just the witness Wheeler had been looking for. Her recall was impressive. Stinson could reenact three-year-old conversations, word for word, as if reading from a script. She could explain exactly how Jess Smith and Harry Daugherty navigated the halls of power together, even how they jointly managed their household finances. She could describe the blank stock certificates, the thousand-dollar bills, the suitcases filled with bootleg liquor that had slowly clued her into her ex-husband's illicit activities. And, most importantly, she could tie those dark deeds back to Harry Daugherty.

"It was enough to convince me," he recalled, "she could blow the case against the attorney general wide open."

However, as the two spoke later inside his private compartment, their DC-bound train rumbling over its tracks, he needed assurances that her testimony was the truth.

Wheeler knew from all his courtroom experience that witnesses with an axe to grind might not volunteer false testimony, but they were willing to be led on by their interrogator. Stinson, by her own admission, felt honor-bound to defend her late ex-husband, whom the attorney general's allies were holding up as a kind of scapegoat. The recent remarks of Senator Willis on the Senate floor, in particular, incensed her: "Is a man to be convicted and his reputation blackened and his life ruined because Senator Wheeler says some friend of his accepts money?" Stinson knew that Harry Daugherty was no innocent party, the victim of a rotten friend he trusted too far. Whatever her dear Jess had been mixed up in, so had Daugherty. These public insinuations against Smith's memory stung, and she wanted revenge.

Wheeler therefore needed to be sure Stinson wasn't just telling him what he wanted to hear. So he tested her.

"Well, didn't Daugherty do this and that?" he asked, again and again, and each time she declined to play along unless she could back up his suggestion with something she'd seen or heard or with something Jess Smith had told her. (Wheeler considered such secondhand testimony admissible, he later wrote, because "in a conspiracy, which is what I was charging, evidence is admissible which might otherwise be deemed hearsay, to establish the terms and conditions under which the conspirators acted.")

She promised to tell the committee everything she knew, but there she drew the line. She simply would not cross the bounds of her own direct knowledge. Wheeler thought she made "an utterly credible witness."

MEANWHILE, WHEELER'S ABSENCE from the capital had not gone unnoticed. Hearings were scheduled to begin later that week, and it was hard to fathom why the man who would be leading them had vanished suddenly and without explanation.

"Senator Burton Wheeler," the Associated Press reported the morning of Wednesday, March 12, "disappeared for twenty-four hours. Wheeler was not at his office Tuesday nor at his home during the night, lending an air of mystery to the final preparations."

Upon his return, Daugherty, who was back in the capital after a vanishing act of his own, was asked for his thoughts. He demurred. "Nothing to say," he told a gaggle of reporters. "Let them start the talking."

Yet by the time the senator's train pulled into Washington's Union Station that Wednesday morning, Wheeler had resolved to get his star witness talking on the record as soon as possible, before the attorney general or his hounds could scare her into silence—or before she did something foolish. Stinson seemed to have second thoughts about testifying and was desperate for outside advice. She begged Wheeler for permission to visit Jess Smith's old golfing buddy—Ned McLean.

"Out of the question," said Wheeler, who knew that McLean and Daugherty were good friends. Instead, he placed Stinson under virtual house arrest at the Washington Hotel—under the watchful eye of his own sister, no less, Maude Wheeler Mitchell, who doubled as his personal secretary. There was no time to waste. The hearings, he decided, would start a day earlier than scheduled, that very afternoon, in fact, with Roxie Stinson on the witness stand.

Later, shortly before they received word that the committee would be convening forthwith, at 4 p.m., reporters spotted Wheeler on the fourth floor of the Senate Office Building.

"Showing up at his office after a mysterious twenty-four-hour absence," a correspondent for the United Press syndicate observed, "Wheeler today was accompanied by the three persons identified to inquirers simply as 'Mr. Fink, Mr. Stern, and Mrs. Stinson.' They hurried into the office with him."

No one was prepared for the bombshell they were about to drop.

18

"Partners in Crime"

B y 4 p.m. on March 12, such a crowd had jammed itself into Room 410 of the Senate Office Building that Wheeler's four colleagues on the committee could barely press their way to their seats.

Every inch of standing room was occupied by reporters, photographers, lawyers, senators and congressmen, congressional staff, and members of the general public. More than half of the spectators were women, a contingent one condescending journalist that day dismissed as "scandal hounds, the types that haunt divorce courts in search of sensations that provide morsels of diversion in their dull lives."

The Senate's Republican leadership had assigned the committee not one of the marble-walled caucus rooms usually reserved for important proceedings but a cramped, fourth-floor meeting space. There was no dais; instead, the committee sat along one end of a conference table, in front of a mirror that framed and reflected the room's three chandeliers. At the other end of the table stood a simple chair for the witness. The accommodations were simple, to be sure, but if banishing the committee to room 410 had been intended as a petty swipe at Wheeler's insurgency, it was already backfiring. The clamor ricocheting off the smaller room's wood-paneled walls, the collective body heat in the air, the heads bouncing and swaying as spectators strained for a better view—all of it only amplified the sense that something big was about to happen.

Although the attorney general wasn't present, he was well represented. Along one side of the conference table sat his two personal attorneys, former Republican congressman L. Paul Howland and former Democratic senator George E. Chamberlain. Next to them was Warren G. Grimes, special assistant to the attorney general and a supervising agent within the Bureau of Investigation. Somewhere in the room, too, was Thomas M. Smith, the undercover special agent still posing as a *New Haven Union* reporter.

A hush fell over the room when Wheeler appeared at the entrance.

"The lady who is to come on the stand," he announced, "does so with the understanding her picture will not be taken."

Stinson had insisted on it. Another legislator, hungry for press coverage, might have seen it as a minor setback, but Wheeler had the media savvy to see that the request cut both ways. Her camera shyness only underscored her reluctance to testify, bolstering her credibility. She was here because the Congress of the United States had commanded her to appear under "pains and penalties"—not to court fame or publicity.

"There will be no picture, then," Chairman Brookhart declared. With a show of reluctance, the photographers in the room picked up their tripods and squeezed their way out through the crowd.

Only then did the assembled throng get its first glimpse of Wheeler's surprise star witness. Dressed in a sealskin coat and metallic turban hat, her hair bobbed over her ears, she was the picture of Roaring Twenties fashion. All eyes followed as, head bowed, she sauntered to the witness chair, patent leather pumps clicking on the floor. When she took her seat, she slipped off her sealskin coat, "revealing herself," one newspaperman leered, "in a graceful black gown with just a suggestion of décolleté, and sleeves short enough to reveal strikingly fine arms."

Wheeler broke the reporter's reverie. "You may state your name to the committee," he said.

"Do I have to stand?" Her voice was soft, with a distinct midwestern twang.

"No, just be seated."

"Roxie Stinson."

HER TESTIMONY SPANNED five days—each one of them validating Wheeler's decision to call her as his star witness. She was credible, yes, but also attractive, witty, charming, poised, and sympathetic.

She delivered confident, perfectly positive answers.

She sobbed at the mention of Jess Smith's death, twisting her tear-soaked handkerchief.

She beamed white-toothed smiles when asked about happier topics.

She bantered with the committee and sent ripples of laughter across the hearing room. Once, when Wheeler asked her what kind of papers had been in Jess Smith's briefcase on one particular occasion, she quipped: "I don't know; I can't read through leather."

Most importantly, she refused to be intimidated. At one point, a gray-haired, stern-faced man pushed his way through the crowd and stood directly behind the attorney general's two lawyers. The man folded his arms and stared coldly through his spectacles at Stinson, who, as it happened, was explaining how she had always promised to tell all if (and *only* if) she were subpoenaed. Noticing the man's menacing gaze, she gestured to him.

"Mr. Daugherty knows that I told him frankly what I am saying about it."

The room stirred at the mention of the name.

"When you say Mr. Daugherty," Wheeler said, pointing at the man, "you mean Mr. Mal Daugherty, standing there?"

"Yes, and he knows I don't fib," she said and then turned to lock eyes with him. "Isn't that so?"

A suddenly unsettled Mal Daugherty broke in. "Does the committee want me to answer that question?" he asked, before Wheeler waved him off.

Stinson was, in short, captivating, and the newspaper correspondents ate it up.

But for all her style, she brought substance, too. Jess Smith may not have told her *everything* about what he and Harry Daugherty were up to, but he'd never held back, either. Stinson complained to the committee that she and her ex-husband, a notorious gossip, "never discussed anybody else but Mr. Daugherty." "That," she added, "is the first thing we talked about and the last thing."

Guided by Wheeler's questions, she related everything she knew. And while anyone hoping for the proverbial smoking gun was disappointed, she painted a devastating picture of a lifelong political dealer who, entrusted with the high office of attorney general and aided by a slavish lieutenant, set about raiding the Justice Department cupboard for favors to dispense.

WHEELER'S FIRST TASK was to establish the contours of a conspiracy between Jess Smith and Harry Daugherty. He knew that, whatever misdeeds his witnesses would reveal, they were unlikely to trace back directly to his investigation's target. The attorney general was simply too savvy a lawyer and too experienced a fixer to leave behind fingerprints; there was a reason men like Harry Daugherty kept men like Jess Smith around. Still, if Wheeler could prove that the attorney general nonetheless directed, approved, or benefited from any illegal or improper transactions executed by Smith, he might have a case. Perhaps not a case that could stand up in a court of law, but that wasn't the point. He only needed one that would prevail in the court of public opinion. If the American people could be persuaded that their attorney general was party to a criminal conspiracy, President Coolidge would be forced to cut him from his cabinet.

He began with the fact that everyone in the room already knew.

"Would you say they were intimate friends?" Wheeler asked Stinson early on.

"Why, Jess Smith was a great admirer of Harry Daugherty all his life," she answered. "I think he was his ideal."

"What position, if any, did he occupy with Mr. Daugherty after Mr. Daugherty was selected as attorney general?"

"Bumper—intimate friend."

She explained that Smith kept a desk in an anteroom just off the attorney general's private office, and part of his role was to "kinda ward off people from Harry Daugherty and call down undesirables."

Their relationship extended far beyond work, however. "He was in constant touch with Harry Daugherty," she testified. "They lived together. They were most intimate friends, and Jess adored him. He wanted to shield him in every possible way. He lived for him, he loved him."

Eventually, Wheeler brought her straight to the point. "Miss Stinson, tell me this: What have you to say as to whether or not Harry Daugherty was a partner of Jess Smith in all their transactions?"

"Oh, Jess Smith would not presume to do anything without authority from Harry Daugherty," she said. "They were absolutely close together in every connection, and in close touch with each other. Socially, in business ways, and every other way. Jess Smith lived for Harry Daugherty."

Once more, bluntly: "Mr. Smith was one of Mr. Daugherty's partners, was he not?"

"Oh, no," interjected Senator Moses, who thought Wheeler was referring to a legal partnership.

"I say," Wheeler repeated, "he was one of Mr. Daugherty's partners, was he not?"

"Partners in law?" Stinson asked.

"Partners in *crime*."

The crowd gasped, and Stinson screwed her face in annoyance.

Wheeler rephrased his question. "He was one of the partners of Mr. Daugherty," he asked, "in these different deals that were pulled off?"

"Yes, sir."

OF COURSE, DAUGHERTY'S legal representatives couldn't allow such talk to go on without protest.

On Stinson's first day before the committee—mere minutes after she was sworn in—Wheeler and his witness had just settled into a staccato rhythm of knowing questions and just-the-facts answers when Paul Howland, counsel for Attorney General Daugherty, tried to derail them.

Wheeler was asking Stinson about a house on H Street, owned by Ned McLean and occupied by Daugherty and Smith during their first year in Washington. "What do you say," he inquired, "as to whether or not they paid any rent for that house?"

"I think not," Stinson answered. "I was not informed by Jess."

Howland jumped in. "Let me ask you if the 'prosecutor,' so-called, will allow or think this competent for the witness to say that she was so informed by Jess Smith; whether he thinks that is competent testimony to go in this record?" Howland had a point—much of her testimony was the textbook definition of hearsay.

Wheeler, however, believed hearsay might be admissible as evidence of a conspiracy between Smith and Daugherty. "I do," he said.

"And you have been admitted to the bar?"

Chairman Brookhart rushed to Wheeler's defense. "We will not have remarks of that kind here."

But Wheeler could defend himself. "I am not going to be bulldozed by you," he thundered at Howland, who had defended Daugherty before the House Judiciary Committee when it was considering Rep. Oscar Keller's articles of impeachment. "I want you to fairly understand that here and now."

"Do not misunderstand me. I am not trying—"

"You bulldozed the committee over on the House side," Wheeler interjected, "but I want to tell you right here and now that you are not going to bulldoze me for one second."

"Do not misunderstand me—"

"I do not misunderstand you. I understand your tactics very well. And I want you to understand right from the start that you are not going to bulldoze me, and I am not going to take any of your petty small abuses."

"That is not it at all."

"Yes, your attitude has been that."

Senator Ashurst, the committee's other Democrat and, incidentally, Wheeler's old law school classmate at the University of Michigan, had heard enough. "Counsel for Mr. Daugherty, we expect from you a large amount of silence until your time to cross examine the witness comes."

"You are here," Wheeler added, "by the courtesy of this committee."

"We have had scant courtesy so far," said Howland.

"Some people," Ashurst replied, "do not know what courtesy is."

Chairman Brookhart finally shut down the exchange. "Proceed with your inquiries, Senator Wheeler."

ON HER SECOND day, Roxie Stinson recounted a trip she took with Jess Smith in the summer of 1921 to New York City. While there, the famed vaudeville performer Joe Weber showered them with theater tickets and other Broadway favors, and at one point she overheard Weber ask Smith about a pending "deal."

"With reference to this matter we were talking about," Weber said, understandably cagey in the presence of a third party, "how is it getting along?"

"Well, I don't know," Smith answered. "We are working on that now."

"Well, you know I am very anxious to have it consummated."

Afterward, Smith decoded the conversation for Stinson. Weber's brother-in-law, he explained, was in the federal penitentiary, and Harry Daugherty himself was working on a pardon, or at least a parole, to free him.

There was a problem, however. "I don't know whether we are going to bother with him or not," Smith said. "He is awful cheap and wants something for nothing. We get a lot of those."

It was a bombshell allegation that Wheeler, of course, would need to confirm with additional evidence. Pardons, however, seemed commonplace next to what else Daugherty and Smith were selling.

"When Mr. Harry Daugherty first went into office," Wheeler asked at one point, following up on a rumor he'd heard, "what have you to say as to conversations Jess Smith had with reference to their getting money out of whiskey deals?"

"Well," Stinson answered, "it was in reference to permits."

"Tell me about it, or tell the committee about it."

"Well, it is not very definite. It is about different permits that they could get through that people could get liquor out of warehouses."

Ever since the Eighteenth Amendment's passage, millions of gallons of pre-Prohibition liquor had sat locked up in government-bonded warehouses—the kind Alexander Fink was offered in return for Stinson's silence. There, the spirits, mostly whiskey, aged and mellowed, guarded by Treasury Department agents. As long as it sat in storage, the liquor was perfectly legal to own—Prohibition didn't abolish property rights, after all, only "manufacture, sale, or transportation"—but getting it out of the warehouse legally was another matter. Just the paperwork alone was daunting. Under the Volstead Act, the Internal Revenue Service had primary authority for enforcing Prohibition, and it made the process of withdrawal more onerous than filing a tax return, requiring at least six confounding forms: 1404, 1405, 1408, 1410, 1410-A, and 1410-D. It also required a legitimate excuse, such as exportation to a foreign country or use in a medicinal or industrial application. And finally, it depended on the signature of a senior Treasury official, which in this case the attorney general of the United States was evidently offering to broker, all under the nose of his chief rival in the cabinet, Treasury Secretary Andrew Mellon.

"That," Stinson added, "was when they were first in office, you understand. But that did not last very long, because they got afraid of it." It was risky business for the attorney general to meddle in another cabinet officer's affairs.

Instead, they allegedly moved on to safer, simpler transactions where Daugherty could rely on his own authority as head of the Justice Department. With Jess Smith as go-between, she said, they struck illicit deals with publicly traded corporations like White Motors and Pure Oil, which both had matters pending before the Justice Department. As payment, they sometimes received unregistered stock certificates, which they deposited in a blind brokerage account at the Washington firm of Hibbs & Co. under the name of W. W. Spaid No. 2.

All this work in the shadows proved quite lucrative. Smith's estate, which had been worth roughly $150,000 when Daugherty took office in 1921, was valued at $250,000 upon his death two years later—and this in the absence of a salary and in spite of the $50,000 annual household expenses he split with Daugherty. At the same time, Smith's generosity became even more lavish. He paid off Stinson's mortgage. He started enclosing $100 or even $500 bills in his letters. A few times, she reported, he gave her stock "to put on the market quickly and quietly."

But Stinson only realized the full scale of graft within the Justice Department, and her ex-husband's role in it, when she once saw him remove seventy-five $1,000 bills from a money belt.

"Seventy-five one-thousand dollar bills?" asked an astonished Senator Wheeler.

"Yes, sir."

"When he showed them to you what, if anything, did he say in reference to them?"

"Nothing."

"How did he come to show them to you?" Senator Jones asked.

"Well, he would just tell me about different deals and of money they would make."

"By 'them' whom do you mean?" Senator Ashurst asked.

"Mr. Daugherty and him."

"Mr. Harry M. Daugherty?"

"Yes, sir."

"When he showed you the seventy-five thousand-dollar bills where had he been—where had he come from?" Wheeler asked.

"He had come from Washington."

"He had brought them with him in his belt from Washington?"

"Yes, sir. Apparently."

"It was not in a black satchel, was it?" Senator Ashurst inquired facetiously. Everyone in the room got the reference—the bag that Edward L. Doheny's son used to transport his cash "loan" to Albert Fall.

"It was not," Stinson said when the chuckles died down. "I did not see it in a satchel."

Nevertheless, for all their evident success in monetizing their roles within the Justice Department, Daugherty and Smith missed out on at least one big opportunity. In the fall of 1922, Smith gossiped that "five men in the past few days have made thirty-three million dollars."

By that point Stinson had learned not to pry; the less she asked, the more he volunteered. But at $33 million, her curiosity was irresistible.

"Were you and Harry in on it?" she asked.

"No," Smith said. "That is what we are sore about. They were our friends, too." (Stinson jumbled a few of the details, but Teapot Dome special counsel Owen Roberts and Atlee Pomerene were already on the case. They would soon learn that five oil executives including Harry Sinclair had conspired to skim the profits from the sale of thirty-three million barrels of oil, defrauding their own shareholders.)

Perhaps the most surprising revelation involved the so-called Fight of the Century. On July 2, 1921, Jack Dempsey and Georges Carpentier met in Jersey City for the most anticipated title bout in history. All across America, millions followed along, huddling around their neighbors' radio sets or swarming their local newspaper offices for ticker-tape updates, as the world's heavyweight and light-heavyweight boxing champions went toe-to-toe. When the American Dempsey landed a hard right hook in the fourth round, sending his French challenger down for the count, an entire nation rejoiced in the news together. But only the eighty thousand who had packed themselves into the wooden arena at Boyle's Thirty Acres (Jess Smith among them) were able to *watch* Dempsey pummel Carpentier into the ropes—to enjoy, with their own eyes, the spectacle of Dempsey strutting around the ring as the referee counted to ten.

Soon after, Roxie Stinson met up with Smith in nearby Atlantic City and learned that millions more might soon have the chance to see the fight—with the unlikely aid of Attorney General Harry Daugherty. It turned out that a motion picture camera crew had been at the bout. Their footage was hastily cut together, and within days of Dempsey's victory, lines snaked around the block from Atlantic City's movie theater to see the resulting hour-long film. Smith took Stinson to see it—twice—and would not stop raving about it. It was "so much better than the real fight," he gushed. "So much more enjoyable."

The only catch was that, by law, the reels couldn't leave the state of New Jersey. A 1912 federal statute, inspired by racist hysteria over the dominance of Black prizefighter Jack Johnson, prohibited the interstate distribution of fight films. If only the promoters could find a way around the law, they stood to make millions. That was where the attorney general came in.

"We have a big thing," Smith whispered to Stinson. Using informal channels within the Justice Department—not binding orders or official memos—he and Daugherty would ensure that anyone who violated the law would only receive a token fine, not prison time. In return, the pair stood to earn $180,000.

"Now, what had Mr. Smith himself to do with it?" asked Senator Jones.

"Well, he was the one that was—what would you call it?—he was the one that was making the deal for them."

"That is," Wheeler interjected, "he was the one that was the go-between?"

"Yes, sir."

Smith was the "bumper," as Stinson described him, who insulated Daugherty from the hard evidence of their graft, not only in the deal-making but in handling their payouts. Daugherty never touched the money; Smith brought it back to Washington Court House, where he deposited it at the town's only federally chartered financial institution—the Midland National Bank. Smith once bragged to Stinson that he'd "just deposited $175,000 of Eastern money there."

And just in case there was ever any trouble with the money, or if the wrong people came asking about it, Smith could always fall back on the bank's leadership. Its president was Mal S. Daugherty.

ROXIE STINSON'S TESTIMONY painted a devastating picture of an attorney general unbound by the rule of law. Certainly, her recollections left many holes for Wheeler's future witnesses to fill in, and Daugherty's staunchest defenders could still dismiss much of her testimony as mere hearsay. But for many who followed the proceedings or even glanced at each day's banner headlines—"DAUGHERTY-SMITH COMBINE DEALT IN PICTURES, WHISKIES, OILS, PARDONS SAYS ROXIE STINSON," screamed the March 14 Atlanta Constitution—there was reason to suspect that Harry Daugherty had violated his oath as the nation's attorney general.

Official misconduct at that level was newsworthy enough. What made Stinson's revelations truly scandalous, though, were the details she offered up about the near-Shakespearean drama Jess Smith endured in his final days.

All throughout the hearings, Stinson danced around the cause of her ex-husband's demise, hinting again and again that her beloved Jess didn't die by his own hand, as if she herself couldn't accept the truth. At one point, she was asked to sum up her thoughts on the matter. In response, she teased the conspiracy theorists and "scandal hounds" in the audience. "So far as I am concerned," she said, tears coursing down her cheeks, "it may not even be true that he committed suicide or passed away in that manner."

Stinson stopped. Deep down, she knew that Smith wasn't murdered in some desperate cover-up. That idea simply didn't match up with everything she'd witnessed in his final days.

"But I am convinced," she continued, now correcting herself, "in view of his preparations, and putting his house in such complete order as he did, and under the great stress to which I have referred before, and his doubts and fears, which I knew, that he did probably—I am sure that he did take his own life."

That didn't exactly capture her thinking, either. In a strictly legal sense, Smith might have been the only one to blame for his death. But Stinson's feelings of moral responsibility weren't bound by legal constructs.

She searched for a way to explain. Finally, she spoke.

"I . . . consider Harry Daugherty as morally responsible for the death of Jess Smith."

As she told the story of Jess Smith's final days, choking back tears, the world began to understand what kind of man Harry Daugherty really was.

19

"They Are Going to Get Me"

Rarely was the mood between the two old friends so icy.
It was early May 1923, the month before the "Voyage of Understanding" was set to embark, and President Harding had summoned Harry Daugherty to the White House for a confidential meeting. Only upon arriving did Daugherty learn that the subject was his closest friend, his most essential aide, his partner in all things, Jess Smith.

"I have been informed," the president announced, "that Jess has been conducting himself rather badly of late."

"What is he doing?" In other words: How much did the president know? Since the election, Smith had been welcomed into Harding's inner circle by virtue of his relationship with Daugherty. He was a regular presence at the White House poker table, as well as at official events. But Harding was never meant to know about Smith's unofficial activities on behalf of the administration.

"He's running with a gay crowd, attending all sorts of wild parties," the president said. "And you should know too that he is using the attorney general's car until all hours of the night."

Those were hardly capital offenses—and most assuredly the least of Smith's misdeeds.

"I'm amazed," Daugherty said, feigning surprise. "I will look into the matter at once."

Harding hesitated and then added regretfully: "I suggest that you tell him it will be impossible for him to go with us on the trip to Alaska. The party is already filled."

149

The meeting's significance began to sink in. Barring Jess from the Alaska trip would publicly signal the administration was making a clean break from the man who had paraded around DC for more than two years, touting his friendship with "Warren," his intimacy with "Harry," and his easy access to the corridors of power.

Daugherty could read between the lines. Some scheme Jess had gotten mixed up in was on the verge of exposure. It would surely drag them all down unless the unbroken chain linking the president of the United States to a shameful world of graft and corruption was snapped. Someone had to take the blame, and Warren Harding didn't want it to be Daugherty.

IF ANYONE HAD earned Harry Daugherty's loyalty, it was Jess Smith.

That past January, after months of fighting political enemies both real (congressmen like Oscar Keller) and imagined (the Bolsheviks who were behind every loud noise, every sudden movement), the nerve-racked attorney general's body gave out. The very day after the House voted down Keller's impeachment charges, 204 to 77, Daugherty grew dizzy and collapsed in his Wardman Park apartment. A concerned President Harding dispatched his White House physicians, who were shocked to find Daugherty's systolic blood pressure hovering around 215—meaning the attorney general was on the brink of a life-threatening stroke. The doctors ordered indefinite bed rest and, to excuse his absence from the Justice Department headquarters, explained to the press that the attorney general had "a heavy cold." Privately, however, there was real concern that his illness would spell the end of his political career, if it didn't kill him first.

Jess Smith would never let that happen. Over the ensuing two-plus months, Smith sat at the attorney general's bedside day and night, shooing away visitors, supervising his medical care. He went days at a time without stepping outside for fresh air. His presence was needed, most importantly, to enforce a strict information quarantine and keep the worries of the world—the demands of the Justice Department, the attacks of his political enemies, even requests from the White House—out of the sickroom. It was several days before Daugherty could so much as sit up in bed and weeks until he could stand, and Smith was there for each milestone. Slowly, the attorney general regained his strength. By March, he was traveling south to convalesce beneath Florida's sunny skies, and on April 30, he triumphantly returned to Washington and resumed his official duties.

Smith celebrated the victory as if his own—but it came at great personal cost. He was himself in bad shape, suffering from advanced diabetes, which only worsened as he focused all his energies on Daugherty's recovery. Smith "absolutely neglected himself physically," his doctor complained. He overate, packed on extra weight, and refused to carry out the stringent treatment plan prescribed for him. Left untreated, his diabetes sapped his energy and thrust him into severe bouts of depression. And it wasn't only his health that suffered. So too did his finances. When Daugherty fell ill, Smith had been in the process of selling his dry goods store in Washington Court House. It was his life's work, the source of whatever personal fortune he could claim to have acquired legitimately. But Daugherty's recovery demanded his full attention, and he paid too little mind to negotiating a good deal for himself. Ultimately, he sold the Jess W. Smith Department Store for a song—$38,000, far less than it was worth.

None of that mattered to Smith, who was genuinely glad to give himself to Harry Daugherty. He expected nothing in return.

Least of all betrayal.

SMITH'S FACE WENT white as Daugherty broke the news. Recounting his conversation with the president, he informed Smith that he would not be going to Alaska. In fact, it would be better for everyone if he left Washington for good.

"I'm sorry, Jess," Daugherty said. "But you do need a rest, you know. You're not a well man. Why don't you enter a hospital back home, rest awhile."

"I'll go home," Smith answered, "but damned if anybody can make me enter a hospital."

He received the news, Daugherty would recall, "as a prisoner receives a death sentence."

Indeed, Smith faced a bleak future. Nothing could ever match his time in the capital, where he'd been a small gear within Washington's biggest wheel, tending day and night to the man he loved. For more than two years he'd basked in the attorney general's reflected glory—only to see his sun suddenly go dark. He'd lived with an almost religious certainty that his devotion would be rewarded. That Daugherty could so casually cast him aside, sacrificing him to protect another man—even if that man was the president of the United States—shattered his worldview.

Desperate for consolation, Smith rushed home to Ohio and to that one light that still flickered: Roxie Stinson. Ordinarily he would greet his ex-wife with a simple kiss. This time, however, he snatched her hand and kissed it hungrily.

"Roxie, you're just beautiful!" he said, throwing his arms around her. "You're the sweetest thing I ever saw! I never was so glad to see anyone in my life."

Though she giggled at his lack of embarrassment, Stinson also noticed a dark undercurrent beneath his joy. "He was in fear," she recalled. "He was in *mortal* fear." In fact, the famously carefree Jess Smith had grown paranoid, suspicious of that random stranger on the train or man sitting alone at the restaurant. "I don't like the looks of that fellow," he would tell her. At one point, he inexplicably insisted that she carry his briefcase, which contained important documents from Washington.

"They are going to get me," he told her.

"No, they won't, Jess."

"They passed it to me."

Stinson thought she knew what he meant—they'd passed the *blame* to him. Evidently, Smith had grasped the implications of his banishment.

He worried about her, too. During a dinner dance at the Scioto Country Club, he made her promise not to go out after dark by herself and to never, ever drive alone, lest some unfortunate "accident" befall her.

At one point, she offered to play the role of a priest in a confessional: "Tell me what the trouble is. You can trust me. Tell me."

"No, no, no," he said. "Just cheer me up. Just brace me up."

DESPITE ALL HIS hurt, Smith couldn't allow even this to come between him and Daugherty. He still loved the man, whatever the nature of their relationship. He longed for his company and craved the opportunity to serve again. Soon his wish was fulfilled. On May 12, the attorney general arrived in Columbus for yet another extended vacation, and the pair were reunited.

By most appearances, the two men fell right back into old habits. Smith looked after Daugherty's health. He accompanied the attorney general to his satellite office at the Columbus federal building. He even wrote personal letters on "Office of the Attorney General" stationery, just as he had in Washington. Smith might have convinced himself that, despite his exile from official power, their personal relations were returning to some kind of normalcy.

Before long, an incident shattered that illusion. On May 23, Smith and Daugherty drove to Deer Creek in nearby Pickaway County to spend a few nights at "the Shack," a rustic two-story cabin that the two men owned along with Mal. For the past two years, the Shack had been their retreat from the troubles of politics. Here there had been blue-sky scheming, bootleg whiskey, and poker games next to a roaring fireplace. Now, it seemed, there was only resentment.

On their third day at the Shack, Harry Daugherty was taking his customary afternoon nap when an old friend from Columbus arrived and asked for an appointment with the attorney general.

"He is asleep," Smith informed the visitor, "and he can't be disturbed."

The man insisted his business was urgent and was so persistent that Smith eventually walked upstairs and roused Daugherty. He regretted his decision immediately.

"You know I won't be disturbed!" Daugherty screamed. The attorney general swore and cursed, a helpless Smith absorbing each verbal blow. He was destroyed all over again. Daugherty had *never* treated him this way.

Seeing Smith's wounds, Daugherty then produced the salt. He dressed, summoned his chauffeur, and threatened to leave Smith—who had no car of his own at the Shack—stranded. It was a ten-mile walk back to Washington Court House.

Eventually, the attorney general's anger cooled, and he arranged for his nephew Ellis to drive Smith back to town. But the damage was done. Smith mumbled the entire way home and at one point tried to jump from the moving automobile. By the time he arrived back in Washington Court House, an idea had formed in his mind—a dark plan that, oddly, also seems to have given him comfort.

Smith marched directly into Carpenter's hardware store and bought a revolver and box of cartridges. The shopkeeper was shocked. Everyone in the small town knew that Jess Smith was deathly afraid of firearms.

"This is for the attorney general," Smith said as he paid.

Later that afternoon, he met up with Roxie. She was surprised to see her dear Jess, so downcast of late, back to his old self, spine straight, head upright. She wondered if there'd been a breakthrough at the Shack.

"Has it been straightened out?" she asked. "Are things all right now, Jess?"

He smiled. "Yes. They are all right now."

A FEW DAYS later, Smith talked Daugherty into letting him return to Washington, ever so briefly, "to see a few friends and wind up a little business." Relations were still frosty between the two men, but after his blowup at the Shack, the attorney general was hard-pressed to say no. After all, Smith had left the capital so abruptly. The least he deserved was a chance to clear out his personal possessions.

On May 28, the two men shared an eastbound train out of Columbus but evidently saw little of each other. The attorney general had to hear from one of their travel companions that Smith was refusing to drink and generally acting "queer."

He might have been thinking of his previous day's visit to the Washington Court House Cemetery. There, beneath a towering Celtic cross inscribed with the name "Smith," he found a granite ledger gravestone inscribed "Laura E. Smith, 1853–1912"—his mother's—and decorated it with a floral wreath. One burial site in the family plot remained unfilled. He must have noticed.

"I've been through hell, just plain hell!" he told an old friend who'd come along. "I don't think I have long to live."

It was the kind of thought he would have shared with Daugherty— if they had still been talking. As it was, upon arriving in Washington the two men went their separate ways, Smith to their suite at the Wardman Park and Daugherty to the White House, where President Harding, aware of their falling out, had invited his attorney general to stay for a few nights.

Daugherty worried about his friend's fragile mental state, however, and dispatched his Justice Department assistant, Warren "Barney" Martin, to sleep in the second bedroom. Smith and Martin had never gotten along, but it was better than leaving a troubled man all alone in an empty hotel suite.

That evening, mortality was still on Smith's mind. Although he'd drawn up a valid will the year before, now he scribbled a new one on a single leaf of Wardman Park stationery. "In the presence of Almighty God," it read, "and being of sound mind, I make this my last will. I give all I possess to Edmund St. John [his cousin], Louise St. John Thompson [another cousin], Roxy R. Stinson, Harry M. Daugherty, and M. S. Daugherty. I ask that M. S. Daugherty be made my executor. Jess W. Smith. May 28–1923." It was unwitnessed.

In the morning, Smith stumbled through eighteen holes with Barney Martin, navy physician Joel Boone, and Peyton Gordon, the US attorney for the District of Columbia—the man who, if it came to it, would ultimately prosecute him for official misconduct. Smith was understandably distracted.

"Jess Smith didn't play the kind of game he was able to play or was accustomed to playing," Boone recalled. "We had to remind him to drive off, putt, to keep his eye on the ball. He seemed to be in a trance."

Afterward Smith went to his office. Instead of clearing out his personal possessions—his stated intention—he stuffed his briefcase with official Justice Department documents and returned with them to the Wardman Park.

Loneliness tortured him that night. This luxury apartment, a site of dealmaking and a symbol of his unparalleled intimacy with the attorney general, had once inspired pride in him. Now, despite Martin's company, its hollow rooms only amplified his despair. Desperate for comfort, he phoned Ned McLean and his wife, Evalyn, who were at their 2,600-acre farm in Leesburg, Virginia. He asked if he could stay over for three or four nights. Evalyn was recovering from an illness but, realizing that something was off, told Smith to come anyway.

Soon, though, a ferocious thunderstorm erupted over Washington. There was no way he could attempt the forty miles to Leesburg over muddy roads and swollen streams. He called the McLeans again around ten to say he'd come first thing in the morning.

Another two hours passed. Outside, sheets of rain drowned the hotel gardens. Smith became disconsolate. At midnight, he phoned Leesburg again. Evalyn McLean took the call.

"Hello, how are you?"

"I am fine but rather nervous."

"Now, now. What's wrong with you?"

"Oh, I'm just a little upset. Ned's asleep, you say?"

"Isn't Mr. Daugherty with you?"

"No, the chief sent for him to come to the White House."

"Who is with you?"

"Barney Martin."

"Well, you get a little sleep now and you'll feel better."

"I'll be at the farm at seven."

"You can stay as long as you like."

"I'm so glad I can come."

It was the last time anyone heard from Jess Smith.

AS THE NIGHT wore on, he must have made peace with what Daugherty had done to him. He could have retaliated, if he'd wanted. A rumor, in fact, later surfaced that he had an appointment the very next day to meet with Montana senator Thomas Walsh, who was at that point beginning to dig into the oil lease irregularities, but the rumor misunderstood the man. Harry Daugherty was capable of betrayal; Jess Smith was not.

Instead, he doubled down on his devotion. He must have known how convenient his death would be—and not only for himself, in offering an escape from the shame of scandal, but also for the man who depended on him. It was the ultimate sacrifice.

Sometime before he raised the revolver to his temple, however, Smith did some housecleaning. He gathered up Daugherty's personal papers—as many bank receipts, letters to friends, and telegrams as he could find—and stuffed them into a big metal wastebasket. To that he added all the files he'd rescued from Justice Department headquarters and lit a bonfire.

As the papers charred and crumbled into ash, little else remained in the world that could link the attorney general to all their misdeeds—with one notable exception.

Jess Smith cocked the revolver and, one final time, made himself indispensable to the man he loved.

20

"This Base Insinuation"

After ten months of Washington speculation, Roxie Stinson's tear-streaked tale more or less resolved the mystery of Jess Smith's death. Although it was only one woman's presentation of the facts, it offered a plausible explanation for why Smith ended his own life, as well as the suspicious circumstances surrounding the suicide. The eagerness of Billy Burns and Dr. Boone to ascribe his act to "brooding over his physical condition"? The crippling guilt that kept Harry Daugherty from his friend's funeral? Those puzzle pieces now fell into place.

The revelations naturally lent themselves to boldfaced banner headlines. "SAYS SMITH DIED FOR DAUGHERTY," shouted the *Akron Beacon Journal*. The *Atlanta Constitution* blasted a double-deck header across its eight columns: "ROXIE STINSON BRANDS DAUGHERTY AS INTRIGUER; NAMES HIM SILENT PARTNER IN FIGHT FILM DEAL." The *Boston Daily Globe* topped its coverage with "SMITH'S EX-WIFE FIRST BIG GUN IN DAUGHERTY'S PROBE" and then, after the jump, "DAUGHERTY INQUIRY STARTS WITH A BANG." The *New York Daily News*, the nation's highest-circulation daily, simply shouted: "DAUGHERTY PROBE SENSATION."

For the impresario of this Capitol Hill spectacle, the headlines gave some measure of satisfaction, but Burton Wheeler couldn't rest too easy. Stinson's disclosures instantly raised the stakes in his battle with the attorney general, painting a truly unsettling portrait of the man. If Harry Daugherty could so profoundly betray his closest and most loyal friend—if he could all but pull the trigger on Smith's suicide weapon—what might he do to his avowed enemy?

Gaston Means had warned Wheeler that his own life and those of his wife and children were in danger.

"Now, you know what they'll try to do if they want to get you," Means told him during one of his many working visits to the Wheeler residence. "They'll run a car into you, drive you into the sidewalk, a pole or something of the kind. You be careful."

Lulu Wheeler wasn't spared Means's dark fantasies. "Don't buy candy from anybody," he told the senator's wife, explaining that assassins might pose as candy peddlers to poison the couple's children.

The Wheelers *had* noticed strange men lurking outside their house, hiding behind the leafy hedge that ringed their front yard. The senator, who bragged that he could "spot a detective at fifty paces," assured himself they were simply keeping an eye on him, watching who came and went. Wheeler tried to write off Means's admonitions as, at best, the paranoia of a man who spent too much time in the criminal underworld or, at worst, psychological warfare by a ruthless operator still working for Harry Daugherty.

But the beguiling detective wasn't the only one whispering caution. So, too, was coolheaded Frank Vanderlip, the retired bank president who was financing much of the committee's investigative work. Vanderlip, who had also made himself Daugherty's enemy, was convinced that his own life was in danger—a fear stoked by an insurance carrier who denied his application for a million-dollar accidental death policy. Vanderlip was taking precautions, and he begged the senator to do the same. Knowing few other multimillionaires willing to bankroll his crusade, Wheeler had little choice but to comply. At the banker's insistence, he abandoned his habit of riding the trolley through the capital. Instead, this champion of the downtrodden began traveling back and forth to Capitol Hill in the splendor of Vanderlip's armored Pierce-Arrow limousine, a chauffeur behind the wheel, seats upholstered in gray shadow-stripe Lusterweave.

Wheeler found the situation absurd. Harry Daugherty might have been a crook, but he was no common gangster. "The idea that my enemies would try to harm me was as silly as it had been in my Montana days," he later recalled. "From a public reaction standpoint, it would be the worst thing they could do."

No, physical violence was too blunt an instrument for Daugherty. The master manipulator typically pursued revenge with more civilized, yet no less effective tools. Wheeler steeled himself for what was to come.

AS IT HAPPENED, Daugherty aimed his first counterpunch not at Wheeler himself but at his star witness. It came in the form of a letter, signed by Daugherty and his two attorneys and addressed to Chairman Brookhart, requesting that the committee subpoena four men from Ohio, including stockbroker Samuel Ungerleider and his own brother, Mal, as witnesses. If allowed to testify, the letter declared, the witnesses would reveal an audacious plot to blackmail a sitting attorney general, sprung in Cleveland the previous month.

"A.L. Fink," it read, "acting as an agent for Roxie Stinson, represented to the above witnesses that the said Roxie Stinson had letters and documentary evidence which would be greatly embarrassing to H. M. Daugherty if given to the public at this time; that the said Roxie Stinson was ready and willing to sell said documentary evidence and her silence to the Attorney General for $150,000, and would deliver said documents to the above named witnesses and leave the country so that they could not be subpoenaed to testify in any investigation that might be had of the Department of Justice at Washington."

His motive in sharing this story was transparent to all who read it. If he could brand Stinson as a blackmailer, he could undermine her credibility as a witness. That much seemed fair play—as the "defendant" before this congressional tribunal, no one would question his right to impeach the prosecution's chief witness.

Daugherty immediately pivoted, however, to deploy some blackmail of his own.

"We allege on information and belief," he and his two attorneys wrote, "that said witnesses if called will testify that on the 18th day of February, 1924, Roxie Stinson and A.L. Fink registered at the Hollanden hotel, in Cleveland, Ohio, under the name of A.L. French and wife; they occupied room 456 in said hotel; that on the next morning they paid their bill and departed."

The formal, lawyerly language obscured a shocking reality. In a letter to a Senate committee, the attorney general of the United States was publicly insinuating an extramarital affair between two private citizens. It was a right hook, aimed squarely at Roxie Stinson's good name—and it landed.

In the looser language of a press statement, Daugherty added a few quick jabs: "She is a disappointed woman who blames me because her divorced husband did not make her sole legatee under his will; an angry woman because the courts have decided against her in litigation over the estate of her divorced husband; a malicious woman because the friends of the attorney general have brushed her aside and disregarded all her tentative efforts to capitalize her silence."

Point, Daugherty.

THE COMMITTEE SPRANG to Roxie Stinson's defense. Addressing Daugherty's two counsel in the hearing room, Chairman Smith Brookhart vowed that he would no longer take the high road by ignoring the attorney general's increasingly combative public statements. "Being a kind of fighting individual myself," Brookhart said with an edge of anger in his voice, "I'm going to strike back at him from now on."

Forceful words, but it was Wheeler who fully voiced the committee's indignation. "If ever a man stooped to a cowardly, low-down trick," he thundered, "it was the attorney general when he attacked this poor, defenseless woman. We have made no effort to go into the attorney general's private life—and we could if we want to."

Daugherty's closet contained at least a skeleton or two, Wheeler was hinting—perhaps something to do with the salacious and persistent gossip about the full extent of his intimacy with Jess Smith, or his alcoholic son's rumored ties to New York gamblers.

"Nobody," he continued, "has wanted to besmirch the character of any woman in this case, and it remained for the attorney general to adopt that kind of tactics in this case."

He went further, reaching for his fighting words: "And I say it was an unmanly and an indecent thing for the attorney general to make the attack that he did. If he had a spark of manhood about him he would retract that statement."

Wheeler's fury made it into nearly every American newspaper, verbatim, but the press also craved a reply from the composed, self-assured woman who had so captivated them from her witness chair.

At first Stinson remained silent. Her actions in Cleveland were hard to explain—but it must have been more than that. Shame, even in a time of loosening sexual mores, still attached itself to an unmarried woman so accused. Having some of the country's most powerful men argue over her sexual virtue would have only added to her embarrassment.

For the better part of a week she sequestered herself in her DC hotel room, feigning illness, mulling over her response. Finally, on March 22,

Stinson returned to the hearing room and boldly accused Harry and Mal Daugherty of engineering a "frame-up."

"This base insinuation of Mr. Harry M. Daugherty's," she declared, "that I occupied that room or another room with this man, is utterly false and impossible." In her telling, they spent only two hours in her room together, dining and discussing his latest stock scheme. The blackmail charge she denied just as vehemently. She reminded the committee that she had not volunteered her testimony but only appeared under subpoena, which wasn't the behavior of someone making good on an extortion threat. When Fink, she said, offered her silence to Mal Daugherty and Sam Ungerleider for $150,000, he was acting without her knowledge or consent.

Her denial was all assertion and no evidence, but—for those inclined to accept it—it was compelling enough.

For what it was worth, Fink offered his own version of events to his hometown press in Buffalo. In his telling, *he* was the real victim of the whole sorry episode. When he arrived in Cleveland, he planned neither to blackmail Harry Daugherty nor coerce Roxie Stinson's silence. It was Daugherty's men, he claimed, who dragged him into the realm of extortion. When their sleuths learned that he'd booked Roxie Stinson's hotel room under the fictitious names of "Mr. and Mrs. A.L. French," Mal Daugherty, Sam Ungerleider, and friends approached him with a carrot and a stick. If he cooperated in pressuring Stinson into silence, he would be awarded a lucrative liquor warehouse license. If he refused, he would be arrested for violating the morality laws of the state of Ohio.

What exactly had transpired in Cleveland? Was Stinson actually a foiled blackmailer or the innocent victim of unscrupulous men? That would forever remain a mystery.

The question, in any case, was rendered moot the moment the attorney general deployed his sly innuendo, accusing an apparently respectable woman who had just charmed America of extramarital relations. When Wheeler denounced Daugherty's public smear as "unmanly," he spoke for millions who considered Stinson's virtue off-limits in political combat, regardless of the facts. Had Daugherty limited himself to the alleged blackmail conspiracy, he might have succeeded in destroying Stinson's value as a witness. Instead, public sympathy swung to her side, and his accusation had the unexpected effect of shoring up her credibility.

Harry Daugherty's first counterattack backfired.

Surely, however, the vindictive attorney general would strike again—and it was a safe bet that, next time, he'd take direct aim.

21

"A Pretty Slick Fellow"

B urton Wheeler was not easily intimidated. He resolved to follow one sensational witness with another—Gaston Bullock Means, who had just phoned the senator and demanded to be put on the stand at once. At last, he was putting his most dangerous trump card on the table.

It was certainly a gamble. The charismatic detective, a shadowy character straight out of a pulp fiction magazine, was sure to captivate the American public. On the other hand, Wheeler would be staking his case to the testimony of a man with a long and well-documented history of mischief.

Long before he entered the world of law enforcement, Gaston Means had all the makings of a master con artist: a southern gentleman's charm, an actor's talent at delivering lines, a psychopath's lack of empathy. He could be unthinkably cruel; as a young boy, according to family lore, he once threw a dog into a fireplace and stood there grinning at the smell of burning fur. His mind could concoct the most outrageous lies that somehow sounded like self-evident truths. Even his commanding presence—he stood well over six feet tall with long, simian limbs—helped him gain the trust of others.

Those tools of persuasion served young "Bud" Means, as he was known in his youth, when he dropped out of college, took a sales job with a North Carolina textile company, and learned that hawking towels for commission was a steep path to fortune. Restless, he promptly reinvented himself as the apprentice-son of his multimillionaire employer and began "borrowing" modest sums from his customers, who reasoned that such a well-endowed heir must be good for a fifty- or hundred-dollar loan. Several thousand dollars later, he was exposed as a fraud and fired.

His next job put his trust-building skills to more constructive use. As a sleuth for the William J. Burns International Detective Agency, a role that satisfied his lifelong love of intrigue, Means effortlessly persuaded servants to inform on their employers and bank clerks to turn over confidential records. Give him a few days and he could uncover a subject's deepest secret. He could don black tie and blend into a society party, winning the confidence of wives of powerful men. Or he could grow a two-day beard, climb into an ill-fitting suit, and infiltrate an underworld gang. Billy Burns called him "one of the best investigators who ever lived," and Means forged a close bond with his boss, who shared his indifference to legal and ethical rules. He was on track for a long, successful career at the Burns agency—until a better-paying employer lured him away.

In 1915, with Europe engulfed in war, Germany's military intelligence service recruited Means to leave the Burns agency and spy on his own country—a declared neutral power—for the hefty fee of a thousand dollars a week. As a secret operative for the Kaiser, code-named Agent E-13, Means skulked around American shipyards, searching for evidence that the United States was violating its purported neutrality. He founded a pro-German front organization, the American Peace Society. He accused prominent Americans who supported the Allied effort, like financier J. P. Morgan and steel magnate Charles Schwab, of circumventing the country's neutrality laws. Most consequentially, he arranged for the transport of crucial wartime supplies like rubber and copper to Germany, which was being strangled by an Allied blockade. His handsome pay, made by dead drop in Lower Manhattan's Trinity Church graveyard, allowed him to rent the entire floor of a New York City hotel, where a life-size portrait of Wilhelm II presided over his dining room.

The moment America entered the war, the ever-honorable Agent E-13 resigned from the Kaiser's service, but by that point, he had located a new employer: Maude King, a beautiful widow of a rich lumberman who was being hounded by fortune hunters and schemers. What Mrs. King needed, Means whispered in her ear, was someone who knew how these unsavory characters worked and could fend them off, a Burns detective—himself, for instance. King promptly hired Means as her business manager, granting him power of attorney over her entire estate. More than $100,000 of her fortune evaporated before she joined Means for a walk in the woods and died from a mysterious pistol "accident." Means was tried for murder—and was almost certainly guilty—but was set free by a jury of his peers. (Rumor had it that two of the jurors were intimidated and another bribed.)

By this point, Means's job prospects might have seemed limited. His association with the Kaiser's intelligence service had become public knowledge, and newspapers across the country had covered his murder trial with sensational headlines. Few employers would take a chance on an admitted German spy and acquitted murderer. But on October 28, 1921, the Bureau of Investigation did. In need of sly but loyal operatives to carry out sensitive assignments, the Bureau's newly installed director, Billy Burns, could think of no one better suited than his old star employee.

To bypass scrutiny of Means's checkered past, Burns hired him as a "Special Employee" through the Bureau's secret "blue slip" system, usually reserved for confidential informants. Despite his seemingly provisional status, however, Means was endowed with all the authority of someone hired through the usual channels. He received a golden badge, numbered 651 and engraved with the screaming eagle of the United States of America, as well as a commission card bearing his own signature and endorsed by both Burns and Attorney General Daugherty. In the hands of a man like Gaston Means, these tools—not to mention a Department of Justice office and telephone, the use of government stationery, and access to official files—could mean only one thing: mischief.

Indeed, he engaged in little else over his next eighteen months as a special agent. As a private detective for the Burns agency, Means had developed investigative sources across the criminal underworld. Now he spread word that, as a newly minted federal law enforcement officer, he would perform extraordinary favors for his old acquaintances. The Jazz Age was in full swing, and criminals knew that everything was fixable for the right price—oil stocks, horse races, boxing matches, the World Series, even criminal proceedings.

Means started small, inviting the targets of federal investigations to his office and selling them a peek at their case files. Later he grew bolder, promising to have criminal defendants' indictments quashed in return for five-figure bribes. His most lucrative schemes, though, revolved around Prohibition, which had spawned a criminal class with deep pockets and little appetite for serving time behind bars.

For several months in the middle of 1922, Means haunted the shadows of America's bootleg capital, New York City. Making no secret of his law enforcement status, he sailed with rumrunners on their yachts and spent long evenings in speakeasies, his long arms draped over the back of his booth, a big black bottle sitting on his table. He signaled that he was open to doing business, but he also made it clear that he was not to be trifled with. Once, Means spent months investigating four brothers who supplied liquor to Manhattan's blue-blooded Racquet and Tennis Club, then approached them with the damning evidence, offering to destroy it for $100,000. When the brothers balked, Means turned an airtight case over to the US attorney for the Southern District of New York. All four brothers served time.

New York's wet crowd was on notice, and soon the money poured in like smooth Canadian whiskey, ten, fifteen, twenty thousand dollars a day, most of it paid in return for Means's promises to help with liquor withdrawal permits, medicinal whiskey prescriptions, and other loopholes through the nation's dry laws. "It's not exactly crooked," he would say, "but it's not exactly legal, either."

Means intimated, falsely, that his scheme had the blessing of the seniormost Harding administration officials and claimed that it was all simply to raise funds for the Republican National Committee, which was struggling to repay its multimillion-dollar campaign debt from 1920. "A man, to raise this amount, has to be a pretty slick fellow, and no angel would be put on such a job," he explained. "That's why I have it, and that's why they have confidence in me. They know what I can do."

He almost always took the bootleggers' cash and almost never delivered on his promises, yet he rarely worried about the consequences. Instead, the consummate con man relied on the bootleggers' own criminal complicity—not to mention the underworld's code of silence—to keep his marks quiet. (He did take one practical precaution: he transformed his Washington home into a virtual fortress, complete with concrete walls and iron bars.)

All the while, Means must have been performing valuable services for his Justice Department superiors, who were willing to overlook his increasingly audacious schemes. He could often be found in the company of Jess Smith, strolling through the department's headquarters with bundles of files under their arms, and on more than one occasion Billy Burns ran interference for Means when his antics got him in trouble.

That all changed in April 1923, however, when one dissatisfied customer, a Pennsylvania bootlegger whom Means had fleeced for fifteen grand, came forward with sworn affidavits and mailed them to Treasury officials, congressmen, and others who had no interest in protecting an outlaw federal agent. Inevitably, the news became public, and a red-faced Burns, who had never revealed that the notorious Gaston Means was on the Bureau's payroll, was forced to cut ties with his most ruthless operative.

The gears of justice began to turn, and there was nothing Burns or even Harry Daugherty could do to stop them. Means went to ground, hiding for several months behind a veil of aliases and disguises while the Bureau's deputy director, John Edgar Hoover, led a nationwide manhunt. Eventually, in the fall of 1923, Means was apprehended and indicted on four counts in the Southern District of New York. Trial was set for the following spring.

By March 1924, when he volunteered his services to Wheeler's investigation, Means could present himself as a free agent, a man without conflicting loyalties and with secrets to spill. A second federal indictment, just handed down on March 7 in a separate case, further signaled that no goodwill remained between Means and his old employer. Under indictment twice over, facing criminal prosecution and perhaps even prison bars, Means's rift with the attorney general gave every appearance of being final and irreparable.

EVEN AS WHEELER formally summoned Means to the Senate hearing room, lingering doubts about his witness nagged at him. Despite all appearances, Wheeler just couldn't shake his suspicion that the detective's cooperation was a ruse—that he was actually spying on the committee's investigation and secretly reporting back to the attorney general.

And if Means's loyalty to the Senate investigation was cause for concern, then so was the man's loyalty to the truth. In his days as a federal prosecutor, Wheeler would have thought twice before putting a serial liar on the witness stand—and then twice more about building a case on such suspect testimony. Even if Means proved himself a cooperating witness after all, he would undoubtedly fabricate information that furthered the investigation's goals. In a sense, Wheeler would become complicit in another man's perjury.

Was it just to convict someone based on false testimony? Not in a courtroom, certainly, where the pursuit of justice demanded a rigid adherence to accepted procedure and ethical principles. But in his investigation of Attorney General Daugherty, Wheeler was pursuing a higher form of justice. The old rules no longer applied.

22

"A Complete Master of Himself"

Never had a congressional witness about to confess his crimes looked so at ease.

Gaston Means mugged for the cameras. He waved to acquaintances in the room. Dressed in a dark three-piece suit and bowtie, two sharpened pencils poking out from his breast pocket, he was the picture of genteel respectability. If the two criminal prosecutions pending against him in federal district court troubled him at all, he showed no sign.

On the morning of Friday, March 14, Means settled into his witness chair, flashed a dimpled smile at Senator Wheeler, and the hearing got underway.

"Mr. Means," Wheeler began, "let me ask you if you claim immunity of any kind or description?"

The committee had just received a letter from Assistant Attorney General Earl Davis, newly installed head of the Justice Department's criminal division, warning that compelling Means to incriminate himself under oath might, under the Compulsory Testimony Act of 1893, constitute an implied grant of immunity. Means could thus give himself an "immunity bath" whereby the Justice Department would be barred from prosecuting him for each crime he confessed to before the committee. The letter made sense in a technical, legal way, but Wheeler chose to read it as an act of political gamesmanship, an attempt to pressure the committee from calling one of its most valuable witnesses.

Whatever its intent, Means immediately rendered the question moot.

"I waive immunity," he answered with an impatient flick of the hand. "I ask for no quarter and my intention is to give no quarter."

He was there, he added, against the advice of his lawyer, a New York attorney who was not only his codefendant in the recent indictment, but who also happened to be Harry Daugherty's former law partner.

"This is the first time," Means said, "I have ever gone contrary to the advice of counsel."

Wheeler then launched into a surprising line of questioning. Critics of the investigation would surely make an issue of Means's character, so Wheeler shrewdly stole their thunder.

"Have you ever been convicted of a felony?" he asked.

Means lit the first of many cigarettes. The smoke would be his plaything for the rest of the hearing.

"I have been accused of every crime in the catalogue," he answered, "but not convicted, so far. I have never been convicted but have been charged with every known crime." He stopped to think for a second and then added: "Oh, I have been convicted once or twice for minor fights."

"How was that?"

Means filled his lungs with smoke and then shot it down through his two nostrils.

"I have been in the mayor's court for hitting some fellow or some fellow hitting me, and licking me, perhaps, or otherwise, or something like that. But I have never called that anything."

"What is your business at the present time?"

"Answering indictments."

The room erupted in laughter.

"I mean, what line of business do you follow?"

With a thrust of the lower lip, Means jetted his cigarette smoke toward the ceiling.

"Oh," he said, "I am an investigator."

For the better part of a half hour, they proceeded through his entire checkered résumé, including his service for the German government during the war and his relationship with Billy Burns.

"What is the relationship like between you and Mr. Burns at the present time?"

"The friendliest in the world. He is a man you can rely on. He is a man who is absolutely honest."

Means was evidently willing to betray the attorney general, but he would never give up his friend and sometimes employer Billy Burns—something he'd made clear to Wheeler again and again. Perhaps there was honor among thieves after all.

THAT HE WAS betraying anyone at all surprised Gaston Means himself. Until an incident the day before, he had never planned to take the witness stand.

Wheeler's suspicions about the wily detective, it turned out, had been well founded—secretly, unofficially, he'd been spying for Harry Daugherty the entire time. Through intermediaries, Means and Daugherty had struck a deal. In return for his discreet investigative services, Means would never have to spend a single night behind bars. As the plan went, Means would be hauled before a pliant judge—presumably someone who owed Daugherty a favor—and plead guilty. That judge would make a big show of his outrage over Means's misdeeds and then announce, regretfully, that he was unable to send the defendant to the penitentiary; the government had informed him that Means was needed as a cooperating witness in an ongoing criminal investigation. Although Means would be fined to the statutory limit, his prison sentence would be suspended.

The deal served all parties' interests. Means, of course, would avoid time behind bars. The Justice Department, embarrassed by the public knowledge that it once employed a sociopathic con man, would score a conviction in open court. And Daugherty, privately, would gain the off-the-books services of a master sleuth.

For some two weeks in late February and early March, Means was a regular visitor to the Wheeler residence, sometimes tantalizing the senator with hints of real leads but mostly probing his knowledge, noting how far his investigation had pierced the truth. After each meeting, Means then reported his findings to the attorney general through their mutual friend, Thomas Woodnutt Miller, who worked closely with the Justice Department as the federal government's alien property custodian.

For a time, Means's dispatches provided Daugherty with real, actionable intelligence. He got advance notice that Wheeler would make an issue of the Dempsey-Carpentier fight film scheme. He became aware that a former Bureau of Investigation agent named Hazel Scaife had been feeding the senator information about the war fraud cases that Daugherty had declined to prosecute. And he learned that the committee, despite these promising leads, was struggling to find competent witnesses willing to go on the record.

And then, quite suddenly, after Wheeler's unexplained overnight absence from the capital, Roxie Stinson appeared on the witness stand. Wheeler, rightfully distrustful of Means, had shrouded his Ohio trip in secrecy, catching Means and hence Daugherty completely off guard.

After Stinson's first day of testimony, Miller came to see Means in his office at 909 16th Street NW.

"The attorney general says for you to go to hell!" he said. "That you've lost your cunning. That you are not the investigator you once were. That you are no good any longer as an investigator. That you are discharged."

Means's face turned purple. "Did Harry M. Daugherty say—for you to tell me—*that*?"

"He did!"

Means reached for the phone and asked the operator for Senator Wheeler's office. As Miller listened, Means told the senator to summon him as a witness. "I am ready to testify," he said.

Hanging up, he turned back to Daugherty's messenger.

"Now you can go and report to Mr. Daugherty, and you can add, for his further information, that I say to him that I am not a Jess Smith!"

Betraying Daugherty was an option of last resort. At this point, however, he had no choice but to ally himself with Senator Wheeler and hope that the investigation would usher in a new attorney general and a reformed Justice Department that might take mercy on a key witness. Even then, he might still face jail time—or worse.

"I had crossed swords with Mr. Harry M. Daugherty, Attorney General of the United States," he later reflected, "and my fate was sealed."

THE CROWDED HEARING room was spellbound. Though Roxie Stinson had set a high bar for theatrics on the congressional stage, Gaston Means somehow cleared it. The detective was "a complete master of himself," observed the *New York Times*, his pudgy face calm and steady, never betraying a hint of evasion or nervousness. For three rollicking hours, he addressed the committee members by name, answered their questions politely, and sometimes tossed back questions of his own, as if he and his inquisitors were old friends. He discussed everything, the *New*

York Tribune reported, "as though he were explaining a complicated and amusing game to a crowd of intensely interested children."

Means's testimony coincided with a nationwide craze over the shadowy world of sleuths, usually glimpsed only through the kind of detective fiction Jess Smith had loved, found in pulp magazines like *True Detective* and the fictional exploits of Dashiell Hammett's Continental Op or Agatha Christie's Hercule Poirot. Now here was the real deal, in the flesh, and everyone, including the five senators of the committee, relished the moment.

Playing against type made Means's performance that much more powerful. "Nothing could be further from Sherlock Holmes or the black-mustached, hissing villain of melodrama than he," observed a writer for *Collier's* magazine. "Imagine a huge, good-natured, big-voiced breeze of a man, with a rich Southern accent—'bo'n on a plantation near Concord, No'th Carolina'—with an impudent wit and devastating candor. Entirely at ease, unembarrassed by the most embarrassing questions, he seems to enjoy himself thoroughly."

Even the legendary Broadway producer David Belasco, among the spectators that day, was blown away. "What I could have done with that man had I gotten him earlier!" he said. "He has the perfect instinct for delivering a line."

And, Belasco might have added, for using a prop.

Not long into his testimony, Means introduced one of the most memorable exhibits in the history of congressional hearings.

He had been asked a simple question—"When did you first go to work for the Department of Justice?"—but Means apparently wanted to supply a precise answer.

"Let me get my records, will you, please, Senator?"

"Certainly," Wheeler said.

Means got up and walked over to an anteroom where he'd stashed his belongings. He soon returned lugging an enormous accordion-style suitcase made of cheap cardboard.

"Here are my records," he said, unable to repress a grin.

He hefted the case onto the table and undid the latches. Inside were copies of letters, photostatic reproductions of official reports, a correspondence file, and eleven loose-leaf binders.

"Let me call your attention to these books here," Wheeler said, referring to the binders. "Will you state to the committee what they are?"

"These are my diaries, hour for hour, minute for minute."

Wheeler walked over to the witness chair. As Means puffed on his cigarette, the senator went through the binders. Ten were labeled with date ranges, the eleventh being an index.

"I will ask that these diaries be introduced in the record for our use and marked for identification."

That accordion case was only the setup. Means delivered the punch line a little later, as he was telling the committee about his suspension from the Department of Justice in February 1922 and his subsequent reinstatement three months later.

"Have you a copy of the letters there showing that fact, Mr. Means?"

"Yes."

"Will you produce the letters?"

"Yes, sir. I have the letter showing my suspension." There was a pause. "I will have to get my other file now for that."

"Please do so."

Means again went to the little anteroom. Moments later he returned with an even bigger cardboard case.

The crowd roared in laughter.

AMUSED AND INTRIGUED, the packed hearing room listened with rapt attention as Means disclosed his dark dealings with Jess Smith.

The detective—if you could believe the stories he spun for the committee, and that was a big if—carried out all sorts of errands on Smith's behalf. He investigated political enemies. He carried out black-bag operations. And he collected cash—lots of it.

In that last role, Means stressed that he was purely a hands-off middleman. Though he was certainly capable of intimidation, he was no thuggish enforcer.

"I had money delivered to me," he told the committee. "I did not go out and hold 'em up."

In 1921, he testified, a man came by his house every two or three weeks with banknotes wrapped in yellow manila paper, which he then turned over to Smith without question. Means later learned that the bundles, thousands of dollars each, were Smith's cut (and perhaps Daugherty's, too) of the profits from the Dempsey-Carpentier fight film. They totaled "thirty, forty, or maybe fifty thousand."

Grand as that was, the figure paled in comparison to a $100,000 bribe he claimed to have once collected.

It was sometime in February 1922, he told the committee, when Jess Smith told him that a man from Mitsui & Co., a Japanese financial conglomerate, would be dropping off a package. Sure enough, Means soon heard a knock on the door of his room at Washington's Bellevue Hotel, where he was then living with his wife and son. It was a Japanese man, who handed the detective a bundle of cash and left without even asking for a receipt. Means counted the money. There were a hundred $1,000 bills—enough to buy ten brand-new Rolls-Royces. Naturally, his curiosity was piqued, but Means knew better than to ask questions. When Smith arrived later that evening to collect the cash, Means handed it over without comment, and Smith went on his way to Washington Court House, Ohio.

Later, Means was able to deduce the purpose of the bribe. Mitsui & Co. was the parent company of Standard Aircraft—the subject of one of the Justice Department's wartime fraud cases. A War Department audit showed that Standard Aircraft, which supplied hundreds of warplanes to the US Army Air Service during the World War, had overcharged by some $6.59 million. For some time, Mitsui & Co. had been locked in a legal battle with the federal government over the return of those millions. Until, that is, the Justice Department suddenly and inexplicably withdrew the case.

If it could be trusted, Means's testimony resolved a longstanding mystery—why the attorney general had been so lax in prosecuting the wartime fraud cases. They should have been an easy way to highlight the mistakes of the Democratic administration that preceded Harding's. And yet, despite strong public sentiment against the "war profiteers" who had lined their pockets at the expense of American servicemen, Daugherty refused to go after them. Means's story finally offered a succinct, if disturbing, explanation for his inaction.

It also dovetailed nicely with Roxie Stinson's testimony. The image of thousand-dollar bills—an uncommon denomination—registered with everyone in the hearing room, where Stinson had just recalled seeing Jess Smith arrive from Washington with seventy-five of the so-called G-notes in his money belt. If the missing bills could be accounted for (a 25 percent commission, perhaps?), the two witnesses' stories seemed to corroborate each other, implicating Jess Smith in felonious graft.

Still, Wheeler was still one link removed from the investigation's actual target. In the court of public opinion, guilt by association was a real thing—but Wheeler wanted something stronger. Try as he might to gather all these loose strands of evidence, he still couldn't connect them back to the attorney general.

That was probably exactly how Smith and Daugherty had planned it.

"They knew the game," Means told the committee.

In matters involving anything but official business, he explained, Harry Daugherty met with no one but Jess Smith, who then worked out the details with other parties. Two-way meetings were the rule. Three-person conferences were forbidden: too many witnesses.

It was almost as if Harry Daugherty had foreseen these very proceedings.

23

"Dope to Smear Wheeler"

Gaston Means's graft allegations would capture most of the headlines. The next morning's *Chicago Daily Tribune*, for instance,
raved about the "MASTER SPY'S BOODLE TALE."

For Wheeler and his Senate colleagues, however, another line of testimony hit closer to home.

As smoke drifted from his cigarette, Means confessed to spying on
two senators in recent years—not on the basis of probable cause in the
course of a lawful criminal investigation but on direct instructions from
Jess Smith, who held no official office at the Justice Department.

The targets had been senators Thaddeus Caraway of Arkansas and Robert La Follette of Wisconsin, two of the Harding administration's sharpest
critics. Both often took swipes at the attorney general from the Senate floor,
taking full advantage of their congressional immunity under the Constitution's speech and debate clause from defamation suits—especially Caraway,
who had a reputation for testing the limits of senatorial decorum.

"At whose direction did you investigate Senator Caraway?" Wheeler
asked.

"I investigated him through Mr. Jess Smith's direction."

"Was that at the time that Mr. Caraway was making some attacks in
the Senate on Attorney General Daugherty?"

"He had made some attacks on President Harding, too, prior to that,"
Means answered, "and he had made attacks on the attorney general, too."

Wheeler asked Means if he'd searched the senator's office himself, or
assigned the task to someone else.

"We didn't go through Caraway that way at all, Senator," he said mysteriously.

The truth was too shocking for even Means to reveal in a public hearing: Caraway became the target of an elaborate blackmail operation by the Justice Department. An investigator working under Means—the detective's own father-in-law, W. R. Patterson—infiltrated the senator's social circle, worming his way into his family life, to confirm rumors that he'd fathered a child with his secretary.

When Caraway eventually learned of this scheme, he naturally withheld the details but publicly accused Daugherty of having him "shadowed."

At the time, the attorney general denied the charge, calling it a "malicious untruth."

"Now, Mr. Means, you also investigated Senator La Follette, did you not?"

"I investigated him in April, right after he introduced his resolution."

"What resolution?"

"To investigate Teapot Dome."

"You went through his office then, as I understand it, for the purpose of ascertaining what information he had relating to the Teapot oil scandal. Is that correct?"

"Anything he had where he could be stopped in what he was doing."

Wheeler asked him to explain what "stopped" meant.

"How it was going to be used, I don't know," Means said, "except this way, I would interpret it. If you found something damaging on a man you would quietly get word to him through some of his friends, or otherwise, that he had better put the soft pedal on the situation. That is the way the information is generally used when you find it."

"You have never gone through my offices yet, have you?" Wheeler asked.

Means grinned. "If somebody will assign me to it, I will do it."

George Moses leaned over and whispered something to Wheeler.

"Senator Moses suggests to me," Wheeler told Means, "that I can save time by asking you what senators you have not investigated."

"Oh, there are lots of them I haven't," Means said. "They are a pretty clean body. You don't find much on them, either. You don't find very much."

Just in case anyone was worried, Means gave the committee a quick tutorial in checking for wiretaps. "I know how to tap," he boasted, "and how to keep from being tapped." As the senators listened intently, he explained how he hooked three bells to all his phones. Typically, the electrical current in a telephone line was just strong enough to ring all three, so if fewer rang he'd know that someone, somewhere, was listening.

All this talk of congressional surveillance reminded Wheeler of some unusual reports from back home regarding Bureau of Investigation agents.

"You have got them in Montana now checking up on my record," Wheeler said as the hearing was wrapping up for the day. "I will say I got three telegrams, one from Butte, one from Great Falls, and one from Helena, saying they are checking up my record in Montana, from the Department of Justice."

Similar reports had reached Chairman Brookhart. "One is out in Iowa checking up on me, too," he said.

Ashurst reassured his colleagues: "I do not think they will find anything on you."

"No," Wheeler said. "I am not worrying the slightest."

PERHAPS HE SHOULD have. Unlike his friend John Glenn's earlier run-in with Special Agent Charles F. Hately, this was no casual fishing expedition he was hearing about; by the time Gaston Means took the witness stand, the Bureau of Investigation had practically invaded the state of Montana.

In Butte, in Helena, in Great Falls, detectives interviewed Burton Wheeler's old enemies, including men whom Wheeler had prosecuted and sent to prison. They pumped his political rivals—top state Republicans, as well as officials of the Anaconda Company—for information, telling them "we must indict him and smear him whether we ever get a conviction or not." They raked over his record as state legislator and federal prosecutor, speculating that he *must* have dipped a toe in Montana's legendary pool of graft. They followed the faintest wisps of scandal, with one investigator reporting to Director Burns his trouble locating "the 'cop' who arrested Wheeler and took the woman he was with to the hospital."

They heard a lot of warmed-up grievances and a few wild tales. But Wheeler seemed justified in his overconfidence. No matter how deep they dug into the senator's past, the agents couldn't hit pay dirt—some personal indiscretion or professional misstep that might give the attorney general leverage over his tormentor and bring that circus of a congressional investigation to an end.

The detectives were so frustrated in their efforts that, by mid-March, one of their most promising leads (if it could be so called) was a complaint

from a disgruntled seasonal ranger at Glacier National Park, where
Wheeler owned a lakeside cabin. Throwing his senatorial weight around,
Wheeler had apparently halted construction on a public campground that
would have spoiled the solitude of his summer retreat. It wasn't the senator's best look, but the allegation would hardly land a fatal blow to his
reputation, let alone justify criminal prosecution. Nevertheless, the complaint eventually landed on Director Burns's desk and was duly placed in
Wheeler's case file for follow-up.

The investigation was spinning its wheels.

AND THEN SUDDENLY, finally, it got traction. The breakthrough
came courtesy of someone not even on the government payroll—a movie
producer moonlighting as an investigator and masquerading as a political
journalist.

Blair Coan, forty years old, pug-faced and Stetson-hatted, had spent
more than a decade ferreting out the Windy City's political secrets, first
as a reporter for the *Chicago Examiner* and then as chief investigator for
several committees of the Illinois state legislature. Coan was no disinterested truth-seeker. Instead, he had an uncanny knack for finding facts
that supported the conclusions his employers desired. He was not above
paying his sources for statements and had a habit of greeting witnesses
with a prewritten affidavit in hand, lacking nothing but a signature
and notary's seal. By 1924, he had reinvented himself as a producer for
Essanay Studios, where Charlie Chaplin once mugged for the cameras,
but he never lost his passion for seeking out facts that aligned with
political priors.

Coan joined the Montana investigation after a series of secret meetings between Billy Burns and Harry Daugherty at the Wardman Park,
where the two men still lived one floor apart and stayed in constant contact about the hunt for Wheeler's dirty laundry. At one of these conferences, they were joined by George Lockwood, secretary of the Republican
National Committee, who offered his own organization's help. Soon the
three men hit upon a plan: the RNC would place a private detective on its
own payroll and then send him to Montana to join the case. This investigator would be able to operate freely of Justice Department regulations
(such as they were), paying witnesses for their testimony, for instance,
rather than work through the Bureau's cumbersome blue-slip system for
confidential informants.

Blair Coan's name came up, likely suggested by Burns. The two detectives had already joined forces once before to topple a US senator. In 1911, when the Illinois state legislature was looking into irregularities behind the election of Sen. William Lorimar, Coan served as the proper, public face of the investigation while, undercover and out of sight, Burns worked his magic. Together, the two men presented a mountain of evidence (both real and manufactured) of bribery and vote rigging, leading to Lorimar's eventual unseating. Burns knew firsthand of Coan's results-oriented ruthlessness. He was a natural choice.

And so, on March 7—five days before Roxie Stinson first took the stand—the Republican National Committee placed Coan on the payroll of its *National Republican* magazine, sent him to Justice Department headquarters to be briefed by Burns himself, and then immediately dispatched him to Montana.

Coan arrived on March 11 with only a thin cover story. In public, he claimed to be gathering string for a *National Republican* article on Wheeler's past. In private, though, he was frank about his purpose. He was looking, he freely admitted, for "dope to smear Wheeler."

Unlike the Bureau agents who tracked down the senator's political enemies only to hear the same old tired rumors about his personal and political lives, Coan dug into Wheeler's professional history. Lawyers like Wheeler, he knew, were sometimes obliged to take positions at odds with their public rhetoric. Find the right case or the right client, and Coan might make Wheeler out to be a hypocrite or even a traitor to his stated values. Tug at that string a little more, and who knew what might fall out.

Soon he zeroed in on one particularly intriguing attorney-client relationship. From his sources in Great Falls, Coan heard all about the struggles of Gordon Campbell, a shrewd geologist but bumbling businessman who had struck oil near Kevin, Montana, in 1922. Without even securing the right to pump the oil he'd discovered, Campbell set up what fast became Montana's largest oil development syndicate—and then found himself teetering on the edge of bankruptcy and fending off at least forty separate lawsuits, including predatory actions from Standard Oil and other national concerns. At this point, Campbell turned to Burton Wheeler, one of the state's most prominent lawyers, for help. In January 1923, shortly after his election to the Senate but before he had taken office, Wheeler agreed to represent Campbell in return for a hefty $10,000 retainer.

There was nothing unusual about a US senator maintaining a private law practice—many senators did the same—but there *was* something unseemly about this supposed champion of the downtrodden carrying water for an oil company. Coan pulled at this thread.

It turned out that Campbell, who had discovered his oil on federal lands, never was able to secure the Interior Department lease required for actually pumping that oil. And yet he'd continued to sell stock in his syndicate, advertising widely in the Montana newspapers without disclosing that he still had no way of extracting the oil. That spelled a different kind of legal trouble for the geologist—and, in fact, US postal inspectors were already working up a mail fraud case against him.

Wheeler's association with such an outfit was a minor scandal in its own right—but could there be more to it? Perhaps. If Campbell had been struggling to secure a lease from the Department of the Interior, might he have asked his distinguished attorney, who also happened to be a US senator, to intervene? And would Wheeler, who had been paid $10,000, have then violated a conflict-of-interest statute that prohibited members of Congress from receiving compensation for participating in federal proceedings? If so, Wheeler had engaged in something beyond political embarrassment—it would have been criminal.

Coan passed along his suspicions to Billy Burns, and before long Bureau of Investigation operatives were rifling through Campbell's offices. Without obtaining a search warrant, they departed with a sheaf of letters and telegrams that, read selectively, suggested that Wheeler had indeed aided Campbell in Washington.

Meanwhile, Coan tracked down someone who could narrate that evidence, someone willing to adjust his recollection to fit the investigation's needs—Gordon Campbell's former secretary, who had fallen out with his employer. As the man spoke, Coan pecked away at his typewriter. The affidavit, sworn and notarized, made its way from Billings, Montana, to the Washington, DC, offices of the *National Republican* and thence, without delay, to the Bureau of Investigation.

The kind of behavior Means had warned Wheeler about, the shady dealing the former detective excelled at himself, now seemed to be paying off for Daugherty.

MEANWHILE, AND NOT coincidentally, another prominent Montana lawyer had come under Justice Department scrutiny.

Since arriving from DC on February 21, two staff attorneys with the Office of the Attorney General had been gathering information on one

John L. Slattery of Glasgow, Montana. Slattery made an odd target for a
Justice Department investigation. Unlike Montana's junior senator, he had
nothing against Harry Daugherty. On the contrary, the former Republican
state senator was Daugherty's hand-picked US attorney for the District of
Montana, a post he'd filled since his appointment by President Harding in
May 1921. By all accounts, Slattery had acted as "a perfect specimen of
the Daughertian juriconsult," as journalist H. L. Mencken put it, a loyal
servant of the Harding and then Coolidge administrations. Never had he
ruffled feathers in Washington or uttered a cross word about the attorney
general.

Instead, what initially brought him under the Justice Department's
microscope was a long-simmering dispute between Slattery and the anti-
saloon crowd in Butte, Montana, a rowdy mining town where bootleggers
and moonshiners operated in flagrant violation of the Eighteenth Amendment. Since assuming office, Slattery had prosecuted 497 such violations,
but groups like the Anti-Saloon League and the Silver Bow Ministerial
Association wanted more. They blasted him for going after low-level conspirators, like two court constables who had been caught accepting bribes
from bootleggers, rather than the "big fish," and they openly asked why.
Their insinuation was thinly veiled. A criminal conspiracy to circumvent
the Volstead Act had captured Montana's legal system—even, possibly, its
top federal prosecutor, Slattery himself.

The charges reached Justice Department headquarters in Washington
at precisely the right moment. It turned out that Attorney General Daugherty, for reasons of his own, desired a full and thorough review of the
allegations against his US attorney. He promptly dispatched one of his top
staff lawyers, Philip H. Marcum, a special assistant to the attorney general, along with Emmett E. Doherty, a twenty-six-year-old lawyer who'd
grown up in Butte and knew the landscape well.

The investigators were in Montana for nearly a month, long enough
to amass damning evidence against Slattery. "We had so much on him,"
was how someone familiar with the investigation described it—proof of
misconduct that might have constituted grounds for immediate dismissal
or even criminal prosecution.

Attorney General Daugherty was in a merciful mood, though. He
would overlook Slattery's shortcomings. He just needed a favor in return.

24

"Victim of a Hostile Welcome"

As Burton Wheeler closed in on Harry Daugherty, his mantra became "Follow the money." If he was ever to prove that the attorney general was a crook, he would need more than hearsay from an accused blackmailer and the suspect testimony of a con man. He would need financial records documenting the graft alleged before the select committee.

To that end, he appointed accountant John Phelon—a former bank examiner for the Federal Reserve who came highly recommended by Frank Vanderlip—as an official investigator for the committee and dispatched him to Washington Court House, Ohio, and that town's only federally chartered bank.

On the afternoon of March 19, Phelon marched into the Midland National's rather unassuming red-brick building on Court Street. There, confronted with a signed congressional subpoena, bank president Mal Daugherty and clerk Vera Neail had no choice—or so it seemed at first—but to open their books for inspection.

Almost immediately, Phelon made some astounding discoveries. Rather than start with the named deposit accounts of Jess Smith and Harry Daugherty (which, common sense suggested, might have been handled with extreme caution), he shrewdly went straight to the bank's record of certificates of deposit, or CDs. What first caught his eye was the grand total of $274,024.86 in CDs—a staggering sum, in his experience, for an institution capitalized at only $100,000. Digging a little deeper, Phelon requested all deposit slips from the November 1920 election onward and found two CDs bearing Harry Daugherty's name, one for $39,500, and another for $41,965, as well as another made out to Jess Smith for $63,000. These, too, were eyebrow-raising amounts, considering that Harry Daugherty earned only $12,000 as attorney general, with Smith famously declining a government salary.

That wasn't all. Phelon found several smaller CDs made out to fictitious names, including four at $5,000 each for "J. E. Grey" but endorsed by Harry Daugherty. Another, for about $3,000, bore the name of the New York State License Commission, the body that sanctioned boxing matches within the Empire State, where the Dempsey-Carpentier fight film had been screened in contravention of federal law. This piqued Phelon's curiosity, not only because it was endorsed by "J. E. Grey" but also because, in his experience, a certificate of deposit from New York was unlikely to have made its way to a small town in Fayette County, Ohio.

These were the most preliminary of findings, made over just four hours of work, but they promised to bolster Senator Wheeler's case against the attorney general. Given enough time, Phelon was confident he would discover much more. Mal Daugherty must have been, too.

On his second day, Phelon was just stepping into the bank building when Mal Daugherty intercepted him.

"Mr. Phelon, sit down for a minute," he said. "I want to talk to you."

Phelon took a seat.

"Mr. Phelon," he said, "I have talked to my attorneys, and we have decided to let the matter stand as it is."

Phelon asked what that meant. As a seasoned examiner for the Federal Reserve, Phelon was unaccustomed to interference from a bank officer. Was Daugherty telling him not to proceed with his examination?

"That is it exactly."

Daugherty offered no explanation for his sudden defiance, but it didn't take a certified public accountant to put two and two together: The investigation was getting too close to something truly damaging.

"I am very sorry you have taken this attitude," Phelon said and then huffed out to report the incident to Senator Wheeler.

"There had been no unfriendly discussion of any kind until then," he wrote. "So the only reason he could have for stopping my work would be to gain a few days' vacation time. I find myself the victim of a hostile welcome and unable to do anything until Washington can enforce its wishes."

Washington would try. Meeting in executive session, the committee immediately issued a new subpoena, commanding Mal Daugherty to appear "forthwith" at the hearing room in Washington and to bring with him "deposit ledgers of the Midland National Bank since November 1, 1920; also note files and transcript of owners of every safety vault; also records of income drafts; also records of any individual account or accounts showing withdrawals of amounts of $25,000 or over during above period."

On March 22 at 8:10 a.m., US Marshal Stanley Borthwick personally served the subpoena on Mal Daugherty. The banker again chose to defy the Senate.

"From advice of counsel, I refuse to comply with the order of the committee," he wrote in a statement. "There is nothing in the bank to confirm the outrageous falsehoods testified to before the committee. For the protection of the individual customers and the stockholders and upon advice of counsel, the bank will test the question."

Wheeler, in response, declared that the committee would "go to the limit" in enforcing its demands.

EVEN AS MAL Daugherty stonewalled, denying the committee access to his brother's financial secrets, the hearings chipped away at Harry Daugherty's reputation.

Witnesses described an attorney general indifferent to corruption and protective of anyone he saw as a political ally. Most persuasive were the former Bureau of Investigation agents forced out after knocking on the wrong doors. One uncovered more than $7 million of fraud in the government's wartime aviation contracts, only to have his findings ignored by higher-ups at the department. Another was fired after his inquiry into Prohibition violations along the US-Mexican border implicated a federal prosecutor. "The Department of Justice," former special agent Hazel Scaife wrote to Daugherty in an angry resignation letter, "is functioning as a first aid to crooks."

This drip-drop of damning testimony, day after day, sapped the strength of Daugherty's staunchest defenders. His two counsel, Paul Howland and George Chamberlain, once alert for any opportunity to steer the proceedings in their client's favor, now slumped resigned in their chairs. Even Republican senator George Moses, the committee's designated critic of its progressive majority, found himself, one commentator wrote, "swept from his moorings by the astonishing evidence which has been offered. Today his air implies that he hardly knows what to do."

Wheeler was winning over the skeptics—but he also let the success go to his head. Drunk on his own publicity, he became even more reckless in his accusations. Knowing that barrels of ink were spilled whenever he opened his mouth, he openly insinuated that Secretary of War John Weeks, hitherto above suspicion, was complicit in the Justice Department's refusal to prosecute the war fraud cases. He asked aloud whether Secretary of the Treasury Andrew Mellon, another cabinet officer of sterling reputation, had conspired with Daugherty in liquor deals.

Republicans cried foul. "We demand," wrote the editors of the Republican-leaning *Chicago Daily Tribune,* "that the process of whole-sale dishonoring carried on by the man Wheeler, with the consent if not approval of the senate, be brought under some decent control."

Even sympathetic commentators called out his carelessness. "It is quite true, of course, that not all of this mountain of evidence will stand critical analysis," Bruce Bliven wrote in the liberal *New Republic.* "The Committee goes down some false trails; and a few of these lead to the doorsteps of innocent men."

Assured of his own righteousness and oblivious to the consequences, Wheeler was leaving a trail of vengeful enemies in his wake—a fact that he would come to regret only much later.

One of these newly sworn enemies was George B. Hayes—not one of Bliven's "innocent men," to be sure, but someone who resented Wheeler's presence on his doorstep nonetheless.

Hayes was a New York attorney who specialized in legal gray areas. Much to his embarrassment, his name got dragged into the hearings on March 21 when a former client, druggist John Gorini, testified about a bootlegging ring connected, tangentially, to Jess Smith.

Back in 1921, Hayes was hired to secure the return of 7,700 cases of Scotch whiskey seized by the government—and utterly failed.

"Mr. Hayes was your attorney?" Gorini was asked.

"Yes, sir, to my sorrow."

Hayes, red faced, was in the hearing room to testify himself that day.

"How much did you pay Hayes?"

"Why, Hayes, I only gave him about three thousand. He never sent me a bill for the trial, because he didn't dare to."

When Hayes later took the witness chair, he struggled to explain his actions as honorable, ethical, legal—but all the public would remember of him was a line from his embittered client: "He would kill his mother for five cents, I think."

George B. Hayes would never forgive Wheeler for the insults aired on such a national stage—and soon sensed his chance at revenge when special agents of the Bureau of Investigation questioned him about his business before the solicitor of the Interior Department, the officer who litigated disputes over oil leases.

More than a year would pass before Wheeler realized his mistake.

FOR THE MOMENT, however, he had bigger problems. Mal Daugherty was in open defiance of the Congress of the United States. As important as Harry Daugherty's financial secrets were to the committee's work, that issue paled in comparison. In rejecting the select committee's subpoena, Mal Daugherty had issued a direct challenge to Congress's power to compel testimony and the production of evidence. If Wheeler let his challenge go unanswered, what would stop other witnesses from doing the same, not just before the select committee but before any congressional panel inquiring into sensitive subjects?

In theory, an enforcement mechanism did exist—contempt of Congress. When a witness like Mal Daugherty ignored a subpoena, either house of Congress could direct its sergeant at arms to hale the contemnor before its bar, where a trial would be conducted. If the full Senate (or House) held the accused in contempt, it could order him imprisoned somewhere within the Capitol until he thought better of his defiance.

This power had long been taken for granted, and few witnesses dared to challenge it. As recently as March of 1921, for example, the Senate successfully resolved a dispute over requested Treasury Department documents when it threatened to try the outgoing secretary of the treasury, David F. Houston, at its bar for contempt. In truth, however, the existing case law on the matter was inconclusive. The Constitution itself said nothing about congressional contempt; the power was only implied by other constitutional prerogatives.

Its first major test came in 1821, when the House of Representatives held one John Anderson in contempt for attempting to bribe one of its members and remanded him to the custody of the House sergeant at arms,

Thomas Dunn. Anderson then filed suit against Dunn, alleging assault, battery, and false imprisonment. The case went to the Supreme Court, where the justices dismissed Anderson's suit, adopted an expansive view of what became known as Congress's "inherent contempt" power, and noted that without it, Congress would "be exposed to every indignity and interruption, that rudeness, caprice, or even conspiracy, may meditate against it."

Unfortunately for Wheeler, *Anderson v. Dunn* wasn't the high court's last word on the matter. In the case of *Kilbourn v. Thompson*, decided in 1880, a House select committee had been investigating the collapse of a Philadelphia bank to which the United States had been a creditor. When one of the bank's former executives, Hallett Kilbourn, refused to honor a subpoena demanding certain documents, the House detained him in a local DC jail until he agreed to comply. Kilbourn challenged his arrest all the way to the Supreme Court—which ultimately rejected many of its earlier holdings in *Anderson*. In their ruling, the justices not only adopted a narrower view of the contempt power; more significantly, they also declared that, unless it was explicitly exercising its "legislative function," Congress didn't possess "the general power of making inquiry into the private affairs of the citizen."

Whether Mal Daugherty's subpoena—and the Senate's ability to enforce it through its contempt power—would hold up in court was therefore an open question. It might hinge on whether Wheeler's investigation of the Midland National's books was an exercise of the Senate's "legislative function," or whether he was merely prying into the attorney general's "private affairs."

If Mal Daugherty proved stubborn enough, in other words, the case might go all the way to the Supreme Court. That was a war Burton Wheeler was ready to wage.

25

"Rid of an Unfaithful Servant"

As the hearings entered their third week, President Calvin Coolidge grew desperate for a way out of his pledge to retain his embattled attorney general.

The unfolding scandal around Harry Daugherty's Justice Department had become one of those Roaring Twenties spectacles, like the Dempsey-Carpentier title bout or Charles Lindbergh's marathon flights, that held the entire nation spellbound. Even if the testimony of Roxie Stinson, Gaston Means, and a parade of witnesses hadn't *proved* wrongdoing by the attorney general, Senator Wheeler had identified, as one *New Republic* writer observed, "half-a-dozen trails of corruption leading straight to the door of the Attorney-General's private office."

For a president facing reelection that November, Daugherty's continued presence within the administration had become an unwelcome distraction.

Just how unwelcome became clear on Tuesday, March 25, when Sen. Hiram Johnson of California, who denounced Daugherty on the campaign trail and repeatedly called on the president to jettison him from the cabinet, defeated Coolidge in the South Dakota Republican primary—the first toe-to-toe matchup between the incumbent and his progressive challenger. For a sitting president, it was a shameful rebuke, and the ensuing rush of panic seemed to clarify his thinking. His principled resolve to retain Daugherty out of deference to the late President Harding crumbled, and Coolidge determined to cut his attorney general loose. All he needed was a pretext.

As if by Providence, Harry Daugherty had just given him one.

On March 25, as South Dakota Republicans were still going to the polls, Daugherty flatly refused the select committee's request for five Bureau of Investigation case files related to gun running along the Mexican border. (The committee was still tracking down rumors that the Bureau had helped foment rebellion in the Mexican province of Baja California on behalf of American oil interests.) The documents, Daugherty protested in his letter to Chairman Brookhart, "are very confidential in their nature and their presentation as requested in your letter would be inimical to the public interests."

The committee assumed that Harry Daugherty, who had previously pledged "every facility which the Department of Justice affords," was now simply stonewalling, defying the committee's requests in concert with his brother Mal.

By a unanimous vote, the five senators formally asked President Coolidge to overrule his attorney general and order the documents' disclosure. They didn't yet know it, but it was just the opening Coolidge had been waiting for.

On the morning of March 26, Coolidge summoned Daugherty to the White House for their first one-on-one meeting in more than a month. The attorney general came prepared with a draft letter for the president to sign, in which Coolidge would concur in Daugherty's refusal and declare not just the Bureau case files at issue but *all* internal Justice Department documents off-limits. This didn't sit well with Coolidge, and the two men failed to reach consensus.

When they reconvened that afternoon, the yawning rift opened further. Coolidge now warned that he might be compelled to ask for Daugherty's resignation if he persisted in his defiance of the committee. Despite this threat, Daugherty refused to budge. He held firm to his legal advice, asserting that the confidential files of the Justice Department—which included privileged information about pending cases and investigations—demanded special care.

Coolidge promised him he'd think it over.

ON THE AFTERNOON of March 27, Harry Daugherty was pulling into the Justice Department's Vermont Avenue headquarters when his bodyguard pointed out a conspicuous vehicle parked outside. It was a Pierce Arrow limousine—the official White House car.

"This probably means something serious," Daugherty commented.

Up in his sixth-floor office suite, he found Coolidge's secretary, C. Bascom Slemp, waiting. Slemp, a slender man with bulging eyes, handed over a letter on White House stationery.

"They got to the President at last?" Daugherty asked—"they" meaning his political enemies.

"Can't say anything under the circumstances," Slemp said. "I'm just bringing you the letter."

Daugherty started reading. Addressed to "My dear Mr. Attorney General," the letter consisted of three dense, legalistic paragraphs.

Later he would learn that it was ghostwritten by Secretary of State Charles Evans Hughes, the former Supreme Court justice now acting as Coolidge's unofficial legal adviser. All morning the two men had huddled up in the White House, searching for a politically acceptable legal rationale to dismiss a sitting attorney general.

In the end, they settled on this fresh dispute over the Bureau of Investigation case files. The committee's formal request for White House intervention, Coolidge and Hughes realized, was sufficient pretext. In order to respond to the committee, Coolidge needed the disinterested legal advice of his attorney general. And yet, Daugherty's advice had become automatically suspect. The Senate investigation was forcing the attorney general to look out for the nation's interests, as well as his own—and those two didn't necessarily align. How could Coolidge know Daugherty's real reason for withholding the documents? Was it because their release would actually jeopardize some ongoing legal action—or simply because they would embarrass Daugherty personally?

The attorney general, the letter declared, had waded into an irresolvable conflict of interest.

"I am not questioning your fairness or integrity," it stated. "I am merely reciting the fact that you are placed in two positions, one your personal interest, the other your office of Attorney General, which may be in conflict. I do not see how you can be acting for yourself in your own defence in the matter, and at the same time and on the same question acting as my advisor as Attorney General. These two positions are incompatible, and cannot be reconciled. I am sure you will see that it is necessary for me to have the advice of a disinterested Attorney General, in order that I may discharge the duties of my office in this and other matters."

It was "the letter of a lawyer," as Chief Justice Taft would describe it. It maintained the pretense that Daugherty was an honorable public servant, and it made no mention of the charges aired before the Senate committee. Nevertheless, as it came to its inevitable conclusion, Coolidge's letter demanded the very action Senator Wheeler had been clamoring for. "I recognize that you are entitled to a full and fair hearing. But as there is no way by which you can divest yourself of the interest you have personally in the investigation, I can see no way but for you to retire as Attorney General, and I am therefore compelled to request your resignation."

As Daugherty put down the letter, the master string puller knew he'd run out of string.

OVER AT 1600 Pennsylvania Avenue, President Coolidge waited.

Word of the president's letter spread among White House officials, accompanied by a palpable sense of relief. For weeks now, mere mention of Daugherty's name had sent shivers down their spines.

Some staffers, overcome by excitement, leaked the news to the press. One informed a reporter that Coolidge "was rapidly approaching a definite decision on whether he would keep the attorney general in the Cabinet, and that it would be announced publicly." Another official "close to the President" was even more specific, promising that the "case of the attorney general will be cleared by nightfall." Journalists sharpened their pencils. Editors envisioned the banner headlines. "COOLIDGE PREPARES GUILLOTINE FOR DAUGHERTY AS EVIDENCE OF UNFITNESS FOR OFFICE PILES," the *Atlanta Constitution* teased as it awaited official confirmation.

And yet, as the hours ticked by, no response came from Justice Department headquarters. The silence was maddening; the president's letter couldn't have made itself more clear. As the afternoon sky darkened into evening, Coolidge directed his secretary to send a terse follow-up note:

March 27, 1924.

My Dear Mr. Attorney General,

The President does not understand the delay in complying with his request. He directs me to notify you that he expects your resignation at once.

VERY TRULY YOURS,
C.B. SLEMP
SECRETARY TO THE PRESIDENT.

Even that failed to procure a reply. Still expecting a letter or tele-gram from the attorney general any minute, Slemp remained in his office well past the customary hour until finally, fifteen minutes past seven, he went up to the executive residence to confer with Coolidge and Secretary of State Hughes. The three men considered their options. Cabinet offi-cers were rarely dismissed outright. Old-fashioned decency dictated that a president would ask for a resignation, and the appointee would then render it, maintaining the pretense of a voluntary departure. Ultimately, however, the attorney general served at the pleasure of the president, who did not need Daugherty's cooperation to effect this simple change in em-ployment status. Was Daugherty actually daring the president to fire him?

Coolidge had no way of knowing, but Daugherty had a secret reason for the delay—one worth trying the president's patience. It was imperative that, while he was still attorney general, he meet with Special Assistant to the Attorney General John S. Pratt, who at the moment was rushing to St. Louis but would not arrive in Washington until early Friday morning, March 28.

A seasoned prosecutor out of Toledo, Ohio, Pratt had proven himself a loyal servant, competent and discreet, since assuming his current post in August 1921, and he made no secret of his fealty to Harry Daugherty. A month earlier, Pratt had publicly denounced the attorney general's perse-cutor. "The charges made yesterday on the floor of the Senate by Senator Wheeler are purely political and based on gossip and hearsay," he said in a speech to his fellow Toledoans on February 20. "He hides behind the immunity of a United States senator and would have the people of the United States believe that Mr. Daugherty is a crook and a grafter on the basis of gossip."

Pratt was the perfect choice for an urgent and sensitive assignment that had just arisen, and Daugherty had summoned him the moment he learned his dismissal was imminent. "Proceed to Washington immedi-ately," Daugherty's March 26 telegram read. "Conference important mat-ter." Asking no questions, Pratt dropped all plans and boarded the next DC-bound train. Until it arrived, all Daugherty could do was stall.

Before he became a private citizen, there was one more case Attorney General Daugherty had to set in motion.

THE NEXT MORNING at ten o'clock, on Friday, March 28, Coolidge had barely settled into the Oval Office for the day when Barney Martin, the attorney general's special assistant, appeared. He handed over a short, formal letter. It was exactly what the president was hoping for.

THE ATTORNEY GENERAL
Washington

March 28, 1924

My dear Mr. President:

I hereby acknowledge receipt of your letter of March 27th, by the hand of your Secretary, requesting my resignation as Attorney General of the United States.

Solely out of deference to your request and in compliance therewith, I hereby tender my resignation. While you do not state when you desire my resignation to become effective, I most respectfully request that it become effective forthwith.

YOURS VERY TRULY,
H. M. DAUGHERTY.
ATTORNEY GENERAL.

If the letter seemed restrained for a man of Daugherty's wrath, there was good reason. What Martin delivered to the Oval Office was only the first, official resignation letter.

A little less than two hours later, the Justice Department released a second missive to the press. This one was combative, even scathing at times, written by "a private citizen" to his president. It lamented that he was the victim of anarchical forces and implied that Coolidge had been fooled into doing their bidding. It complained about his persecution at the hands of Burton Wheeler. It railed against the character of Wheeler's witnesses. It noted the senator's failure to observe any discernible rules of evidence.

Most pointedly, Daugherty warned that Coolidge had just invented a "dangerous doctrine" by asserting that an attorney general under attack must be disqualified from service. "If a member of the cabinet," he wrote, "is to be incapacitated or disqualified by the preferment of charges against him, no matter how malicious and groundless, and he is compelled to give up his responsible position and sacrifice his honor for the time being because of such attack, no man in any official position is safe, and the most honorable, upright, and efficient public servant could be swept from office and stable government destroyed by clamor."

President Coolidge ignored the letter, and the press buried it below the fold. Daugherty might have had a point, but by now nearly everyone could acknowledge that he was not the "honorable, upright, and efficient public servant" he claimed to be.

As Daugherty left the Justice Department building one final time, an aide carrying his smoking pipes and other personal possessions in a bundle, the shouts of newsboys announcing his resignation filled his ears. Despite the feisty tone of his letter, to the *Chicago Daily Tribune*'s correspondent he appeared "a dejected and disappointed man."

BURTON WHEELER WAS interrogating his witness when the news reached the hearing room.

There was a brief stir, interrupting former Republican congressman J. Van Vechten Olcott, who was telling how someone once dangled a federal judgeship before him in exchange for a $10,000 bribe. For a moment, Wheeler became visibly elated. And then, determined to conclude the day's business as planned, he composed himself and resumed his questioning.

Only after Chairman Brookhart gaveled the hearing to a close would Wheeler permit comment on the news.

"The country has gotten rid of an unfaithful servant," he boasted. He was careful, however, not to sound too triumphant. Some on the committee were already making noises about winding down the inquiry now that it had achieved its principal goal. Wheeler made it clear that he wanted the panel to continue "in its work of uncovering crooks."

"There should be a general house cleaning," he explained, "in the Department of Justice."

Wheeler might have shrunk from self-congratulation, but the significance of the moment wasn't lost on him. He'd proven the naysayers wrong, authoring and then realizing his own implausible storyline. As a Washington novice, a freshman senator from the Rocky Mountains, Wheeler had picked a fight with the capital's most ruthless political operator—and won. By any standard, his was a meteoric rise. "Senator Wheeler has been in Washington about three months and in that time has set a record," columnist Julian Street opined for the United Press syndicate. "The oldest of old timers agree that no other senator has ever got himself before the nation as Wheeler has, in anything like the same space of time."

Already there was talk that he might earn a place on a presidential ticket that fall—if not as the Democratic vice presidential nominee, then perhaps as running mate to the progressive Sen. Robert La Follette, who was eyeing a third-party bid.

His hometown newspaper, meanwhile, couldn't contain its joy. On March 29 the *Butte Miner* ran an editorial celebrating "Senator Wheeler's Victory":

> Score one for Senator Wheeler!
>
> In spite of all the abuse and personal attacks that have been levied against the Montana gentleman by republican agencies he has succeeded in making President Coolidge see the light.
>
> Those who have watched the course of the investigation, and who are open and fair-minded about it, will give Senator Wheeler credit for accomplishing what he set out to do in the public interest . . .
>
> The Montana gentleman has been the target of partisan traducers of high and low degree, but he has not been diverted from the serious work he had in hand and, for the most part, he has not paid any attention the attacks levied against him.
>
> Apparently he has concluded that deeds always speak more convincingly than words, and by adopting this course he has triumphed over his enemies.

It was an occasion to rejoice, to be sure. But the *Miner*—not to mention Senator Wheeler himself—had no idea that the fight was just beginning.

PART III

26

"One of the Darkest Pages in American History"

B y outward appearances, there was nothing irregular about the federal grand jury meeting in Great Falls, Montana. It convened on Tuesday, April 8, 1924, inside the city's brick-and-sandstone federal building, under the auspices of Judge Charles N. Pray, appointed to the US District Court for the District of Montana by the president and confirmed by the Senate. Witnesses swore to tell the truth. Jurors took their customary oath of secrecy. The courtroom decor—the red oak wainscoting, the heavy wooden furniture, the Stars and Stripes—imparted an air of official dignity to the proceedings.

For those inside the grand jury room, however, some details raised eyebrows. No court reporter made a transcript. The foreman was the defendant's sworn enemy. A private investigator on the Republican National Committee payroll, rather than a sworn federal law enforcement officer, summarized his findings for the jury.

Even the identities of the prosecutors suggested something unusual. The local US attorney who formally brought the charges, John Slattery, had until very recently been under investigation by the attorney general's office—until that inquiry was quietly hushed up. Stranger still was how Slattery took a back seat in presenting the evidence to an out-of-state prosecutor, a lawyer from Washington, DC, who had reported directly to Harry Daugherty until the latter's resignation.

That lawyer, Special Assistant to the Attorney General John S. Pratt, didn't overwhelm the grand jury with evidence. The standard of proof was lower than in a trial; to indict, the grand jury only needed to find reason to believe that a crime had been committed ("probable cause"), not proof beyond a reasonable doubt. Several witnesses did testify, including a former secretary of the defendant's coconspirator, and Pratt did introduce a pile of telegrams, a packet of letters, and a number of canceled checks to back up their recollections, but the entire case took only a couple hours to present. When they finished around 11 a.m., Pratt and Slattery presented a ten-page indictment to the jury and withdrew.

The seventeen jurors deliberated. A few mounted a spirited opposition to the indictment. The foreman, former Great Falls mayor N. T. Lease, steered waverers in the other direction. After a time, they cast their first ballot. The vote was ten for, seven against—just two shy of the required twelve for returning a true bill, as approved indictments were known in legal circles.

At noon they broke for lunch, during which several grand jurors were reportedly taken out to lunch by Republican politicians and told that it was "necessary to indict" the defendant, a prominent Democrat. They reconvened around one thirty for another round of votes. One juror switched sides, leaving the indictment one vote short of approval. After a final, heated argument, a tenth ballot was taken just before three in the afternoon—twelve for, five against. The requisite majority having been achieved, a motion to make the vote unanimous was carried.

The judge and prosecutors were notified and US Attorney Slattery—his debt to Attorney General Daugherty paid in full—affixed his signature.

Thus was born the case of *United States of America v. Burton K. Wheeler.*

TWO THOUSAND MILES away in Washington, Wheeler learned the news from an Associated Press correspondent seeking comment.

For a moment, the senator was uncharacteristically without words. True, the news did not come as a complete surprise. Ten days earlier, he had learned from Frank Vanderlip, who in turn had heard from a friend at the Republican National Committee, that the Department of Justice was working up an indictment against him. At the time, he put little stock in the rumor. He found it hard to believe that the embattled department, under the temporary stewardship of Solicitor General James Beck until President Coolidge selected a new attorney general, would dig itself an even deeper hole by abusing its prosecutorial authority. "That's crazy," he told Vanderlip then.

Now he was outraged—and a little hurt. "It was the first time in my life," he reflected much later, "that I had been accused of doing something illegal."

The ten-page indictment accused him of representing Gordon Campbell in matters before the Department of the Interior, in violation of Section 1782 of the Revised Statutes of the United States—a conflict-of-interest law that prohibited members of Congress from accepting compensation in return for "any service rendered . . . in relation to any proceeding, contract, claim, controversy, charge, accusation, arrest, or other matter or thing in which the United States is a party." If convicted, he faced a $10,000 fine or two years in prison, or both, and would be disqualified from holding further office.

The statute was enacted in 1864, during the Civil War, when members of Congress were overwhelmed with pleas to represent defendants before military tribunals or help clients procure federal contracts, but it codified a more general principle. Federal officeholders, it said, should look out for the public interest of the nation rather than the private interest of the highest bidder. The influence that attached to their office should not be for hire.

Only one member of Congress had ever been convicted of violating the statute—Sen. Joseph R. Burton of Kansas, who in 1902 was hired by the Rialto Grain and Securities Company of St. Louis to intercede on the company's behalf in an ongoing mail fraud investigation. In return for $2,500 in legal fees, Burton met with the US postmaster general and his chief postal inspector, and the investigation was soon dropped. A federal grand jury later indicted Burton, who was convicted, had his conviction overturned by the Supreme Court, was retried and reconvicted, had his second conviction upheld by the high court, and finally resigned his Senate seat days before his colleagues were set to expel him. He served five months of a six-month sentence in a Missouri jail.

Burton had crossed a bright line, but the statute was so broadly written that an unwary senator or congressman might innocently stumble into legal jeopardy. Wheeler, however, was no naive politician. He knew the statute in question well from his days as a federal prosecutor, and when he agreed to represent Campbell he crossed his t's and dotted his i's, conditioning his employment (and his $10,000 retainer) on his representing Campbell only in *state* proceedings, not federal.

Only once as Campbell's attorney had he approached the line dividing legal from illegal—and while he might have tiptoed right up to it, he believed he'd never crossed it.

On March 14, 1923, ten days after assuming office as senator, and three days before sailing for Europe, he got a telegram from Campbell asking him to arrange a meeting with the solicitor of the Interior Department, who happened to be an old friend of Wheeler's from Montana. Wheeler obliged; he stopped by the solicitor's office, said that Campbell had "some difficulties with oil lands, including some government lands," and suggested the two men should discuss the oil leases in person. Campbell later came out to Washington, where Wheeler's Senate aide introduced him to the solicitor.

As Wheeler saw it, he'd acted purely as a senator on behalf of his constituent, not in his capacity as Campbell's attorney. Perhaps the grand jury, under the sway of federal prosecutors hell-bent on revenge, had overlooked that subtle distinction?

Blinded by the irrepressible optimism of a man who knew he was on the right side of history, Wheeler couldn't see how damning it all looked and—technical questions of the law notwithstanding—how his actions gave the distinct appearance of a conflict of interest. He couldn't acknowledge that he might have made a mistake; instead, his mind turned to how he'd been framed. Had the prosecutors steamrolled the grand jury by misconstruing the facts? Or had some witness possibly lied, puffing up Wheeler's simple favor to a constituent into something criminal?

"Who in the name of God?" he started to think. But did it really matter? He knew who ultimately stood behind this legal charade. Never mind that Harry Daugherty was already telling the press that he had "nothing whatever to do" with the indictment—and how could he, he protested, having been out of office at the time? Wheeler knew better. The Department of Justice was temporarily leaderless, yes, but Daugherty's loyal appointees still occupied positions of power.

Wheeler finally found a few words for the Associated Press reporter. "That is palpably a frame-up," he declared. "It is the culmination of a campaign, backed up by the Republican National Committee, to get me because of my activities in the Senate in connection with the graft and corruption in the Department of Justice. They wanted an interruption in these exposures."

For good measure, Wheeler added his emphatic denial of the charges— without wading into the weeds of what specifically he'd done for Campbell. "I have never represented anyone," he said, "before any department of this government since my election to the United States Senate."

At the moment, the indictment was an immediate concern—a knife to the throat of his political career. Only much later, with the benefit of time, would he calmly and rationally reflect on its greater significance. The law, divorced from its pursuit of justice, had become something quite monstrous, an instrument of the powerful and corrupt. His indictment represented, he said then, "one of the darkest pages in American history."

27

"The Most Damnable Conspiracy"

That evening, before the full significance of the indictment could sink in, Wheeler had to wrestle with a more trivial concern: whether to keep some longstanding dinner plans.

Weeks earlier, Supreme Court justice Louis Brandeis had reached out with an invitation, apparently eager to meet the maverick senator foolhardy enough to take on Harry Daugherty. At the time, Wheeler was beyond flattered. Brandeis was one of his legal heroes—a champion of civil liberties, a pathfinding Jewish jurist, and, in the words of a noted critic, "a militant crusader for social justice."

Now, with more on his plate than he could have imagined, Wheeler considered whether to cancel. Had the invitation come from almost anyone else, he might have.

He kept the appointment.

After the meal, Lulu Wheeler and Brandeis's wife, Alice, excused themselves, and the justice invited the senator into his library for a private chat.

"Are you worried?" Brandeis asked.

Wheeler confessed that he was "a little shaken." It wasn't just the threat of jail time. One of his essential qualities had been called into question. He had "never before been called a crook," he explained to Brandeis, "not even by my bitterest enemies in Montana."

The senator intimated that he wanted to return immediately to his home state and demand, as was his constitutional right, a speedy trial.

No. Brandeis was firm. By leaving the capital and halting the important work of his investigation, he would only be playing into Daugherty's
hands.

"They're trying to stop you," Brandeis said. "Don't let them. That's all
they want to accomplish."

The justice's advice made a deep impression. In the eleven days since
Daugherty's resignation, Wheeler had struggled to articulate a reason for
continuing with the investigation. After all, the attorney general's dismissal
had been the explicit objective of his original Senate resolution and the
driving goal of the committee's hearings. Colleagues like Senators Jones
and Ashurst wavered, suggesting that it might be time to wrap things up.
Wheeler, however, sensed that there was still more to accomplish—more
corruption to uncover, more evidence of criminal wrongdoing that might
someday put Daugherty behind bars. Justice Brandeis agreed—and such
validation from the legal luminary steeled Wheeler's resolve.

Moreover, the Montana indictment now gave him a powerful rationale for probing further. Here was proof that the rot at the Justice Department had spread far beyond the office of the attorney general. Daugherty
was gone, but clearly others still did his bidding. And if the department
would abuse its prosecutorial power to settle a political score, as appeared
to be the case here, who could say how else its integrity was compro-
mised? More than just his own political career was on the line. So was the
rule of law—the principle articulated just two decades prior by President
Roosevelt that "no man is above the law, and no man is below it."

Suddenly, the committee's investigation burned with urgency once
again. Keep up the fight and don't give in, Brandeis told him. "This will all
come out all right."

It was just the pep talk Wheeler needed. Before retiring for the night,
he released another statement for the morning papers.

"This indictment is merely the latest illustration of the corruption of
the Department of Justice," it read. "The machinery of Federal justice has
been utterly prostituted."

Swayed by Brandeis, he vowed to stay in the capital and fight on.

"This action," his statement concluded, "is the most convincing evidence that the investigation of the Department of Justice should go on—
and it will go on—because it shows that even with Daugherty out of office
his malign influence still moves his old pawns."

THE NEXT DAY, the Senate chamber was unusually crowded when Burton Wheeler stepped inside early in the afternoon. Eighty-two senators sat at their desks beneath galleries jammed with spectators.

It was an uncommon if not unprecedented moment in the Senate's history. Wheeler was only the sixth sitting senator ever indicted on federal charges, joining a list that included John Smith of Ohio, charged in 1807 for conspiring with the treasonous Aaron Burr; John Hipple Mitchell of Oregon, charged in 1904 for helping timber barons fraudulently claim large swaths of public land; and Truman Newberry of Michigan, charged in 1919 for exceeding the statutory campaign spending limit by a factor of forty-six. But none of his predecessors in infamy had ever so publicly antagonized an attorney general. None of those previous indictments appeared, on their face, so nakedly political. Within the confines of their personal feud, it seemed almost natural for Daugherty to strike back against Wheeler with criminal charges—but, in the grand sweep of history, it was an extraordinary action.

"An atmosphere of intense interest," wrote the *New York Times*, filled the chamber, with everyone wondering how Wheeler would respond and whether the Daugherty investigation would go on.

Wheeler didn't leave his audience waiting long. After shaking hands with a few concerned colleagues, he rose from behind his desk and began a fight to save his political career.

"Mr. President and members of the Senate, I have risen to a point of personal privilege," he began, invoking a parliamentary rule that allowed a senator to respond to a charge of misconduct and which almost automatically granted control of the Senate floor.

Wheeler began by expressing his shock that Daugherty, with the aid of his minions still at the Justice Department, had sunk this low.

"In all of my political fights in the state of Montana," he said, "in all of the bitterness that has ever existed, never has anybody had the temerity to stand up and charge me with having accepted money illegally upon any occasion. They have differed with me; they have differed with my political philosophy; they have charged me with many things, among these that I favored labor too much. I want to say in that connection that I plead guilty, perhaps, to having been friendly to labor, and I always intend to be; but my honesty or integrity has never been attacked before by my worst political enemies. This has evidently been done solely for the purpose of injuring me before the country and delaying, if possible, this investigation of the conspiracy that has been conducted right under the dome of this Capitol and right under the eyes of the Senate of the United States and the occupant of the White House."

Emotion stirred behind nearly every word, tempered by a steely self-confidence. Newspaper correspondents in attendance observed that Wheeler, in spite of the circumstances, had never appeared so dignified, so statesmanlike. His rhetoric rose to match his countenance.

"I ask you, and not for my sake but for the sake of every man who starts an investigation, and for the sake of this investigation, and for the sake of every other investigation, to put a stop to this spy system, to put a stop to this framing of every man. Why, testimony has come out in the committee investigating the Department of Justice—and it has not been controverted—that the lives of members of the United States Senate are constantly being investigated, and then, if they find something on them, it is held over them to intimidate them in the discharge of their duty.

"I want to ask this body, the members of the Senate who start in to investigate crime when the Department of Justice fails to show it up; the members of the Senate who attempt to show up crookedness and corruption when the Burns Detective Agency fails to uncover it, are they to be subjected to this kind of treatment? Are our homes to be searched? Are our offices to be ransacked?"

This case, he was telling his colleagues, was about more than the guilt or innocence of one man. The future of congressional oversight hung in the balance. Would Congress be free to ask pointed questions of the executive branch and probe deeply into allegations of misconduct? Or would the executive branch be allowed to intimidate its congressional pursuers and thus shield itself from scrutiny?

In his case, he declared, the "miserable sleuths of the Department of Justice sent their minions out to Montana absolutely and unqualifiedly to frame a member of the United States Senate in order that he may be stopped from carrying on this investigation and unearthing fraud and corruption and conspiracy here in the city of Washington, such as never before been unearthed in the history of the United States."

Wheeler professed innocence—but he didn't expect his colleagues to take his word for it.

"Let me say to you senators here today," he explained, "that you are the judges of the qualifications of the members of this body. I should be delighted to have this body appoint any committee, any members of the United States Senate, to investigate these charges that have been filed against me, and I venture the assertion that after you have done it you will see a report that there is not a scintilla of evidence casting the slightest reflection upon my honesty or upon my integrity."

It was a risky proposal. Any such committee would be appointed by the president pro tempore, a Republican, and if the committee somehow sustained the charges, Wheeler would almost certainly face expulsion from the Senate. Regardless of how they felt about Daugherty, by this point few Senate Republicans would shed a tear if Wheeler's six-year term were cut short; his cantankerous ways hadn't exactly endeared him to his stodgy colleagues.

It also would not have been lost on Wheeler that the last politician to invite a Senate investigation—Harry M. Daugherty—didn't fare too well.

Nevertheless, he believed strongly enough in his own innocence to place the matter in his colleagues' hands. And in truth it was probably less a gamble than an actual trial in a court of law. In a case that would turn on a technical reading of the statute, he was better off with a jury of his actual (rather than theoretical) peers.

Meanwhile, he vowed, as the Senate considered his fate, he would fight on against corruption within the Department of Justice.

"I am going on with this investigation," he declared, "and I am not going to be stopped by threats, nor am I going to be stopped by clouds; and I sincerely hope that you will believe me when I say that there is not one scintilla of truth in the things with which they have charged me."

Anger—or was it fear?—welled up inside him. Those dark fantasies of Gaston Means, of his enemies running him off the road in a "car accident," or selling poisoned candy to his children, no longer seemed so far fetched. Even if it never came to that, this frame-up could still put him behind bars, unable to provide for his family.

"But they have not stopped with their attack upon me. They have tried," he said, choking on his words—and stretching the truth, "to injure my wife and my babes. They have done it through the most damnable conspiracy that has ever been perpetrated upon a man in the United States Senate."

And with that he sat down, brushing tears from his eyes.

WITHOUT DELAY AND without dissent, the Senate took up Wheeler's request that it investigate the charges against him. Moments after the conclusion of his speech, his colleague from Montana, Tom Walsh, introduced S. Res. 206:

> *Resolved*, That a committee consisting of five Members of the Senate to be appointed by the President pro tempore to investigate and report to the Senate the facts in relation to the charges made in a certain indictment returned against Senator Burton K. Wheeler in the United States District Court for the State of Montana.

The Senate immediately adopted it by unanimous consent.

The next day, President pro tempore Albert Cummins appointed three Republicans and two Democrats to the Select Committee on Investigation of Charges Against Senator Burton K. Wheeler of Montana.

Sen. William Borah of Idaho, who had advised President Coolidge to dismiss Daugherty long before most other Republicans, would hold the gavel.

"A serious charge has been made against a senator," Borah declared, "and we are going to get to the bottom of it."

In Borah's selection, Wheeler could find reasons for both hope and anxiety. In terms of integrity and legal acumen, he could trust the so-called Lion of Idaho more than perhaps any other colleague. On the other hand, the westerner's fierce independence (not unlike his own) also made the outcome unpredictable; neither Borah's past kindness nor their ideological kinship had any predictive power.

Wheeler's future was now in Borah's hands. Within a few short months, the forty-two-year-old had emerged from the obscurity of Rocky Mountain politics and made himself a household name across America. Given his current trajectory, there was no telling how high he might climb. Even the White House seemed within reach—but only if he could survive this assassination attempt on his political career.

28

"The Straight Path of Justice"

On the same day a US senator cried that he'd been framed by the Department of Justice, Harlan Fiske Stone, fifty-one, stern faced, and built like a bull, raised his right hand, took his oath of office as the fifty-second attorney general of the United States, and promised to remake that same department into "the shield of innocence but the swift avenger of guilt."

Stone's rhetoric gave Wheeler reason for hope. With the stroke of a pen, the new attorney general could direct the US attorney's office in Montana to dismiss the charges, immediately bringing an end to the greatest crisis of the senator's career.

"The nation," Stone went on, "must be kept in the straight path of justice, under the law."

After being helmed for three years by an attorney general who weighed the political consequences of every decision, now the pendulum of the Justice Department swung in the other direction. Daugherty had served the private interests of the Harding administration; Stone would (in theory) serve the law. Harry Daugherty craved power his entire life; Stone had never before sought government office. Daugherty cut his teeth as a lobbyist; Stone was a legal scholar, dean of Columbia Law School for the past fourteen years.

Coolidge chose Stone, an old friend and classmate from Amherst College, after telling reporters that he wanted "to get a $75,000 or $100,000 man for a salary of $12,000"—in other words, a lawyer who would offer sterling credentials and outstanding abilities at a deep discount, all in the

name of public service. Stone fit the bill. He'd recently retired from Columbia to accept a lucrative partnership heading up litigation at the Wall
Street firm of Sullivan & Cromwell, where his new salary indeed ran into
the six figures. His name might have been unfamiliar on Capitol Hill, and
he was certainly a stranger to the halls of the Justice Department, but in
the wake of Harry Daugherty, those counted as pluses rather than mi-
nuses. On the morning of April 1, after a hearty White House breakfast
of fried eggs and bacon that doubled as a job interview, Coolidge invited
Stone upstairs for cigars. The president lit his, puffed it in silence for some
time, and then finally said: "Well, I think you'll do."

The next day, Stone's nomination was sent to Capitol Hill. It sailed
through the Senate, where establishment conservatives and insurgent progressives both found something to like. On the one hand, there were his
solid business ties—his board seat with the Atlanta and Charlotte Air Line
Railroad, his retainer as advisory counsel to J. P. Morgan & Co. On the
other hand, there were his undeniable liberal tendencies—his defense of
conscientious objectors during the war, his public protest against the Justice Department's anticommunist Palmer raids. On April 4, without dissent, the Senate Judiciary Committee gave Stone its blessing. Three days
later, after only minimal discussion and with no recorded vote, the full
Senate confirmed Stone's nomination in executive session.

He assumed office the morning of April 9—mere hours before Burton Wheeler's impassioned defense on the Senate floor—with no illu-
sions about the challenge before him. Trust in the Department of Justice
had never ebbed so low. In this job, perceptions mattered. If any executive department must be seen as politically neutral, it was the one that
enforced the nation's laws. But these days a growing chorus of critics
second-guessed nearly every decision it made—and Stone could hardly
blame them. Whatever one thought of his methods, Wheeler had turned
up some shocking revelations. A particular concern of Stone's was the
Bureau of Investigation, which was, he later recalled, "in exceedingly
bad odor."

Stone needed wise counsel and knew just who could provide it: Harvard Law professor Felix Frankfurter, cofounder of the American Civil
Liberties Union and a former Justice Department lawyer in the Theodore
Roosevelt administration. Even before Stone took office, the two men had
struck up a steady correspondence, with Frankfurter dispensing blunt
advice.

"The key to [your] problem is, of course, men," Frankfurter wrote. "Everything is subordinate to personnel, for personnel determines the governing atmosphere and understanding from which all questions of administrative organization take shape." In other words, a fresh face in the attorney general's office was a start, but the changes couldn't stop there.

Stone agreed. Daugherty had stocked the department's upper ranks with friends and sycophants, most of them chosen for their loyalty, not their ability. Assistant Attorney General Rush Holland, for instance, who oversaw personnel matters for the department, had gotten his job not because of a distinguished legal career—he had none—but because he'd edited a weekly newspaper out of Zanesville, Ohio, in the 1890s that had been friendly to Daugherty. He was "a politician pure and simple" in the words of one of his less-than-impressed colleagues. Stone wanted such appointees out. Although he considered it unfair to clean house in one fell swoop, he promised to review his subordinates' records and résumés one by one, dismissing those who fell short of his standards.

And then there was the matter of the Wheeler indictment. Stone made a full review of the case soon after taking office and didn't like what he saw. To begin with, as he complained to prosecutor John S. Pratt, he "doubted whether there was sufficient evidence to secure a conviction."

Questions of evidence aside, the indictment appeared to be a gross abuse of the Justice Department's powers. It was, he confessed to one of his assistant attorneys general, "part of a political fight" and "an improper use of the federal process to serve a political purpose." Each new puzzling detail he came across only further aroused his suspicion. The telegrams, letters, and other papers submitted as evidence to the grand jury, for example, were kept not in the department's case files, as was standard, but in a safe deposit box at Liberty National Bank. And yet, despite his misgivings about the case, Stone vowed restraint.

"There is only one question presented to me," he wrote to a friend, "and that is whether I should allow the law to take its course in the customary manner, or whether I should do something to interfere." The latter would have won him praise from liberal circles. It also would have been bad form, he believed, coming so soon after his predecessor "had been publicly charged with such personal interference."

Harlan Fiske Stone was no Harry Daugherty.

The case of *United States of America v. Burton K. Wheeler* would proceed.

29

"We Anticipate Contempt Proceedings"

His passions stirred by the indictment, his confidence buoyed by Justice Brandeis's encouraging words, Burton Wheeler plunged back into his work with renewed vigor. The Select Committee on Investigation of the Attorney General could not afford to slow down.

Triumph though it was, Harry Daugherty's dismissal did not quench Wheeler's thirst for justice. If anything, the Great Falls indictment had proved that simply decapitating the beast would not slay it. Even after the arrival of a new, ostensibly reform-minded attorney general, Daugherty appointees still filled the upper echelons of the Justice Department. Daugherty's hand-picked special prosecutor, John S. Pratt, continued to oversee the Wheeler case. Assistant Attorney General Rush Holland, Daugherty's political enforcer within the department, remained in office, as did Billy Burns, who had used the Bureau of Investigation as an instrument of vengeance on behalf of his boss and old friend. Those plain facts propelled Wheeler forward. His hearings would continue until they exposed the full extent of the rot within the federal government's law enforcement apparatus. Only then might the Department of Justice live up to its name.

But that wasn't all. Justice also demanded an appropriately severe punishment for the man who had betrayed the public trust of his office; forced retirement was too mild. And while Wheeler alone was powerless to initiate criminal proceedings, he knew that his committee was the only body actively seeking evidence that might someday put Harry Daugherty behind bars.

Thus loomed a showdown with banker Mal Daugherty, who had ejected the committee's forensic accountant from the premises of his Midland National Bank and ignored a later subpoena to bring the bank's books to Washington. Without the financial secrets hidden in the bank's ledgers, all those unconfirmed allegations of graft and self-dealing against Jess Smith and Harry Daugherty would remain just that—mere allegations.

Thankfully, Wheeler had a plan to break through. If Mal Daugherty refused to go before the committee in Washington, then the committee would go to Mal Daugherty. That Friday, April 11, Wheeler and Brookhart would travel to Ohio and convene an extraordinary hearing of the committee in the Daughertys' hometown of Washington Court House. Summoning the legal authority of the US Senate, brandishing Congress's contempt power as they would a cudgel, the two senators would personally demand access to the Midland National's records and dare the obstinate banker to say no.

FIRST, HOWEVER, WHEELER seized the opportunity to shine his committee's spotlight on the developments in Montana. On the morning of Thursday, April 10, he hauled Billy Burns into the hearing room and grilled the Bureau of Investigation director about the circumstances leading up to the grand jury's indictment. Burns was, as usual, guarded and cocky. He was not, however, about to perjure himself—not when there had been multiple witnesses to the conversations he was now forced to recount under oath.

His face went ashen when, under Wheeler's grilling, he admitted that he'd sent three men to Montana to investigate Wheeler's past. He reluctantly agreed that Blair Coan, on the Republican National Committee payroll, was also part of the investigation. Wheeler then elicited an even more damaging admission.

"Did you discuss it with Mr. Daugherty?"

Harry Daugherty told every reporter who asked that he'd had "nothing whatever to do with" the indictment.

"I may have discussed it with Mr. Daugherty."

Belaboring the point, Wheeler forced Burns to confess that he and Harry Daugherty had "talked a great deal" about it, both before and after the attorney general's dismissal, despite a clear conflict of interest.

Chairman Brookhart asked a pointed follow-up. "He wanted you to get something on Wheeler?"

Burns, visibly uncomfortable, answered softly, "He did not say that."

Not a soul believed him—including his new boss. Over at the Justice Department, Harlan Fiske Stone was already quietly searching for a new director who wouldn't allow politics to seep into the important work of the Bureau of Investigation. Americans, Stone believed, shouldn't have to fear detectives snooping around their private lives just because of an unkind word about someone in power—even an attorney general.

THE NEXT MORNING, Wheeler watched from the window of his sleeping compartment as his most unlikely and unwanted travel companion imaginable finally disembarked and climbed into a waiting taxi at Columbus, Ohio.

For the past sixteen hours, Wheeler—as he headed west with Chairman Brookhart, a deputy sergeant at arms, and a stenographer to "invade," as the press put it, the Daughertys' stronghold of Washington Court House—had been forced to share a Pullman car with none other than Harry Daugherty himself. It must have been the most awkard train ride of either man's life, where every trip to the washroom risked an encounter with his sworn enemy. In fact, it had nearly come to that the previous day at Washington's Union Station, where Daugherty, trailed by porters carrying heavy trunks and golf clubs, brushed past the senatorial party as he boarded the train. Everyone wisely pretended not to notice one another.

Daugherty told a reporter that his presence on the same train as his adversary was "merely a coincidence." He was on a personal mission, he explained—his house in Columbus had been burglarized, and the thieves had apparently taken all his personal papers from his years before becoming attorney general. (Although the stolen documents hadn't yet been subpoenaed, the timing of the theft was curious, to say the least. Curiouser still, police never received an official report of the supposed crime, and neighbors reported that they'd neither seen nor heard signs of a break-in.)

Now relieved of Daugherty's toxic presence, the senators continued on several stops to Washington Court House, where two automobiles ushered them to the Cherry Hotel, site of that day's hearings. Outside, a curious crowd, tickled by the thought that a congressional committee would convene in their little town, waited for a glimpse. Inside, the hotel's owner greeted them. He was thrilled to host the hearing, he reported, and had set aside for the committee a prized southeast corner room, large enough to host an official proceeding. An adjacent room was reserved for the traveling press corps, outfitted for the occasion with newly strung telephone and telegraph wires.

Wheeler had important business to attend to but, upon check-in, was intercepted by Philip Kinsley, Washington correspondent for the *Chicago Daily Tribune*. That paper, unabashedly Republican, had spared no criticism of Wheeler's investigation. Kinsley himself, however, must have had a soft spot for the senator.

"Are you going to stay here tonight?" the reporter asked.

"Yes."

"I wouldn't," Kinsley told him. "They're going to have someone get into your room."

Kinsley was describing an effective if unoriginal blackmail ploy— contrive a situation whereby the blackmail target momentarily occupies the same hotel room as some hired stooge of the opposite sex. Suddenly, a photographer bursts in, or perhaps a police officer. Scandal is assured— unless the target pays up or performs some coerced favor.

Wheeler wanted to shrug it off, but Kinsley was emphatic. "Don't stay here tonight," he warned.

UPSTAIRS IN ROOM 12, a large corner guest room outfitted for the occasion with a conference table, Chairman Brookhart gaveled the Select Committee on Investigation of the Attorney General to order. Anticipation and cigarette smoke filled the air as a crowd pressed in at the doorways and hung around the hallway outside.

As the subcommittee of two waited to see if its defiant witness would finally submit to the Senate's authority, it heard testimony from some of Frank Vanderlip's investigators who had been poring over the local public records for information on Harry Daugherty's finances. It had just sworn in its second witness when four men strode in.

"May I interrupt the proceedings for a moment?" one of them asked.

"State your name," Wheeler said.

"We are attorneys for M. S. Daugherty and the Midland National Bank," the man answered. "We desire to question the jurisdiction of this committee to examine the books of the bank and to call as witnesses persons who are connected with the bank. Our purpose in appearing here at this time is to see whether the committee desires to cooperate with us in getting this question into court with a view to having it properly heard and adjudicated." In other words, Daugherty's attorney wanted the committee to stand down until a judge could settle the outstanding legal questions surrounding the dispute.

Brookhart wasn't having it. "Our desire," he said, "is to see the books, and we are going to proceed as quickly as we can to see them. We want to see what these accounts show. That is what we came out here for."

The committee needed an answer, on the record, to its subpoena. "They decline to obey our subpoena at all and decline to appear before us?" Brookhart asked, as a stenographer transcribed his words. "Is that it?"

"Yes, sir."

Wheeler broke in. "All right," he said, "I guess that makes it clear." He then reminded the attorneys that the committee had ways to enforce its own subpoenas: "We, of course, anticipate contempt proceedings in the Senate."

"We anticipated that would be the course," Daugherty's attorney said with haughty confidence before storming out of the room with his three colleagues.

As if on cue, at the very moment the committee called a recess to discuss this latest development, another man barged in.

"Wheeler!" he yelled. "Brookhart!"

It was Fayette County sheriff W. L. Lewis. Pressing his way through the crowd, the husky lawman strode to the table where the two senators were sitting and shoved a sheaf of papers into their hands.

They read hastily. The select committee had been served with a temporary restraining order from the Fayette County Court of Common Pleas, signed by one Judge Nye Gregg. The injunction barred Wheeler and Brookhart from "entering into said banking room and from taking, examining, or investigating any of the books, records, &c., and from in any manner molesting or interfering with the business and affairs of said bank, its officers, agents, &c."

Pandemonium nearly broke out at the notion of a county judge trying to assert his power over the US Senate. Caught up in the drama of the moment, some in the room mistakenly thought that Sheriff Lewis also meant to march the two senators to the local jail at once. But as the commotion subsided and as Wheeler and Brookhart perused the document more carefully, they clarified for the crowd that the court was merely summoning them to appear one month later to argue why the restraining order should be withdrawn.

They also learned, with the help of a local lawyer in the room, a sensational fact about Judge Gregg—he was Harry Daugherty's former law partner at the Columbus firm of Gregg, Worthington, & Daugherty. Gregg, it turned out, wasn't even a regular member of the court of common pleas; he was a mere probate judge, sitting in place of another judge who had conveniently left town on the day of the committee's arrival.

Somewhere out of sight, Harry Daugherty was still pulling strings.

AFTER THE COMMITTEE adjourned, Wheeler began charting a course forward. The outrageous charade redoubled his resolve to hold Mal Daugherty in contempt and press the committee's right to compel his testimony. Judge Gregg's summons, on the other hand, required no response; procedural irregularities aside, the Constitution's Supremacy Clause cast doubt on a county court's ability to order around a committee of the US Senate.

Standing in the hotel lobby, Wheeler might have been preoccupied with such legal thoughts when, as he later recalled, a "good-looking bleached blonde" approached him with a smile. Something about this woman brought back to mind Philip Kinsley's earlier warning.

Introducing herself as a beauty parlor operator, the woman confessed her lifelong dream of opening her own shop in the nation's capital, a place she knew absolutely nothing about. Perhaps a senator could offer some advice—and maybe he'd like to discuss the DC business landscape somewhere more private? Harry Daugherty had arranged quite a welcome for him indeed.

The woman's eyes begged Wheeler. Her lips enticed. It was exactly the kind of honey trap an unguarded man might have fallen for—but Wheeler merely gave her the cold shoulder.

"I don't know anything about the hairdressing business," he told her. "Or anything of the kind."

When that didn't immediately discourage her, Wheeler made an excuse and walked away. He left Daugherty's hometown that very night, his hotel bedsheets unwrinkled.

30

"Young Man"

On May 10, 1924, John Edgar Hoover received an urgent summons to Attorney General Stone's office.

On his meticulously polished desktop, the assistant director of the Bureau of Investigation kept only one framed photograph. It was of his closest friend, someone whose loyalty was beyond reproach—his black Airedale terrier, Spee Dee Bozo. A simple glance at it, especially in moments of professional challenge, could recharge his spirits.

This was one of those moments.

Two days earlier, Hoover's direct supervisor had received a similar summons. Upon arriving, the attorney general informed Director William J. Burns that his resignation was desired. That idea didn't appeal to Burns, who replied he had no intention of resigning.

"Perhaps you'd better think that over," Stone suggested. Burns could resign voluntarily and exit the department gracefully—or he could be fired, the news announced without any of the usual platitudes about faithful service to the government. Burns needed only one night to think it over. He handed in his resignation the next morning.

With that sequence of events in mind, Hoover mustered all his courage, took the elevator four floors up, and found Stone in his sixth-story corner office. Inside, the official portraits of former attorneys general gazed down from the walls. In the middle of the room stood the massive mahogany desk of the nation's top law officer.

Harlan Fiske Stone somehow made the desk feel small. Though his college days were thirty years behind him, Stone still resembled the starting center for the Amherst football team that he'd once been—square head, massive forehead, bushy eyebrows, broad shoulders, muscular chest.

Hoover, five foot seven, was a study in contrast. Slim and bony cheeked at twenty-nine, wavy dark hair slicked back, he could have been mistaken for an office boy, except for his serious—some might say menacing— brown eyes that seemed capable of staring down a charging bull.

A bull, perhaps, but not Harlan Stone, not today.

"Sit down," the attorney general commanded.

Hoover dared not refuse the order.

HOOVER WAS A survivor. When Attorney General A. Mitchell Palmer, a Democrat, handed the reins of the Justice Department to Harry Daugherty, a Republican, on March 5, 1921, Hoover's job security evaporated in an instant.

Having spent the past four years cataloguing the left-wing threats to American capitalism and carrying out raids on radical groups, the young lawyer had established his bona fides as America's top Red hunter. Unfortunately, that was the last thing his new boss wanted. Like the rest of the incoming administration, guided by Harding's campaign pledge of a "return to normalcy," Harry Daugherty was prepared—at first—to turn the page on the excesses of the Red Scare. The new attorney general seemed not to share Hoover's grave concerns about the radical threat to the American way of life. Almost immediately upon taking office, Daugherty undertook a review of Eugene Debs's conviction on sedition charges. That process culminated for the socialist leader (who, campaigning from his prison cell, had won nearly a million votes in the 1920 presidential election) in an Oval Office meeting and a full presidential pardon.

With his Red-hunting prowess undervalued in Daugherty's Justice Department, Hoover could have simply left the government rolls and taken a private sector job, but that simply wasn't his way. Instead, the Wilson administration holdover vowed never to become as replaceable as the curtains in the Oval Office. If Daugherty didn't understand the threat posed by America's radical elements, then it would become his mission to correct the new attorney general's thinking. Over several months, Hoover fed Daugherty a steady diet of weekly intelligence reports on every radical threat, real or imagined, against the United States—strikes, bomb plots, direct support from Moscow. Memo by alarming memo, a creeping paranoia overcame the attorney general, who began to see his young subordinate's worth. By August 22, 1921, Daugherty had committed himself to fighting the Red Menace, and Hoover claimed as his reward the Bureau's assistant directorship.

Now, not even three years later, Hoover's job security was again in doubt. Attorney General Stone had made his reformist tendencies clear, and—despite occasional misgivings—Hoover had served for three years as a loyal number two to Billy Burns. He'd had a finger in nearly every investigation, including that most political and controversial inquiry of all—the Wheeler case. Although Burns maintained personal oversight of the agents in Montana, Hoover dutifully helped from time to time, fielding reports and responding to inquires while Burns was out. At one point he even helped turn Justice Department intelligence over to the Republican National Committee. Such a brazen case of political retribution wasn't his idea of the best use of Bureau resources, but he did what it took to survive—always.

A CLOCK TICKED on the wall of the attorney general's office.

Stone peered at Hoover over his glasses, and the two men locked eyes across the huge desk. Stone made his request.

"Young man," the attorney general said, "I want you to be acting director of the Bureau of Investigation."

Unbeknownst to Hoover, Stone had been asking around about him. Assistant Attorney General Mabel Walker Willebrandt, the second woman to hold that title and one of Daugherty's few incorruptible lieutenants, informed him that Hoover was "honest and informed and one who operates like an electric wire, with almost trigger response."

"Everybody says he's too young," Stone replied, "but maybe that's his asset. Apparently he hasn't learned to be afraid of the politicians, and I believe he would set up a group of young men as investigators and infuse them with a will to operate independent of congressional and political pressure."

The Bureau needed political independence, and also a better sense of organization, a stronger chain of command. Might this twenty-nine-year-old former library cataloguer, a true believer in the virtue of classification and filing systems, be just the man for the job? Stone deplored how, under the Daugherty regime, investigations were regularly initiated from the office of Director Burns, or even by Jess Smith, who technically didn't even work for the department. Hoover, he sensed, would not abide such outside meddling.

The ranks needed a thorough cleaning, as well. "The Bureau [at the time] was filled with men with bad records," Stone recalled years later, "and many of them had been convicted of crime. The organization was lawless, maintaining many activities which were without any authority in federal statutes, and engaging in many practices which were brutal and tyrannical in the extreme."

Hoover's service under Burns and Daugherty were red flags, to be sure—but Stone was willing to take a chance on this temporary appointment. And Hoover sensed exactly what Stone needed to hear.

"I'll take the job, Mr. Stone, on certain conditions."

"What are they?"

"The Bureau must be divorced from politics and not be a catch-all for political hacks," Hoover answered. "Appointments must be based on merit. Second, promotions will be made on proved ability and the Bureau will be responsible only to the attorney general."

Stone forgave the transparent sycophancy.

"I wouldn't give it to you under any other conditions," he said. "That's all. Good day."

ALTHOUGH HOOVER WOULD manage day-to-day affairs as acting director, Stone considered himself, for now, the true head of the Bureau. "I am not much of a detective," he quipped to a reporter, "which ought to qualify me."

Over these next few months, which would be so critical for transforming the troubled agency into "the greatest detective force in the world," as he described his goal to the press, the attorney general would personally supervise its major investigations, approve all hiring decisions, and, most importantly, steer the Bureau through a series of major policy changes.

He wasted little time. Three days after his meeting with Hoover, Stone ordered the acting director to carry out sweeping reforms:

May 13, 1924

MEMORANDUM FOR MR. HOOVER, ACTING DIRECTOR OF THE BUREAU OF INVESTIGATION

FROM THE ATTORNEY GENERAL.

Confirming my conversations with you and with Mr. Holland, and until further instructed, I desire that the following policies should be adopted with respect to the Bureau of Investigation:

(1) The activities of the Bureau are to be limited strictly to investigations of violation of law, under my direction or the direction of an Assistant Attorney General regularly conducting the work of the Department of Justice.

(2) I desire that the personnel of the Bureau be reduced so far as is consistent with the proper performance of its duties.

(3) I request that you go over the entire personnel of the Bureau, as conveniently as may be done, and discontinue the services of those who are incompetent or unreliable.

(4) I, some time ago, gave instructions that the so-called "dollar a year men" should be discontinued, except in those cases where the appointees are in the regular employment of this Department. Please see that these instructions are carried out with all convenient speed.

(5) Until further instructed, I desire that no new appointments be made without my approval. In making appointments please nominate men of good character and ability, giving preference to men who have had some legal training.

(6) I am especially anxious that the morale of the Bureau be strengthened and I believe that a first step in that direction is the observation of the foregoing suggestions.

HARLAN STONE
ATTORNEY GENERAL.

The memo amounted to a complete dismantling of the "spy system," to use Senator Wheeler's term, that had menaced critics of the government through politically or personally motivated investigations. To all the Burns and Daugherty holdovers within the Bureau, the message was clear. There would be no more rifling through congressmen's desks, no more fishing expeditions to senators' home states, no more Red raids.

Stone trumpeted his reforms in a series of press interviews.

"The Bureau of Investigation is not concerned with political or other opinions of individuals," he told one reporter. "It is concerned only with their conduct and then only with such conduct as is forbidden by the laws of the United States. When a police system passes beyond these limits, it is dangerous to the proper administration of justice and to human liberty, which it should be our first concern to cherish. Within them it should rightly be a terror to the wrongdoer."

Stone confessed sympathy with those who argued that mere reform didn't go far enough, who called for the Bureau's outright abolition. "There is always the possibility," he acknowledged, "that a secret police may become a menace to free government and free institutions because it carries with it the possibility of abuses of power which are not always quickly apprehended or understood."

Necessity, however, outweighed the risks. "The enormous expansion of federal legislation," he explained, "both civil and criminal, in recent years, has made a Bureau of Investigation a necessary instrument of law enforcement."

Stone would do his best to set the Bureau on its proper course—but maintaining it would require eternal vigilance on the part of future attorneys general and, ultimately, their bosses.

AS JOHN EDGAR Hoover arranged his belongings on Billy Burns's old desk, a new piece of jewelry glistened from his left hand. The day after his promotion happened to be Mother's Day, a sacred occasion within the house that Hoover shared with his sixty-four-year-old mother. This year, apparently overcome by her son's good news, Annie Hoover flipped the gift-giving custom on its head, presenting her son with a diamond-studded sapphire ring. Every day for the rest of his life, Hoover would wear it on his left ring finger, a potent symbol of his devotion to his new role.

After settling into the director's office, one of his first acts was to fire Gaston Means, officially and finally. Nearly everyone, including Hoover himself, thought Means had been sacked months earlier, but a careful review of the personnel files showed that Burns had merely changed his status to "temporarily suspended." Hoover, who had always despised Means and, in fact, once asked Director Burns to ban Means from snooping around his office, was mortified. He wrote to the attorney general, suggesting that Means's name be expunged from the rolls immediately. "Please do this," was Stone's answer.

With that one monumental error corrected, Hoover plunged headlong into Stone's more substantive reforms. He dismissed every dollar-a-year special agent who wasn't a regular Justice Department employee, requesting the return of their badges and credential cards. He duly instructed his division heads in Washington and his fifty-four field offices across the nation "that the activities of the Bureau are to be limited strictly to investigations of violations of the federal statutes." He pored over the records of the Bureau's 607 employees and boasted in a memo to Stone that he'd "already recommended a number of Special Agents whose services may be discontinued for the best interests of the service." All this work he accomplished within three days of the attorney general's memo.

Hoover, on his own initiative, enacted further reforms. He forbade special agents from drinking whiskey, either publicly or privately, out of respect for the nation's Prohibition laws. He demanded they "be neat in dress and discreet in habit." Most significantly, he strengthened the Bureau's chain of command. Previously, special agents across the country had operated with extraordinary autonomy, their investigations often supervised from afar by Washington. That naturally opened doors to mischief. Hoover now slammed them shut, ordering all special agents to report directly to their local field office supervisors.

In theory, these reforms would recenter the Bureau of Investigation around the limited purpose for which it had been founded in 1908: assisting the Department of Justice in gathering evidence and prosecuting lawbreakers, be they bootleggers, monopolists, or foreign spies.

In theory, Americans could now enter the political arena and voice unpopular opinions—even antagonize an attorney general—without worrying about government detectives rummaging through their private lives as retribution.

In theory, Acting Director Hoover welcomed these new shackles on his agency.

At least, that was the impression he gave on May 17, when he raised his right hand and swore to tell the truth before Wheeler's Senate select committee. He was there to answer allegations that the Bureau had conspired with American oil companies to overthrow the government of Baja California. Hoover, however, who claimed to know little about "this Mexican matter," quickly steered the interrogation toward Stone's reforms.

"I want to say," he interjected at one point, "that the new attorney general has just recently charged me, upon assuming the duties of acting director, to initiate no investigation except upon his specific approval, and that is the policy the Bureau is following today."

Wheeler couldn't hide his surprise. "No investigation without his approval?"

"All matters must be taken up with him," Hoover answered, "and he must be advised in detail concerning it."

Swept away by these unexpected revelations, committee members prodded Hoover for basic facts that Burns had refused to disclose, from the Bureau's annual budget to its current staffing levels. The Bureau operated on a budget of $2.25 million, Hoover answered, and employed 607—a number he was in the process of shrinking.

"The attorney general has instructed me," Hoover explained, "to reduce the personnel of the bureau in every way possible, and that is being done. I have already made a number of recommendations for reducing the force."

"I am glad to hear that," said Senator Jones.

"So am I," added Chairman Brookhart.

The character of the Bureau's special agents also came up.

"Prior to the war," Wheeler asked, "most of the men that were in the Bureau of Investigation were young lawyers, graduates of law schools?"

"That is correct, and that is the policy we are following today," Hoover said. "We are making no recommendations for appointments except of persons with legal training."

Brookhart then jumped in: "The policy, then, will be to get rid of those professional double-crossing detectives?"

If that snide remark rubbed Hoover the wrong way, he suppressed his reaction.

"Most positively," he answered. "We do not intend to have anybody in the service of that character."

In a matter of minutes, the acting head of the Bureau of Investigation had managed to charm the most skeptical audience imaginable. He answered his questions with no hint of evasion. He cited specific figures and even volunteered information. It was not what the five senators were accustomed to from officers of the Justice Department.

Before Brookhart could gavel the meeting closed, Hoover had one thing to add. "The bureau," he pledged, "is ready and willing to respond to any request of the committee for files or information."

Wheeler was so impressed that, afterward, he invited Hoover to his office for a private chat. As the two men settled into well-worn wooden chairs, surrounded by mementos of Wheeler's career in Montana, the senator admitted that he was "very glad to note" the policy changes but wanted Hoover's word on one important matter. The committee's witnesses had been shadowed, their families watched, persons entering or leaving their homes followed and reported to the Justice Department of Justice. Would Hoover promise that there would be no further intimidation of witnesses?

Hoover assured Wheeler that, going forward, the committee would "have no grounds for rendering any complaint against the Department of Justice or the Bureau in going without its proper confines."

PUBLICLY, HOOVER WAS saying all the right things. Privately, however, his actions cast doubt on whether he actually believed the words coming from his mouth.

On May 21, the select committee heard testimony from Jessie Duckstein—one of the Bureau's three female special agents at the time— about her prior employment as stenographer to Jess Smith. Duckstein recalled typing letters concerning whiskey permits and fight films, and she distinctly remembered Smith ordering members of Congress placed under surveillance.

By corroborating the statements of earlier witnesses, Duckstein struck yet another blow against Harry Daugherty. Yet while she certainly didn't come off as loyal to the Department of Justice, she wasn't crossing any professional lines, either: her testimony strictly concerned a time prior to her employment with the Bureau, and it divulged nothing about her confidential work as a special agent.

Hoover resolved to fire Jessie Duckstein anyway. That very day, he set her dismissal in motion. The paperwork made the timing appear a mere coincidence. In his memorandum, Hoover framed her discharge as part of a general "reduction of the force" ordered by the new attorney general. As if that wasn't enough, he cited a letter from Duckstein's immediate supervisor suggesting that the request had nothing to do with the agent herself (or her testimony). The problem was her *gender*. "There is no particular class of work adaptable for women Agents in the Washington Field Office," Special Agent in Charge E. R. Bohner wrote in this supporting document. "In fact, it is not advisable to have any assigned to this office."

Five days later, for the crime of aiding the Senate committee in its investigation of the Justice Department, Jessie Duckstein was out of a job.

Duckstein's firing came with a plausible (if sexist) cover story, but there was little doubt that politics had influenced another of Hoover's early decisions as acting director. In a speech delivered shortly before Hoover assumed the top job, former attorney general Harry Daugherty claimed that Moscow had orchestrated the "present investigative mania at Washington" (and hence his downfall)—and further insinuated that Senator Wheeler was a secret agent of the Soviet Union. The senator, Daugherty reminded his audience, had in the spring of 1923 made a "pilgrimage" to the Russian capital. "There, no doubt," the former attorney general brayed, "new inspirations were advanced as to what steps should be taken to cripple the government of the United States and crumble the columns that support it."

At this, even many of Daugherty's staunchest supporters winced, concerned that the former attorney general had climbed too far out on too shaky a limb. Hoover's Bureau of Investigation, on the other hand, took the outlandish charge seriously. Under the acting director's supervision and at the direction of prosecutor John S. Pratt, a special agent traveled to Omaha, Nebraska, and interviewed Paul Grenning, captain of the ocean liner that had transported Wheeler back from Europe. Was it true, Special Agent E. B. Hazlett asked, that Senator Wheeler traveled with a Russian envoy? That he praised Lenin? And disparaged America?

The captain's answers could have no bearing on the pending conflict-of-interest case against the senator, but they had the potential to destroy his once-promising political future. In any case, Captain Grenning could only disappoint; contrary to Daugherty's fevered imagination, Senator Wheeler was apparently no closet Bolshevik. As Special Agent Hazlett reported to Hoover:

> Considerable discussion was carried on among various passengers as to the propriety of certain United States Senators visiting Russia. Capt. Grenning states that he made it a point to discuss the matter with SENATOR WHEELER and attempted to draw SENATOR WHEELER out as to his impressions of Russia at the present day. The SENATOR stated that he was not impressed with the present government of Russia and that it was his opinion that it could not exist for any great length of time, as it was not founded upon substantial rules of recognized government.

The Bureau promptly closed this secret investigation, but Hoover had already showed his hand. Mere weeks had passed since he insisted to Stone that "the Bureau must be divorced from politics." If the new attorney general's reforms were to succeed, someone would need to shepherd them into the future—and under Hoover, the Bureau was already slipping back into its old ways. If that happened, what would Wheeler's whole crusade amount to?

31

"It Would Be Well
to Suspend Judgement"

ashington had become a hall of mirrors. From April 10 to May 12, 1924, a Senate committee investigated the Justice Department investigation of the senator who had been investigating the Justice Department.

Despite a new attorney general with liberal tendencies and a shake-up at the top of the Bureau of Investigation, Wheeler remained in legal jeopardy. The charges against him were still pending, and Attorney General Stone had made no move to dismiss them. At the moment, his best hope for redemption was this Senate panel, created at Wheeler's request.

Chaired by Sen. William Borah of Idaho, who enjoyed a sterling reputation for evenhandedness, the Select Committee on Investigation of Charges Against Senator Burton K. Wheeler of Montana (as it was formally called) functioned as a sort of extrajudicial court. It sifted through the same evidence presented to the Montana grand jury. It called the same witnesses and heard testimony from the same investigators and prosecutors. Technically, the committee was only to judge whether Wheeler was fit to remain a member of the Senate. Effectively, however, that meant this committee of five senators—three Republicans and two Democrats—would render a verdict on his guilt or innocence.

The basic facts were not in dispute; instead, the case turned on a question of interpretation. When Wheeler interceded on behalf of Montana oilman Gordon Campbell at the Interior Department, setting up a meeting with the solicitor of the department, was he a lawyer representing a client, or merely a senator serving a constituent? The former was illegal; the second was commonplace, especially among senators from western states, where the federal government was the largest landowner.

Borah and his colleagues probed the matter with what now seemed, after all the spectacle of the Daugherty investigation, remarkable sobriety. There was no gossip, no hearsay, no innuendo. When witnesses volunteered more than a senator's question demanded, Borah stopped them in their tracks. When a senator's line of questioning strayed from the committee's charge, Borah politely admonished them.

In place of theatrics, the committee studied every shred of evidence the Justice Department had presented, weighing the relative strength of each witness, scrutinizing every telegram or letter. It also steered clear of dissecting the motives behind the indictment; Wheeler's charge of a "frame-up" was a separate issue that could wait another day.

Compared with the Teapot Dome and Daugherty hearings, these were tepid proceedings, if not downright boring. But if any investigation needed to maintain a no-nonsense, nonpartisan appearance—if any stood a chance of rising above politics and breaking what had become a vicious cycle of recrimination—it was this one.

AS THEY HEARD from seventeen witnesses whose testimony spanned 185 printed pages, Borah's hearings cast doubt on the veracity of three crucial affidavits, collected by Blair Coan of the Republican National Committee, that prosecutors had used to secure the indictment. The affidavits, Borah learned, relied exclusively on hearsay to suggest that Wheeler and Campbell had come to an informal understanding about Interior Department permits, and the witnesses had sworn to them only after being treated to lavish accommodations in Denver and Billings.

More importantly, no witness ever offered proof positive that Wheeler—a former federal prosecutor who knew the conflict of interest statute inside and out—had crossed a legal or ethical line. While Wheeler did defend Campbell in Montana state court, a different lawyer represented the oilman in proceedings before the Interior Department. Another of Campbell's attorneys testified that Wheeler rebuffed him when asked for advice about an Interior Department permit. "I don't know a goddamned thing about government permits," he recalled Wheeler saying. "I wouldn't know one of the damned things if I saw it. Besides, I told Campbell I would not have anything to do with his government land."

The closest Wheeler had come to representing Campbell before the federal government in violation of the law, the available evidence showed, was when he set up a meeting between Campbell and the solicitor of the Interior Department—a service his office (as well as Borah's, or indeed any western senator's) performed for citizens of Montana almost every day.

On May 14, a Senate clerk read Borah's report aloud as Wheeler listened from his desk on the Senate floor. As befitting its author, the report was measured and lawyerly—but it was unequivocal in its exoneration. A point-by-point recital of the committee's evidentiary findings, it directed its readers to an inevitable conclusion. It was, of course, different from a jury verdict; a jury of twelve ordinary, impressionable people could be persuaded or even fixed. Nevertheless, by the time the clerk reached the conclusion, Wheeler was as giddy as a schoolboy.

"The committee wholly exonerates Senator Burton K. Wheeler from any and all violations of Section 1782 of the Revised Statutes of the United States," the clerk recited. "Senator Wheeler was careful to have it known and understood from the beginning that his services as an attorney for Gordon Campbell, or his interests, were to be confined exclusively to matters of litigation in the state courts of Montana, and that he observed at all times not only the letter but the spirit of the law."

Reaction within the Senate was mixed. Borah's impartiality was unimpeachable, and his conduct throughout the investigation impressed his colleagues. No one questioned his methods, and few could question his conclusions. A few stalwart Republicans, still smarting from Wheeler's relentless attack on their copartisan, refused to concede anything about the defendant's innocence, but their numbers were small.

There was, however, considerable pushback against the very idea of the Senate conducting its own trial while the matter was still pending before an actual court of law. That was the concern embodied in a minority report issued by the lone dissenter on Borah's committee, Republican senator Thomas Sterling of South Dakota. Sterling contended that the evidence presented to the panel was sufficient to justify the indictment and that any Senate action at this point would prejudice the court proceedings to come. Precedent was certainly on Sterling's side. In the four previous instances where the Senate investigated the conduct of an indicted senator, it pointedly waited until after the case had made its way through trial and appeal.

An editorial in the *St. Paul Dispatch* echoed Sterling's objection—adding, with a note of irony, that while Wheeler blasted the indictment as an assault against the rule of law, the Senate now threatened to undermine that same principle.

"Hitherto," the *Dispatch*'s editors wrote, "it has been presumed that Senators and representatives, like all other citizens, were subject to the laws of the land, and liable to punishment if caught disobeying them. But apparently not. Of course, Senator Wheeler still faces trial in Montana. But whatever the result of that trial may be it will be said that he already had been acquitted by the Senate. The Senate has gone as far as it could go toward directing a verdict in the trial court, and has done everything it could do to place Senator Wheeler above the law."

That argument carried weight with many mainstream Republicans. When the time came to vote on Borah's report, thirty-five senators abstained—most of them guided by such reasoning. Nevertheless, a majority of Borah's colleagues concurred in his verdict. By a vote of fifty-six to five, his report was adopted and approved.

The US Senate had found Burton Wheeler not guilty.

ALL EYES NOW turned to Harlan Fiske Stone.

For the new attorney general, no other case on the federal docket loomed as large as that of *United States of America v. Burton K. Wheeler*. The Senate had reviewed the evidence and found it lacking, and the defendant had made credible charges of a politically motivated frame-up. In the wake of Borah's report, progressives from both sides of the aisle, joined by most Democrats, clamored for a swift dismissal. To Wheeler's sympathizers, it seemed inevitable that Stone, the avowed reformer, would correct this grave injustice.

Even stodgy establishment newspapers called on Stone to act. "Today," wrote the editors of the *New York Journal of Commerce*, "there is a prevailing belief that the Department of Justice is very rotten in many of its branches. There is a prevailing lack of confidence in the Federal prosecuting officials in numerous districts. In these circumstances, it is a first and paramount duty of Attorney-General Stone to give to the country convincing proof that there has been a change of heart in the department and that these evils will not recur. He should obviously discontinue the proceedings against Senator Wheeler. This has nothing to do with what we may think of Wheeler or his methods; it is a question of protecting individual rights against invasion."

Stone left them all as puzzled as they were disappointed. On May 15, the attorney general announced that he saw "no reason for a change in the department's attitude" and that "no reason appeared for dismissing the proceedings." He did not elaborate.

Felix Frankfurter counted himself among the flabbergasted. Through a flurry of letters, the Harvard law professor had been showering Stone with friendly, confidential advice. Now he picked up his pen to register his disapproval.

"The circumstances under which the indictment was brought," he told Stone, "are suspicious beyond peradventure, and raise a *prima facie* case that the instruments of justice were resorted to for personal and partisan reasons, to obstruct or break the efforts of one who was performing a great and needed public service."

In his reply, Stone acknowledged that Borah had reasoned his way to one conclusion, but held out the possibility that a jury, in such a technical case, might reason in the other direction. Further, he hinted that there was more to the case than Borah had known. After all, Borah never attempted to gather facts beyond what had been presented to the grand jury. Justice Department prosecutors, on the other hand, were still building their case against Wheeler—and they would be assisted by a team of Bureau of Investigation agents in search of more persuasive evidence.

"I think it would be well," Stone warned Frankfurter, "to suspend judgement about the Wheeler indictment. A senatorial committee is not just the place to determine the guilt or innocence of a man charged with crime."

Premature or not, the Senate's rush to judgment presented other problems. Stone sympathized with the minority report's view that, by effectively exempting one man from the standard criminal process, the Senate was undermining the principle of equality before the law. Moreover, with so much at stake, this case above all others demanded a proper resolution. More than just one senator's political career hung in the balance. As Wheeler himself had argued, his fate would determine whether members of Congress would feel free to criticize the executive branch without fearing legal retribution. Even more importantly, Wheeler's indictment had called into question whether the American legal system could render impartial justice—whether political passions, rather than law, ruled the nation.

And if Stone believed those matters too important to place before ninety-six gray-haired politicians, he certainly wouldn't entrust them to a single lawyer occupying the office of attorney general. America needed to reaffirm its bedrock legal principles. The proper venue for that, he judged, was a courtroom.

32

"Take into Custody the Body of M. S. Daugherty"

A s Wheeler awaited trial, the Senate Select Committee on Investigation of the Attorney General entered the final phase of its inquiry in May of 1924.

Now two months in, the hearings were no longer a national sensation. Daugherty was gone; the novelty had worn off. Headlines that once spanned entire front pages now fit neatly within a single column, and now and then an empty seat could be found in the hearing room. Despite the waning public interest, however, Wheeler was determined to leave no stone unturned. He was exposing fresh new scandals in increasingly obscure corners of the federal government.

Among them was the Office of the Alien Property Custodian, an independent executive branch agency that worked in close collaboration with the Department of Justice. It was run by Thomas Woodnutt Miller, a former Republican congressman whose last-minute change of allegiance at the 1920 Republican National Convention helped swing the nomination to Warren Harding. (Miller had also served as the secret intermediary between Harry Daugherty and Gaston Means while the latter was spying on the Senate investigation.) As alien property custodian, Miller managed some $300 million in assets seized from German nationals at the outbreak of the recent war—"alien property" that would be eventually be repatriated once the German government made good on its war reparations. Much of Miller's work was mundane—investing the millions, collecting the interest, and so on—but occasionally claimants would come forward alleging some misunderstanding, demanding the immediate return of their property. In those instances, the attorney general got involved, and one such case had long aroused suspicion.

IN JULY OF 1921, a German industrialist named Richard Merton appeared in the Office of the Alien Property Custodian with an outlandish claim.

At the outbreak of war with Germany in April 1917, the US government had seized 33,360 shares of the American Metal Company, a 49 percent stake in the firm, that belonged (or so it was presumed at the time) to the Metallgesellschaft corporation of Frankfurt, Germany. Four years later, Merton had come to Washington to challenge that seizure. On the eve of America's declaration of war, he claimed, Metallgesellschaft had actually transferred its interest in the stock—by oral agreement, he said with a straight face—to an investment firm in neutral Switzerland. Acting as an agent for these Swiss investors, Merton was now demanding the return of nearly $7 million, which represented the proceeds, plus interest, from the government's sale of the company's stock.

The story was far-fetched. And yet the Office of the Alien Property Custodian held no hearings, called no witnesses, and made no attempt to controvert Merton's claim. With little scrutiny at all, Miller confirmed Merton's application for the return of the seized property and forwarded the file to the Justice Department for final approval. There, in September 1921, one of Daugherty's underlings authorized the repayment of $6.5 million in US Treasury checks, representing the principal, plus another $500,000 in Liberty bonds, representing the interest.

At the time, there was no public announcement of the transaction. The news did leak out the following year—"$7,000,000 PAID BY DAUGHERTY IN 'QUEER' DEAL" read the headline when the *Louisville Courier Journal* broke the story in May 1922. But at that time Congress, then still firmly under Republican control, had no appetite for an investigation.

Wheeler, armed with congressional subpoena power and a battalion of Frank Vanderlip's private investigators, now made up for lost time.

It developed that Merton, upon arriving in Washington, had first approached John T. King, a Republican national committeeman and close friend of Harry Daugherty's, for help. Merton wanted to find a lawyer—the right lawyer with the right connections. King told him he wouldn't need an attorney to press his claim; the American Metal matter could be handled in a less adversarial fashion. King then introduced him to Jess Smith, and before long $7 million had disappeared from the US Treasury and reappeared in Merton's bank account.

How exactly Smith performed this magic trick remained a mystery: it was only established that he personally asked the Office of the Alien Property Custodian to expedite the "praiseworthy" case. But rumor had it that, shortly thereafter, Merton hosted a fabulous champagne dinner for Miller, King, and Smith at the Ritz-Carlton in New York, where he presented each of his guests with a gold cigarette case.

Wheeler got a chance to ask Miller about this gathering during the hearings.

"Did you attend a dinner at the Hotel Ritz-Carlton, at which—"

"No, sir," interrupted Miller, pince-nez clasped to the bridge of his nose. "I have heard that I did, and I am glad you brought that out."

Wheeler repeated himself: "You were not present at any dinner at which Mr. Merton was present? Would you say you never met him at the Ritz-Carlton Hotel in New York?"

"I am sure I never did," Miller answered. "When I go to the Ritz it stands out in my memory."

Miller's memory, however, seemed to fail him over and over again. He claimed to have no recollection of handling the American Metal case, aside from a general awareness of its existence, and could not recall how many times he'd met with Jess Smith.

"Senator, I really can not say how many times Mr. Smith has been in my office," Miller said. "But he was never there at my office on any specific matter, because I knew he was not a lawyer."

"Did he not come there and tell you that the attorney general wanted certain things done?"

"Yes, sir," said Miller, backtracking a bit. "I want to get that plain. I also know that while Mr. Smith said at times what you have indicated I did not take any orders from Mr. Smith or consider them in that light, because I ran that office."

That was about as frank as Miller would get. The alien property custodian admitted to nothing improper. Wheeler called several other witnesses connected to the American Metal matter, and none offered hard evidence of wrongdoing, either. In the end, Wheeler found plenty of smoke but never could locate the proverbial fire.

Even as he moved on to the next scandal, one tantalizing rumor, never corroborated but never contradicted, either, nagged at him. Sometime after the American Metal claim went through, a disgruntled attorney within the Office of the Alien Property Custodian had written to President Harding alleging that "somebody or some group divided a $500,000 fee for getting this claim allowed."

Could Harry Daugherty have been among that group? The fee had apparently been paid in Liberty bonds, an unregistered government security with no records kept of ownership or transactions involving ownership. And so without access to Daugherty's financial records, there was no way to trace the bribe to the former attorney general—or so Wheeler thought at the time.

He had no way of knowing that over at the Justice Department, Attorney General Stone had already opened his own investigation into the matter—one that eventually would lead to the fire itself.

IN LIGHT OF the American Metal revelations, the committee's ongoing dispute over access to Harry Daugherty's bank records pulsed with renewed urgency. But even more fundamental concerns drove Wheeler to action, as well.

After Mal Daugherty's stunt in Washington Court House, where he not only ignored his subpoena but also induced an Ohio state court to obstruct an official congressional proceeding, Wheeler followed through on his threat to invoke Congress's contempt power. Such a naked challenge to the Senate's authority could not go unanswered; not only Wheeler's investigation but every future congressional inquiry depended on its ability to compel testimony. To protect the Senate's rights, Wheeler could choose one of two paths.

One led toward what was known as *statutory* contempt of Congress. In that event, the full Senate would certify a contempt citation to the US District Court for the District of Columbia, after which Mal Daugherty's case would be treated like any other criminal matter. A federal statute, enacted in 1857, required the local US attorney to prosecute the matter, and Daugherty, if convicted of contempt of Congress, would face "imprisonment in a common jail for not less than one month nor more than twelve months."

The other path promised drama and spectacle along the way. It led toward *inherent* contempt of Congress, whereby the Senate sergeant at arms would arrest Daugherty, hale him before the bar of the Senate, and, if he still refused to speak, imprison him somewhere inside the Capitol until he thought better of his defiance.

Few were surprised when Wheeler chose the more dramatic and spectacular option, but in fact inherent contempt offered one major advantage over the statutory route. It was more likely to compel compliance with the subpoena; once convicted of statutory contempt, Daugherty would be jailed whether he produced the bank records or not, leaving him little incentive to cooperate. In any case, Wheeler's colleagues were in no mood to resist. On April 26, the full Senate adopted, without dissent, S. Res. 215:

> *Resolved*, That the President of the Senate pro tempore issue his warrant commanding the Sergeant at Arms or his deputy to take into custody the body of . . . M. S. Daugherty wherever found, to bring the said M. S. Daugherty before the bar of the Senate, then and there to answer such questions pertinent to the matter under inquiry as the Senate may order the President of the Senate pro tempore to propound; and to keep the said M. S. Daugherty in custody to await the further order of the Senate.

Within hours, deputy sergeant at arms John J. McGrain was Ohio-bound, a signed arrested warrant in hand. Alerted to the news, Daugherty fled Washington Court House for Cincinnati, where he offered to give himself up voluntarily inside the federal courthouse so that he could immediately challenge his detention in district court.

McGrain agreed to the plan. On the morning of April 28, he formally placed Mal Daugherty under arrest inside the office of the local assistant US attorney, who offered to represent the Senate's interests in the matter. No handcuffs, no shackles, no striped jumpsuits were involved. The arrest was a mere formality and promised to be brief.

Within minutes, McGrain, Mal Daugherty, and four lawyers all crammed into the chambers of US District Court judge Smith Hickenlooper, who took up Mal Daugherty's petition for a writ of habeas corpus—an ancient legal procedure, inherited from the English common law, whereby courts could review the legality of a person's imprisonment. And the legality of the Senate's action, for which there were few precedents and no explicit constitutional authorization, was very much an open question.

After hearing brief statements from counsel on both sides, the judge granted Daugherty's petition and issued the writ. Until the court could fully weigh the arguments and issue a final ruling, Daugherty would be transferred to the custody of the court—but that was a mere technicality. Mal Daugherty immediately posted a $5,000 personal bond, promised to appear at a hearing the following month, and was—temporarily, at least—a free man.

The matter came up for a full hearing on May 20 before a different judge, Andrew M. J. Cochran, who confessed that he was in a tight spot. The Supreme Court's prior decisions in *Anderson* and *Kilbourn* were in apparent conflict, and with such fundamental constitutional questions at stake, a higher court would almost certainly review his ruling.

"Whichever way I decide this case," he told attorneys for Daugherty and McGrain, "it will go to the Supreme Court of the United States before being finally decided."

Eleven days later, Cochran announced his ruling from the bench.

"I am compelled to hold that the Senate's action in attempting to compel the petitioner to testify is absolutely void," he said. The problem, as he saw it, was the lack of any legislative intent behind the committee's investigation, echoing the high court's ruling in *Kilbourn*. Its demand for access to the Midland National's books wasn't in service of some new banking legislation or a review of the Justice Department's annual appropriations bill. The committee was simply prying into Harry Daugherty's personal affairs—in the interest of public integrity, perhaps, but without any explicit constitutional authority.

"The Senate has no power to impeach any federal officer at the bar of public opinion, no matter what good may come of it," the judge declared. "That the Senate has in contemplation the possibility of taking action other than legislation would seem of itself to invalidate the entire proceedings."

Cochran's ruling, if allowed to stand, promised to undermine an important constitutional check on the executive branch. Congress's oversight power would be gutted, its subpoena power limited to witnesses who could provide information about specific legislative proposals. Wide-ranging investigations into general misconduct, even if they promised to inform future legislation, would be powerless to compel testimony. Scandals like Teapot Dome would, in effect, be shielded from public scrutiny.

Wheeler immediately vowed to appeal directly to the Supreme Court, an action the full Senate—fiercely jealous as always of its institutional prerogatives—promptly authorized by a vote of seventy to two. Attorney General Stone, citing federal law, declared that he was obligated to defend congressional officers like McGrain in their official duties and pledged his department's support.

The fate of Mal Daugherty, as well as Congress's authority to investigate the executive branch, would be decided by the nation's highest court.

33

"Double Crossed"

D espite its setback in the courtroom, the select committee pushed on toward its conclusion, introducing, along the way, one final, sensational witness.

On the morning of Friday, May 16, a stout, bald man, immaculately dressed in a tailored gray suit with a white silk shirt, black bow tie, and tan shoes, stepped into the hearing room. Had he walked in alone, his entrance might have escaped notice; aside from his jitteriness, and perhaps the grandeur of his clothes, there was little to set him apart from the average spectator. As it was, this man was flanked on either side by an armed, uniformed guard, and that was an escort that turned heads. Wheeler's latest witness, it turned out, was a convicted felon who'd been granted extraordinary parole from the Atlanta federal penitentiary to dish about his secret dealings with Jess Smith.

The man's name was George Remus, and he'd been, for a time, the largest supplier of bootleg liquor in the United States. An enterprising pharmacist-turned-lawyer who opportunistically switched careers again when the country banned intoxicating liquors in 1919, Remus had exploited a loophole in the Volstead Act to become the nation's so-called bootleg king, moving some nine hundred thousand gallons of booze in deals exceeding $25 million. His fabulous wealth became the stuff of legends. He threw lavish parties at his Cincinnati mansion, dispensing diamond-studded jewelry and brand-new Pontiacs as party favors, earning a reputation for extravagance that reportedly inspired F. Scott Fitzgerald to create that quintessential Roaring Twenties literary figure, Jay Gatsby.

Prohibition had created plenty of sudden millionaires, but what set apart Remus from other operators who relied solely on luck and muscle was how he conducted his business behind a legal facade, withdrawing perfectly lawful medicinal spirits from government-bonded warehouses (like the one Alexander Fink had been offered), all with the approval of permits signed by Prohibition officials within the Treasury Department. The committee listened with rapt attention as he explained how it all worked.

"Now, these permits that you speak of that you got," Wheeler asked, "they were for medicinal purposes, were they not? Not for beverage purposes?"

"For medicinal purposes." Remus looked at Wheeler with piercing blue eyes. "Of course, that is a farce. Pardon me, Senator."

"Tell us why it is a farce. Will you explain that?"

"I don't think there is one scruple of liquor ever prescribed by physicians that is used absolutely for medicinal purposes. That is my opinion."

"In other words," Wheeler said, "you think this provision in the Volstead Act, allowing whiskey for medicinal purposes, is a joke?"

"It is the greatest comedy, the greatest perversion of justice, that I have ever known of in any civilized country in the world. Pardon me for that, if you will. And I have never had a drop of liquor in my whole life, personally."

Teetotaler or not, Remus had kept the liquor flowing across the eastern half of America, and he used the fiction of medicinal alcohol as legal cover. Buying first one pharmacy and then a series of them, Remus withdrew as much legal, medicinal whiskey as he could, with the full approval of the Prohibition authorities, and then had his own men hijack the delivery trucks. The stolen goods were then sold on the black market at a huge profit. Soon he realized he could double his income by owning the distilleries, too, which he bought at distressed prices from owners less savvy than he. Eventually, he came to own seven of them.

Even still, Remus couldn't keep up with demand. No matter how much he produced, his supply bottlenecked on its way out of the warehouse. He just couldn't secure enough withdrawal permits, which required the signature of a high-ranking Prohibition Bureau official.

And that's where Jess Smith came in. The two men met in the spring of 1921 in the lobby of Manhattan's Commodore Hotel.

"What did he say to you," Wheeler asked, "with reference to being able to get these permits through for you?"

"He had heard of me as being a reasonably large operator from the viewpoint of the whiskey industry. Of course that was pursuant to the meeting, that was so understood."

"That was the reason he met you?"

"Yes, absolutely."

The two men struck a "gentleman's agreement," Remus explained, whereby Smith, leveraging all his connections, would procure the necessary permits in return for a fee of $1.50 to $2.50 per case, depending on the number of cases—and Remus ultimately withdrew tens of thousands of cases.

To Wheeler's delight, Remus didn't expect the committee to take his word for it; as proof he presented canceled checks, written out to "cash" but endorsed by "J.S." on the back. The evidence, though still circumstantial, corroborated Roxie Stinson's earlier, hazier charge that Smith and Daugherty had been involved in "whiskey deals."

As Stinson had testified, Smith soon pulled out of the liquor permit racket because he "got afraid" of meddling in the affairs of the Treasury Department, where Daugherty held little sway. Nevertheless, Smith and Remus continued to transact business.

"You had no other purpose for meeting Mr. Smith?" Wheeler asked Remus, steering his witness to a subject even more serious than subversion of the Volstead Act.

"Other than to do what he could from the viewpoint of holding a person harmless in the event of legal entailments," Remus answered. "He was pretty close to the attorney general."

In other words, Smith was selling that ultimate favor available to the nation's legal authorities—a get-out-of-jail-free card. The understanding, Remus went on to explain, was that Attorney General Daugherty would personally intervene to spare him the indignity of prison stripes.

"How much did you pay him on the first occasion?"

"I think it was $50,000."

"How much did you pay him in the aggregate, altogether, on these different occasions?"

"Oh, between $250,000 and $300,000," Remus answered. "That is my best judgment at this time."

"And that money was paid to Jess Smith for protection, was it not?"

"Yes."

"What did he say with reference to your being indicted in these matters, or prosecuted?"

"That there never would be any conviction—maybe a prosecution, but no ultimate conviction, that no one would have to go to the penitentiary."

Evidently, something had gone wrong; Remus now spent his days shelving books at the prison library and his nights behind bars in Atlanta's federal penitentiary. Tears came to his eyes as he described his predicament, locked in a cell block with common criminals. "All the money in the world would not tempt me again," he told the committee.

Wheeler addressed the elephant in the room. "You've been double crossed, haven't you?" he asked.

The witness had a habit of referring to himself in the third person—a defense mechanism when confronting difficult facts, perhaps, or a way to stress his own importance. "Remus has been betrayed by everyone he had trusted," he said, for example, on one occasion. At this moment, however, he managed to suppress his verbal quirk.

"Well, the dead don't speak," he replied, sidestepping Wheeler's provocative question, "so what is the use of having to answer that?"

WHEELER'S SUGGESTION OF a double-cross put a dramatic spin on Remus's story, but the truth was more complicated. Unlike his sometimes-associate Gaston Means, Jess Smith was no common swindler. It was always possible (though not entirely plausible) that Smith collected the bribes without Daugherty's knowledge and then proved powerless, given his lack of official position at the Justice Department, to steer the legal proceedings in Remus's favor. A more likely explanation, however, was that Daugherty was in on the deal as Smith had claimed and yet found even his own influence as attorney general constrained by one ill-considered appointment to the Justice Department's upper ranks.

When Mabel Walker Willebrandt was sworn in as assistant attorney general in charge of Prohibition enforcement on August 29, 1921—three months after the first protection money changed hands between Remus and Smith—Harry Daugherty might have allowed himself a moment of smug satisfaction. In choosing a woman for that role, the Harding administration was currying favor with the twenty-six million female voters (newly enfranchised by passage of the Nineteenth Amendment) who overwhelmingly supported Prohibition. And at the same time, in selecting an inexperienced, thirty-two-year-old public defender—just four years out of the University of Southern California law school—he ensured that he would maintain control over Volstead Act prosecutions, which, as Jess Smith was learning, could be quite lucrative indeed. Certainly, few expected Willebrandt to wage a successful war against the well-financed and increasingly brazen operators in the black market for intoxicating spirits. For their part, the Washington press corps refused to take her seriously, commenting on her choice of shoes ("black strap pumps of the very latest style") rather than her formidable legal skills, referring to her condescendingly as a "pretty woman lawyer." Bootleggers, reporters speculated, must have been toasting her appointment.

If George Remus was among them, he soon would soon learn just how badly he'd underestimated her. Although she personally disagreed with Prohibition, once in office Willebrandt pursued scofflaws with the conviction of Carrie Nation, and it wasn't long before she turned her hatchet on America's bootleg king. Within two months of taking office, she sent undercover Bureau of Investigation agents to Cincinnati to investigate Remus's operation and then traveled to the Queen City herself to present the case to the grand jury.

Daugherty, meanwhile, had no other choice but to leave Willebrandt alone. Where he'd once expected her to be a pliable lieutenant, she had proven herself fiercely independent and, worse, beyond reproach, one of those rare Prohibition officials who would not even countenance the thought of a bribe. If his interactions with her ever strayed into the irregular—if he asked her to go easy on a certain defendant, for example, or to drop a pending investigation—she was exactly the kind who would raise holy hell. And so Harry Daugherty found himself powerless to fulfill the promises Jess Smith had made on his behalf. With Daugherty sidelined, Willebrandt obtained a conviction against Remus for conspiracy to violate the National Prohibition Act and fought his appeals all the way to the Supreme Court. In the end, Remus received the maximum statutory penalty—a $10,000 fine and two years in prison.

In the case of George Remus, justice was ultimately obtained, but the bootlegger's testimony before the select committee amounted to a staggering allegation nonetheless. For a prosecutor, there was no more sacred duty than deciding whom to throw into the maw of the criminal justice system and whom to spare. Someone in the office of the nation's highest prosecutor—whether Daugherty himself, his most intimate friend, or the two of them conspiring together—had sold it for cash.

34

"He Did Not Dare"

From the very beginning, Harry Daugherty clamored for an opportunity to defend himself before the select committee. If only given the chance to testify, he promised, he could expose every accusation aired against him as a vicious lie. For the former attorney general's dwindling supporters, it remained a rallying cry—Daugherty was innocent, and he could prove it.

Wheeler was not moved. He remembered how Daugherty, pulling levers behind some curtain, had turned his own impeachment hearings into an attack on the congressman who had introduced the articles of impeachment in the first place. Wheeler had learned from poor Oscar Keller's mistakes. He would not allow Daugherty to control the select committee's hearings, at least not until the "prosecution" had rested. Only at that point would the "defense" be allowed to present its own case.

The time, it seemed, had finally come. Witness by witness, Wheeler had laid out his evidence, from the testimony of Roxie Stinson and Gaston Means to that of George Remus—115 witnesses in all and 3,338 pages of transcripts. Hard, incontrovertible proof would remain elusive for as long as his banker brother stonewalled the committee, but there was reason to believe that Harry Daugherty, through his coconspirator Jess Smith, had accepted bribes in return for a variety of favors—from liquor permits, to immunity from prosecution, to the approval of a $7 million alien property claim. The Department of Justice had become, in the words of Wheeler's colleague Senator Ashurst, "the Department of Easy Virtue." In the court of public opinion, it amounted to a damning case.

With Congress scheduled to adjourn in early June, the committee was now eyeing a summer recess. Newspaper correspondents who salivated over the prospect of one final, titanic clash—a face-to-face showdown between Burton Wheeler and Harry Daugherty—would soon be rewarded.

On Saturday, May 31, coincidentally the very same day as Judge Cochran's decision in the Mal Daugherty contempt case, the committee revealed that it was finally Harry Daugherty's turn to answer the charges against him.

"I wish to make the announcement," Chairman Brookhart said at the close of the day's hearing, "that probably about Friday we desire to ask Mr. Daugherty himself to appear here."

"About Friday of this week, did you say?" asked Paul Howland, Daugherty's legal counsel.

"Yes," Brookhart said. "And that he waive his claim as to immunity."

"Oh, he has not got any immunity to waive."

"Well, you understand what I am saying. We will ask to examine him at that time. And if that date is not satisfactory, if he can set some other date about that time, no doubt we can agree on it."

"In other words, the committee is not going to issue process on him and treat him as a regular live Cabinet member, even if he is an ex-Cabinet member?"

Howland was referring to a longstanding courtesy afforded to cabinet officers whereby committees would merely *request* their presence rather than command it by subpoena.

"Well," Brookhart began to say, "if you want us—"

Howland cut him off. "I will advise you if the date is satisfactory to him."

Four days later, on Wednesday, June 4, Howland and his cocounsel, former senator George Chamberlain, returned the committee room with a lengthy letter from the former attorney general. Wordy in style, aggrieved in tone, it declared that he would neither testify nor allow counsel to represent him before the committee, after all.

Indeed, he had hoped to be called earlier, his letter claimed, but as he followed the proceedings he came to detect "a feeling of antagonism entertained toward me by certain members of your committee, and that these members of your committee, instead of prosecuting a fair and impartial inquiry into my official conduct as Attorney General of the United States, have made a desperate attempt to blacken my reputation."

"I have never been able to understand," he wrote, "why your investigation was conducted upon such unusual and peculiar lines, and with such bitter personal feeling toward me on the part of certain members of your committee."

Wheeler had never hidden his personal animosity toward Daugherty, making it easy for the former attorney general to dismiss the investigation's conclusions as something other than impartial findings. But by lamenting the committee's focus on his "reputation" rather than his "official conduct," Daugherty elided a basic fact. If the committee was blackening his reputation, it was doing so by exposing his alleged misdeeds as attorney general.

Daugherty hastened to deny those allegations. "At this point," he continued, "I take occasion to contradict and deny any inference, surmise, or supposition that I profited in any illegal, corrupt, or unethical way, directly or indirectly by reason of any activities of political associates or friends, at any time, or that my conduct, either official or personal, was directly or indirectly influenced at any time, in any way, by venal or corrupt motives."

In other words: *I am not a crook.*

Daugherty went on to complain that the only testimony suggesting wrongdoing on his part came "by way of the grave," through hearsay attributed to the late Jess Smith, and how could he counter that? "The silence of the tomb," he wrote, "has forever rendered the direct denial of these slanders impossible."

Grasping for one final excuse, Daugherty cited Judge Cochran's decision in his brother's contempt case. The judge, he noted, had ruled that the investigatory powers of the committee were "absolutely void and without constitutional authority." It would therefore be unseemly for him, a former attorney general, to lend his credibility to what the federal judiciary had held to be a kangaroo court.

WITH DAUGHERTY'S REFUSAL, the work of the Select Committee on Investigation of the Attorney General effectively came to an abrupt and unsatisfying end. There would be no ultimate war of words, nor a formal report to the Senate. Congress was set to adjourn for its summer recess, the "prosecution" had already laid out its case, and in reality— even if Daugherty had chosen to mount a defense—the court of public opinion had already rendered its judgment. In truth, by withdrawing from

the proceedings, the former attorney general only calcified the collective
moral sanction against him.

"Mr. Daugherty's legal position," wrote the editors of the *New York
Times*, "may be entirely correct and defensible, but there can be no mis-
taking the judgement which the public will form of his moral position. His
decision not to testify will seem to many a tacit admission that some at
least of the sinister suspicions thrown upon his course and his companions
at Washington are not without foundation. Those who from the first insisted that all his rights should be respected by the Senate committee have
now to reckon with the fact that when the time came for him to maintain the greatest of all his rights—the right to an unsullied reputation—he
chose to resort to legal avoidance."

Wheeler was in Missouri when the news reached him. Immediately,
he grasped that Daugherty's decision would spell a quiet, anticlimactic
end to his hearings—and that evidently put the senator in a feisty mood.
He would never have the chance to put the former attorney general under oath and grill him about all the unresolved mysteries surrounding his
three years in office.

That evening, Wheeler interrupted his speech before a St. Louis Democratic club to taunt the former attorney general with the questions he'd
now never have the chance to ask.

"He did not dare to take the witness stand," he roared, "and under
oath tell why he could afford to pay $25,000 a year for an apartment in
Washington, all upon a salary of $12,000 a year.

"He did not dare come before the committee and explain how it was
that the man who ate with him, slept with him, was his constant companion, nearer and closer to him than his own wife, how it was that that man
could graft a million dollars and he not know about it.

"He did not dare come before the committee and explain how much
money he had collected himself upon various cases that had been dismissed.

"He did not dare submit himself to cross-examination because he
had a guilty knowledge and a guilty conscience, and with all his boldness
and all his bravery he did not have the temerity to go on there and raise
his hand before God and testify under oath."

Wheeler then turned to the upcoming presidential contest, which was
just getting underway. The stakes this time, he argued, went beyond the
basic question of who would occupy the White House.

"The Republican Party is soon to meet in Cleveland, and we all know that the nominee of that party is going to be Calvin Coolidge," he said. The incumbent president had beaten back challenges by Henry Ford, Gifford Pinchot, and Hiram Johnson. "We all know that if this administration is re-elected to office that they will go back into office feeling that they have the stamp of approval for all of the misdeeds, for all of the corruption that has been exposed in the Republican Party, because you cannot go out and elect Mr. Coolidge and the Republican Party next fall without saying that you put your stamp of approval upon the corruptionists and the crooked-ness that has taken place in the national capital."

For months, Wheeler had been declaiming against Harry Daugherty. Now, with the attorney general out of office and the investigation into Daugherty's misconduct effectively closed, Burton Wheeler marked as his enemy the whole of the Republican Party itself and, in particular, the man at the top.

35

"Look Elsewhere for Leadership"

F our years earlier, American voters had rejected the progressive spirit that once animated so much reform under the Taft, Roosevelt, and Wilson administrations. With President Harding's inauguration, as journalist Lincoln Steffans observed, Washington became "the kept woman of Wall Street," and now, under President Coolidge, who famously declared that "the chief business of America is business," the two had evidently married. Ironing out social and economic inequalities was no longer a priority of the federal government; such goals were replaced by cutting taxes and eliminating troublesome regulations.

By exposing the corruption of a department that, in the same spirit, doled out "justice" to the highest bidder, Wheeler had given the American people a reason to reconsider their decision. He hoped the November election would become a referendum on America's "return to normalcy."

Many felt the same—and wondered why Wheeler, having catapulted himself to national fame, shouldn't be out front and center, making the case for a course correction. Thus, in the summer of 1924, despite facing a serious indictment, Wheeler found himself on not one but two parties' shortlists for vice president.

First were the Democrats, who met at Madison Square Garden on June 24 for a nominating convention that would become a marathon event, dragging on for sixteen days and 103 rounds of balloting, revealing deep rifts between, on one side, western progressives and northeastern liberals and, on the other, southern conservatives. When the deadlock broke, the party finally chose John W. Davis, a conservative lawyer and diplomat from West Virginia whose hard-line politics would lock up the Old South. To balance out the ticket, party leaders turned to Wheeler, now the face of the party's progressive wing. Sen. Tom Walsh, serving as convention chairman, asked Wheeler if he would accept the vice presidential nomination. Davis himself echoed this request.

Wheeler rebuffed all offers. He was disgusted that Democrats had chosen a lawyer for the "House of Morgan" as their standard-bearer and simply couldn't bring himself to shill for a candidate who shared virtually none of his values, whatever Davis's party affiliation. Instead, Wheeler declared that the party had "forfeited any right it may have to the support of the progressive Democrats of the country."

"When the Democratic Party goes to Wall Street for a candidate," he announced, "I must refuse to go with it. Between Davis and Coolidge there is only a choice for the conservatives to make. The uncontrolled, liberal, and progressive forces must look elsewhere for leadership."

Having scorned the Democrats, Wheeler soon fielded overtures from a new, insurgent movement that hoped to follow in the footsteps of the People's Party (which carried five states in 1892, placing third) and the Progressive "Bull Moose" Party (which carried six states in 1912 under its standard-bearer, former president Theodore Roosevelt, placing second). In mid-July, leaders representing labor unions, farmers, women, civil rights activists, socialists, and northeastern intellectuals convened in Cleveland to organize a third-party bid around Wisconsin senator Robert M. "Fighting Bob" La Follette. When their first pick for vice president, Justice Louis Brandeis, politely declined, they adjourned their convention and left the choice of a running mate up to La Follette himself.

The next weekend, La Follette appeared at Wheeler's doorstep in Washington with a request: Would he join him on the Progressive ticket as its vice presidential nominee?

Though tired and, at sixty-nine, one of the oldest presidential candidates in US history, La Follette looked as combative as ever beneath his enormous pompadour of white hair. Wheeler was tempted by the offer; he admired La Follette above almost any other politician, and he could not deny the generational logic behind the pairing. The Wisconsin senator was the progressive movement's outgoing leader. He was in poor health, and everyone understood this would be his last hurrah. Wheeler, forty-two, was now widely seen as La Follette's successor. Fit, handsome, bursting with energy, he would carry the progressive torch into the future—all the

while continuing his crusade against corruption before untold thousands
of Americans on the campaign trail.

Still, Wheeler couldn't bring himself to say yes. He just wasn't the
right man for the job.

"Listen, I can get out and talk to the farmers and labor people in
Montana," he told La Follette. "But hell, I couldn't go into Boston and
New York and Chicago and those places. I just couldn't do it."

Despite the hundreds or thousands of public addresses he'd given
across his career in law and politics, Wheeler had never once spoken from
a script. Whether in the courtroom, atop a campaign podium, or on the
Senate floor, he always said what came to mind, organizing his thoughts
and choosing his words on the fly. He simply couldn't recite the same
stump speech, day after day, in front of complete strangers.

"Oh, yes you can," was La Follette's response.

Outside, the Wheelers' yard was a riot of color—forsythia, lilac, and
azalea, all enclosed by a neat hedge, shaded by elms, oaks, and maples. After spending half a year sifting through the filth of the Justice Department,
and with a federal indictment hanging over his head, did he really want
to spend the next three months in a series of hotel rooms and railcars? All
for a quixotic campaign that could hope, at best, to deadlock the Electoral
College and throw the election to the House of Representatives?

At the moment, home seemed far more inviting.

"No," he said with finality. "I just haven't a chance. You ought to get
somebody else."

Word of Wheeler's decision, however, apparently did not spread too
widely, and in the days that followed, his political enemies conspired
to keep him off the campaign trail.

Soon after La Follette's visit, Wheeler learned that Special Assistant to
the Attorney General John S. Pratt—Daugherty's loyal prosecutor, still on
the Department of Justice payroll despite Stone's reforms—was preparing
a second indictment against him, this one in the District of Columbia,
where federal juries and judges were typically more deferential to prosecutors. Wheeler asked his friend Ray Baker, a former director of the US Mint
with extensive Republican connections, to verify the story.

Baker soon returned to Wheeler's Senate office with a disturbing report. The rumors were true, but with a twist—the indictment would never
materialize if Wheeler simply refused to join the Progressive ticket.

"Is that so?" Wheeler was infuriated. Obviously, Daugherty's friends (and most Republicans for that matter) would not want Wheeler out on the campaign trail, fulminating against the corruption of the past four years. But did they really expect to blackmail him for the rest of his life? To control his political destiny? No, Wheeler would not allow himself to be moved like a pawn on a chessboard.

He marched straight to La Follette's office.

America didn't deserve another four years of "normalcy"—of the common laborer taking a back seat to Wall Street, of public integrity losing out to partisan loyalty. Mustering all the political capital he'd accumulated through his crusade against corruption, Wheeler would launch a new crusade for his dearest political values.

"I've changed my mind," he told La Follette. "I've decided that I'll run for vice president"—adding, almost as an afterthought—"if the offer is still available."

36

"The Usual Silence"

T hunderclaps announced the start of his campaign.

On Labor Day, September 1, Burton Wheeler mounted the podium on Boston Common and surveyed the sea of straw hats. Some five thousand had braved this horrid weather—sweltering heat alternating with drenching rain—to hear from the man who'd vanquished Harry Daugherty. It was an impressive turnout, even more so considering that Massachusetts was President Coolidge's home state.

As thunder pealed, Wheeler denounced "this den of iniquity called the Department of Justice" and defended his decision to hear testimony from gangsters and convicts.

"I am willing," he said, "to admit that some of the witnesses we called belonged to the underworld, and I am willing to go further and say that the Department of Justice, the duty of which is to see that the law is enforced impartially against the strong as well as the weak, was being run by the underworld, by the gang, if you please, from Ohio."

The ensuing cheers were reassuring; this was exactly the kind of crowd he'd thought he couldn't relate to. Wheeler could only go on for so long, however, about the misadventures of Harry Daugherty, who was not on the GOP ticket, of course, and would never hold public office again. Wheeler's role, as he well knew, was to link the corruption he'd uncovered to the actual Republican standard-bearer, and so he reserved some of his most sarcastic language for Silent Cal—whom the *Christian Century*, in a widely circulated editorial, had recently hailed as "a strong, silent man, who never speaks unless speech is required, but who, when he speaks, utters words of wisdom and power."

Wheeler now ridiculed that notion. "This mythically great, strong, silent careful man," he sneered, "as vice president and then chief executive of the United States, stood by and allowed all these things to go on without a lift of an eyebrow. And not even then, when the unspeakable slime of departmental corruption was exposed to his official gaze, did this mythically courageous, strong, silent, careful man by word or gesture disapprove of the crimes or of the criminals, but on the contrary he joined in the hue and cry against the Senate for exposing the dark deeds of his Cabinet."

For an hour and a half he roared on. When the heat became unbearable, he asked for his audience's indulgence to continue in his shirtsleeves. As he whipped off his coat, his listeners howled their approval.

By the time he was carried off the stage on the shoulders of Boston police officers, his doubts about rallying a big-city crowd had evaporated into the steamy air.

WHEELER'S FUTURE LOOKED promising. But it all might amount to nothing if a jury put him behind bars. On the same day as his speech in Boston, half a continent away in Great Falls, Montana, two attorneys entered a federal courtroom to formally answer charges on his behalf in the case of the *United States of America v. Burton K. Wheeler.*

In what the Progressives' campaign manager branded as "an attempt to prostitute the processes of justice for political purposes" and "a clear indication that the Department of Justice is to be used as an adjunct of the Republican National Committee in this campaign," US Attorney John Slattery had scheduled Wheeler's arraignment to coincide with the opening day of his vice presidential campaign—on purpose, Wheeler and his fellow Progressives presumed.

Wheeler was outraged over Slattery's dirty trick but nonetheless ready to proceed with a trial. La Follette had given his blessing: Wheeler would step away from the campaign trail for as many days or even weeks as he needed to prove his innocence. The ensuing publicity, the two men agreed, would surely make up for his absence—unless, of course, the jury returned a verdict of guilty.

As it turned out, they wouldn't have to take that risk. As soon as Wheeler's defense counsel gave his answer to the charges—"Your Honor, we demur to the indictment"—the judge announced that he was recusing himself. A member of the federal bench since 1912, Judge George M. Bourquin had presided over numerous cases where Wheeler had been the federal prosecutor. Later, despite their frequent clashes in the courtroom, the judge rushed to Wheeler's defense when his character was called into question during his 1922 senatorial campaign. Given that history, Bourquin wrote in his disqualification statement, he was "unable to preside in this cause with absolute impartiality."

The recusal spelled a delay of at least several months. For Wheeler, it was just as well. With his court date pushed to 1925, he could turn his full attention to the task at hand: the November election.

"IN A CAMPAIGN," Wheeler told his crowd, "a candidate ought to tell you where he stands on important issues, but up to this time President Coolidge has never told you where he stands on any issue in the campaign."

Thus began the unlikely centerpiece of his stump speech—a one-man comedy sketch about the nation's famously reticent president, who had, in line with his reputation, made few public campaign appearances, allowing surrogates to make the case for his reelection.

"Tonight," Wheeler continued, "I'm going to bring him before you, and I'm going to ask him where he stands."

Wheeler dragged an empty chair to the front of the platform. Confusion and curiosity swept over the crowd. Wheeler stroked his bowtie, tugged at each of his coat sleeves, and then extended his hands in an imploring gesture toward the empty chair.

"Why, Mr. Coolidge—"

Men and women in the back strained to see if the president was really there.

"—why did you wait for Congress to expose the vile details of corruption in the Department of Justice before you consented to remove Attorney General Daugherty from office, when you, as well as all Washington, knew he was crooked?"

There was scattered applause as a few quick wits realized the gag.

"Tell me, Mr. Coolidge, why in the name of common sense you permitted detectives to shadow my house by day and by night and to follow—to shadow me from the office to the house and back again?"

The cheers grew louder, mixed with laughter.

"Oh, tell us, Mr. Coolidge, why you visited Ned McLean's party at his house when the Dempsey-Carpentier fight films first were shown, if you believe in law enforcement?"

More applause.

"Mr. Coolidge," he said with finality, "I ask you to tell the American people where you stand on any single issue."

A standing ovation followed, and Wheeler let it run its course. Only after the last whistle pierced the air did he turn to his audience.

"There, my friends," he concluded with a sweeping gesture, "is the usual silence that emanates from the White House. They don't dare come upon the public platform and discuss the record of the last three years of their administration."

The crowd roared its approval.

Over his ten months as a US senator, Wheeler had learned a thing or two about staging a spectacle. His campaign rallies rivaled anything a vaudeville producer or revivalist minister could muster, filling cavernous auditoriums at lunchtime and sports arenas at night. He paced the stage, back and forth, telling the sordid tale of corruption in the nation's capital. He spoke in a low voice with nervous intensity and then shocked the crowd with outbursts of verbal thunder. He welcomed hoots and hollers and even invited hecklers, soaking in the applause as he cut them down. One reporter likened the sound of a Wheeler rally to that of a baseball game.

Although a felony prosecution still hung over his head, the indictment turned out to be an asset on the campaign trail. Republicans did, of course, try to make an issue out of the pending charges. "There is the possibility," Coolidge's war secretary, John W. Weeks, mused in a speech broadcast nationally over the airwaves, "that the people of the United States will have a vice president found guilty of violation of the laws he has taken his oath to sustain." But despite his private worries about the impending trial, Wheeler attributed the size of his crowds, in part, to how his indictment bolstered his progressive credentials: "I believe they came out to see the man who had driven Harry Daugherty from office [and] who had been indicted by the Justice Department in return."

Over the course of a single day in Minneapolis, his five speeches reached the ears of twenty-five thousand voters. In Puyallup, Washington, some twenty thousand packed the state fairgrounds to hear him. And in Southern California, he drew a capacity crowd to the Hollywood Bowl, the open-air amphitheater where the Los Angeles Philharmonic staged summertime concerts. Rave reviews followed. "No prima donna, no golden throated tenor, no orchestra leader with a magic wand," concluded the *Los Angeles Examiner*, "has ever known the depth of applause that reverberated through the Hollywood hills about the Bowl when Senator Wheeler was finished."

Showered with adulation, optimism overcame him. Initially, Wheeler had expected the Progressive campaign to be little more than a symbolic protest against the two-party system. Now he felt assured of victory in the western states and believed he and La Follette had a fighting chance in New England. Impressive endorsements only boosted his newfound confidence. Activists like W. E. B. Du Bois, Jane Addams, John Dewey, and Helen Keller stood side-by-side with politicians like Smith Brookhart, Fiorello La Guardia, and Harold Ickes in backing the La Follette–Wheeler bid.

His hopes were further bolstered when a poll showed them winning six to nine states—enough to deny President Coolidge an Electoral College majority, throwing the presidential election to the House of Representatives and the vice presidential contest to the Senate.

That aroused speculation that the House, split three ways among Republicans, Democrats, and Progressives, might itself deadlock and fail to elect a president. Were that to happen, the Senate's choice as vice president— possibly Wheeler himself, who had already proven his ability to piece together an unlikely majority in Congress's upper chamber—would become acting president under the Constitution's Twelfth Amendment.

That prospect, however remote, inspired reverie among his supporters. "What will happen under the administration of Burton K. Wheeler as President of the United States?" asked the left-leaning *Nation*, in all seriousness. "A new kind of Attorney General certainly."

THE NEWS WAS encouraging, but Wheeler's greatest test as a candidate came on the evening of September 18, when he took the stage at the Ohio state fairgrounds just outside of Columbus—the last redoubt of a mortally wounded but still dangerous Harry Daugherty.

He steeled himself for the worst.

One persistent rumor held that Daugherty himself would be in the audience. Another suggested that a process server would mount the podium and interrupt his speech by serving him with official notice of a civil suit, filed by a woman who claimed to have been a passenger in his car when it went over the edge of the road outside Butte, Montana. (The implication was that Wheeler and the plaintiff had been romantically involved.)

Under the circumstances, some candidates might have pulled their punches. Not Wheeler, who declared that "blackmail suits and framed indictments will not stop me in this campaign." Instead, he unleashed a ferocious barrage against "the Daugherty system" and the band of political lackeys he termed the "Ohio gang."

The crowd's reaction astonished him. These five thousand Ohioans shouted and cheered and roared in laughter. At Wheeler's first utterance of the name "Daugherty," he heard hisses. When he denounced the "corrupt practices" of the former attorney general, he heard applause.

"I expected to be run out of the city when I came," he told his audience. "But I find that you are as well acquainted with the record of some of your residents as we investigators in Washington."

By now Wheeler had honed his theatrical instincts, and he paused to survey the crowd.

"I challenge Daugherty himself if he is in this hall," he said finally, "or any of his friends to come forward on this platform and point out to you one administration in the history of this government so venal and corrupt as the administration which they participated in for a time."

A hush fell over the assembly. Heads swiveled. If Daugherty did appear on the platform, he might plausibly point to the scandal-plagued administrations of James Buchanan or Ulysses S. Grant. Then again, Daugherty would not willingly invite such comparisons.

In the event, no one stepped forward; the former attorney general had opted to spend a quiet night at home.

The next day, Daugherty released a statement denouncing the Progressives' vice presidential nominee as "a common liar."

"Wheeler has come and gone," it added, "and Columbus still stands."

THE SAME COULD have been said for the country's two-party system.

Wheeler electrified his audience and energized the American Left, but all that enthusiasm was not enough to overcome the challenges common to most third-party bids. Hampered by shoddy organization at the state level, Progressives struggled to convert genuine passion into actual votes. La Follette and Wheeler failed to qualify for the ballot in West Virginia and in California were forced to run as the nominal candidates of the Socialist Party of America—a real handicap amid lingering anti-Red sentiment. A huge disparity in fundraising also dragged down the ticket; Republicans raised $4 million, the Progressives little more than $200,000.

An uneven performance by the head of the ticket only compounded its woes. To preserve his health, La Follette opted for radio addresses over in-person rallies but never could master the emerging medium, shouting into the microphone rather than speaking calmly and directly to the listener on the other end (as Coolidge managed to do). Over the final weeks of the election, when the time came for La Follette to address crowds in the flesh, he made a disastrous last-minute change in campaign strategy. The plan had always been for La Follette to follow Wheeler's route through the rural West and Midwest, where the Progressives' supporters were concentrated; Wheeler had made the initial sales pitch there, and the head of the ticket was to close the deal. With dwindling campaign funds, however, La Follette opted instead to barnstorm through East Coast cities where the Progressives were long shots, at best.

In the end, despite the optimistic polling and fanatical crowds, hopes for an Electoral College deadlock proved a pipe dream. With the twenties roaring and postwar prosperity booming, American voters were not ready to rock the boat. A majority didn't even show up to the polls on November 4, 1924, but those who did—slightly less than half the eligible electorate—returned silent Mr. Coolidge to the White House in a landslide vote for "normalcy." The Progressives won only one state, La Follette's native Wisconsin, and its thirteen electoral votes, though they finished second, ahead of Democrats, in another eleven states. Overall, President Coolidge won a commanding majority of 382 electoral votes—including, in a stinging loss for Wheeler, the four from Montana.

Even as Wheeler had always known that pocketbook issues decided most elections, he had hoped that 1924 would be different. In an election night statement, he sounded a note of despair: "The people voted . . . for what they believed would mean material gain to themselves," it read. "The exposure of corruption here in Washington apparently made no impression upon them."

He immediately departed on a long-delayed hunting trip, in what seemed like his last chance to relax for some time. His criminal case would come to trial sometime in the next year, and on top of everything else, his wife Lulu was now three and a half months pregnant with their sixth (and presumably last) child.

After two months of nonstop campaigning, he would need to regain his strength for the battle to come. Even after all his travails, Burton Wheeler was not out of the woods yet.

37

"He Is Asking Justice"

When Judge Frank Dietrich finally gaveled the trial of *United States of America v. Burton K. Wheeler* to order on the morning of April 16, 1925, six months had passed since the election and twelve since Daugherty's resignation. But the criminal charges against Montana's junior senator, alleging that he'd illegally helped an oilman secure drilling rights from the Department of the Interior, had yet to fade from the national conversation. It wasn't just that a trial of a sitting senator was exceedingly rare, though of course it was: Wheeler's was only the fifth in US history. No, what really animated public interest in the case were the fundamental principles wrapped up in Wheeler's fate.

There was the freedom of Americans to criticize (or even slander) officers of their government: if a US senator was not free from what appeared to be a nakedly vindictive, politically motivated prosecution, no one would be.

There was Congress's oversight power: if the jury found Wheeler guilty, future legislators would surely think twice before investigating the Department of Justice, or any organ of the executive branch, for that matter.

Finally, there was rule of law: if the legal system failed to repel this injection of politics into the criminal process, the once-twinned concepts of law and justice would continue to drift apart, casting doubt on the notion that America was, to quote John Adams, "a government of laws, not of men."

With the entire country watching, the site of this great test of principles—the town of Great Falls, Montana, straddling the upper Missouri River—had taken on the appearance of a traveling circus. Crowds swarmed the entrance to the federal building, hoping for a courtroom seat. Newly strung telegraph wires converged on the US Customs office, the temporary headquarters for the dozen or so national press correspondents covering the case. Some seventy-five subpoenaed witnesses fought with 120 prospective jurors over the city's few remaining hotel rooms. A spiritualist minister who claimed to have predicted Wheeler's election to the Senate years in advance, just as clearly as she could foretell oil strikes, advertised for her lecture series. And, on the outskirts of town, a group of Blackfeet camped out in support for "Chief Bearshirt," as they affectionately called the man who had defended the interests of their tribe as their attorney (and now as their senator) for more than a decade.

Among all the outsiders, though, most conspicuous were the Bureau of Investigation agents—an entire platoon of them—who had swarmed into town a week before. "Great Falls is busy trying to solve the puzzle of why there are so many Department of Justice agents in the city," reported the *New York Times*. "What they are doing here and what possible emergency makes their presence necessary are matters of conjecture." US Attorney John Slattery, the lead prosecutor in the case and the top-ranking Justice Department official in Montana, would only tell the *Times* that "agents are always on hand when cases of importance are about to be called for trial."

Not necessarily. This surge of detectives—orchestrated by John Edgar Hoover in Washington via telegram and long-distance telephone—was both extraordinary and at the same time entirely predicable. Senator Wheeler had shown no mercy in his inquiry of the Department of Justice, and the Bureau was now returning the favor.

As their confidential reports revealed, some agents were there on anodyne assignments: one was tasked with keeping Hoover informed about the latest courtroom developments, and others were standing by to track down new investigative leads raised during the trial. But most were there to vacuum up any information that might give the prosecution a leg up. As Special Agent W. W. Spain reported, he was "checking hotel registers, tracing telephone calls, examining newspaper files." Special Agents George Costello, J. H. Smart, and W. F. Scery, on the other hand, were busy with "surveillance of persons whose activities might be prejudicial to the Government." Many others described their activities in more cryptic terms, writing that they were "engaged in under cover work" or, simply, "confidential matters." All told, some twenty-five special agents had converged on this town of twenty-five thousand.

Wheeler tried to make light of the situation, quipping that Great Falls looked "like a Justice Department convention." Jokes aside, however, the trial was no laughing matter—and Wheeler knew it. A guilty verdict would spell immediate death to his political career. By statute, he'd be legally disqualified from holding future office, and the Senate would almost certainly expel him, no matter what Senator Borah had found. A guilty verdict might also claim his freedom, with the statute carrying a maximum penalty of two years behind bars.

The possibility of a prison sentence was a terrible thing to live with, especially when Lulu Wheeler was nine months pregnant back in Washington. The questions must have gnawed at his sense of fatherhood. Would he miss the child's entire infancy? How would he provide for his growing family? Lulu had always been by his side at his most difficult moments, and it pained him to be two thousand miles away in her time of need. Though in good health, Lulu had just turned forty, and any pregnancy at that age, no matter how seemingly free from complications, warranted special concern. Naturally, he worried.

It wasn't that he lacked confidence in his case. Wheeler believed wholeheartedly in his own innocence, and he relished the chance to deny the charges on the witness stand, under oath. Nor did he lack faith in his counsel. Assembled at the defense table was a legal dream team. There was Sam Ford, a former state attorney general who, as a leading Montana Republican, was crossing party lines to defend his friend. There was William F. O'Leary, a legendary criminal defense attorney from Great Falls and undisputed master of cross-examination; and James H. Baldwin, Wheeler's law partner and his successor as one of Butte's preeminent litigators. Those three formidable attorneys were a match for any prosecutor, but to lead his defense Wheeler had enlisted a true heavyweight—Sen. Tom Walsh, hero of the Teapot Dome hearings. Walsh brought a sharp legal mind and decades of experience in private practice to the proceedings, to be sure, but his greatest contribution was his public stature. It was exceedingly rare for a sitting senator to act as a defense attorney in a criminal trial, and Walsh's appearance by Wheeler's side, his bushy mustache and permanently arched eyebrows instantly recognizable to any Montanan, spoke volumes.

And yet, despite Wheeler's confidence, not even the legal services of Montana's senior senator could guarantee an acquittal in this case.

This was no murder trial, where the jury was asked to decide a simple question of fact. In this case, the basic facts were not in dispute. Wheeler had received a legal retainer from Gordon Campbell, and he had intervened on Campbell's behalf at the Interior Department. Set against the statute, which prohibited members of Congress from accepting compensation in return for "any service rendered . . . in relation to any proceeding or claim . . . in which the United States is a party," those facts looked incriminating enough. It took more than a little nuance to understand that neither fact on its own constituted a crime; the law required the prosecution to prove *a connection between the two.*

It remained to be seen whether the twelve laymen now empaneled—four merchants, three farmers, two smelter operators, a coal operator, an apartment house manager, and a factory worker—could really be expected to apply the same supple legal reasoning to the case as Senator Borah. Most ordinary Americans weren't even aware that it was perfectly normal for members of Congress to maintain a private legal practice while in office. The judge would do his best to explain the relevant law to the jurors, but the decision was ultimately their own.

Even if the jury could be trusted to reason its way through the law, however, experience made it painfully clear that a fair trial was no guarantee. With his railway injunction, Harry Daugherty had shown that a court proceeding could act as a fig leaf for the naked exercise of power. More recently, Wheeler's indictment was proof positive that the Justice Department could pervert the criminal process for political ends, and his enemies had clearly not moved on. A bitter Harry Daugherty had recently announced that he was writing a tell-all memoir to "answer all my critics." Billy Burns, meanwhile, with his history of jury tampering, was now back in command of the Burns International Detective Agency.

And even if those two men chose to stay on the sidelines, there were still the twenty-five Bureau of Investigation agents who were making themselves at home in Great Falls. Judge Dietrich himself had wondered about them and took the extraordinary precaution of sequestering the entire jury at a local hotel for the duration of the trial. Supervised by two special deputies under instruction to never leave them unattended, the jurors would be allowed no contact with the outside world. No newspapers, no phone calls—and certainly no conversations with detectives.

There was a still more troubling concern that Wheeler, in all his hubris, couldn't acknowledge. Daugherty had been out of office for a full year, and yet the Department of Justice continued to pursue a conviction, first under Attorney General Stone, a lawyer whose integrity was beyond reproach, and now under Stone's handpicked chief of the department's criminal division, Assistant Attorney General William J. "Wild Bill" Donovan. Upon arriving in Washington in August of 1924, Donovan (who as US attorney in Buffalo had played a role in bringing Alexander Fink and hence Roxie Stinson to Wheeler's attention) undertook a thorough review of the Wheeler case. After reviewing the evidence, Donovan not only ordered the Montana prosecution to move forward. With the avid help of Special Assistant to the Attorney General John S. Pratt, he also sought and obtained a long-threatened second indictment against Wheeler in the District of Columbia for conspiracy to defraud the government.

The actions of Stone and Donovan, neither of whom had any history of personal animus toward Wheeler, were hard to square with Borah's sweeping exoneration or with Wheeler's own protestations of a frame-up. A haunting possibility hung over the trial's opening moments. Did the Department of Justice know something about the case that everyone else did not?

Now, as the trial got underway, US Attorney John Slattery seemed to answer that question when he rose for his opening statement and announced a sensational development. Indeed, the public didn't know all the facts. The prosecution, he promised, would introduce damning new evidence of Wheeler's guilt in the form of testimony from a surprise witness, a lawyer from New York who was not under subpoena and whose identity the prosecution could therefore keep secret.

"I won't divulge his name," Slattery told reporters after court adjourned for the day, "because I don't want to tip off the defense. The lawyer will be here. Wheeler knows his name."

"GEORGE B. HAYES!"

The trial had entered its fourth day, and everyone in the courtroom was beginning to wonder when Slattery would make good on his threat. Over the preceding days, a parade of prosecution witnesses had merely rehashed the old evidence without offering proof that Wheeler had accepted compensation for prosecuting a claim before the Interior Department, in violation of federal law.

Now, as Slattery called out the name of his mystery witness, he smiled broadly. His cocounsel, an experienced Justice Department litigator, winked at the newspaper reporters, as if to say, "Here's the moment you've been waiting for."

George B. Hayes. The name didn't register at first with Wheeler. In unison with the rest of the crowd, the defendant turned to see who would answer the call. And then, as he watched a gray-haired man with sharp, angular features, built like a middle-aged boxer, stride toward the witness chair, it hit him. It had taken him a moment because the Brookhart-Wheeler committee had interviewed 115 separate witnesses, but now he remembered clearly. Hayes was the New York lawyer who had gotten mixed up in a bootlegging ring—who told the select committee about Jess Smith's forays into the illicit liquor trade—who sat there, red faced, while his dissatisfied client, bootlegger John Gorini, told the committee that Hayes "would kill his mother for five cents, I think."

Anyone who remembered would surely have wondered what this disreputable attorney could add to the prosecution's case.

It didn't take long for Hayes and Slattery to get to the point.

"Do you know the defendant in this case?"

"I do."

"When and where did you meet him?"

"In the lobby of the Waldorf-Astoria Hotel, New York City, March 16, 1923, between four and seven." Hayes spoke at a machine-gun pace, almost shouting his words. "It was sometime between then. I can not tell you what hour exactly."

The meeting, he said, had been set up by their mutual friend Eddie Booth—the solicitor of the Interior Department and the same lawyer Wheeler had asked to look into Gordon Campbell's case.

"I went to the Waldorf and had him paged," Hayes said of Wheeler. "I think I met him near the main desk. After a moment or two Wheeler said something about some oil leases claimed by one Gordon Campbell, who he told me was in Montana."

The essence of Hayes's story was this: Wheeler and Booth wanted to "fix" Campbell's oil leases in return for a handsome commission. The problem was Wheeler's status as a senator. Under the law, Wheeler himself could not represent Campbell before the Interior Department and needed a "figurehead" or "dummy" to stand in his place. And because he was sailing for Europe the very next day, it was urgent that he find someone right away.

Hayes protested that he knew "nothing about oil litigation or land laws." Never mind that, Wheeler told him. He and Booth had it all figured out. When the leases came up for argument, Booth would tell Hayes exactly what to do—which motions to file, which statutes to cite. If they all just worked together and kept their lips sealed, the leases would be fixed in Campbell's favor, and the Montana oilman would shower them with generosity.

That brought Hayes to that most crucial issue—the question of compensation. Hayes and Wheeler, the senator allegedly told him, could split the fees "fifty-fifty."

"Did he say there was millions in it?" Slattery asked.

"I think he stated it would run into a very substantial figure," Hayes said. "I think he mentioned millions."

Wheeler just stared at the witness. If he couldn't find a way to prove that the story was a complete fabrication, he'd soon be behind bars.

IT WAS A humbling moment, and Wheeler might have used it to reflect on his actions since February 19, 1924, the date he launched his crusade against Harry Daugherty from the floor of the Senate. His intentions had always been virtuous, no question, but he'd indulged in questionable tactics along the way. Charges made on the basis of distorted truths. Baseless allegations aired under the protection of congressional immunity. Innocent parties tainted by a careless word. Now it seemed as if the entire trial had been designed to teach him a lesson—to give him a taste of his own medicine. Did Wheeler, understanding in this instant better than anyone how it felt to be unjustly accused, feel a pang of remorse?

If he did, he quickly moved on; mounting his defense was as urgent as ever. Wheeler's private knowledge that Hayes had perjured himself didn't make his testimony any less damning. And damning it was. As if to emphasize the point, the instant Hayes stepped down from the stand, the prosecution rested its case.

At this moment, the jury would have almost certainly voted to convict. Hayes had filled in a gaping hole in the prosecution's case, painting the picture of a senator who, far from simply performing a favor for one of his constituents, had intervened at the Interior Department for his own personal benefit. Unless his story was discredited, the jurors would have little reasonable doubt that Wheeler had violated the conflict-of-interest statute.

But the testimony cut beyond those immediate concerns. For Wheeler's critics—and especially his enemies—Hayes offered up a delicious irony. That self-righteous senator who denounced Harry Daugherty for circumventing the regular legal process in the name of personal gain now stood accused of the same thing. All those who had swum so shamelessly in Washington's pond of corruption, only to be called out by Wheeler, now had reason to gloat.

Wheeler couldn't wait to wipe the smirk off their faces. How exactly to accomplish that, though, wasn't clear. He huddled with Walsh and his other lawyers.

The defense team first turned to the date of his alleged meeting with Hayes: March 16, 1923. The witness hadn't pulled it out of thin air. Wheeler really had been at the Waldorf Astoria that day, having checked in alone early that morning. He realized that whoever at the Department of Justice was orchestrating this frame-up had seized on the fact that his was the only name on the hotel register. They must have assumed he'd have trouble proving an alibi.

But Wheeler hadn't been alone for long. That same morning, a few hours after he checked in, Lulu Wheeler had arrived from Montana. After the long train journey, Lulu never bothered to stop at the front desk and add her own name to the register, but she was with him for the rest of the day. During the afternoon of March 16, when the senator was supposedly inviting a complete stranger into a criminal conspiracy, the Wheelers were actually in the shops of Fifth Avenue, building up a wardrobe for their impending trip to Europe. After rushing back to change their clothes, they dined at the home of socialite Florence Jaffray "Daisy" Harriman, then saw an opera at the Met with Colonel Edward M. House, former confidential adviser to President Wilson.

Those three people could account for nearly every minute of his day—a solid alibi indeed—if only Walsh could put them on the witness stand. Unfortunately, all three were on the East Coast, a two-day train ride away, and Lulu Wheeler, at nine months pregnant, would be unable to travel at all. Walsh could always ask the court for a recess, but the delay would only give Hayes's story more time to sink in with the jury. It wasn't ideal.

Next the defense team considered witness impeachment. Wheeler already knew that Hayes had been mixed up in a bootlegging conspiracy; that was the reason he'd testified before the select committee in March of 1924. Now a flood of telegrams from friendly sources in New York revealed that Hayes was under a mountain of legal trouble. At the time the Justice Department recruited him as a voluntary witness, there had been four outstanding income tax judgments against him. Having neglected to file returns for the years 1917 to 1920, Hayes owed the US Treasury the fantastic sum of $292,191.33. And his legal woes didn't end there. Two former clients were suing him in federal court for the recovery of $15,000, alleged to have been "obtained under false pretenses," and the Manhattan district attorney was investigating three separate complaints alleging that he'd withheld funds from his clients. Hayes was in so much trouble that he'd recently relocated to Havana, Cuba, seeking refuge from litigants and tax collectors.

Would the jury really believe the testimony of a man who cheated his clients and swindled the government? Especially once they knew how much leverage the Department of Justice had over him? A man might say anything, even under oath, to avoid tax evasion charges and the repayment of more than a quarter million in back taxes.

Within hours, the defense team had lined up five witnesses, one from Buffalo, two from New York, and one more from Washington, DC, who they hoped would destroy Hayes's credibility with the jury. These witnesses, however, came with the same drawback as those who could establish Wheeler's alibi—they were a two day's journey from Montana. Nothing would stop the prosecution from using that time to summon its own character witnesses, while the jurors spent two nights locked in a hotel, replaying Hayes's story in their minds.

In the end, Wheeler and his counsel made the risky decision to forgo any delay. Instead, they would strike back at once with the witnesses already on hand.

The jury would hear Eddie Booth, the Interior Department solicitor who supposedly brokered the meeting between Hayes and Wheeler at the Waldorf Astoria, deny that any such thing ever happened.

They would hear Arthur B. Melzner, the law clerk for the select committee, explain that when he introduced Hayes to Wheeler before the select committee's hearing of March 21, 1924—a year after their supposed conference at the Waldorf Astoria—the two men acted as if they'd never met before.

Finally, they would hear William G. Feely, an experienced Washington, DC, litigator, testify that he and he alone had represented Gordon Campbell's interests before the Interior Department and that Wheeler had never been involved, through a "dummy" attorney or otherwise.

Important testimony, all of it. Ultimately, however, the defense's case would hinge on the testimony of its star witness—the defendant himself. Burton Wheeler would take the stand, swear to tell the truth, and offer the jury his full-throated refutation of George B. Hayes's story.

In this Great Falls courtroom, it would be the word of a Montana senator against that of a New York lawyer. After a year of fighting in Washington, at least Wheeler was now on home turf. As usual, he liked his odds, but overconfidence can be a fatal flaw.

WITH A SMILE, Wheeler settled into the witness chair late in the morning of April 22. The other defense witnesses had just given their testimony, sowing the seeds of reasonable doubt in the jurors' minds.

Now it was his turn, and he angled his body toward the jury box. Whenever possible, he would directly address the twelve men who held his fate in their hands. No one had to tell him the importance of eye contact.

Walsh, in charge of direct examination, got right to the point. "Now, Senator," he said, "were you present on Monday when the witness Hayes testified?"

"I certainly was."

"What have you to say to having met him in the corridor of the Waldorf Astoria hotel in the city of New York—"

Wheeler was so eager to deny Hayes's tale that he interrupted his own lawyer.

"I will say that I—" he started, before Walsh cut him off with, "Just a moment please."

Wheeler was used to asking the questions, not answering them. But in this one instance he would need to learn a little restraint.

Walsh then finished his question: "—just immediately prior to your departure for Europe, in the spring of 1923."

"I will say," Wheeler began again, "that I never met him in the hotel corridor of the Waldorf Astoria hotel in the city of New York. I never met this man Hayes but once in my life. The only time I ever met him was when he was subpoenaed before the committee in the Daugherty investigation down there in the city of Washington. The first time I ever heard his name was when it was mentioned in the course of the Daugherty investigation by a witness named Gorini, a bootlegger, and Hayes was Gorini's attorney, and was mixed up, as I recall the testimony—"

"Just a moment!" interjected Slattery.

"—with the bootleg ring in New York."

Slattery turned to the judge. "Now," he said, "we object to that as a voluntary statement, and not responsive to any question."

Judge Dietrich sustained the objection—he would not allow gratuitous narratives from the witness—but Wheeler had lost nothing in trying.

Walsh had the next question ready, anyway.

"All right," he said. "Who introduced Hayes to you when he was called before the committee?"

"I was introduced to him in the anteroom of the committee by Mr. Melzner, the clerk of the committee."

"Did you ever discuss with Hayes the affairs of Gordon Campbell?"

"Never, at any time in my life."

"What of the engagement that Mr. Hayes says he made for you?"

"Why, there wasn't a blessed thing to that at all. There was no such engagement."

"Now," Walsh said, "I want you to tell this jury how you spent the day of March 16, 1923, the day you were in New York, and the day prior to your departure for Europe."

Looking straight into the eyes of the jurors, Wheeler shared his entire alibi, sparing no detail. He told the jurors about the letters of introduction that Colonel House had written for them, to be presented at American embassies and consulates in Europe. About dinner at Daisy Harriman's. About the Hartman trunk Wheeler bought for their belongings. About how Lulu tried on so many hats that they remained at Avedon's Fifth Avenue well past closing.

When he finished, it was clear that he'd never had a moment—let alone half an hour, as Hayes had alleged—to forge a baroque criminal conspiracy to defraud the government. And by invoking the names of House, Harriman, and his wife, he strongly implied that they would back up his story, if only they could be present.

"Where is Mrs. Wheeler at the present?" Walsh asked, just to drive the point home.

"Mrs. Wheeler is confined at home, because we are expecting the arrival of a baby at the house."

"When?"

"Well, any day."

"Is her physical condition such as to permit her to be present here?"

"No. She—we have a nurse at the house at the present time who is staying with her and she is expecting to be confined any moment."

Direct examination went on for several hours. Walsh was beyond thorough, shrewdly asking every question he expected Slattery to put to his witness, stealing the prosecutor's thunder. In the process, Wheeler got a chance to explain everything in his own terms, including, crucially, why he had intervened on Gordon Campbell's behalf at the Interior Department and why it didn't constitute a crime.

"You did tell Campbell," Walsh asked, "that after you got to Washington you would take this permit up?"

"Certainly, just what I would do for any constituent."

"Did you tell him you were going to take it up with Solicitor Booth of the Interior Department?"

"I probably did. What I did was as a United States senator, not as Campbell's attorney."

"You were still his attorney when you went to Washington?"

"Absolutely—the firm was," Wheeler answered. "That did not bar me from doing for Campbell a favor any more than for one of these jurymen."

By the time Walsh turned the courtroom over to the prosecution for cross-examination, there was little for Slattery to go over.

That didn't stop sparks from flying.

"On the occasion," Slattery said at one point, "when you landed in Washington—"

"I did not *land* in Washington," Wheeler corrected the prosecutor. The way Slattery said "landed" had a bite to it, as if he were suggesting that Wheeler had been there on a nefarious mission. "I *arrived* there."

In his retort, Slattery invoked Harry Daugherty's old charge that Wheeler was secretly in Moscow's employ: "Perhaps I have that mixed with when you landed from Russia."

"I did not land from Russia," Wheeler growled. "I landed from England."

All their verbal fencing accomplished little, aside from giving Wheeler another chance to denounce Hayes's story as perjury.

"Nothing was ever more false than that statement," Wheeler declared, "if it was made to you or anybody else."

"It was made right on the stand there in this court," Slattery shot back. "It was false."

"You heard it made right in front of you there, didn't you?"

"Yes, and I say it was false, and it is false."

"I understand why you take your version of it, Senator."

"Yes, and I understand why you make some of the statements you do, Mr. Slattery."

WHEELER WAS DINING at his hotel when the US marshal found him. The verdict was in.

In his closing arguments, Slattery had admonished the jury not to fall prey to sympathy. "A jury's duty is a solemn one," he reminded them. "A juror's oath is not an idle oath. Sympathies and prejudice are enemies of justice. The government has been fair. I say to you the government has proved all that it said it would prove."

Walsh had offered his retort: "The district attorney tells you he is fair. Whenever I hear a man tell me that he is honest, I then begin to doubt his integrity." He then addressed Slattery's comment about sympathy. "Senator Wheeler is not asking sympathy; he is asking justice, and acquittal of a baseless charge. Were he even, gentlemen of the jury, capable of entertaining such a thought, I would not be here to represent him. He disdains it, as do I."

"In my judgement, gentlemen, there is no case here," Walsh continued. "There is no evidence upon which you could condemn a jail bird or a street walker. Much less a man who through the way he has commended himself to the people of the state of Montana, has been elevated by them to the highest position, official position in their gift, and who, for four years with distinction represented the government of the United States as its legal representative in this court." Walsh told the jury that none of the telegrams, letters, or contracts the prosecution had introduced before calling Hayes as a witness proved Wheeler's guilt. "There is nothing whatever in this evidence on which you would hang a dog. If that had been all the prosecution had to offer I would have asked the court to direct you, and I honestly believe he would have instructed you, to return a verdict of acquittal. But if you find a verdict of guilty you will find it on the testimony of George B. Hayes and make a perjurer out of Wheeler. Hayes's story is perjury or a pipe dream, one way or the other."

As Wheeler hurried out of his hotel, bound for the courthouse, he was handed an urgent telegram from Washington, DC. Just before entering the packed courtroom, he peeked at the message, and an irrepressible smile lit up his face.

The jury had already filed in its box, and as Wheeler approached the front of the room, one juror noticed the senator's beaming face. The juror smiled back.

Judge Dietrich gaveled the courtroom to order and turned to the jury. "Have you agreed upon a verdict?"

"We have, your honor," said the foreman, Albert E. Fousek.

The jury had been out for nearly two hours—most of which they used to dine on the tab of the district court. In fact, the jurors had taken less than half an hour for their actual deliberations. Evidently, there'd been no struggle toward unanimity.

A slip of paper was passed up to the court clerk. The judge warned the courtroom against demonstrations, and the silent crowd waited for the clerk to read the verdict. Wheeler's fate, bound up with more abstract notions of justice and the rule of law, hung in the balance.

Not guilty on all three counts.

Before the clerk could even finish, there was a rush toward the bench. Friends crowded around a smiling Wheeler, offering their congratulations.

Even Slattery held out his hand. "It was just a case for me," he said. "I am the district attorney and had no choice other than to prosecute." There were a lot of things Wheeler might have wanted to say or do to the prosecutor. As it was, he found himself in a forgiving mood and simply shook Slattery's hand.

A huge crowd swarmed Wheeler, and a smaller one encircled Senator Walsh. The hero of Teapot Dome had now corrected a second historic injustice.

"I want to say," Wheeler shouted, "no man ever had an abler defender than I did in Senator Walsh. I can never repay him for what he has done for me, and what I say about the senator applies to my other counsel."

Amid the scrum, an old friend—a butcher he'd known in Butte, who now lived in Seattle and had traveled out for the trial—pressed close to Wheeler. "I've got someone," he whispered, "who'll throw Hayes into the Missouri River, and no one will ever know about it."

Wheeler hesitated for a moment. These people had put him through unbelievable, unnecessary trials. And the things he'd proven himself capable of would have shocked his younger self. He'd aired baseless allegations and put a sociopathic liar on the witness stand. But murder?

"No," was all he said.

The butcher was persistent. "Well," he pressed, "you find out what his haunts are in New York and I'll have someone take care of him there."

Wheeler just shook his head again.

The celebration raged on for more than twenty minutes. The crowd's joy redoubled when it learned the contents of Wheeler's telegram, the message that had brought a smile to his face even before he'd learned his fate.

It was the kind of thing a Hollywood screenwriter might dream up.

The cable was from their family physician, Dr. Daniel Davis, of Washington, DC. At 6:45 p.m., just as the jury was about to cast its first and final ballot, Lulu Wheeler had delivered a baby girl, seven pounds, four ounces.

Mother and child were both "doing nicely."

Epilogue

"The Triumph of Justice"

J ustice prevailed in Great Falls, Montana.

    The case of *United States of America v. Burton K. Wheeler*, declared the editors of the *Philadelphia Record* shortly after the verdict, had been "one of the most contemptible and vindictive political persecutions ever known in this country." Reflecting on the decision, they considered what might have been its legacy had Wheeler lost: "The speedy acquittal clears the air of a good deal of hypocrisy and crooked partisanship."

    Exactly why the Department of Justice so doggedly pursued its case against Wheeler, going so far as to frame him with perjured testimony, would forever remain a mystery. For his part, Wheeler was willing to give Harlan Fiske Stone the benefit of the doubt, reasoning that someone had misled the reformist attorney general with false evidence. Suspicion naturally fell upon prosecutor John S. Pratt, whom Stone had kept on despite his ties to Harry Daugherty. Pratt was the first Justice Department official to interview George B. Hayes, and together the two of them had every opportunity to concoct a story that, at face value, offered proof of Wheeler's guilt. Whoever doctored the evidence, however—and Wheeler himself suspected Assistant Attorney General Donovan, no stranger to dirty tricks later in his career as America's wartime spymaster—the act ultimately underscored the case for taking the department in a new direction.

    After four years of Daughertyism, the Department of Justice now had the chance to make a clean break—to declare its independence from political tug-of-war and, going forward, simply enforce the law of the land. No more black-bag operations to avenge political slights. No more vendettas disguised as criminal prosecutions. No more fixers propping up their feet on the attorney general's desk. Though it would forever remain an arm of the executive branch and thus under the control of a politically minded president, the department could, if it policed itself, pursue justice with near-judicial impartiality.

That was certainly the goal of Attorney General Stone, who—as if to advertise his department's commitment to reform—placed his own predecessor in his legal crosshairs.

Although Stone deplored Wheeler's penchant for unfounded allegations and hearsay evidence, he followed the Daugherty hearings with intense interest, and one line of inquiry in particular aroused his suspicions—that of the American Metal Company. There were rumors that several Washington power brokers had received a cut of the $7 million payout, which Alien Property Custodian Thomas W. Miller had approved on the basis of flimsy evidence. During the hearings, Wheeler implied that Harry Daugherty, who had apparently intervened in the case through the person of Jess Smith, must have been among them.

Stone realized he could verify Wheeler's charge even without access to the bank accounts Mal Daugherty was still jealously guarding. Although the Liberty Bonds issued in the transaction were bearer bonds with no record kept of their ownership, they did included coupons that their owners would clip out every six months and deposit at their local banks. Acting on his own initiative, Stone began tracing those coupon payments through the records of the Treasury Department. "As far as I know," he told a friend, "it had never occurred to anyone else that they could be traced in this fashion." It was extraordinary for an attorney general, with all the demands of his high office, to conduct his own investigation, but these were extraordinary times. Eventually, credentialed accountants at the Bureau of Investigation took over, tracing $50,000 worth of Liberty bonds to Miller; $112,000 to John T. King, the Republican party official who brokered the alleged bribe; and $224,000 to the Midland National Bank of Washington Court House, Ohio, and accounts belonging to Jess Smith and Harry Daugherty.

Finally—incontrovertible proof.

In January 1926, US Attorney Emory Buckner of the Southern District of New York hauled the former attorney general before a grand jury to explain himself. Daugherty demurred and filed the handwritten statement which appears as the epigraph to this book. "I refuse to testify and answer questions put to me," it concluded, "because the answer I might give or make and the testimony I might give might tend to incriminate me." As if that statement wasn't enough to stoke suspicions, it was also revealed that he'd recently taken the relevant ledger sheets from his brother's bank to "the Shack" at Deer Creek, Ohio, where, inexplicably, he'd burned them.

Despite these challenges—lip-sealed witnesses, destroyed evidence, not to mention the fact that the statute of limitations had run out for a bribery charge—prosecutors managed to build a conspiracy case, and in September of 1926, Daugherty and his codefendant Miller stood trial in a New York federal courtroom. (King was also indicted but died of pneumonia before the case came to trial.) The jury voted nine to three for conviction but could not reach unanimity, with some jurors reporting that they would have convicted the defendants for bribery but found the conspiracy charge too technical. The judge declared a hung jury. US Attorney Emory, determined to claim justice, retried the case the following February. This time, the jury unanimously found Miller guilty but deadlocked again over Daugherty, voting eleven to one to convict. A lone holdout, described in contemporary accounts as "the florist at the Hotel Astor," could not be persuaded to send the former attorney general to prison.

Emory saw the writing on the wall. If two juries had failed to reach consensus, a third probably would, as well, and he had to weigh his thirst for justice against the great demands on his office's resources. In open court he declared a *nolle prosequi*—effectively, a request to dismiss the case. "I have never tried a case three times in my life," he said wanly. The judge granted the motion. Daugherty was a free man.

The former attorney general rose to address the court. Choking back tears and leaning on a cane, he was a shadow of the man who once commanded an entire Chicago courtroom by simply setting foot inside it. "May it please the court," he said, "perhaps I am taking a liberty few men could take. I am the only attorney general, I believe, except one that has ever been tried for a felony. I am innocent of this charge." Until his death in 1941 at the age of eighty-one, Harry Daugherty would live a bitter existence dedicated to salvaging his legacy—an impossible project he began at this moment.

Two hundred miles away, in Washington, Burton Wheeler would not let his old nemesis have the last word on the matter. "The jury," Wheeler said in a statement, "in convicting Miller and disagreeing on Daugherty, convicted the man who was merely one of the pawns through which

Daugherty worked. Daugherty was the real brains of the conspiracy and should have been convicted."

He put his best face on the muddled result. "He is, of course, convicted in the eyes of the public," he said, "and the verdict is a further vindication of the work of the investigating committee here in Washington."

IN THE END, Thomas W. Miller's eleven-month stay at the Atlanta penitentiary (shortened by parole from an eighteen-month sentence) was the only prison time arising from Wheeler's Senate hearings. Daugherty would never face trial again, and while federal prosecutors, to their credit, did seek and obtain convictions against five coconspirators behind the Dempsey-Carpentier fight film, the judge in their case ultimately levied fines in lieu of jail time.

For Tom Walsh, the results from the government's Teapot Dome prosecutions were nearly as disappointing, despite the earnest efforts of President Coolidge's special counsel. Of the three principals in the scandal—former Interior secretary Albert Fall and oil executives Edward L. Doheny and Harry Sinclair—only Fall was ever convicted. In 1929, a jury found him guilty of bribery and conspiracy to defraud the government. He served nine months of a one-year prison sentence. The following year, a jury acquitted Doheny, declaring the oilman not guilty of offering the same bribe that Fall had been found guilty of accepting. Sinclair, meanwhile, won his own acquittal on the underlying charges—although he later served six months in the District of Columbia jail for contempt of court, having hired William J. Burns to shadow members of his jury. (One was offered "a car as long as this block" if he voted to acquit.)

More encouraging were the outcomes of the twin civil suits arising from the oil-lease scandal. In 1927, a unanimous Supreme Court voided the Teapot Dome and Elk Hills leases as "made fraudulently by means of collusion and conspiracy" among Fall, Doheny, and Sinclair. The oil-rich lands in Wyoming and California were returned to the Navy Department, and the nation's highest court went out of its way to condemn Fall as "a faithless public officer."

WHEELER, TOO, COULD claim one unalloyed victory. On January 17, 1927, the Supreme Court of the United States handed down its unanimous opinion in the case of *John J. McGrain v. Mal S. Daugherty*. It was a landmark decision that gave teeth to Congress's oversight power and sanctioned future investigations of executive branch misconduct. On the narrow question of whether the Senate could arrest a defiant witness for contempt of Congress, the court was unambiguous.

"We conclude," Justice Willis Van Devanter wrote for the court, "that the investigation was ordered for a legitimate object; that the witness [Mal Daugherty] wrongfully refused to appear and testify before the committee and was lawfully attached; that the Senate is entitled to have him give testimony pertinent to the inquiry, either at its bar or before the committee; and that the District Court erred in discharging him from custody under the attachment."

On the broader and more significant question of whether Congress properly possessed the power to investigate, the court was just as clear. In order to legislate effectively, the court reasoned, both houses of Congress needed good information and were therefore entitled to hold hearings, issue subpoenas, and punish those who obstructed their investigative work.

"We are of opinion," the justices declared, "that the power of inquiry—with process to enforce it—is an essential and appropriate auxiliary to the legislative function."

Those words would come to sustain generations of congressional investigators as they compelled testimony, punished recalcitrant witnesses, and exposed shocking misconduct by cabinet secretaries, White House officials, and even presidents of the United States.

HINDSIGHT CAN OFTEN make victory declarations appear painfully premature—and the April 15, 1926, testimonial dinner hosted by three hundred of Burton Wheeler's closest friends offers a classic example.

Even before *McGrain*, and despite all the hung juries and acquittals to come, a celebratory mood filled Washington's City Club. Officially, the occasion was a District of Columbia judge's recent dismissal of the second indictment against Wheeler, but the toasts that evening suggested victory on a grander scale. The keynote speaker, Sen. Henrik Shipstead of Minnesota, touted "the triumph of justice over the Department of Justice," a sentiment echoed in the congratulatory letters and telegrams that were read aloud from journalist H. L. Mencken, Rabbi Stephen Wise, former Harvard president Charles W. Eliot, and legal scholar Felix Frankfurter.

If the speakers that evening could be believed, Wheeler's victory over Harry Daugherty was a watershed moment. Corruption within the Justice Department was banished to the past. The future appeared bright. To raised glasses of sparkling cider, one toast maker practically thanked Wheeler's enemies for elevating the stature of America's most promising progressive icon since Theodore Roosevelt. "The most hopeful thing of the last few years," declared Alabama congressman George Huddleston, "is that Wheeler, running for vice president, polled four and a half million votes."

To many in the room, Burton Wheeler seemed destined for greatness. Someday soon, they hoped, he might even lead a transformational presidency that would realize their most cherished political values—economic justice for farmers and laborers, social equality, civil liberties, integrity in public office.

Those who clung to such fantasies were only setting themselves up for disappointment. By the time a primary challenge unseated the four-term incumbent in 1946, Wheeler was widely seen at best as a maverick who defied all labels and at worst as a cranky conservative—the senator who helped derail President Franklin D. Roosevelt's court-packing plan and then bitterly fought US intervention in the Second World War. After leaving the Senate on January 3, 1947, Wheeler spent his remaining years in private practice in Washington, DC, a political nonentity until his death in 1975 at the age of ninety-two.

The origins of his later undoing were already visible in his early successes—his stubborn, unyielding idealism; his tendency to court publicity with controversial opinions; his willingness to forsake lesser principles in the pursuit of some higher goal. Though such qualities were at first put to noble purposes and endeared him to many, these flaws were amplified later in his career, reaching their peak when his strident anti-interventionism led him to the America First movement, Charles Lindbergh, and charges of Nazi sympathy.

Decades later, relatively few Americans remember him as the fiery freshman who took down a corrupt attorney general; or the progressive icon who gave Roosevelt's 1932 presidential bid an early and crucial push; or the seasoned senator who was briefly favored for the 1940 Democratic nomination until Roosevelt broke with precedent and sought a third term. Instead, he's most likely to be remembered via his most prominent depiction in modern popular culture, as a caricature from the 2004 alternate history novel (and 2020 HBO limited series) *The Plot Against America*. In the best-selling novel, Philip Roth reimagined Wheeler as a vile anti-Semite who, once in the White House, dismantles civil liberties and jails prominent Jewish dissidents.

Certainly few Americans would recognize Wheeler as the inspiration for 1939's *Mr. Smith Goes to Washington*—originally titled *The Gentleman from Montana*—wherein a young, naive senator is framed with corruption charges after spurning an older, crooked politician. When Wheeler and director Frank Capra shared a box at the film's October 17, 1939, world premiere in Washington's Constitution Hall, the similarities were lost on no one. It went on to garner an impressive eleven Academy Award nominations, winning for Best Original Story. Some eight decades later, *Mr. Smith* endures as one of the most famous films about American government, selected by the Library of Congress in 1989 as one of the first twenty-five titles to be preserved in the National Film Registry (and inspiring not one but two episodes of *The Simpsons*). The real-life saga that inspired it has, however, been almost completely forgotten.

And to the eventual dismay of the celebrants that April evening in 1926, the "triumph of justice over the Department of Justice" would in its own way be forgotten as well. In the short term, of course, Wheeler did set the Department of Justice and the Bureau Investigation on better paths. The nation needed an extreme counterexample like Harry Daugherty to know what it really wanted in an attorney general—someone who would steer the federal government's legal machinery not in his own interests, or those of the president who appointed him or of his political party, but in the interests of the United States, full stop. Wheeler's investigation shocked the American people into caring whether the Department of Justice was actually pursuing justice, or something else entirely. And within the department itself, greater public scrutiny and the leadership of reformers like Attorney General Stone encouraged professionalization among the ranks and gave rise to new institutional norms around political neutrality and prosecutorial independence.

Ultimately, however, Wheeler's hearings produced no new legislation, prompted no structural changes to the Department of Justice, and imposed no statutory restrictions on the Bureau of Investigation. In the absence of those measures, only institutional norms stood in the way of a

Daughterian relapse—and history would prove just how precarious norms alone could be.

EVEN WHEELER COULDN'T see that amid his greatest successes, the seeds were already being sown for the kind of perversion of justice he had so feared upon returning from the Soviet Union.

On December 10, 1924, Attorney General Stone summoned the acting director of the Bureau of Investigation to his office.

For the past seven months, Stone had peered over John Edgar Hoover's shoulder as the young man remade the Bureau of Investigation into a politically neutral, law-abiding crime detection force. Hoover had impressed him as "a man of exceptional intelligence, alertness, and executive ability." He not only trimmed the force, cutting 155 from the payroll; he transformed it, so that half of its 352 special agents had legal training. He enforced discipline among the ranks. He rooted out the political hacks and hardboiled detective types. At Stone's behest, Hoover even held a series of cordial meetings with leaders of the American Civil Liberties Union, an organization he'd once investigated for subversive activities.

Hoover seemed especially keen to restore the Bureau's good name. "This Bureau cannot afford to have a public scandal visited upon it," he wrote in a "personal and confidential" memo to all special agents. "What I am trying to do is to protect the force of the Bureau of Investigation from outside criticism and from bringing the Bureau of Investigation into disrepute." (Hoover just as closely guarded his own reputation; he was now going by J. Edgar after a Washington department store, in rejecting his charge account application, confused his creditworthiness with that of a similarly named Mr. John E. Hoover.)

As Stone nodded with approval at Hoover's performance as acting director, he knew his own time at the Department of Justice was running short. Within weeks, President Coolidge would nominate him to fill a vacancy on the Supreme Court. Before handing the reins to another attorney general, Stone needed to install a director who could realize his best hopes for the once-troubled Bureau. Although he considered several candidates, none measured up to Hoover. The acting director, he wrote to a friend, showed "far greater promise than any other man."

In a private letter to Harvard law professor Felix Frankfurter, Stone laid out his rationale for making Hoover's appointment permanent.

"Hoover has been zealous in the reform of the Bureau and has done his work with a thoroughness and intelligence which has been most gratifying," wrote Stone. "If given a chance, he will make good in a way which would be gratifying to all those who have liberal ideas about the administration of that branch of the Department of Justice and who believe that there is a better way of conducting investigations than by old-fashioned detective methods."

Frankfurter's reply counseled caution. If Stone had forgotten about Hoover's role in the Palmer raids of 1919–1920—the thousands arrested and hundreds deported for nothing more than leftist political sympathies—then Frankfurter felt obliged to remind him. "Hoover," he warned, "might be a very effective and zealous instrument for the realization of the 'liberal ideas' which you had in mind for the investigatorial activities of the Department of Justice when his chief is a man who cares about these ideas as deeply as you do, but his effectiveness might be of a weaker coefficient with a chief less profoundly concerned over these 'ideas.'"

In other words, who was the real J. Edgar Hoover? Where Stone imagined a liberal reformer, Frankfurter saw only a chameleon—an unlikely survivor of the Wilson administration who adjusted his politics as his surroundings and supervisors changed. How else had he survived first a presidential transition and then the greatest scandal in Justice Department history?

Frankfurter's concerns were not enough to sway Stone. When Hoover arrived in the attorney general's office that chilly December day, Stone announced what would come to be seen as a fateful decision, although at the time it received only a single column-inch on page thirty of the *New York Times*. He informed Hoover, without any trace of a smile, that he could drop the word *acting* from his title.

Thus ensconced at the head of America's largest domestic intelligence gathering operation, J. Edgar Hoover marveled at the powers of his new office. He could crack down on threats to what he defined as the American way of life. He could keep America's enemies in check—and also his own. He could make himself indispensable to his superiors—attorneys general and presidents alike. Just twenty-nine at the time, Hoover would serve as the fifth director of the Bureau of Investigation and then the first director of the Federal Bureau of Investigation, as the agency was rechristened in 1935, for another forty-seven and a half years, through seventeen attorneys generalships and eight presidencies.

WHEELER MIGHT HAVE been responsible for Hoover's reign—but only incidentally. The senator could hardly have foreseen that, in toppling a crooked attorney general who used the Bureau of Investigation as his own personal spy ring, he would be opening the door for the man described by a leading historian of the FBI as the "architect of the modern surveillance state."

A more direct legacy can be found in the uses and abuses of the congressional investigation. More than anyone, Wheeler pioneered the modern political scandal as a weapon against potentates who purport to stand above the law. To be sure, American politics boasts a tradition of scandal as old as the republic itself—just ask Hamilton and Burr. But it was Wheeler who, as the impresario of a Capitol Hill spectacle, first yoked the public's eternal fascination with moral stumbling to a free press that was, by the 1920s, capable of stoking outrage across the entire nation.

Future legislators would freely borrow from his playbook, and not all would use it for such noble purposes. From 1950 to 1954, Sen. Joseph McCarthy weaponized scandal and commanded congressional hearings in a way that distinctly recalled Wheeler's performance three decades prior. Levying bold accusations against public figures with little or no proof to back them up, McCarthy ruined the careers and blackened the reputations of dozens of government officials—most of whom, unlike Harry Daugherty, never committed crimes against the United States. Wheeler's own detractors levied charges against the Daugherty investigation that would be familiar to critics of modern, partisan hearings—and given all his bravado and bombast, his overt hostility to the target of his inquiry, and his elastic interpretation of the rules of evidence, the objections were understandable.

Ultimately, though, they misunderstood the man and his mission. Although he framed his crusade against corruption in idealistic terms, Wheeler's direct appeal to the American people betrayed an astute cynicism about the judicial process. A powerful crook, he realized, could exploit the procedural safeguards that typically protected the accused from an abusive state. "No man is above the law" was a sound and sonorous principle but one that became mere platitude as it approached the apex of political and legal power—especially in an era of exceptional public corruption. Attorney General Daugherty, by virtue of his high office, not to mention his cunning at manipulating official proceedings in his favor, seemed beyond the reach of a court of law.

Wheeler's particular genius—which seems almost counterintuitive today—was to seek justice instead in the court of public opinion. There, unbound by the rules of the criminal justice system, his freewheeling investigation forced Daugherty's retirement from public life and consigned America's most corrupt attorney general to the judgment of history. Daugherty never spent a single night behind bars, but a certain kind of justice was served.

For all his successes, Burton Wheeler couldn't guarantee that another Harry Daugherty or William J. Burns would never undermine justice again. But he did show that it was a fight worth undertaking.

Acknowledgments

As a public television host, I've known the embarrassment of serving as the lone public face for an undertaking that was, in truth, the product of dozens of hard-working, creative people. That familiar feeling now overwhelms me again. It's my name on the cover, but you wouldn't be holding *Crooked* in your hands without the help of so many others.

I'll be forever grateful to editor Sam Raim for taking a flier on a first-time author. Sam was my trusted collaborator from acquisition to transmittal, and the book is so much better for his contributions. And when it came time to part ways, Carrie Napolitano took the baton from Sam and ran with it. I was lucky to find in Carrie someone who truly understands my passion for historical storytelling. I'm also in debt to Michelle Aielli, Michael Barrs, Fred Francis, Michael Giarratano, Amanda Kain, Ashley Kiedrowski, Kate Mueller, Mary Ann Naples, Monica Oluwek, Niyati Patel, Sara Pinsonault, Jeff Williams, and the entire team at Hachette Books who helped transform my words into something people would want to buy, as well as to the Hachette Book Group sales department that went and sold it.

Crooked would never have found its way to Hachette were it not for my agent, Samantha Shea. Like Sam, she bet on an unproven author, and I can only hope to prove the wisdom of her wager. With a publishing neophyte for a client, Samantha fielded my beginner's questions with grace and understanding and sent me on the search for a compelling book concept. After I eventually wrote her in August 2019 with a half-baked idea about corruption in the Harding administration, she nudged me in the right direction, helped draft a formal proposal, and found the perfect home for what became *Crooked*. I'm also grateful to Valerie Borchardt, Cora Markowitz, and everyone else at Georges Borchardt, Inc.

This book is based on extensive primary-source search, and I couldn't have written it without the help of the archivists, reference librarians, and staff members at the National Archives and Records Administration in College Park, Maryland; the Library of Congress Manuscript Division in Washington, DC; the Montana Historical Society in Helena; and the Montana State University Library in Bozeman. Special thanks are due to archivist Cody White at the National Archives at Denver, who graciously provided me with a copy of the indictment against Burton Wheeler when COVID-19 made travel there an impossibility, as well as Jayne Davis of JLD Research, who was my capable proxy at the Ohio History Connection. At the Library of Congress, Ryan Reft made a stranger in town feel welcome and steered me to several indispensable collections. I'm also grateful to the staff of the FBI's Information Management Division, which processed dozens of my Freedom of Information Act requests; as well as the USC Libraries' indispensable Interlibrary Loan and Document Delivery team.

I'm lucky to belong to a community of friends and fellow writers. Geoff Manaugh has inspired and encouraged me throughout the years. Greg Nichols and Matthew Pearl of *Truly*Adventurous* not only tutored me in the craft of narrative nonfiction but also connected me with my agent. Several friends also generously offered to read the unfinished manuscript. Aaron Thompson provided a much-needed boost in confidence, as well as suggestions that only an actual litigator could have given. Likewise, John Metzidis steered me around pitfalls, corrected my legal terminology, and helped me pin down the closing thoughts of the epilogue. In fact, many of the insights in those final pages are his (but only the good ones, of course).

Finally, there's not enough room between two covers (unless, perhaps, we're talking about a tome of Tolstoyan proportions) to properly acknowledge my wife, Kseniya Melnik. On countless occasions she took our infant-turned-toddler son off my hands so I could write—as did my ever-helpful parents-in-law, Vladimir and Larissa Melnik. But Kseniya is so much more than a babysitter. She's a brilliant fiction and television writer who stokes my ambition, edits like a pro, and supports my writing goals with a patience that passes all understanding. From encouraging me to pursue a book project in the first place, to helping me break the plot as I outlined it, to reviewing the near-finished manuscript while nine months pregnant—she has been my partner in everything. Without her, this book would not exist.

Select Bibliography

Books and Periodicals

Abbott, Karen [Abbott Kahler]. *The Ghosts of Eden Park: The Bootleg King, the Women Who Pursued Him, and the Murder That Shocked Jazz-Age America.* New York: Crown, 2019.

Ackerman, Kenneth D. *Young J. Edgar: Hoover, the Red Scare, and the Assault on Civil Liberties.* New York: Carroll and Graf, 2007.

Adams, Samuel Hopkins. *Incredible Era: The Life and Times of Warren Gamaliel Harding.* Boston: Houghton Mifflin, 1939.

Alderfer, H. F. "The Personality and Politics of Warren G. Harding." PhD thesis, Syracuse University, 1926.

Alexander, Gregory J., and Paul K. Williams. *Wardman Park Hotel.* Charleston, SC: Arcadia, 2017.

Alexander, Jack. "Profiles: The Director—I." *New Yorker*, September 25, 1937, 20–25.

———. "Profiles: The Director—II." *New Yorker*, October 2, 1937, 21–26.

———. "Profiles: The Director—III." *New Yorker*, October 9, 1937, 22–27.

Allen, Frederick Lewis. *Only Yesterday: An Informal History of the Nineteen Twenties.* New York: Harper and Brothers, 1931.

Amberg, Alicia. "Smith Wildman Brookhart of Iowa: Republican Insurgent." Master's thesis, Kansas State Teachers College of Emporia, 1971.

Anthony, Carl Sferrazza. *Florence Harding: The First Lady, the Jazz Age, and the Death of America's Most Scandalous President.* New York. William Morrow, 1998.

Ashby, LeRoy. *The Spearless Leader: Senator Borah and the Progressive Movement in the 1920's.* Urbana: University of Illinois Press, 1972.

Bagby, Wesley M. "The 'Smoke Filled Room' and the Nomination of Warren G. Harding." *Mississippi Valley Historical Review* 41, no. 4 (March 1955): 657–674.

Baker, Nancy V. *Conflicting Loyalties: Law & Politics in the Attorney General's Office, 1789–1990.* Lawrence: University of Kansas Press, 1992.

Batchelor, Bob. *The Bourbon King: The Life and Crimes of George Remus, Prohibition's Evil Genius.* New York: Diversion Books, 2019.

Bates, J. Leonard. *Senator Thomas J. Walsh of Montana: Law and Public Affairs, from TR to FDR*. Urbana: University of Illinois Press, 1999.

Beezley, Ray O. "The Political Career of Burton K. Wheeler." Master's thesis, University of Southern California, 1951.

Belknap, Michal R. "The Mechanics of Repression: J. Edgar Hoover, the Bureau of Investigation, and the Radicals, 1917–1925." *Crime and Social Justice* no. 7 (Spring/Summer 1977): 49–58.

Bliven, Bruce. "Tempest over Teapot Dome." *American Heritage*, August 1965, 20–23, 100–05.

———. "Wheeler's Way and Walsh's: The Senate Committees at Work." *New Republic*, April 2, 1924, 148–50.

Blythe, Samuel G. "A Calm Review of a Calm Man." *Saturday Evening Post*, July 28, 1925.

Boatmon, Ellis Grey. "Evolution of a President: The Political Apprenticeship of Warren G. Harding." PhD diss., University of South Carolina, 1966.

Britton, Nan. *The President's Daughter*. New York: Elizabeth Ann Guild, 1927.

Brown, Anthony Cave. *The Last Hero: Wild Bill Donovan*. New York: Times Books, 1982.

Brown, Dorothy M. *Mabel Walker Willebrandt: A Study of Power, Loyalty, and Law*. Knoxville: University of Tennessee Press, 1984.

Butler, Anne M., Wendy Wolff, and Sheila P. Burke. *United States Senate Election, Expulsion, and Censure Cases, 1793–1990*. Washington: Government Printing Office, 1995.

Cahan, Richard. *A Court That Shaped America: Chicago's Federal District Court from Abe Lincoln to Abbie Hoffman*. Evanston, IL: Northwestern University Press, 2002.

Cameron, Donald John. "Burton K. Wheeler as Public Campaigner, 1922–1942." PhD diss., Northwestern University, 1960.

———. "Burton K. Wheeler, Spokesman for the Progressive Movement." In *Landmarks of Western Oratory*, vol. 34, edited by David H. Grover. Laramie: University of Wyoming Publications, 1968.

Ciment, James, ed. *Encyclopedia of the Jazz Age: From the End of World War I to the Great Crash*. London: Routledge, 2015.

Clayton, Cornell W. *The Politics of Justice: The Attorney General and the Making of Legal Policy*. Armonk, NY: M. E. Sharpe, 1992.

Coan, Blair. *The Red Web: An Underground Political History of the United States from 1918 to the Present Time Showing How Close the Government Is to Collapse and Told in an Understandable Way*. Chicago: Northwest, 1925.

Coffey, Justin P. "Harding Biographies." In *A Companion to Warren G. Harding, Calvin Coolidge, and Herbert Hoover*, edited by Katherine A. S. Sibley, 79–93. West Sussex, UK: Wiley, 2004.

Coffey, Thomas M. *The Long Thirst: Prohibition in America, 1920–1933*. New York: W. W. Norton, 1975.

Cole, Cyrenus. *I Remember, I Remember: A Book of Recollections*. Iowa City: State Historical Society of Iowa, 1936.

Colman, Elizabeth Wheeler. *Mrs. Wheeler Goes to Washington: Mrs. Burton Kendall Wheeler, Wife of the Senator from Montana*. Helena, MT: Falcon Press, 1989.

Cook, Fred J. *The FBI Nobody Knows*. New York: Macmillan, 1964.

Coolidge, Calvin. *The Autobiography of Calvin Coolidge*. New York: Cosmopolitan, 1929.

Crawford, Kenneth G. "J. Edgar Hoover." *Nation*, February 27, 1937, 232–233.

Crichlow, Donald T. *American Political History: A Very Short Introduction*. Oxford: Oxford University Press, 2015.

Cummings, Homer, and Carl McFarland. *Federal Justice: Chapters in the History of Justice and the Federal Executive*. New York: Macmillan, 1937.

Dale, Porter H. II, and Christopher D. Dale. "The Calvin Coolidge Inauguration Revisited: An Eyewitness Account by Congressman Porter H. Dale," *Vermont History* 62, no. 3 (1994): 214–222.

Daugherty, Harry M., and Thomas Dixon. *The Inside Story of the Harding Tragedy*. New York: Churchill, 1932.

Davis, Colin J. *Power at Odds: The 1922 National Railroad Shopmen's Strike*. Urbana: University of Illinois Press, 1997.

Davis, Margaret Leslie. *Dark Side of Fortune: Triumph and Scandal in the Life of Oil Tycoon Edward L. Doheny*. Berkeley: University of California Press, 1998.

Dean, John W. *Warren G. Harding*. American Presidents Series, edited by Arthur M. Schlesinger Jr. New York: Times Books, 2004.

Diner, Hasia. "Teapot Dome, 1924." In *Congress Investigates: A Documented History, 1792–1974*, edited by Arthur M. Schlesinger Jr. and Roger Bruns, 199–217. New York: Chelsea House, 1975.

Downes, Randolph C. "The Harding Muckfest." *Northwest Ohio Quarterly* 39, no 3 (1967): 5–37.

Dunlop, Richard. *Donovan: America's Master Spy*. Chicago: Rand McNally, 1982.

Dunne, Finley Peter. "A Look at Harding from the Sidelines." *Saturday Evening Post*, September 12, 1936, 24–25, 74–75, 79.

Emery, Edwin, and Henry Ladd Smith. "From Jazz Journalism to Interpretive Reporting." In *The Press and America*, 1st ed., 621–649. New York: Prentice-Hall, 1954.

Emery, Michael, and Edwin Emery. "The Twenties: Radio, Movies, Jazz Journalism." In *The Press and America: An Interpretive History of the Mass Media*, 7th ed., 265–299. Englewood Cliffs, NJ: Prentice-Hall, 1992.

Federal Bureau of Investigation. *The FBI: A Centennial History, 1908–2008*. Washington, DC: Government Printing Office, 2008.

Ferrell, Robert H. *The Presidency of Calvin Coolidge*. American Presidency Series, edited by Donald R. McCoy, Clifford S. Griffin, and Homer E. Socolofsky. Lawrence: University Press of Kansas, 1998.

———. *The Strange Deaths of President Harding*. Columbia: University of Missouri Press, 1996.

Findlay, James G. " Memorandum for the Director: Early History of the Bureau of Investigation, United States Department of Justice." FBI History, November 19, 1943. https://web.archive.org/web/20041019232040/http:/www.fbi.gov/libref/historic/history/historic_doc/findlay.htm.

Fox, John F., Jr. "The Birth of the Federal Bureau of Investigation." Federal Bureau of Investigation, July 2003. https://www.fbi.gov/history/history-publications-reports/the-birth-of-the-federal-bureau-of-investigation.

Frankfurter, Felix. "Hands off the Investigation." *New Republic*, May 21, 1924, 329–331.

Frederick, Richard G. "The Front Porch Campaign and the Election of Harding." In *A Companion to Warren G. Harding, Calvin Coolidge, and Herbert Hoover*, edited by Katherine A. S. Sibley, 94–111. West Sussex, UK: Wiley, 2004.

Fuess, Claude M. *Calvin Coolidge: The Man from Vermont*. Boston: Little, Brown, 1940.

Gardner, Gilson. "Our Next President: La Follette or Wheeler." *Nation*, September 17, 1924, 279–280.

Garvey, Todd. *Congress's Contempt Power and the Enforcement of Congressional Subpoenas: Law, History, Practice, and Procedure*. Congressional Research Service, report RL34097, May 12, 2017.

Gentry, Curt. *J. Edgar Hoover: The Man and the Secrets*. New York: W. W. Norton, 1991.

Giglio, James Nickolas. *H. M. Daugherty and the Politics of Expediency*. Kent, OH: Kent State University Press, 1978.

———. "The Political Career of Harry M. Daugherty." PhD diss., Ohio State University, 1968.

Goodfellow, Guy Fair. "Calvin Coolidge: A Study of Presidential Inaction." PhD diss., University of Maryland, 1969.

Gould, Lewis L. *The Most Exclusive Club: A History of the Modern United States Senate*. New York: Basic Books, 2005.

Green, Bruce A., and Rebecca Roiphe. "Can the President Control the Department of Justice?" *Alabama Law Review* 70, no. 1 (2018): 1–76.

Greenberg, David. *Calvin Coolidge*. The American Presidents Series, edited by Arthur M. Schlesinger, Jr. New York: Times Books, 2006.

Gutfield, Arnon. "Years of Hysteria, Montana, 1917–1921: A Study in Local Intolerance." PhD diss., University of California, Los Angeles, 1971.

Hamilton, James. *The Power to Probe: A Study of Congressional Investigations*. New York: Random House, 1976.

Harper, Robert S. "Before Revelry." *Plain Talk*, July 1928, 44–51.

Harris, Ray Baker. *Warren G. Harding: An Account of His Nomination for the Presidency by the Republican Convention of 1920*. Washington, DC: privately published, 1957.

Haste, Richard A. "Burton K. Wheeler." *American Review of Reviews*, October 1924, 407–409.

Hernon, Joseph Martin. *Profiles in Character: Hubris and Heroism in the US Senate, 1789–1990*. Armonk, NY: M. E. Sharpe, 1997.

Hoover, Herbert. *The Memoirs of Herbert Hoover: The Cabinet and the Presidency, 1920–1933*. New York: Macmillan, 1952.

Hoover, Irwin Hood (Ike). *Forty-Two Years in the White House*. Boston: Houghton Mifflin, 1934.

Hoover, J. Edgar, and Courtney Ryley Cooper. "The Amazing Mr. Means." *American Magazine*, December 1936.

Howard, Joseph Kinsey. "The Decline and Fall of Burton K. Wheeler." *Harper's*, March 1947, 226–236.

———. *Montana: High, Wide, and Handsome*. Lincoln: University of Nebraska Press, 2003.

Hoyt, Edwin P. *Spectacular Rogue: Gaston B. Means*. Indianapolis: Bobbs-Merrill, 1963.

Hudiburg, Jane A. *Senate Floor Privileges: History and Current Practice.* Congressional Research Service, report R46257, March 5, 2020.

Hunt, William R. *Front-Page Detective: William J. Burns and the Detective Profession, 1880–1930.* Bowling Green, OH: Bowling Green State University Popular Press, 1990.

Huston, Luther A., Arthur Selwyn Miller, Samuel Krislov, and Robert G. Dixon Jr. *Roles of the Attorney General of the United States.* Washington, DC: American Enterprise Institute for Public Policy Research, 1968.

Hynd, Alan. "Gaston Bullock Means: Con Cum Laude." In *Murder, Mayhem, and Mystery: An Album of American Crime.* New York: A. S. Barnes, 1958.

———. "The Man Who Swindled the President." *True,* December 1949, 122–136.

Jackson, Justin F. "Railroad Shopmen's Strike of 1922." In *Encyclopedia of the Jazz Age,* edited by James Ciment. London: Routledge, 2015.

Jeffreys-Jones, Rhodri. *Cloak and Dollar: A History of American Secret Intelligence.* New Haven, CT: Yale University Press, 2002.

———. *The FBI: A History.* New Haven, CT: Yale University Press, 2007.

Johnson, Claudius O. *Borah of Idaho.* New York: Longmans, Green, 1936.

Johnson, Marc C. *Political Hell-Raiser: The Life and Times of Senator Burton K. Wheeler of Montana.* Norman: University of Oklahoma Press, 2019.

Kin, David George [David George Plotkin]. *The Plot Against America: Senator Wheeler and the Forces Behind Him.* Missoula, MT: John E. Kennedy, 1946.

Koessler, Mary Lou Collins. "The 1920 Gubernatorial Election in Montana." Master's thesis, University of Montana, 1971.

La Follette-Wheeler Campaign Headquarters. *The Facts: La Follette-Wheeler Campaign Text-book.* Chicago: La Follette-Wheeler Campaign Headquarters, 1924.

Langeluttig, Albert. *The Department of Justice of the United States.* Baltimore: Johns Hopkins Press, 1927.

Link, Arthur S. "What Happened to the Progressive Movement in the 1920's?" *American Historical Review* 64, no. 4. (July 1959): 833–851.

Longworth, Alice Roosevelt. *Crowded Hours: Reminiscences of Alice Roosevelt Longworth.* New York: Charles Scribner's Sons, 1933.

Lowenthal, Max. *The Federal Bureau of Investigation.* New York: William Sloane Associates, 1950.

Luff, Jennifer. *Commonsense Anticommunism: Labor and Civil Liberties Between the World Wars.* Chapel Hill: University of North Carolina Press, 2012.

Lynch, Megan Suzanne, and Richard S. Beth. *Parliamentary Reference Sources: Senate.* Congressional Research Service, report RL30788, April 21, 2008, 70–71.

Mack, Vicki. *Frank A. Vanderlip: The Banker Who Changed America.* Palos Verdes, CA: Pinoles Press, 2013.

MacKay, Kenneth Campbell. *The Progressive Movement of 1924.* New York: Octagon Books, 1972.

MacMahon, Edward B., and Leonard Curry. "Harding: Scandal, Sudden Death and Questions." In *Medical Cover-Ups in the White House,* 78–89. Washington, DC: Farragut, 1987.

MacNeil, Neil, and Richard A. Baker. *The American Senate: An Insider's History.* Oxford: Oxford University Press, 2013.

Manly, Basil. *The Leading Facts in the Wheeler Case*. Washington, DC: Wheeler Defense Committee, 1925.

Mason, Alpheus Thomas. *Harlan Fiske Stone: Pillar of the Law*. New York: Viking Press, 1956.

Maxwell, Robert S. "The Progressive Bridge: Reform Sentiment in the United States Between the New Freedom and the New Deal." *Indiana Magazine of History* 63, no. 2 (June 1967): 83–102.

Mayer, Martin. *Emory Buckner*. New York: Harper and Row, 1968.

McCartney, Laton. *The Teapot Dome Scandal: How Big Oil Bought the Harding White House and Tried to Steal the Country*. New York: Random House, 2008.

McCoy, Donald. *Calvin Coolidge: The Quiet President*. New York: Macmillan, 1967.

McFedries, Archie. "Gaston Means: Colossus of Crime." *Coronet*, December 1945, 102–106.

McKenna, Marian Cecilia. *Borah*. Ann Arbor: University of Michigan Press, 1961.

McLean, Evalyn Walsh. *Father Struck It Rich*. Boston: Little, Brown, 1936.

Means, Gaston B., and May Dixon Thacker. *The Strange Death of President Harding*. New York: Guild, 1930.

Means, Julie. "My Life with Gaston Means." Serial running in four Sunday editions of the *Philadelphia Inquirer*, September 10 to October 1, 1939.

Mels, Edgar. "Daugherty at the Bar." *Nation*, October 27, 1926, 423–424.
———. "Fate and the Ohio Gang." *Nation*, August 25, 1926, 173–174.
———. "Harry Daugherty's Past." *Nation*, May 19, 1926, 551–553.

Messick, Hank. *John Edgar Hoover: An Inquiry into the Life and Times of John Edgar Hoover, and His Relationship to the Continuing Partnership of Crime, Business, and Politics*. New York: David McKay, 1972.

Miller, Nathan. *New World Coming: 1920s and the Making of Modern America*. Cambridge, MA: Da Capo Press, 2003.
———. *Stealing from America: A History of Corruption from Jamestown to Reagan*. New York: Paragon House, 1992.

Morrison, John, and Catherine Wright Morrison. *Mavericks: The Lives and Battles of Montana's Political Legends*. Moscow: University of Idaho Press, 1997.

Murray, Robert K. *The Harding Era: Warren G. Harding and His Administration*. Minneapolis: University of Minnesota Press, 1969.

Nation. "The History of William J. Burns." November 23, 1927, 561.

National Magazine. "Uncle Sam's Law Office: The Functions of the Department of Justice and the Scope of Its Work." January 1922, 417–419, 425.

National Popular Government League. *To the American People: Report upon the Illegal Practices of the United States Department of Justice*. Washington, DC: National Popular Government League, 1920.

Neuberger, Richard L. "Wheeler of Montana." *Harper's*, December 1, 1939, 608–618.

Nevins, Allan. *Hamilton Fish: The Inner History of the Grant Administration*. New York: Dodd, Mead and Company, 1936.

New Republic. "Daugherty Declares War." September 13, 1922, 57–58.

New Republic. "A Lawless Department of Justice." March 29, 1922, 126–127.

Nichols, Christopher McKnight. "The Wilson Legacy, Domestic and International." In *A Companion to Warren G. Harding, Calvin Coolidge, and Herbert Hoover*, edited by Katherine A. S. Sibley, 9–33. West Sussex, UK: Wiley, 2004.

Noggle, Burl. *Teapot Dome: Oil and Politics in the 1920's*. New York: W. W. Norton, 1962.

Nugent, Walter. *Progressivism: A Very Short Introduction*. Oxford: Oxford University Press, 2010.

O'Keane, Josephine. *Thomas J. Walsh: A Senator from Montana*. Francestown, NH: Marshall Jones, 1955.

Okrent, Daniel. *Last Call: The Rise and Fall of Prohibition*. New York: Scribner, 2010.

Olssen, Erik. "The Progressive Group in Congress, 1922–1929." *Historian* 42, no. 2 (February 1, 1980): 244–263.

Payne, Phillip G. "The Harding Presidency." In *A Companion to Warren G. Harding, Calvin Coolidge, and Herbert Hoover*, edited by Katherine A. S. Sibley, 112–131. West Sussex, UK: Wiley, 2004.

Pietrusza, David. *1920: The Year of the Six Presidents*. New York: Carroll and Graf, 2007.

Pinals, Robert S., and Harold Smulyan. "The Death of President Warren G. Harding." *American Journal of the Medical Sciences* 348, no. 3 (September 2014): 232–237.

Powers, Richard Gid. *Secrecy and Power: The Life of J. Edgar Hoover*. New York: Free Press, 1987.

Pringle, Henry F. *The Life and Times of William Howard Taft*, vol. 2. New York: Farrar and Rinehart, 1939.

Quint, Howard H., and Robert H. Ferrell, eds. *The Talkative President: The Off-the-Record Press Conferences of Calvin Coolidge*. Amherst: University of Massachusetts Press, 1964.

Riedel, Richard Langham. *Halls of the Mighty: My 47 Years in the Senate*. Washington, DC: Robert B. Luce, 1969.

Roberts, Jason. "The Biographical Legacy of Calvin Coolidge and the 1924 Presidential Election." In *A Companion to Warren G. Harding, Calvin Coolidge, and Herbert Hoover*, edited by Katherine A. S. Sibley, 193–211. West Sussex, UK: Wiley, 2004.

Rogin, Michael P., and Kathleen Moran. "Mr. Capra Goes to Washington." *Representations* 84, no. 1 (November 2003): 213–248.

Rorabaugh, W. J. *Prohibition: A Very Short Introduction*. Oxford: Oxford University Press, 2020.

Rosenberg, Albert, and Cindy Armstrong. *The American Gladiators: Taft Versus Remus*. Hemet, CA: Aimwell Press, 1995.

Rosenberg, Morton. *Congressional Investigations of the Department of Justice, 1920–2007: History, Law, and Practice*. Congressional Research Service, report RL34197, October 3, 2007.

Ross, Shelley. *Fall from Grace: Sex, Scandal, and Corruption in American Politics from 1702 to the Present*. New York: Ballantine Books, 1988.

Roth, Philip. *The Plot Against America*. Boston: Houghton Mifflin, 2004.

Ruetten, Richard T. "Burton K. Wheeler and Insurgency in the 1920s." In *The American West*, edited by Gene M. Gressley. Laramie: University of Wyoming Press, 1966.

———. "Burton K. Wheeler of Montana: A Progressive Between the Wars." PhD diss., University of Oregon, 1961.

——. "Burton K. Wheeler and the Montana Connection." *Montana: The Magazine of Western History* 27, no. 3 (Summer 1977): 2–19.

——. "Burton K. Wheeler, 1905–1925: An Independent Liberal Under Fire." Master's thesis, University of Oregon, 1957.

Russell, Francis. *The Shadow of Blooming Grove: Warren G. Harding in His Times*. New York: McGraw-Hill, 1968.

Savage, Hugh James. "Political Independents of the Hoover Era: The Progressive Insurgents of the Senate." PhD diss., University of Illinois, 1961.

Schmidt, Regin. *Red Scare: FBI and the Origins of Anti-communism in the United States*. Copenhagen: Museum Tusculanum, 2000.

Schultz, Jeffrey D. *Presidential Scandals*. Washington, DC: CQ Press, 2000.

Shields, Kristoffer. "The Opposition: Labor, Liquor, and Democrats." In *A Companion to Warren G. Harding, Calvin Coolidge, and Herbert Hoover*, edited by Katherine A. S. Sibley, 132–150. West Sussex, UK: Wiley, 2004.

Shugerman, Jed Handelsman. "The Creation of the Department of Justice: Professionalization Without Civil Rights or Civil Service." *Stanford Law Review* 66, no. 1 (2014): 121–171.

——. "Professionals, Politicos, and Crony Attorneys General: A Historical Sketch of the U.S. Attorney General as a Case for Structural Independence." *Fordham Law Review* 87, no 5. (2019): 1965–94.

Sibley, Katherine A. S., ed. *A Companion to Warren G. Harding, Calvin Coolidge, and Herbert Hoover*. West Sussex, UK: Wiley, 2004.

Sobel, Robert. *Coolidge: An American Enigma*. Washington, DC: Regnery, 1998.

Starling, Edmund W., and Thomas Sugrue. *Starling of the White House: The Story of the Man Whose Secret Service Detail Guarded Five Presidents from Woodrow Wilson to Franklin D. Roosevelt*. New York: Simon and Schuster, 1946.

Stevens, Rosemary. *A Time of Scandal: Charles R. Forbes, Warren G. Harding, and the Making of the Veterans Bureau*. Baltimore: Johns Hopkins University Press, 2016.

Stevenson, Elizabeth. *Babbitts and Bohemians: The American 1920's*. Ann Arbor: University of Michigan Press, 1967. See esp. chapter 7, "Surface Solutions."

Stockham, Aaron J. "Lack of Oversight: The Relationship Between Congress and the FBI, 1907–1975." PhD diss., Marquette University, 2011.

Stoddard, Henry L. *As I Knew Them: Presidents and Politics from Grant to Coolidge*. New York: Harper and Brothers, 1927.

Sullivan, Mark. *Our Times: The United States, 1900–1925*. Vol. 6, *The Twenties*. New York: Charles Scribner's Sons, 1935.

Summers, Anthony. *Official and Confidential: The Secret Life of J. Edgar Hoover*. New York: G. P. Putnam's Sons, 1993.

Taylor, Telford. *Grand Inquest: The Story of Congressional Investigations*. New York: Simon and Schuster, 1955.

Thacker, May Dixon. "Debunking 'The Strange Death of President Harding': A Complete Repudiation of the Sensational Book by the Author." *Liberty*, November 7, 1931.

——. "Gaston B. Means—Master Bad Man." Serial in *Liberty*, April 17 to June 12, 1937.

Theoharis, Athan G., ed. *The FBI: A Comprehensive Reference Guide*. Phoenix, AZ: Oryx, 1999.

Thomas, Henry, and Dana Lee Thomas. "The Strange Story of Gaston Means." In *Strange Tales of Amazing Frauds*, 175–190. Garden City, NY: Permabooks, 1950.

Tucker, Ray Thomas, and Frederick Reuben Barkley. *Sons of the Wild Jackass*. Boston: L. C. Page, 1932.

Ungar, Sanford J. *FBI*. Boston: Little, Brown, 1975.

US Department of Justice. *Annual Report of the Attorney General of the United States for the Fiscal Year 1924*. Washington, DC: Government Printing Office, 1924.

———. *200th Anniversary of the Office of Attorney General: 1789–1989*. Washington, DC: US Department of Justice, 1990.

Weiner, Tim. *Enemies: A History of the FBI*. New York: Random House, 2012.

Werner, M. R. *Privileged Characters*. New York: Robert M. McBride, 1935.

Werner, M. R., and John Starr. *Teapot Dome*. New York: Viking, 1959.

Wheeler, Burton K., and Paul F. Healy. *Yankee from the West: The Candid, Turbulent Life Story of the Yankee-Born U.S. Senator from Montana*. Garden City, NY: Doubleday, 1962.

White, William Allen. *The Autobiography of William Allen White*. New York: Macmillan, 1946.

———. *Masks in a Pageant*. New York: Macmillan, 1928.

———. *A Puritan in Babylon: The Story of Calvin Coolidge*. New York: Macmillan, 1938.

Whitehead, Don. *The FBI Story: A Report to the People*. New York: Random House, 1956.

Wilbur, Ray Lyman. *The Memoirs of Ray Lyman Wilbur*. Stanford, CA: Stanford University Press, 1960.

Wilcox, Thomas A., ed. *Congressional Procedures*. New York: Nova Science, 2009.

Williams, David J. "The Bureau of Investigation and Its Critics, 1919–1921: The Origins of Federal Political Surveillance." *Journal of American History* 68, no. 3 (December 1981): 560–579.

Williams, David J. "'Without Understanding': The FBI and Political Surveillance, 1908–1941." PhD diss., University of New Hampshire, 1981.

Yalof, David Alistair. *Prosecution Among Friends: Presidents, Attorneys General, and Executive Branch Wrongdoing*. College Station: Texas A&M University Press, 2012.

Congressional Transcripts and Directories

Charges Against Senator Burton K. Wheeler of Montana: Hearings Before the Select Committee on Investigation of Charges Against Senator Burton K. Wheeler, of Montana, US Senate, 68th Cong. (1924).

Charges of Hon. Oscar E. Keller Against the Attorney General of the United States: Hearings Before the Committee on the Judiciary, US House of Representatives, 67th Cong. (1922).

Congressional Record, 67th Cong., 2nd sess. (1922–1923).

Congressional Record, 68th Cong., 1st sess. (1923–1924).

Investigation of the Attorney General: Hearings Before the Select Committee on Investigation of the Attorney General, US Senate, 68th Cong. (1924).

Official Congressional Directory, 67th Cong., 2nd sess., 2nd ed. (February 1922).
Official Congressional Directory, 67th Cong., 2nd sess., 3rd ed. (July 1922).
Official Congressional Directory, 67th Cong., 4th sess., 2nd ed. (January 1923).
Official Congressional Directory, 68th Cong., 1st sess., 1st ed. (December 1923).
Official Congressional Directory, 68th Cong., 1st sess., 2nd ed. (January 1924).

Document and Manuscript Collections

Columbia Center for Oral History, Columbia University Libraries

Wheeler, Burton Kendall, oral history interview, 1969

Harvard Law School Library

Frankfurter, Felix, papers

National Archives at College Park, Maryland

Department of Justice straight numeric files
187919 (Robert M. La Follette)
191307 (Gaston B. Means)
226225 (Senate investigation of Harry M. Daugherty)
226469 (Burton K. Wheeler)
228730 (American Metal case)
Department of Justice litigation case files
5-844 (George B. Hayes)
22-44-42 (John L. Slattery)
Records of the Miller-Daugherty trials

National Archives at Denver

Criminal case files, 1924–1968, US District Court of the District of Montana, Great Falls Term

Library of Congress Manuscript Division

Boone, Joel Thompson, papers, 1755–1971
Borah, William Edgar, papers, 1905–1940
Coolidge, Calvin, papers, 1915–1932
La Follette family papers, 1781–1988
Lenroot, Irvine Luther, papers, 1858–1971
McLean, Evalyn Walsh, papers, 1874–1948
Miller, Hope Ridings, papers, 1887–1998
Pinkerton's National Detective Agency records, 1853–1999
Stone, Harlan Fiske, papers, 1889–1953
Wadsworth, James, family papers, 1730–1959
Walsh, Thomas James, and John Edward Erickson papers, 1910–1934

Montana Historical Society

Wheeler, Burton Kendall, papers, 1909–1916 [MC 198]
Wheeler, Burton Kendall, papers, 1910–1972 [MC 34]

Montana State University Library

Wheeler, Burton K., collection, 1924–1973 [collection 2214]
Wheeler, Burton K., files, 1924–1945 [collection 2206]
Wheeler, Burton K., papers, 1922–1975 [collection 2207]
Wheeler, Burton K., papers, 1924–1947 [collection 2411]
Wheeler, Burton Kendall, photograph collection, 1909–1958 [lot 004]

Ohio History Connection

Daugherty, Harry, papers
Harding, Warren G., papers

Princeton University Library

Beck, James M., papers

UCLA Library

Britton (Nan) papers

FBI Files

61-3546 (William E. Borah)
62-534 (Blair Coan)
62-725 (Gaston B. Means)
62-2123 (Thaddeus Caraway)
62-3088 (Albert B. Fall)
62-3264 (Roy O. Woodruff)
62-3552 (Veterans' Bureau)
62-5481 (John W. H. Crim)
62-5565 (Gaston B. Means)
62-6216 (Warren G. Harding)
62-7824 (Senate investigation of Harry M. Daugherty)
62-7903 (Burton K. Wheeler)
62-8782 (Harlan Fiske Stone)
67-149 (personnel file of Lucien Wheeler)
67-159 (personnel file of Emilio Kosterlitzky)
67-561 (personnel file of John Edgar Hoover)
67-5159 (personnel file of William J. Burns)
67-24617 (personnel file of Jessie B. Duckstein)
67-102324 (personnel file of Hazel B. Scaife)

Lawsuits and Court Opinions

Ex parte Daugherty, 299 F. 260 (S.D. Ohio 1924)
Mammoth Oil Co. v. United States, 275 U.S. 13 (1927)
McGrain v. Daugherty, 273 U.S. 135 (1927)
Trump v. Mazars USA, LLP, 140 S.Ct. 2019 (2020)

Notes

Prologue: "I'll Get Daugherty"

1   **Only the president:** Not even Daugherty's fellow cabinet members were told of the attorney general's plans. See "Rail Strikers Curbed by Drastic Injunction," *Cincinnati Enquirer*, September 2, 1922; and "Injunction Suit Surprises Cabinet," *New York Times*, September 2, 1922.

1   **credulously reported:** See "Washington Society," *Washington Herald*, September 1, 1922; and "Society," *Washington Times*, September 1, 1922.

1   **courtroom 627:** Richard Cahan, *A Court That Shaped America*, 53.

1   **audible tremor:** "U.S. Obtains Drastic Order in Rail Tieup," *Chicago Daily Tribune*, September 2, 1922.

1   **marble and mahogany walls:** Cahan, *A Court That Shaped America*, 53.

1   **Reporters scampered:** "U.S. Obtains Drastic Order in Rail Tieup."

2   **"The Court observes":** Harry M. Daugherty and Thomas M. Dixon, *The Inside Story of the Harding Tragedy*, 143.

2   **nationwide strike:** Justin F. Jackson, "Railroad Shopmen's Strike of 1922," in *Encyclopedia of the Jazz Age,* ed. Ciment, 432–433.

2   **aim of the Red agitators behind the strike:** Daugherty and Dixon, *Inside Story*, 127.

2   **fifty-one typewritten pages:** The full text of the bill of equity in the matter, captioned *United States of America v. Railway Employees' Department of the American Federation of Labor, et al.,* can be found at *Congressional Record,* 67th Cong., 2nd sess., September 1, 1922, 12097-111.

2   **most sweeping temporary restraining order:** Colin J. Davis, *Power at Odds*, 131.

2   **"It is with great regret":** "U.S. Obtains Drastic Order in Rail Tieup."

2   **great show of his reluctance:** "U.S. Ready to Use Power General Strike Proposal," *Boston Daily Globe*, September 2, 1922.

2   **"The government of the United States":** "Gompers to Put up General Strike Plan to Federation Council as U.S. Enjoins Railway Shopmen," *New York Tribune*, September 2, 1922.

3   **face of Abraham Lincoln:** William Walton, "The Field of Art: Van Ingen's New Mural Decorations in Chicago," *Scribner's*, July 1909.

3   **plucked Wilkerson:** Daugherty and Dixon, *Inside Story*, 142.

3   **At Daugherty's insistence,** "Wilkerson to Succeed Landis, Capital Hears," *Chicago Daily Tribune*, June 27, 1922.

3   **sent an emissary:** "Notables of Bar See Wilkerson Don the Ermine," *Chicago Sunday Tribune*, July 23, 1922.

3   **had its intended effect:** Jackson, "Railroad Shopmen's Strike of 1922."

3   **pledged revenge:** "Labor Council Asks Resistance of Injunctions," *New York Tribune*, September 10, 1922.

4   **entertained articles of impeachment:** "Move to Impeach Daugherty Is Made," *Baltimore Sun*, September 12, 1922.

4   **fellow cabinet members voiced outrage:** In particular, Secretary of State (and future chief justice) Charles Evans Hughes and Secretary of Commerce (and future president) Herbert Hoover objected to the curtailment of civil liberties. See James N. Giglio, *H. M. Daugherty*, 150–151.

4   **escaped a lynch mob:** John M. Paxson, "The Candidate and the Company: The 1920 Gubernatorial Campaign of Burton K. Wheeler and Its Treatment by the Montana Press," thesis about Burton K. Wheeler, Box 3, Folder 13, Burton K. Wheeler Papers, 1922–1975, Montana State University Library, 17–18.

4   **wily blue eyes:** Richard T. Ruetten, "Burton K. Wheeler, 1905–1925," 160.

4   **"Daughertyism":** "Big Audience Hears Wheeler," *Billings Gazette,* October 25, 1922.

4   **"This is your fight":** "Wheeler Makes His Address to Largest Audience Seen in Margaret This Campaign," *Butte Miner*, November 5, 1922.

5   **refused to prosecute antiwar dissenters:** Burton Kendall Wheeler and Paul F. Healy, *Yankee from the West*, 135–164 (hereafter cited in the notes as Wheeler and Healy, *Yankee*).

5   **overcharged the War Department by $2,267,342:** La Follette-Wheeler Campaign Headquarters, *The Facts*, 56.

5   **"protecting the profiteers":** "Big Audience Hears Wheeler."

5   **one congressman's feeble attempt:** Giglio, *H. M. Daugherty*, 152–153.

6   **a nervous breakdown:** "Daugherty's Accuser Collapses; House Grants Leave of Absence," *New York Tribune*, December 24, 1922.

6   **"I'll get Daugherty":** Blair Coan, *The Red Web*, 125.

Chapter 1: "Something Terrible Has Happened"

8   **gunshot rang out:** "J.W. Smith Suicide in Apartment of Attorney General," *Washington Evening-Star*, May 30, 1923.

8   **first law enforcement officer on the scene:** "Daugherty's Friend Suicide in His Room," *New York Times*, May 31, 1923.

8   **nation's most famous detective:** For background on Burns, see William R. Hunt, *Front-Page Detective*.

8   **bent the rules or broke the law:** Hunt, *Front-Page Detective*, 151.

8   **tracked down the most accomplished counterfeiter:** Hunt, 11–12.

8   **infamous 1910 bombing of the Los Angeles Times building:** For the story of the *Times* bombing and Burns's role in apprehending the perpetrators, see Howard Blum, *American Lightning: Terror, Mystery, the Birth of Hollywood, and the Crime of the Century* (New York: Three Rivers Press, 2008).

8   **crumpled at the foot of one of two beds:** Joel T. Boone, unpublished memoirs, Joel Thompson Boone papers, Library of Congress (hereafter cited as Boone memoirs), chapter 18, 69.

8   **.32-caliber revolver:** "J.W. Smith Suicide in Apartment of Attorney General."

9   **through Smith's right temple:** "Smith, Suicide, Mystery Man of Harding Administration," *Baltimore Sun*, May 31, 1923.

9   **purple silk pajamas:** Alan Hynd, "The Man Who Swindled the President," 133.

9   **heavy carpers:** Details about the Wardman Park's decor and furnishings come from "Ballrooms Masterpiece of Modern Architecture," *Washington Post*, June 1, 1919.

9   **inside a metal wastebasket:** Boone memoirs, chapter 18, 69.

9   **Jesse Worley Smith:** Smith's seldom-reported middle name comes from his World War I draft card. NARA via Ancestry.com.

9   **invalid wife:** Carl Sferrazza Anthony, *Florence Harding*, 589.

10   **"most intimate friends":** *Investigation of the Attorney General: Hearings Before the Select Committee on Investigation of the Attorney General*, US Senate, 68th Cong. (hereafter cited as *Investigation*), 16.

10   **"A word of praise":** Boone memoirs, chapter 18, 62b.

10   **flurry of telegrams:** Samuel Hopkins Adams, *Incredible Era*, 44.

10   **"your little friend, Jesse":** Smith to Daugherty, April 2, 1923, reprinted in *Investigation*, 600.

10   **rumors of a sexual component:** Anthony, *Florence Harding*, 294, 409.

10   **always the best-dressed man:** Adams, *Incredible Era*, 43.

10   **"symphony of gray and lavender":** Adams, 43.

10   **matching the color:** Anthony, *Florence Harding*, 589.

10   **treated them as "a duo":** Anthony, 294.

10   **his education stopped at high school:** Adams, *Incredible Era*, 42.

10   **voracious reader of detective stories:** Harry M. Daugherty and Thomas M. Dixon, *The Inside Story of the Harding Tragedy*, 244.

10   **"whaddyaknow":** Robert K. Murray, *The Harding Era*, 431.

10   **"get out your umbrella":** Francis Russell, *President Harding*, 336.

10   **spent his entire career before coming east in retail:** "Smith, Mystery Man of Daugherty Inquiry," *New York Times*, March 30, 1924; and Russell, *President Harding*, 336.

11   **relocated with Daugherty to the capital:** Adams, *Incredible Era*, 238.

11   **considered appointing Smith:** James N. Giglio, *H. M. Daugherty*, 135.

11   **March 5, 1921:** Many sources (including the most visible, Wikipedia) incorrectly give the date as Friday, March 4, 1921, the date that President Harding took office. In fact, President Wilson's outgoing attorney general, A. Mitchell Palmer, remained on as attorney general until Saturday, March 5, when Daugherty took his oath of office at Justice Department headquarters, his predecessor standing beside him. See "New Department Heads Take Reins," *Washington Post*, March 6, 1921.

11   **ensconced himself in an anteroom:** *Investigation*, 33.

11   **common sight inside Justice headquarters:** "Smith, Mystery Man of Daugherty Inquiry."

11   **third floor:** Richard Gid Powers, *Secrecy and Power*, 159; and Athan G. Theo-
      haris, *The FBI*, 250.
11   **kept their political patronage files:** Giglio, *H. M. Daugherty*, 136–137.
11   **removed the revolver:** Anthony, *Florence Harding*, 406.
11   **found a last will:** *Investigation*, 27.
11   **"Will you please come":** Hynd, "The Man Who Swindled the President," 133.
12   **in his dressing gown and slippers:** Hynd, 133.
12   **"I'd better call Dr. Shoenfeld":** Hynd, 133.
12   **made the first medical examination:** Boone memoirs, chapter 18, 69–70.
12   **Harry J. Dougherty:** "Mortimer's Story of $5,000 Payment to Forbes Re-
      futed," *Washington Post*, December 19, 1924.
12   **alerted police:** "J.W. Smith Suicide in Apartment of Attorney General."
12   **followed by Coroner J. Ramsay Nevitt:** Nevitt's own account can be found in
      "Suicide Is Alleged in Smith's Case," *Washington Evening-Star*, December 21,
      1926.
12   **apparently "misplaced" it:** Francis Russell, *The Shadow of Blooming Grove*, 569.
13   **"How ... could a man shoot himself":** M. R. Werner and John Starr, *The
      Teapot Dome Scandal*, 100.
13   **discouraged a thorough search:** That was the recollection of the hotel's house
      doctor, Dr. Schoenfeld. See Hynd, "Gaston Bullock Means: Con Cum Laude,"
      399.
13   **afford their lavish lifestyle:** *Investigation*, 50.
13   **deathly afraid of firearms:** *Investigation*, 545.

Chapter 2: "What a Bolshevist Really Looked Like"

14   **could not miss the news:** To be clear, there's no positive documentation that
      Wheeler read about Smith's death aboard the *President Harding*, but given the
      presence of an onboard newspaper it seems unlikely that he didn't.
14   *Oceanic Edition*: "United States Lines to Issue Daily Newspaper," *Marine
      Journal*, May 19, 1923.
14   **"Daugherty's Chum Dies By Own Hand":** *Austin Statesman*, May 30, 1924.
14   **"Itching to try out my toga":** Wheeler and Healey, *Yankee*, 198.
14   **"Warren G. Harding era of complacency":** Wheeler and Healy, 198.
15   **Senate Office Building:** The building has subsequently been named for the
      long-serving Georgia senator, Richard Russell Jr. See Architect of the Capitol,
      "Russell Senate Office Building," https://www.aoc.gov/explore-capitol-campus
      /buildings-grounds/senate-office-buildings/russell.
15   **"We're going to Europe":** Wheeler and Healy, *Yankee*, 198–199.
15   **shopping on Fifth Avenue:** "Hayes' Story of N.Y. Meeting Untrue, Says Sena-
      tor on Stand," *Great Falls Tribune*, April 23, 1925.
15   **black-shirted fascists:** Wheeler misremembered the fascists as wearing brown
      shirts. Transcript of Wheeler dictation for autobiography, Box 23, Burton
      Kendall Wheeler papers, 1910–1972 [MC 34], Montana Historical Society
      (hereafter cited as Wheeler dictation), E-28.
15   **"driven into the streets":** Wheeler dictation, E-30.
15   **"I have been called a Bolshevist":** "Senator B. K. Wheeler Tells Flathead Farm-
      ers of Russia," *Helena Independent Observer*, August 2, 1923.

15   **gutted him:** Wheeler would describe the Soviet regime as "the most dictatorial and cruel government in the world today." Ray Beezley, *The Political Career of Burton K. Wheeler*, 47.

15   **another fifty years of "re-education":** Wheeler and Healy, *Yankee*, 200.

16   **Even Orthodox priests:** Wheeler and Healy, 201.

16   **arrested for boarding a train:** Wheeler dictation, E-45 to E-46.

16   **released with an official apology:** Dayton Stoddard, unpublished manuscript for Burton K. Wheeler biography, Burton Kendall Wheeler papers, 1910–1972 [MC 34], Montana Historical Society, B-8.

16   **dreamed of living in the "wild west":** Wheeler and Healy, *Yankee*, 57.

16   **"anywhere . . . that was wide and open with opportunity":** Wheeler and Healy, 57.

16   **losing his shirt to a couple of card sharps:** Wheeler and Healy, 58–63.

17   **"rough, tough, dirty" town of Butte:** Wheeler and Healy, 65.

17   **his first criminal trial:** Wheeler and Healy, 71–73.

17   **Anaconda Mining Company:** Marc C. Johnson, *Political Hell-Raiser*, 7–8.

17   **all but three daily newspapers:** Wheeler and Healy, *Yankee*, 98.

17   **specialize in personal injury suits:** Johnson, *Political Hell-Raiser*, 9; and Wheeler and Healy, *Yankee*, 89.

17   **one term in the state legislature:** Wheeler and Healy, *Yankee*, 83–96.

17   **as chief federal law officer:** Wheeler and Healy, 97–114.

18   **stood firm against popular sentiment:** Wheeler and Healy, 135–164.

18   **attempted to strangle his campaign:** Wheeler and Healy, 165–184.

18   **brush with mob violence:** John M. Paxson, "The Candidate and the Company: The 1920 Gubernatorial Campaign of Burton K. Wheeler and Its Treatment by the Montana Press," thesis about Burton K. Wheeler, Box 3, Folder 13, Burton K. Wheeler Papers, 1922–1975, Montana State University Library, 17–18; and Wheeler and Healy, *Yankee*, 173–175.

18   **"I'll shoot anyone full of lead":** Wheeler and Healy, *Yankee*, 174.

18   **ship's "milk steward":** "Cat Mascot of S.S. Harding Is Given Rating of 'Milk Steward,'" *Rutland News*, June 19, 1923.

18   **daily pogo stick races:** "Pogo Stick Racing Excites Younger Set on Big Ocean Liners," *Norman Transcript*, August 28, 1923.

19   **"His purpose and activities in Washington":** "Harding Aid's Suicide Mystery," *New York Daily News*, May 31, 1923.

19   **Charles F. Cramer:** Samuel Hopkins Adams, *Incredible Era*, 301–302.

19   **left a news clipping:** Francis Russell, *The Shadow of Blooming Grove*, 563.

19   **handwritten letter to Warren G. Harding:** Adams, *Incredible Era*, 302.

19   **avoided the shame of an unfolding scandal:** Adams, 301.

19   **Founded in 1870:** Jed Handelsman Shugerman, "The Creation of the Department of Justice," *Stanford Law Review* 66, no. 1 (January 2014): 121–172.

19   **That office was as old as the republic itself:** For an overview of the history of the office of attorney general, see Nancy V. Baker, *Conflicting Loyalties*; J. H. Shugerman, "Professionals, Politicos, and Crony Attorneys General: A Historical Sketch of the U.S. Attorney General as a Case of Structural Independence," *Fordham Law Review* 87, no. 5 (2019); and US Department of Justice, *200th Anniversary of the Office of Attorney General*.

19   **One notable exception was George H. Williams:** The best account of this little-known episode can be found in Allan Nevins, *Hamilton Fish*, 662–664, 769–772, and 818.

20   **penned anonymous letters:** Nevins, *Hamilton Fish*, 818.

20   **reached far beyond its original domain:** Albert Langeluttig, *The Department of Justice of the United States*; and US Department of Justice, *Annual Report of the Attorney General of the United States for the Fiscal Year 1924*.

20   **eighty US attorneys:** "Fight Will Be Made for Extra U.S. Judge," *Baltimore Sun*, January 30, 1924.

20   **Created by executive action:** For accounts of the Bureau's creation, see John F. Fox Jr., "The Birth of the Federal Bureau of Investigation"; Tim Weiner, *Enemies*, 7–12; Aaron J. Stockham, "Lack of Oversight," 17–69; "Bonaparte Founded G-Men," *Washington Star*, August 18, 1935; and James Findlay, "Memorandum for the Director: Early History of the Bureau of Investigation."

21   **sweeping raids:** Weiner, *Enemies*, 29–32.

21   **continued to infiltrate:** Weiner, 60.

21   **spying on anyone who dared to criticize the Harding administration:** "Caraway Declares Spy Is Set on Him," *New York Times*, May 28, 1922.

Chapter 3: "Very Bad News"

22   **"Harry, Boone has some news":** Joel T. Boone, unpublished memoirs, Joel Thompson Boone papers, Library of Congress (hereafter cited as Boone memoirs), chapter 18, 71–73.

22   **risen well above his official station:** Carl Sferrazza Anthony, *Florence Harding*, 247.

23   **chance encounter at a shoeshine stand:** Another version of this story places Harding and Daugherty in a line for an outdoor privy. The account placing them at a shoeshine stand might be a bowdlerized version of the dirty truth— but no conclusive evidence points either way. Details from this telling come from Mark Sullivan, *Our Times*, 16–19; and Francis Russell, *The Shadow of Blooming Grove*, 108–109.

23   **formidable political marriage:** For background on Daugherty's relationship with Harding (and on his own political career), see Sullivan, *Our Times*, 16–49.

23   **"seven crisp $500 bills":** James N. Giglio, *H. M. Daugherty*, 12. The "important matter" was the election of a US senator, which was the prerogative in those days of the state legislatures.

24   **"I found him sunning himself like a turtle":** Morris Robert Werner, *Privileged Characters*, 5.

24   **"Mother of Presidents":** Robert H. Ferrell, *The Strange Deaths of President Harding*, 148.

24   **cajoled, pressured, and persuaded:** Giglio, *H. M. Daugherty*, 106–107.

24   **"I don't expect":** "Hays Arouses Wood Leaders, Clash Averted," *New York Tribune*, February 25, 1920.

25   **bickering in a backroom hazy with cigar smoke:** The best account of this episode, complete with much-needed myth-busting, can be found in Wesley M. Bagby, "'The Smoke Filled Room' and the Nomination of Warren G. Harding," *Mississippi Valley Historical Review* 41, no. 4 (March 1955).

25   personified the values of small town America: Robert K. Murray, *The Harding Era*, 41.
25   "fifteen men in a smoke-filled room": Sullivan, *Our Times*, 37.
25   mistresses was blackmailing the nominee: Anthony, *Florence Harding*, 202–204.
26   clean up this mess: Anthony, 254–256.
26   "not heroics but healing": "Asks Return to Simpler Living," *Indianapolis Star*, June 29, 1920.
26   pledged to roll back: For a succinct summary of the 1920 campaign, see Nathan Miller, *New World Coming*, 61–80.
27   promote a slogan of "America First": "'America First,' Harding's Slogan," *Boston Daily Globe*, October 10, 1920.
27   offered Harry Daugherty the cabinet position of his choice: Giglio, *H. M. Daugherty*, 117.
27   a dedicated phone line: Anthony, *Florence Harding*, 390.
27   Floral tributes: "Jess W. Smith Laid to Rest," *Cincinnati Enquirer*, June 3, 1923.
27   official day of mourning in Washington Court House: "Tribute Paid Jess Smith," *Marion Star*, June 2, 1923; and "Business Suspended for Funeral of Jesse W. Smith," *St. Louis Post Dispatch*, June 3, 1923.
27   recited the attorney general's tribute: "Eulogy Is Read," *Dayton Daily News*, June 3, 1923.
28   Smith's considerable estate: Werner, *Privileged Characters*, 251–252; and Russell, *Shadow of Blooming Grove*, 569.
28   burning its contents on the spot: M. R. Werner and John Starr, *The Teapot Dome Scandal*, 101.

Chapter 4: "Rumors of Irregularities"

29   discussed long-delayed Justice Department business: Harry M. Daugherty and Thomas M. Dixon, *The Inside Story of the Harding Tragedy*, 261–262.
29   party of sixty-seven: The full guest list and schedule can be found in "The Tour of the President to Alaska," Joel Thompson Boone papers, Box 68, Library of Congress.
29   speak directly to the American people: Francis Russell, *The Shadow of Blooming Grove*, 565.
29   the world's first disarmament conference: John W. Dean, *Warren G. Harding*, 130–135.
29   balancing the federal budget: Dean, *Warren G. Harding*, 105–106.
30   broadcast to both coasts: "Harding Talks to Nation," *Kansas City Times*, June 23, 1923. See also Carl Sferrazza Anthony, *Florence Harding*, 424.
30   announced the president's traveling party: "Speaker Gillet to Go to Alaska," *Boston Daily Globe*, June 9, 1923.
30   chronic hypertension: Boone memoirs, chapter 17, 120.
30   mild stroke in January: Transcript of oral history interview with Joel T. Boone, 28, Joel Thompson Boone papers, Box 89, Library of Congress.
30   "heavy cold": "Daugherty Has Cold; Doctors Order Rest," *Miami Herald*, January 28, 1923.
30   his office on Vermont Avenue: "Need for Justice Building Hastened by Order to Move," *Washington Evening Star*, October 7, 1925.

30   **drifting out of Harding's inner circle:** James N. Giglio, *H. M. Daugherty*, 160–161.

30   **Postmaster General Harry New . . . had succeeded Daugherty in those roles:** "Illness Sounds Knell to Daugherty's Power," *Akron Beacon Journal*, May 19, 1923.

30   **Anxiety washed over Daugherty:** The look on Harding's face, Daugherty wrote, "distressed me." Daugherty and Dixon, *Inside Story*, 261–269.

31   **Harding's private demeanor matched his public image:** Frederick Lewis Allen, *Only Yesterday*, 109.

31   **"Now . . . I want to get some law business":** Daugherty and Dixon, *Inside Story*, 262.

31   **selling his ownership stake:** "Harding Sells Control of His 'Marion Star,'" *New York Tribune*, June 21, 1923.

31   **agreed to represent Harding in the transaction:** Mark Sullivan, *Our Times*, 244.

31   **steamed into the copper mining settlement:** "Greeting of Loyal Citizens Tribute to Nation's Chief and to Genial Personality of Mr. and Mrs. Harding," *Butte Miner*, June 30, 1923.

31   **struck up a tune:** "Greeting of Loyal Citizens Tribute to Nation's Chief."

32   **group of local dignitaries:** "Butte Extends Welcome to President and Party," *Butte Miner*, June 30, 1923.

32   **"whether to commiserate with you":** Burton K. Wheeler, "Reminiscences of Burton Kendall Wheeler, 1969" [transcript of oral history interview], Columbia Center for Oral History Research, 89.

32   **"We have witnessed":** "Greeting of Loyal Citizens Tribute to Nation's Chief."

32   **nationwide straw poll:** "Ford in Front, Harding Next in 'Collier's' Tally," *New York Tribune*, May 23, 1923.

33   **At Clark Park:** "Crowd Greets President at Clark's Park," *Butte Miner*, June 30, 1923.

33   **"Till We Meet Again":** "Crowd Greets President at Clark's Park."

33   **strange, unexplained symptoms:** Details on Harding's symptoms from Edward B. MacMahon and Leonard Curry, *Medical Cover-Ups in the White House*, 81–82.

33   **pulled aside Colonel Edmund Starling:** Starling, *Starling of the White House*, 189.

34   **had no business treating the chief executive:** Details on Sawyer's malpractice and Harding's declining health from Robert S. Pinals and Harold Smulyan, "The Death of President Warren G. Harding," *American Journal of the Medical Sciences* 348, no. 3 (June 2014).

34   **mistrusted his doctor's judgment:** Anthony, *Florence Harding*, 424.

34   **190 wooden stairs:** Anthony, 434.

34   **diagnosed him with a sunburn:** "Swelling from Sunburn Curtails Harding Program," *Boston Globe*, June 23, 1923.

35   **The case of . . . Gaston Means had unsettled him:** Russell, *Shadow of Blooming Grove*, 565.

35   **"I have no trouble":** William Allen White, *A Puritan in Babylon*, 239; and White, *Autobiography of William Allen White*, 619.

35   **"If you knew of a great scandal":** Hoover, *The Memoirs of Herbert Hoover*, 49.

35   "some rumors of irregularities": Hoover, 49.

35   a long, coded message from Washington: William Allen White, *Masks in a Pageant*, 432.

35   "what a president was to do": Adams, *Incredible Era*, 372.

36   streetcar nearly plowed: Anthony, *Florence Harding*, 427.

36   motorcar went off a cliff: "President Is Saddened by Auto Accident," *Selma Times Journal*, June 25, 1923.

36   wrecked the Union Pacific locomotive: "Portland's Owl Train Is Wrecked," *Medford Mail Tribune*, July 5, 1923.

36   sudden jolt rattled the ship: Anthony, *Florence Harding*, 437.

36   "All hands on deck": Anthony, 438.

36   "I hope this boat sinks": Anthony, 438.

36   chose to materialize, quite unexpectedly, in Seattle: Hoover, *The Memoirs of Herbert Hoover*, 50.

36   by way of . . . the Canadian Pacific Railway: "A.-G. of U.S. Pays a Visit to City," *Vancouver Sun*, July 30, 1923.

37   presidential standard flapping: "Harding Predicts Prosperous Alaska; Statehood Soon," *New York Times*, July 28, 1923.

37   "listless": Pinals and Smulyan, "The Death of President Warren G. Harding," 234.

37   natural wonders of "Nebraska": Anthony, *Florence Harding*, 440.

37   Hoover, who had actually written the speech: Hoover, *The Memoirs of Herbert Hoover*, 49–50.

37   suffered a mild heart attack: Anthony, *Florence Harding*, 440.

37   cleared his schedule: Pinals and Smulyan, "The Death of President Warren G. Harding," 234.

37   Yosemite, its original destination: "President Harding Spends Sunday in Yosemite Valley," *Long Beach Press-Telegram*, July 29, 1923.

37   His diagnosis? Food poisoning: Pinals and Smulyan, "The Death of President Warren G. Harding," 234.

37   walked under his own power: Anthony, *Florence Harding*, 443.

38   "Everything troublesome was turned away": Wilbur, *The Memoirs of Ray Lyman Wilbur*, 381.

38   paused by a cluster of reporters: "All Reports from Palace Sickroom Are Encouraging," *Modesto Evening News*, August 1, 1923.

38   propped up in bed: Russell, *Shadow of Blooming Grove*, 591.

38   "A Calm Review of a Calm Man": Samuel G. Blythe, *Saturday Evening Post*, July 28, 1923.

38   "That's good": Russell, *Shadow of Blooming Grove*, 591.

38   official cause of death: Daugherty and Dixon, *Inside Story*, 272–273.

38   Tears coursed down his cheeks: "President's Death Is Shock to Daugherty," *Akron Beacon Journal*, August 3, 1923.

Chapter 5: "The Hardest Blow of My Life"

39   "Calvin!": Details of Calvin Coolidge's first moments as president come from Coolidge, *The Autobiography of Calvin Coolidge*, 173–174; Mark Sullivan, *Our Times*, 265–271; "Calvin Coolidge Becomes President as He Sleeps at Father's Home in Little Village of Plymouth," *Vermont Tribune*,

August 10, 1923; and Christopher D. Dale and Porter H. Dale II, "The Calvin Coolidge Inauguration Revisited," *Vermont History* 62, no. 4 (Fall 1994): 214–222.

40   **measured conservatism:** Jason Roberts, "The Biographical Legacy of Calvin Coolidge and the 1924 Presidential Election," chapter 10 in *A Companion to Warren G. Harding, Calvin Coolidge, and Herbert Hoover,* 194–195.

40   **far less calculating:** Robert Sobel, *Coolidge,* 62.

40   **earned him the trust:** Roberts, "The Biographical Legacy of Calvin Coolidge," 195.

40   **"the sly and laconic Yankee rustic":** Nathan Miller, *New World Coming,* 135.

40   **contributed little:** David Greenberg, *Calvin Coolidge,* 40.

41   **eating alone:** Roberts, "The Biographical Legacy of Calvin Coolidge," 196–197.

41   **conventional wisdom:** Roberts, 197.

41   **his father . . . would do it:** Attorney General Daugherty was not convinced that Coolidge's father, a state magistrate, was qualified to administer the oath to a federal official. At Daugherty's urging, Coolidge immediately took the oath a second time upon arriving in Washington, DC. This time, it was administered by Justice A. A. Hoehling of the Supreme Court of the District of Columbia, a federal tribunal. This second oath taking remained a secret for nearly a decade. "Tells of Coolidge and Second Oath," *New York Times,* February 3, 1932.

42   **outpouring of national grief:** Russell, *Shadow of Blooming Grove,* 593–596.

42   **sheer shock:** Phillip G. Payne, "The Harding Presidency," chapter 6 in *A Companion to Warren G. Harding, Calvin Coolidge, and Herbert Hoover,* 117.

42   **In Cheyenne:** Harry M. Daugherty and Thomas M. Dixon, *The Inside Story of the Harding Tragedy,* 273–276.

42   **watched the tributes:** Daugherty and Dixon, *Inside Story,* 273–276.

42   **"hardest blow of my life":** Daugherty and Dixon, 271.

43   **Daugherty would resign:** "Expect Daugherty Will Resign Soon," *Hartford Courant,* August 4, 1923.

43   **Boston Daily Globe observed:** "Coolidge Is Mystery Man," *Boston Daily Globe,* August 4, 1923.

43   **elaborated on the rumors:** "Shakeup Looms in Officialdom at Washington," *Akron Beacon Journal,* August 4, 1923.

43   **"I would rather":** "Daugherty Often Works at His Desk at Capitol Till 2 A.M.—Jane Dixon Reveals New Facts About Busy Attorney-General," *Boston Sun,* July 17, 1921.

43   **Custom dictated:** Boyden Sparkes, "Coolidge Keeps Cabinet and Harding Aids for Present; West Pays Silent Tribute as the Funeral Train Passes," *New York Tribune,* August 5, 1923.

44   **expecting a resignation announcement:** J. F. Essary, "Party Leaders Rally Around New President," *Baltimore Sun,* August 8, 1923.

44   **spared no pageantry:** Russell, *Shadow of Blooming Grove,* 596–599.

44   **six-star rank:** While General of the Armies of the United States is today generally considered a six-star rank, senior to the five-star General of the Army, Pershing never wore more than four. Also, George Washington was promoted to General of the Armies in the 1978 but never actually held the rank in his lifetime.

44 **gulped and choked:** "Daugherty Sobs; Seems Desolate at Harding Bier," *New York Daily News*, August 9, 1923.

45 **social anxiety:** James N. Giglio, *H. M. Daugherty*, 139.

45 **disconsolate:** "Daugherty Sobs; Seems Desolate at Harding Bier."

45 **feeling the pressure:** Claude Fuess, *Calvin Coolidge*, 332.

45 **New Willard Hotel, the Coolidges' temporary lodgings:** Fuess, *Calvin Coolidge*, 314.

45 **"get rid of Daugherty":** Claudius O. Johnson, *Borah of Idaho*, 288–289.

45 **perceived as a repudiation:** Fuess, *Calvin Coolidge*, 332.

46 **Chief Justice Taft:** Samuel Hopkins Adams, *Incredible Era*, 412.

46 **unsolicited career advice:** William Allen White, *A Puritan in Babylon*, 252.

46 **Taft felt:** White, *Puritan in Babylon*, 272.

46 **"Indeed . . . he is very sensitive":** White, 252.

47 **an overture:** Giglio, *H. M. Daugherty*, 165.

47 **the president refused it:** "Daugherty to 'Stand By' Coolidge Administration," *New York Tribune*, August 18, 1923.

47 *New York Tribune*: "Daugherty to 'Stand By' Coolidge Administration."

47 **Ohio's *Akron Beacon Journal*:** "Daugherty to Stick as Attorney General," *Akron Beacon Journal*, August 18, 1923.

Chapter 6: "This Teapot Dome Thing"

49 **Billings, Montana:** Mark Guizlo, "Billings, Montana," Encyclopedia of the Great Plains, http://plainshumanities.unl.edu/encyclopedia/doc/egp.ct.005.

49 **Tom Arthur:** "Tom Arthur," *Missoulian*, March 14, 1921; and "Oil Man in Role of Walsh Spokesman Jars Democrats," *Billings Gazette*, February 20, 1924.

49 **stopped in Billings:** "Wheelers Entertained at Albin Home," *Billings Gazette*, November 26, 1922.

50 **"This Teapot Dome thing":** Burton K. Wheeler, "Reminiscences of Burton Kendall Wheeler, 1969" [transcript of oral history interview], Columbia Center for Oral History (hereafter cited as Wheeler oral history), 89.

50 **conservationists cried foul:** M. R. Werner and John Starr, *The Teapot Dome Scandal*, 68–69.

50 **attend a conference:** Wheeler oral history, 89.

50 **class of insurgent freshmen:** Erik Olssen, "The Progressive Group in Congress, 1922–1929," *Historian* 42, no. 2 (February 1980): 244–263.

51 **"yahoos of the west":** The phrase was William Howard Taft's. The chief justice bemoaned their presence on the Senate Judiciary Committee. See LeRoy Ashby, *The Spearless Leader*, 34.

51 **"The time has come":** Olssen, "The Progressive Group in Congress," 250.

51 **recounted all the irregularities:** "Big Oil Lease Profit Charged by La Follette," *New York Tribune*, April 29, 1922.

51 **persuade a unanimous Senate:** "Senate Orders Sweeping Quiz in Oil Leases," *San Francisco Chronicle*, April 30, 1922.

52 **got an idea:** Wheeler and Healy, *Yankee*, 217.

52 **When they first met:** Transcript of interview with Burton K. Wheeler, July 7, 1949, Burton Kendall Wheeler papers, 1910–1972, Box 27, Montana Historical Society (hereafter cited as 1949 Wheeler interview), 9–10.

52   "Young man": 1949 Wheeler interview, 9.

52   championed Walsh's candidacy: Marc C. Johnson, *Political Hell-Raiser*, 9–10.

52   orchestrated Wheeler's appointment: Johnson, *Political Hell-Raiser*, 11.

52   could not have been more different: 1949 Wheeler interview, 1–3.

53   "Irishman without a sense of humor": Ray Thomas Tucker and Frederick Reuben Barkley, *Sons of the Wild Jackass*, 146.

53   "not the back-slapping, baby-kissing kind": 1949 Wheeler interview, 1.

53   "People voted for him": 1949 Wheeler interview, 1.

53   neighboring lakefront homes: Laton McCartney, *The Teapot Dome Scandal*, 230.

53   "I can't do everything": 1949 Wheeler interview, 5.

53   accepted more committee assignments: *Congressional Directory*, December 1923.

53   didn't get along with La Follette: 1949 Wheeler interview, 5.

53   friends with Edward L. Doheny: J. Leonard Bates, *Senator Thomas J. Walsh of Montana*, 223.

54   "Walsh, I don't know anything about this": Wheeler oral history, 89.

54   the burden of prep work: Bates, *Senator Thomas J. Walsh of Montana*, 213–214; and Mark Sullivan, *Our Times*, 285.

54   heard from two consulting geologists: McCartney, *Teapot Dome Scandal*, 171.

54   slowly sucking Teapot Dome dry: As Daniel Plainview (loosely based on Edward L. Doheny Jr.) explained in the 2007 film *There Will Be Blood*: "Drainage! Drainage! . . . If you have a milkshake, and I have a milkshake, and I have a straw . . . and my straw reaches across the room and starts to drink your milkshake, I drink your milkshake . . . I drink it up!" See Jonathan P. Thompson, "Oil, Milkshakes, and DRAINAGE!," *The Land Desk* (blog), March 19, 2021, https://www.landdesk.org/p/oil-milkshakes-and-drainage.

54   his first major witness: McCartney, *Teapot Dome Scandal*, 171–173; M. R. Werner and John Starr, *The Teapot Dome Scandal*, 110–113; and Sullivan, *Our Times*, 288–293.

55   next two witnesses: McCartney, *Teapot Dome Scandal*, 173–174; and Sullivan, *Our Times*, 300–301.

55   "a hundred million dollar profit": Sullivan, *Our Times*, 300.

55   traveled to the Kentucky Derby: McCartney, *Teapot Dome Scandal*, 101.

55   known each other since the 1880s: Margaret Leslie Davis, *Dark Side of Fortune*, 14–15.

55   nothing to hang his suspicions on: McCartney, *Teapot Dome Scandal*, 174.

56   evidence would trickle in: Sullivan, *Our Times*, 301–302.

56   flooded with so many tips": They're preserved to this day within Boxes 210–214 of the Library of Congress's Thomas James Walsh and John Edward Erickson papers.

56   rumors of a $1 million transaction: McCartney, *Teapot Dome Scandal*, 135–141.

56   "He tells me": Sidney B. Whipple to Thomas J. Walsh, October 30, 1923, Thomas J. Walsh papers, Box 213, Library of Congress.

56   summoned Stackelbeck: Stackelbeck to Walsh, October 31, 1923, Thomas J. Walsh papers, Box 213, Library of Congress.

57   called one witness after another: Bates, *Senator Thomas J. Walsh of Montana*, 217–218.

57   "There had been pillars built up": Committee on Public Lands and Surveys, US Senate, *Leases upon Naval Oil Reserves*, 3 vols. (Washington, DC: GPO, 1924), 840.

57   no longer acting like a bankrupted rancher: Sullivan, *Our Times*, 302–304.

57   local tax records: Sullivan, 304.

58   evidence of staggering corruption: Robert H. Ferrell, *The Strange Deaths of President Harding*, 114–121; and Frederick Lewis Allen, *Only Yesterday*, 129–130. Although Veterans' Bureau director Charles Forbes was assigned the brunt of the blame at the time, modern historians have reassessed his culpability in the affair. See Rosemary Stevens, *A Time of Scandal*.

58   sold $7 million worth of surplus supplies: Nathan Miller, *New World Coming*, 106.

58   "mystery men": See "Veterans' Quiz Unveils Some Mystery Men," *Dayton Daily News*, November 21, 1923; "Mystery Men Linked with U.S. Scandal," *Miami News*, November 22, 1923; and "National Capital's 'Mystery Men' Revealed in Veterans' Bureau Quiz," *Nashville Tennessean*, November 22, 1923.

58   "These men drop quietly": Veterans' Quiz Unveils Some Mystery Men," *Dayton Daily News*, November 21, 1923.

58   the talk of the town: Burl Noggle, *Teapot Dome*, 110.

58   "Intrigue, Debauchery, Corruption": *Atlanta Constitution,* October 25, 1923.

59   "No one above ground or below": "The Mob Spirit," *New York Herald-Tribune*, February 15, 1924.

59   all the more glaring: Giglio, *H. M. Daugherty*, 166–167.

59   "somebody ought to be handling": Crim to Daugherty, November 21, 1923, Department of Justice Straight Numerical File 225387-2, NARA.

59   "This is the situation": Daugherty to Crim, November 21, 1923, Department of Justice Straight Numerical File 225387-2, NARA.

59   "Among their acquaintances": "Mystery Men Linked with U.S. Scandal," *Miami News*, November 22, 1923.

59   "Harry Daugherty has a hand": This quote comes from a conversation Walsh had with Coolidge administration special counsel Owen Roberts, but Walsh also shared his suspicions about Daugherty with Wheeler. Quoted at Werner and Starr, *Teapot Dome Scandal*, 159.

60   disquieting reports from Walsh: Werner and Starr, *Teapot Dome Scandal*, 159–160.

60   "rotten to the core": Werner and Starr, 159.

Chapter 7: "I Object!"

61   "take his seat in the last row": Wheeler and Healy, *Yankee*, 206.

61   convened for a new session: "Radicals Force Deadlock in House as Congress Opens," *New York Times*, December 4, 1923.

61   "Is there objection?": The Senate floor dialogue comes from 68th Cong., 1st sess., *Congressional Record*, December 10, 1923, 157.

61   unanimous consent was the lubricant: Megan Suzanne Lynch and Richard S. Beth, *Parliamentary Reference Sources: Senate*.

62   **heads swiveled:** Wheeler and Healy, *Yankee*, 208.

62   **"This is the time to follow the leader":** Paul Y. Anderson, "And, Now, a Democratic Bloc in Senate, Led by New Member from Montana!," *St. Louis Post-Dispatch*, January 27, 1924.

62   **substantive objection:** Wheeler and Healy, *Yankee*, 208–209.

63   **51 to 45 majority:** There were a total of 96 senators at the time: 51 Republicans, 43 Democrats, and 2 Farmer-Laborites from Minnesota. That state's Farmer-Labor Party would later merge with the Democratic Party. See "Revised List of Congress Members," *Hartford Courant*, December 1, 1923.

63   **deadlocked:** "Radical Senators Force a Deadlock," *New York Times*, December 11, 1923.

64   **"Wheeler . . . there's a chance for you":** Burton K. Wheeler, "Reminiscences of Burton Kendall Wheeler, 1969" [transcript of oral history interview], Columbia Center for Oral History, 8.

64   **Lion of Idaho:** Richard Langham Riedel, *Halls of the Mighty*, 273.

64   **entitled only to a small personal staff:** US Senate, "About Committee & Office Staff: Historical Overview," accessed August 23, 2022, https://www.senate .gov/about/officers-staff/committee-office-staff/overview.htm.

64   **"with an exceedingly bad and threatening cold":** Fall to Lenroot, December 13, 1923, reprinted in Committee on Public Lands and Surveys, *Leases upon Naval Oil Reserves*, 1704.

65   **long, rambling letter:** Committee on Public Lands and Surveys, *Leases upon Naval Oil Reserves*, 1432.

65   **McLean's turn to feign illness:** Morris Robert Werner, *Privileged Characters*, 116.

65   **the telegraph wires:** Mark Sullivan, *Our Times*, 310–311.

66   **"poor Ned's health":** Sullivan, *Our Times*, 310.

66   **"a subcommittee of one":** James Leonard Bates, *Senator Thomas J. Walsh of Montana*, 221.

66   **"Mr. McLean, did you loan":** Bates, *Senator Thomas J. Walsh of Montana*, 221–222.

67   **continued to work its chaos:** "Senate Deadlock Holds," *New York Times*, December 20, 1923.

67   **"You can say for me":** Anderson, "And, Now, a Democratic Bloc in Senate."

67   **proved elusive:** "Senate's Deadlock on Cummins Holds," *Baltimore Sun*, January 4, 1924.

67   **voting as a bloc:** Six progressive Republicans still could not stomach "Cotton Ed" Smith and voted instead for Senator Couzens of Michigan. See "Senate's 32d Vote Elects E.D. Smith," *New York Times*, January 10, 1924.

67   **no senator could remember:** "Smith Elected by G.O.P. Rebel Votes," *Boston Daily Globe*, January 10, 1924.

68   **"If I were to pick":** Quoted at Wheeler and Healy, *Yankee*, 211.

Chapter 8: "Mere Bagatelle"

69   **refused to lift a finger:** James N. Giglio, *H. M. Daugherty*, 166–167.

69   **had yet to open a case file:** The first serial in FBI case file 62-3088 [on the Teapot Dome matter] is dated January 25, 1924.

69   **"I have been both detective and prosecutor":** "No Aid from Federal Bureau, Says Walsh," *Yonkers Herald*, February 23, 1924.

69 **"I rather imagine"**: "Charges Fall Sold Teapot Dome Lease," *New York Times*, January 17, 1924.

70 **"do nothing"**: The quote is adapted from a letter from Taft to his brother Horace, cited at Henry F. Pringle, *The Life and Times of William Howard Taft*, 1019.

70 **stiff intraparty challenge looming**: David Greenberg, *Calvin Coolidge*, 89–93.

70 **"I have visited six states"**: "Johnson Camp Says Oil Fight Halts Coolidge," *Chicago Daily Tribune*, January 20, 1924.

71 **rainy January day**: "The Weather," *Washington Evening-Star*, January 24, 1924, 19.

71 **ordered him to send a representative**: "Coolidge Would Be Ready to Act if Necessary," *St. Louis Post Dispatch*, January 22, 1924; and Giglio, *H. M. Daugherty*, 167.

71 **flee the country by steamship**: Report of Special Agent C. J. Estopinal, January 25, 1924, FBI file 62-3088-1.

71 **a newly helpful Director Burns**: Burns to Dellette, January 20, 1924, FBI file 62-3088-3.

71 **"Ascertain immediately whether he has booked passage"**: Burns to Shanton, January 20, 1924, FBI file 62-3088-4.

71 **placed him under surveillance**: Shanton to Hoover, January 23, 1924, FBI file 62-3088-2.

71 **"I don't suppose it needs to be stated"**: Howard H. Quint and Robert H. Ferrell, *The Talkative President*, 59–60.

72 **"all phases of this matter"**: Giglio, *H. M. Daugherty*, 167.

72 **word had spread**: James Leonard Bates, *Senator Thomas J. Walsh of Montana*, 223; and Laton McCartney, *The Teapot Dome Scandal*, 202.

72 **most conspicuous sight**: "President Orders Justice Agent to Watch Oil Inquiry," *Washington Post*, January 23, 1924.

72 **"I asked the committee"**: All dialogue from Doheny's testimony comes from Committee on Public Lands and Surveys, *Leases upon Naval Oil Reserves*, 1771–1823.

72 **gold-rimmed glasses**: Francis Russell, *The Shadow of Blooming Grove*, 616.

72 **his lawyer, Gavin McNab**: McCartney, *Teapot Dome Scandal*, 200–201; and Sullivan, *Our Times*, 318.

73 **invitation to invest**: Bates, *Senator Thomas J. Walsh of Montana*, 223–224.

73 **"This may be squeamishness"**: Bates, 224.

74 **invoking his Fifth Amendment rights**: M. R. Werner and John Starr, *The Teapot Dome Scandal*, 147.

74 **about to recommend the appointment of special counsel**: Werner and Starr, *Teapot Dome*, 141.

75 **huddled with his advisers**: Robert Sobel, *Coolidge*, 261.

75 **if not unprecedented**: For instance, President Taft interfered in an ongoing criminal investigation amidst the Ballinger-Pinchot controversy of 1909. His intervention was not uncontroversial at the time. See Bruce A. Green and Rebecca Roiphe, "Can the President Control the Department of Justice?," *Alabama Law Review* 1, 22, no. 107 (2018): 58.

75 **scrambled to get ahead of the news**: Giglio, *H. M. Daugherty*, 168.

75 **"May I again urge"**: "Daugherty Urged Naming of Special Counsel, Telling Coolidge He Did Not Wish to Serve," *New York Times*, January 28, 1924.

Chapter 9: "Resolved"

76   rose from his desk to offer a resolution: 68th Cong., 1st sess., *Congressional Record*, January 29, 1924, 1591.

76   "Whereas several weeks have transpired": 68th Cong., 1st sess., *Congressional Record*, January 29, 1924, 1591.

77   "saucer": Neil MacNeil and Richard A. Baker, *The American Senate*, 150.

77   "Republican leaders were predicting": "Bare Oil Scandal," *Weekly Kansas City Star*, January 30, 1924.

78   "I am here to play": "Daugherty Serene," *Los Angeles Times*, January 30, 1924.

78   flooded with private suspicions: Wheeler and Healy, *Yankee*, 217.

78   some of Wheeler's best sources: Burton K. Wheeler, "Reminiscences of Burton Kendall Wheeler, 1969" [transcript of oral history interview], Columbia Center for Oral History (hereafter cited as Wheeler oral history), 92.

78   whistleblower at the Federal Trade Commission: Wheeler oral history, 90.

78   "Tips came to me in bunches": Wheeler and Healy, *Yankee*, 217.

79   "My Dear Senator": "Daugherty Demands Inquiry by Senate Before Taking Action on Hostile Resolution," *New York Times*, February 12, 1924.

80   recalled what had happened: Wheeler and Healy, *Yankee*, 214.

80   fourteen articles of impeachment: See *Charges of Hon. Oscar E. Keller Against the Attorney General of the United States: Hearings Before the Committee on the Judiciary, US House of Representatives, 67th Cong.*

80   strange things started happening: Werner, *Privileged Characters*, 235.

80   badgered Keller about his sources: Giglio, *H. M. Daugherty*, 152; and Jennifer Luff, "Six Surveillance Scandals and the Downfall of the Bureau of Investigation," chapter 6 in *Commonsense Anticommunism*, 103.

80   "comic opera proceeding": "Keller, Angry, Quits Daugherty Hearing, Calling It a Farce," *New York Times*, December 15, 1922.

81   collapsed from a nervous breakdown: "Daugherty's Accuser Collapses; House Grants Leave of Absence," *New York Tribune*, December 24, 1922.

81   the time had come: Bates, *Senator Thomas J. Walsh of Montana*, 228.

81   introduced a joint resolution: "Text of Walsh's Resolution to Cancel Teapot Dome Lease," *Baltimore Sun*, January 29, 1924.

81   two accomplished and undeniably impartial lawyers: Werner and Starr, *Teapot Dome Scandal*, 152–157.

81   "If you are confirmed": Werner and Starr, 154.

82   Walsh was satisfied: Although he was understandably skeptical at first. Bates, *Senator Thomas J. Walsh of Montana*, 228.

Chapter 10: "The Least Embarrassed Person Here"

83   Republicans fretted: James N. Giglio, *H. M. Daugherty*, 169.

83   began lobbying President Coolidge: Donald R. McCoy, *Calvin Coolidge*, 214–215.

83   "First, it is a sound rule": William Allen White, *A Puritan in Babylon*, 267.

84   When Sen. William Borah arrived: This scene is drawn from several accounts: White, *Puritan in Babylon*, 268–269; Claude Fuess, *Calvin Coolidge*, 339–340; Claudius O. Johnson, *Borah of Idaho*, 289; and Harry M. Daugherty and Thomas M. Dixon, *The Inside Story of the Harding Tragedy*, 287–289.

86   **"carry the issue to the country"**: 68th Cong., 1st sess., *Congressional Record*, 2980.

86   **"If it would be of any help"**: McCoy, *Calvin Coolidge*, 213.

Chapter 11: "A Bigger Fool"

87   **five in the afternoon:** Unsigned Bureau of Investigation memo dated February 19, 1924, FBI file 62-7824-99X.

87   **deliver his first full speech:** This scene is drawn from several accounts: Transcript of interview with Burton K. Wheeler, November 13, 1961, Burton Kendall Wheeler papers, Box 27, Montana Historical Society, 5; Burton K. Wheeler, "Reminiscences of Burton Kendall Wheeler, 1969" [transcript of oral history interview], Columbia Center for Oral History, 90; and Wheeler and Healy, *Yankee*, 213–215.

87   **"I want to be frank":** All dialogue from Wheeler's Senate speech comes from 68th Cong., 1st sess., *Congressional Record*, 2769–2770.

87   **courteous, low-pitched voice:** As reported in the *North Adams Transcript*, March 15, 1924.

88   **taken a back seat to the House:** Neil MacNeil and Richard A. Baker, *The American Senate*, 230–244.

89   **biting off the ends of his words:** As reported in the *North Adams Transcript*, March 15, 1924.

89   **rattled that august body:** Wheeler and Healy, *Yankee*, 214–215.

89   **"most sensational speech":** "Wheeler Demands Inquiry," *New York Times*, February 20, 1924.

90   **"an attack so savage":** Quoted at Wheeler and Healy, *Yankee*, 214–215.

90   **Republican senators shared their concerns:** "Wheeler Demands Inquiry."

90   **"take care of this upstart":** Wheeler and Healy, *Yankee*, 218.

90   **a tradition stretching back:** "Washington's Farewell Address," United States Senate, February 22, 1862, https://www.senate.gov/artandhistory/history /minute/Washingtons_Farewell_Address.htm.

91   **the atmosphere inside the chamber became electric:** This scene is drawn from several newspaper accounts: "Daugherty Electrifies Critics by Appearing on Senate Floor," *Washington Evening Star*, February 22, 1924; "Washington Observations," *Washington Evening Star*, February 23, 1924; "G.O.P. Chiefs Split on Daugherty," *Sentinel* (Carlisle, PA), February 23, 1924; "Daugherty Visits Senate Chamber for Half Hour and Chats with Friends," *St. Louis Post-Dispatch*, February 22, 1924; and "Daugherty Visits Senate Chamber," *Stockton Daily Evening Record*, February 22, 1924.

91   **enjoyed Senate floor privileges:** There were no formal rules governing floor privileges in the Senate's first decades, but "Heads of the Executive Departments" were included when the Senate codified its rules in 1859. Although the attorney general did not technically head an executive department until 1870, that term was interpreted to mean cabinet officers, which would have included the attorney general. See Jane A. Hudiburg, *Senate Floor Privileges*.

91   **"The alternate domination":** The full text of Washington's Farewell Address can be found in Senate document no. 106–21, available at https://www .govinfo.gov/content/pkg/GPO-CDOC-106sdoc21/pdf/GPO-CDOC -106sdoc21.pdf.

Chapter 12: "How Secure I Am"

93   **started with a bang:** An allusion to T. S. Eliot's "The Hollow Men."

93   **passed by a vote of sixty-six to one:** 68th Cong., 1st sess., *Congressional Record*, 3410.

93   **"Naive observers exclaim":** Quoted in Dayton Stoddard, unpublished manuscript for Burton K. Wheeler biography, Burton Kendall Wheeler papers, 1910–1972 [MC 34], Montana Historical Society, D-5 to D-6.

94   **once again at the White House:** "Daugherty Defies Critics," *New York Times*, February 28, 1924.

94   **held up by the railroad authorities:** "Daugherty Defies Critics."

94   **"surprised and displeased":** "Daugherty, Still on Job, in Chicago Today," *Chicago Daily Tribune*, February 28, 1924.

94   **"I am here on government business":** "'I'm No Quitter,' Declares Daugherty, Now in Chicago," *Baltimore Evening Sun*, February 28, 1924.

94   **speculation turned to a grand jury:** "Aide in Dark," *Los Angeles Times*, February 28, 1924; and "May Be on Veterans' Bureau Business," *New York Times*, February 28, 1924.

94   **resigned as assistant attorney general:** "Crim Prosecutor for Veterans' Bureau," *Boston Daily Globe*, December 2, 1923.

95   **As the jury foreman would report:** Text of the report from "Forbes Took Bribe, Grand Jury Says," *New York Times*, March 1, 1924.

95   **four-page letter:** Harry Daugherty to Calvin Coolidge, February 28, 1924, Calvin Coolidge Papers, Library of Congress.

Chapter 13: "Pull Wheeler off Daugherty"

98   **strictly personal mission:** Details on Hately's trip to Nashville and dialogue from his interview with John S. Glenn come from several sources: *Investigation*, 1744–1746; Hately's unsigned memo, March 7, 1924, FBI file 62-7824-23X; Hately's handwritten notes on Maxwell House stationery, undated, FBI file 62-7824-24X; "Tried to 'Get' Wheeler Here," *Nashville Banner*, April 10, 1924; "Burns Man Here," *Nashville Banner*, April 10, 1924; "Work Done on Wheeler Case," *Nashville Banner*, April 10, 1924; "Evidence Against Wheeler Sought from J. S. Glenn," *The Tennessean*, April 10, 1924; and "Crooks, Thieves and Stoolpigeons Poison the Washington Ozone as Graft Cesspool Is Probed Deeper," *Daily Worker*, May 12, 1924.

98   **egg-bald with a well-trimmed moustache:** A somewhat dated portrait of Hately appears in "Supply Trade News," *Railway Age Gazette*, September 1, 1916.

98   **Charles Furness Hately:** See a biographical thumbnail of Hately in: Albert Nelson Marquis, ed., *The Book of Chicagoans* (Chicago: A. N. Marquis, 1911), 310.

98   **fashionable Maxwell House hotel:** Ophelia Paine, "Maxwell House Hotel," Tennessee Encyclopedia, https://tennesseeencyclopedia.net/entries/maxwell-house-hotel/.

98   **a retired federal agent:** For background on Glenn's career, see *Investigation*, 1746, 2222.

99   **put together what had happened:** "Tried to 'Get' Wheeler Here," *Nashville Banner*, April 10, 1924.

99 red, leather-bound memorandum book: "Burns Man Here," *Nashville Banner*, April 10, 1924.

100 his office in the Stahlman Building: "Burns Man Here."

100 founded in the waning days: For accounts of the Bureau's creation, see Fox, "The Birth of the Federal Bureau of Investigation"; Tim Weiner, *Enemies*, 7–12; Aaron J. Stockham, "Lack of Oversight," 17–69; Don Whitehead, *The FBI Story*, 17–25; "Bonaparte Founded G-Men," *Washington Star*, August 18, 1935; and James Findlay, "Memorandum for the Director," FBI History, November 19, 1943.

101 "create an investigative service": Findlay, "Memorandum for the Director."

101 "Foucheism": "Secret Service," *Boston Globe*, December 12, 1908.

101 "grew so powerful": Quoted at Max Lowenthal, *The Federal Bureau of Investigation*, 4.

101 "Anybody can shadow me": Fred J. Cook, *The FBI Nobody Knows*, 54.

102 employed only 265 agents: A table with the FBI's annual personnel count and appropriations appears at Athan Theoharis, *The FBI*, 4–5.

102 its detective force doubled: Theoharis, *The FBI*, 4.

102 list of suspected German sympathizers: Hank Messick, *John Edgar Hoover*, 12.

102 campaign of repression: Weiner, *Enemies*, 13–25.

102 full-fledged domestic intelligence agency: On the creation of the General Intelligence Division, see Lowenthal, *The Federal Bureau of Investigation*, 83–92.

102 General Intelligence Division: It was initially called the Radical Division before its renaming in 1920.

102 former Library of Congress clerk: Curt Gentry, *J. Edgar Hoover: The Man and the Secrets*, 67.

102 cataloging those threats: Gentry, *J. Edgar Hoover*, 79.

102 sweeping and controversial raids: Weiner, *Enemies*, 26–46.

103 579 sworn field agents: Theoharis, *The FBI*, 4.

103 still did not carry guns: Special agents were not authorized to carry firearms until 1934.

103 announced a shake-up: "Daugherty Plans Big Reorganization," *Washington Post*, August 19, 1921.

103 the new director's qualifications: Burns's biography is told in William R. Hunt, *Front-Page Detective*.

103 "America's Sherlock Holmes": Benjamin Welton, "The Man Arthur Conan Doyle Called 'America's Sherlock Holmes,'" *Atlantic*, November 20, 2013, https://www.theatlantic.com/entertainment/archive/2013/11/the-man-arthur -conan-doyle-called-americas-sherlock-holmes/281618/.

103 a cryptic marking on a scrap of burlap: Dana Gatlin, "Great Cases of Detective Burns: Tracking Anonymous Letter Writers," *McClure's*, April 1911, 652–662.

104 captured William "Long Bill" Brockway: Hunt, *Front-Page Detective*, 11–12.

104 its "best man": Hunt, 21.

104 employed shady characters: For example, Gaston Bullock Means. See Edwin P. Hoyt, *Spectacular Rogue*.

104 accused of fixing a jury: Hunt, *Front-Page Detective*, 107–108.

104 their forty-year friendship: "W. J. Burns Named Director of Federal Secret Service," *New York Call*, August 19, 1921.

104   **blackmail campaign against Warren Harding:** Carl Sferrazza Anthony, *Florence Harding*, 202–204, 254–256.

105   **returned from his fishing expedition:** As a matter of fact, Hately died soon after his return to Washington, DC, on March 16, 1924. See "Died," *Washington Post*, March 18, 1924.

105   **swarmed the Capitol complex:** Morris Robert Werner, *Privileged Characters*, 312.

105   **tapping into the Capitol phone lines:** Testimony of William O. Duckstein, *Investigation*, 2505.

105   **in the building's ladies' room:** Duckstein, *Investigation*, 2505.

105   **supposed reporter for the *New Haven Union*:** Thomas M. Smith's story is pieced together from his reports in FBI file 62-7824.

106   **ingratiated himself with Senator Wheeler's harried secretary:** Smith to Burns, February 13, 1924, FBI file 62-7824-100X.

106   **Allen Olds Myers:** For background on Myers, who signed his Bureau correspondence as "A.O.M.," see "Arrest Barlow on Libel Charge," *Buffalo Courier*, February 18, 1923; "A True Detective Story . . . 'The Case of the Screaming Parrot,'" *Des Moines Register*, September 5, 1937; and "Burns Detectives at Kiwanis Luncheon," *Evening News* (Wilkes-Barre, PA), July 24, 1918.

106   **"dollar-a-year men":** A full list of such agents appears in *Investigation*, 2453. See also Alpheus Thomas Mason, *Harlan Fiske Stone*, 149; and "Prominent Men Secret Agents," *Evening Journal* (Wilmington, DE), May 13, 1924.

107   **"It is reported":** Memo by A.O.M. (Allen Olds Myers), February 21, 1924, FBI file 62-7824-100X.

Chapter 14: "If She Can Be Kept Quiet"

108   **monitoring her calls and movements:** *Investigation*, 508.

108   **"nervous and jumpy and annoyed":** *Investigation*, 508.

108   **an old flame:** Affidavit of Alexander L. Fink, DOJ Straight Numerical File 226225, NARA (hereafter cited as Fink affidavit), 1.

108   **calling long-distance:** *Investigation*, 508–509.

108   **Stinson, 38:** Stinson habitually lied about her age, first subtracting five years, then seven. Government records confirm that she was born in 1885, not 1890 or 1892, as she later claimed.

108   **"irresponsible boy":** *Investigation*, 626.

109   **strolled into the lobby of the Hollenden Hotel:** Details of Stinson's rendezvous with Fink come from *Investigation*, 504–559, 566–592, 618–637; Fink affidavit; Statement of Irving Frankel, March 26, 1924, FBI file 62-7824-10 (hereafter cited as Frankel statement); "Rochester Sheriffs Here with Warrant for Alexander Fink," *Buffalo Enquirer*, March 25, 1924; and "Checking Up on Fink and Roxie Stinson Here in Buffalo," *Buffalo Enquirer*, March 18, 1924.

109   **Crystal chandeliers:** Details about the Hollenden Hotel and its decor come from historic postcards as well as "Hollenden Hotel," Encyclopedia of Cleveland History, https://case.edu/ech/articles/h/hollenden-hotel; and Allison V. Newbold, "Hollenden Hotel," Cleveland Historical, https://clevelandhistorical .org/items/show/818.

110   **"a way out"**: "Rochester Sheriffs Here with Warrant for Alexander Fink."

111   **knocking on her front door**: *Investigation,* 506.

111   **years of mutual resentment**: The *Chicago Daily Tribune*'s Philip Kinsley reported that Stinson "has long had a feud with the Daughertys" and that she "was always jealous of every one who cared for Jess." See "Roxie Called a Mere Pawn of Daugherty Foes," *Chicago Daily Tribune,* March 16, 1924.

111   **Roxie Stinson's marriage to Jess Smith**: Details on their relationship come from Adams, *Incredible Era,* 44–46; Russell, *Shadow of Blooming Grove,* 336–337; Werner, *Privileged Characters,* 243–244; "Ohio Villagers Recall Romance of Roxie Stinson," *Chicago Daily Tribune,* March 15, 1924; Julian Street, "Tells Story of Smith's Suicide," *Los Angeles Record,* April 4, 1924; "Smith, Mystery Man of Daugherty Inquiry," *New York Times,* March 30, 1924; "Roxie Stinson, Who Starred in 'Scandal,'" *Brooklyn Daily Eagle,* April 6, 1924; "Roxie Called a Mere Pawn of Daugherty Foes," *Chicago Daily Tribune,* March 16, 1924; "'I'll Have My Revenge' Cried Roxie—And She Did!" *Houston Post,* April 13, 1924; and R. H. Jones, "Roxie Stinson's Shattered Romance," *Knoxville News,* April 2, 1924.

111   **solemnized on November 10, 1908**: Marriage license of Jess W. Smith and Roxy R. Stinson, Ancestry.com.

112   **"extreme cruelty"**: R. H. Jones, "Roxie Stinson's Shattered Romance," *Knoxville News,* April 2, 1924.

112   **townsfolk scoffed**: Adams, *Incredible Era,* 45.

112   **advised her on gentlemen suitors**: Werner, *Privileged Characters,* 243.

112   **"a queerer aftermath to divorce"**: The friend was Aileen Hess Harper, paraphrased by Adams, 46.

112   **block her admission**: "Roxie Called a Mere Pawn of Daugherty Foes," *Chicago Daily Tribune,* March 16, 1924.

112   **resented the time Jess spent with her**: "'I'll Have My Revenge' Cried Roxie—And She Did!" *Houston Post,* April 13, 1924. See also Anthony, *Florence Harding,* 75.

112   **proceeded to flirt with her**: Anthony, *Florence Harding,* 254.

113   **"very much better off"**: *Investigation,* 23.

113   **their total household expenses**: *Investigation,* 49–50.

113   **"just loose in an envelope"**: *Investigation,* 582.

113   **stock in the Pure Oil Company**: *Investigation,* 28.

113   **White Motor Company stock**: *Investigation,* 21.

114   **handed the page from the hotel register**: Unsigned and undated memorandum for Director Burns, FBI file 62-7824-X4.

114   **this delicate transaction**: Details and dialogue from Fink's visit to Ungerleider and his subsequent attempt to blackmail Harry Daugherty are sourced from Frankel statement; Statement of Samuel Ungerleider, undated, DOJ Straight Numerical File 226225, NARA (hereafter cited as Ungerleider statement); Fink affidavit; "Fink Back in Buffalo, Reveals His Position in Daugherty Inquiry," *Buffalo Times,* March 25, 1924; "Rochester Sheriffs Here with Warrant for Alexander Fink," *Buffalo Enquirer,* March 25, 1924; and "Star Witness in Daugherty Probe Bares Testimony to Be Given Soon," *Buffalo Courier,* March 25, 1924.

114   **"a young fortune staring me in the face"**: Statement of Irving Frankel, March 26, 1924, 1, FBI file 62-7824-10.

114 **indicted for grand larceny:** "Buffalo Man Held for Grand Larceny," *Buffalo Times*, December 8, 1921.

114 **the executive suddenly dropped dead:** "Frank G. Curtis of Jamestown Dies Suddenly," *Buffalo Courier*, March 16, 1922.

114 **again charged with grand larceny:** "Fraud Charges Against Brokers Heard by Jury," *Democrat and Chronicle* (Rochester, NY), October 13, 1923.

115 **"a man big enough to expose Daugherty":** "Star Witness in Daugherty Probe Bares Testimony."

115 **"had the goods":** "Star Witness in Daugherty Probe Bares Testimony."

116 **twenty-eight such warehouses:** "Survey of the Alcoholic Liquor Traffic," testimony of R. A. Haynes, February 16, 1925, 17.

117 **"I know this will prevent her":** Statement of Samuel Ungerleider, undated, DOJ Straight Numerical File 226225, NARA.

117 **when she heard a knock:** Details and dialogue from the meeting in Stinson's hotel room are sourced from *Investigation,* 504–559, 566–592, 618–637; Fink affidavit; and Ungerleider statement; and Frankel statement.

117 **the hotel decor:** Details about the Hotel Statler decor come from Molly Winger Berger, "The Modern Hotel in America: 1829–1929," PhD diss., Case Western University, 1997, 318.

118 **the Axminster carpet:** Berger, "The Modern Hotel in America," 207.

119 **"absolutely closed":** *Investigation,* 515.

119 **a detective on her tail:** *Investigation,* 516.

119 **her hotel bill of $10.80:** Unsigned and undated memorandum for Director Burns, FBI file 62-7824-X4.

120 **"plain":** *Investigation,* 516.

120 **John V. Ryan:** Ryan to Burns, March 23, 1924, FBI file 62-7824-53X; and "New Inspector," *Dayton Herald*, October 4, 1921.

120 **Ryan's report:** Unsigned and undated memorandum for Director Burns, FBI file 62-7824-X4.

Chapter 15: "The Peculiar Nature of This Inquiry"

121 **its first executive session:** "Wheeler to Lead Daugherty Probe as Chief Counsel," *Atlanta Constitution*, March 4, 1924.

121 **unusual step of nominating:** Wheeler and Healy, *Yankee*, 216.

122 **denying the attorney general:** "Wheeler to Lead Daugherty Probe as Chief Counsel."

122 **"subcommittee of one":** M. Jay Racusin, "'Hushing' of Daugherty Witnesses Charged as Senate Inquiry Opens," *New York Tribune*, March 4, 1924.

122 **"prosecutor":** "Wheeler to Lead Daugherty Probe as Chief Counsel."

122 **"One must see":** Racusin, "'Hushing' of Daugherty Witnesses."

122 **a single law clerk:** His name was Arthur B. Melzner, a Montana lawyer. Wheeler and Healy, *Yankee*, 219.

122 **"Because of the vast power":** Racusin, "'Hushing' of Daugherty Witnesses."

123 **turned on his own party:** For Vanderlip's apostasy and the resulting backlash, see Vicki Mack, *Frank A. Vanderlip*, 313–339.

123 **"moral crusade against corruption":** *Chicago Daily Tribune*, February 23, 1924.

123 **murdering the ghost of President Harding:** "Vanderlip a Coward," *Lyons Republican*, quoted in Mack, *Frank A. Vanderlip*, 332.

123   found himself on the receiving end: Wheeler and Healy, *Yankee*, 219.
123   a *New York World* correspondent: His name was Charles Michelson. Burton
      K. Wheeler, "Reminiscences of Burton Kendall Wheeler, 1969" [transcript of
      oral history interview], Columbia Center for Oral History (hereafter cited as
      Wheeler oral history), 103.
123   "I want to serve you": Mack, *Frank A. Vanderlip*, 334.
123   "voluntary assistance" behind the scenes: For Wheeler's early meetings with
      Gaston Means, see Wheeler oral history, 92–96; Wheeler and Healy, *Yankee*,
      225–227; transcript of interview with Burton K. Wheeler, November 13, 1961,
      Burton Kendall Wheeler papers, Box 27, Montana Historical Society, 11–12;
      Dayton Stoddard, unpublished manuscript for Burton K. Wheeler biography,
      Burton Kendall Wheeler papers, 1910–1972 [MC 34], Montana Historical
      Society (hereafter cited as Stoddard manuscript), D-9 to D-10; and "Daugh-
      erty investigation," topical card file, Burton K. Wheeler Papers, 1922–1975,
      Montana State University Library, cards 3–6.
124   Washington, DC, neighborhood of Chevy Chase: The neighborhood spans the
      District of Columbia-Maryland border. The Wheelers lived on the DC side.
124   hired him to spy on the young woman: As it would turn out, this off-the-
      books investigation probably actually happened. Anthony, *Florence Harding*,
      300.
124   "Go after Mellon on whiskey": Wheeler oral history, 93.
125   "I'm a radical": Wheeler oral history, 93.
125   "He gave me some really good tips": Wheeler oral history, 95.
125   "Means had a brilliant mind": Wheeler and Healy, *Yankee*, 227.
125   dynamiting the sun porch: Stoddard manuscript, 9–10.

Chapter 16: "A Three-Ring Circus"

126   encouraged a 1921 rebellion: "Daugherty Hearing Puts Mexico First," *New
      York Times*, March 10, 1924; and "Oil Men Refute Charge They Aided Mex-
      ican Rebels," *Christian Science Monitor*, March 10, 1924.
126   installed questionable characters: "Daugherty Hearing Puts Mexico First."
126   ignored fifty-five antitrust cases: Thomas Stokes, [no title], *Atlanta Constitu-
      tion*, March 6, 1924.
126   even more salacious gossip: Wheeler wrote that "tips came to me in bunches
      that Daugherty was up to his neck in massive graft." Wheeler and Healy, *Yan-
      kee*, 217.
126   "Ohio crowd": Before Burton Wheeler later popularized "Ohio gang," this
      term was in common currency. See "Ring That Lived on 'Graft,'" *Irish Times*,
      March 4, 1924; "Daugherty's Ohio 'Friends' to Be Grilled," *New York Tribune*,
      March 5, 1924; and "Revelations to Shock U.S.," *Vancouver Sun*, March 3,
      1924.
127   "The hurried visit": Arthur Sears Henning, "Quick 'Ohio Graft Ring' Next,"
      Chicago Daily Tribune, March 3, 1924.
127   "ex-convicts, men under indictment": "Things Heard and Seen in Washing-
      ton," *Pawnee Courier Dispatch and Times Democrat*, May 1, 1924.
127   "Montana scandalmonger" and "assassin of character": "Daugherty Ousted,
      Hits Back at Coolidge; Borah or Kenyon May Succeed Him; Mellon Under
      Fire," *New York Tribune*, March 29, 1924.

128 **"hearts-and-flowers style"**: Wheeler and Healy, *Yankee*, 74.

128 **"It seemed to me"**: Wheeler and Healy, 74.

128 **formal training at the University of Michigan law school**: Wheeler and Healy, 47, 54–56.

128 **first major corruption case**: Johnson, *Political Hell-Raiser*, 11–12; Richard T. Ruetten, "Burton K. Wheeler, 1905–1925," 18–23; and Ruetten, "Burton K. Wheeler of Montana: A Progressive Between the Wars," 10.

129 **"If you have not shown enough letters already"**: Ruetten, "Burton K. Wheeler, 1905–1925," 19.

129 **"It was now possible in the United States"**: Frederick Lewis Allen, *Only Yesterday*, 162.

129 **"as a three-ring circus"**: Allen, *Only Yesterday*, 70.

130 **"jazz journalism"**: Michael Emery and Edwin Emery, *The Press and America*, 265–267, 281–287; and Edwin Emery and Ladd Smith, *The Press and America*, 625–628.

130 **"The result"**: Allen, *Only Yesterday*, 164.

130 **announced that hearings would begin**: "Open Daugherty Probe Thursday," *Boston Daily Globe*, March 11, 1924.

131 **formally subpoenaed**: "Committee Sifts Data on Daugherty," *Baltimore Sun*, March 11, 1924.

131 **found two strangers**: Wheeler and Healy, *Yankee*, 219.

Chapter 17: "You Are Hereby Commanded"

132 **under cover of darkness**: His train departed Washington at 7 p.m. and arrived in Columbus the following morning around 10 o'clock. Affidavit of Alexander L. Fink, DOJ Straight Numerical File 226225, NARA (hereafter cited as Fink affidavit), 5.

132 **"You mustn't do that"**: Transcript of interview with Burton K. Wheeler, November 13, 1961, Burton Kendall Wheeler papers, Box 27, Montana Historical Society (hereafter cited as 1961 Wheeler interview), 8.

132 **his political mentor**: Richard Dunlop, *Donovan*, 143.

133 **staunch ally of President Harding**: Wadsworth and Harding formed a strong friendship as freshmen senators. Francis Russell, *The Shadow of Blooming Grove*, 264.

133 **extreme secrecy**: Fink affidavit, 5.

133 **threatened with arrest and even deportation**: "Fear of 'Deportation' Made Roxie Stinson Talk," *New York Tribune*, March 15, 1924.

133 **445 East Gay Street**: 1924 Columbus, Ohio, City Directory, Ancestry.com.

133 **"a statuesque redhead"**: Wheeler and Healy, *Yankee*, 220.

133 **a striking resemblance**: "Looks Like the Girl on a Silver Dollar," *Boston Daily Globe*, March 14, 1924.

134 **"Probably if you discuss this matter"**: Dialogue from Wheeler's and Stinson's conversation comes from 1961 Wheeler interview, 8; and *Investigation*, 53–54.

134 **"Pursuant to lawful authority"**: Text of subpoena from FBI file 62-7824-38.

134 **"I have persuaded the little lady"**: Fink affidavit, 5.

135 **drop off her dog**: Fink affidavit, 5.

135 **Nose Bud**: *Investigation*, 578.

135 **"I can't get her to loosen up"**: Fink affidavit, 5.

135   ordered a bottle of ginger ale: Affidavit of Gaston Lecollier, DOJ Straight
      Numerical File 226225, NARA.
135   lowered her guard: Fink affidavit, 6.
135   affectionate toward the senator: Fink affidavit, 6.
135   Her recall was impressive: *Investigation*, 2–34.
136   "it was enough to convince me": Wheeler and Healy, *Yankee*, 220.
136   willing to be led on: 1961 Wheeler interview, 9.
136   "Is a man to be convicted": 68th Cong., 1st sess., *Congressional Record*, 2771.
136   "Well, didn't Daugherty do this": 1961 Wheeler interview, 9–10.
136   "in a conspiracy": Wheeler and Healy, *Yankee*, 225.
136   "an utterly credible witness": Wheeler and Healy, 221.
136   "disappeared for twenty-four hours": "Fight to Oust Daugherty Takes Myste-
      rious Turn," *Buffalo Enquirer*, March 12, 1924.
137   "Nothing to say": "Telegrams of Jesse Smith Called For," *Stockton Daily Eve-
      ning Record*, March 12, 1924.
137   begged Wheeler for permission: Wheeler and Healy, *Yankee*, 220.
137   "Out of the question": Wheeler and Healy, 220.
137   virtual house arrest: 1961 Wheeler interview, 9.
137   "Showing up at his office": "Fight to Oust Daugherty Takes Mysterious Turn."

Chapter 18: "Partners in Crime"

138   such a crowd: According to "Details of Daugherty Deals," *Boston Daily Globe*,
      March 13, 1924, the hearing was actually delayed as the committee members
      struggled to get to their seats. Other scene-setting details come from "Smith's
      Ex-Wife First Big Gun in Daugherty Probe," *Boston Daily Globe*, March
      13, 1924; "Roxie Stinson, on Stand, Capital's Biggest Attraction in Many
      Years," *Baltimore Sun*, March 14, 1924; "Roxie Stinson Brands Daugherty
      as Intriguer; Names Him Silent Partner in Fight Film Deal," *Atlanta Constitu-
      tion*, March 13, 1924; "Accuses Attorney General," *New York Times*, March
      13, 1924; Carter Field, "Suicide's Widow Involves Daugherty in His Deals;
      M'Lean Admits Deception," *New York Tribune*, March 13, 1924; "Daugherty
      Took Part in Stock Deals with Smith, Woman Tells Committee," *Baltimore
      Sun*, March 13, 1924; and Arthur Sears Henning, "Smith Fortune Grew Rap-
      idly as Friend Took Office," *Chicago Daily Tribune*, March 13, 1924.
138   "scandal hounds": Cleveland Rodgers, "Roxie Stinson, Who Starred in 'Scan-
      dal,'" *Brooklyn Daily Eagle*, April 6, 1924.
138   intended as a petty swipe: That was certainly how Wheeler took it. Wheeler
      and Healy, *Yankee*, 218–219.
138   sat his two personal attorneys: Field, "Suicide's Widow Involves Daugherty in
      His Deals."
139   Warren G. Grimes: Grimes attended all sessions of the committee as Daugh-
      erty's eyes and ears. See "Plot to Bar Inquiry on Mexico, Charged," *New York
      Times*, May 18, 1924.
139   "The lady who is to come on the stand": "Daugherty Took Part in Stock Deals
      With Smith, Woman Tells Committee."
139   "revealing herself": "Roxie Stinson, on Stand."
139   "You may state your name": Unless otherwise noted, all dialogue from Stin-
      son's testimony comes from *Investigation*, 9–34, 38–68, 504–559, 566–592,
      and 618–637.

139   **Her voice was soft:** Rodgers, "Roxie Stinson, Who Starred in 'Scandal.'"

139   **tear-soaked handkerchief:** Field, "Suicide's Widow Involves Daugherty in His Deals."

140   **"I can't read through leather":** *Investigation,* 540.

140   **stern-faced man pushed his way:** Carter Field, "Tells of Attorney General's Trips Back to Ohio with Smith, Carrying Weekend Cases Full of Liquor," *New York Tribune,* March 14, 1924.

140   **waved him off:** "Smith-Daugherty 'Deals' Ran Gamut from Oil to Shirts, Says Miss Stinson," *Washington Evening Star,* March 14, 1924.

142   **screwed her face in annoyance:** Field, "Tells of Attorney General's Trips Back to Ohio with Smith."

142   **tried to derail them:** Howland's interruption and the ensuing back-and-forth can be found at *Investigation,* 12–13.

144   **locked up in government-bonded warehouses:** Thomas M. Coffey, *The Long Thirst,* 31; and Edwin Palmer Hoyt, *Spectacular Rogue,* 154–156.

144   **six confounding forms:** Hoyt, *Spectacular Rogue,* 155.

145   **deposited in a blind brokerage account:** Adams, *Incredible Era,* 354.

145   **valued at $250,000 upon his death:** *Investigation,* 15.

145   **enclosing $100 or even $500 bills:** *Investigation,* 582.

146   **conspired to skim the profits:** Bates, *Senator Thomas J. Walsh of Montana,* 268.

146   **most anticipated title bout in history:** James Ciment and Kevin Grace, "Boxing," in *Encyclopedia of the Jazz Age,* ed. Ciment, 112–113.

146   **resulting hour-long film:** Werner, *Privileged Characters,* 282–283.

146   **"so much better than the real fight":** *Investigation,* 19.

146   **A 1912 federal statute:** Giglio, *H. M. Daugherty,* 137.

147   **"We have a big thing":** *Investigation,* 18.

147   **"deposited $175,000 of Eastern money":** *Investigation,* 32.

148   **"So far as I am concerned":** *Investigation,* 566.

148   **choking back tears:** "Roxie Stinson Stars at Probe of Daugherty," *Baltimore Sun,* March 27, 1924.

Chapter 19: "They Are Going to Get Me"

149   **"I have been informed":** May Dixon Thacker, "Gaston B. Means—Master Bad Man" (part 5), *Liberty* 14, no. 20 (May 15, 1937): 49.

149   **"What is he doing?":** Harry M. Daugherty and Thomas Dixon, *The Inside Story of the Harding Tragedy,* 248.

149   **"running with a gay crowd":** Daugherty and Dixon, *Inside Story,* 248.

150   **blood pressure hovering around 215:** Jess Smith to Ned and Evalyn McLean, January 29, 1923, Evalyn Walsh McLean papers, Box 8, Library of Congress.

150   **"a heavy cold":** "Daugherty Is Laid Up by Cold," *Boston Daily Globe,* January 28, 1923.

150   **supervising his medical care:** Smith's role as nurse is glimpsed through telegrams reprinted in the select committee's transcripts at *Investigation,* 593–607.

151   **suffering from advanced diabetes:** Joel T. Boone, unpublished memoirs, Joel Thompson Boone papers, Library of Congress (hereafter cited as Boone memoirs), chapter 18, 67–68.

151   "absolutely neglected himself physically": Boone memoirs, chapter 18, 68.
151   selling his dry goods store: Smith to Stinson, January 3, 1923, reprinted at *Investigation*, 576.
151   far less than it was worth: *Investigation*, 31.
151   face went white: Thacker, "Gaston B. Means," part 5, 49.
151   "I'm sorry, Jess": Thacker, part 5, 49.
151   "as a prisoner receives a death sentence": Daugherty and Dixon, *Inside Story*, 261.
152   "Roxie, you're just beautiful": Julian Street, "Tells Story of Smith's Suicide," *Los Angeles Record*, April 4, 1924.
152   "He was in fear": *Investigation*, 540.
152   "They are going to get me": *Investigation*, 540.
152   "passed the blame": *Investigation*, 541.
152   "Tell me what the trouble is": *Investigation*, 542.
152   arrived in Columbus: "Cincinnatians Selected," *Cincinnati Enquirer*, May 12, 1923.
153   wrote personal letters: See Box 29 of the Joel Thompson Boone papers, Library of Congress, for examples.
153   spend a few nights at "the Shack": *Investigation*, 543.
153   "He is asleep": *Investigation*, 544.
153   mumbled the entire way home: James N. Giglio, *H. M. Daugherty*, 158.
153   marched directly into Carpenter's: Francis Russell, *The Shadow of Blooming Grove*, 568.
154   "This is for the attorney general": *Investigation*, 544.
154   "Has it been straightened out?": *Investigation*, 543.
154   "to see a few friends": Daugherty and Dixon, *Inside Story*, 249.
154   refusing to drink and generally acting "queer": Daugherty and Dixon, 249.
154   previous day's visit: "Smith Visited Cemetery Before Going to Washington," *Boston Daily Globe*, June 3, 1923.
154   "I've been through hell": M. R. Werner and John Starr, *The Teapot Dome Scandal*, 99.
154   dispatched his Justice Department assistant: Daugherty and Dixon, *Inside Story*, 249.
155   "In the presence of Almighty God": Daugherty reprinted a photographic copy of the will in his memoirs at Daugherty and Dixon, *Inside Story*, 250.
155   "stumbled through eighteen holes": Giglio, *H. M. Daugherty*, 158.
155   "Jess Smith didn't play the kind of game": Giglio, *H. M. Daugherty*, 158; and Boone memoirs, chapter 18, 62a.
155   stuffed his briefcase: Werner and Starr, *Teapot Dome Scandal*, 99.
155   phoned Ned McLean and his wife: The dialogue from Smith's final phone calls come from Evalyn Walsh McLean, unpublished manuscript of *Father Struck It Rich*, Evalyn Walsh McLean papers, Library of Congress, 394–395. McLean ultimately cut several details from this account in the final, published version of her memoirs.
156   A rumor, in fact, later surfaced: Werner and Starr, *Teapot Dome Scandal*, 99.
156   gathered up Daugherty's personal papers: Daugherty recalled that "Jess had destroyed all my house accounts and my personal correspondence. In fact there was hardly anything left pertaining to my personal affairs." Daugherty and Dixon, *Inside Story*, 249.
156   lit a bonfire: Samuel Hopkins Adams, *Incredible Era*, 308.

Chapter 20: "This Base Insinuation"

158   "Now, you know what they'll try to do": Burton K. Wheeler, "Reminiscences of Burton Kendall Wheeler, 1969" [transcript of oral history interview], Columbia Center for Oral History (hereafter cited as Wheeler oral history), 104.

158   "Don't buy candy from anybody": Wheeler oral history, 104.

158   strange men lurking outside their house: Wheeler and Healy, *Yankee*, 227.

158   psychological warfare: Wheeler and Healy, 226.

158   denied his application: Vicki A. Mack, *Frank A. Vanderlip*, 334.

158   begged the senator to do the same: Dayton Stoddard, unpublished manuscript for Burton K. Wheeler biography, Burton Kendall Wheeler papers, 1910–1972 [MC 34], Montana Historical Society, D-7.

158   his habit of riding the trolley: Julian Street, "Senator Wheeler Like a Tarkington Hero," *Binghamton Press*, April 7, 1924.

158   in the splendor of Vanderlip's armored Pierce-Arrow limousine: "Daugherty investigation," topical card file, Burton K. Wheeler Papers, 1922–1975, Montana State University Library, card 3. For the make of Vanderlip's limousine, see "Luxurious Simplicity in the Car Interior," *Harper's Bazaar*, July 1923, 77.

158   "The idea that my enemies": Wheeler and Healy, *Yankee*, 227.

159   in the form of a letter: The text of the letter appears in Carter Field, "Roxie Stinson Is Accused by Daugherty of Hold-Up Plot," *New York Tribune*, March 18, 1924.

159   "She is a disappointed woman": "Daugherty Makes Denial," *New York Times*, March 15, 1924.

160   "Being a kind of fighting individual myself": "Heaps Fire on Daugherty," *Kansas City Star*, March 22, 1924.

160   "If ever a man stooped": "Heaps Fire on Daugherty."

160   "besmirch the character": Morris Robert Werner, *Privileged Characters*, 251.

160   "And I say it was an unmanly": *Investigation*, 502.

160   engineering a "frame-up": *Investigation*, 507.

161   "This base insinuation": *Investigation*, 510.

161   Fink offered his own version of events: "Star Witness in Daugherty Probe Bares Testimony to Be Given Soon," *Buffalo Courier*, March 25, 1924.

Chapter 21: "A Pretty Slick Fellow"

162   Gaston Bullock Means: There are numerous sources of varying credibility about the life of Means and his activities in the Harding administration. With limited exceptions, I have disregarded Means's own account—full of half-truths, harmless fabrications, and malicious lies—in *The Strange Death of President Harding*. Most reliable is Edwin P. Hoyt's 1963 biography, *Spectacular Rogue: Gaston B. Means*, based in large part upon the private files of the federal prosecutor who put Means behind bars. J. Edgar Hoover (writing with Courtney Ryley Cooper) offered his own profile, titled "The Amazing Mr. Means," for *American Magazine*'s 1936 issue. Other useful (though not entirely reliable) sources include a 1939 series of syndicated newspaper articles by his wife, Julie P. Means, entitled "My Life with Gaston Means," and a 1949 profile in *True* magazine by Alan Hynd titled "The Man Who Swindled the President."

162   **threw a dog into a fireplace:** May Dixon Thacker, "Gaston B. Means—Master Bad Man" (part 1), *Liberty* 14, no. 16 (April 17, 1937): 10.

162   **his commanding presence:** J. Edgar Hoover with Courtney Ryley Cooper, "The Amazing Mr. Means," *American Magazine*, December 1936.

162   **long, simian limbs:** Hoover with Cooper, "The Amazing Mr. Means."

162   **"Bud" Means:** Samuel Hopkins Adams, "The Criminal and the Genius," *Los Angeles Times*, April 16, 1950.

162   **reinvented himself as the apprentice-son:** Thacker, "Gaston B. Means," part 1, 12.

163   **sleuth for the William J. Burns International Detective Agency:** Edwin P. Hoyt, *Spectacular Rogue*, 35.

163   **blend into a society party:** "Midnight Raids, Frame Ups Used as Clubs on Senators," *Atlanta Constitution*, March 15, 1924.

163   **spy on his own country:** Hoyt, *Spectacular Rogue*, 36.

163   **a thousand dollars a week:** Henry Thomas and Dana Lee Thomas, "The Strange Tale of Gaston Means," in *Strange Tales of Amazing Frauds*.

163   **accused prominent Americans:** "To Prove Neutrality Violation to Bryan," *Washington Herald*, May 2, 1915.

163   **transport of crucial wartime supplies:** Hoyt, *Spectacular Rogue*, 44.

163   **made by dead drop:** Hoyt, 42.

163   **Maude King:** Hoyt, 46–50.

164   **mysterious pistol "accident":** Hoyt, 74–75.

164   **two of the jurors were intimidated:** Hoyt, 106.

164   **public knowledge:** "Means Admits Part as Enemy Secret Agent," *Indianapolis Star*, July 18, 1918.

164   **Burns hired him:** Hoyt, *Spectacular Rogue*, 143–144.

164   **these tools:** Hoyt, 144.

164   **spread word . . . that he would perform extraordinary favors:** J. Edgar Hoover and Courtney Ryley Cooper, "The Amazing Mr. Means," *American Magazine*, December 1936, 80.

164   **selling them a peek at their case files:** Hoyt, *Spectacular Rogue*, 147–148.

164   **most lucrative schemes:** Hoyt, 167.

165   **haunted the shadows of America's bootleg capital:** Hoyt, 161.

165   **investigating four brothers:** Hoyt, 162–164.

165   **money poured in:** Julie P. Means, "Amazing Intrigues of a Diabolic Grafter" [part of the syndicated series titled "My Life with Gaston Means"], *Philadelphia Inquirer*, September 24, 1939.

165   **"It's not exactly crooked":** Alan Hynd, "Gaston Bullock Means: Con Cum Laude," 401.

165   **the blessing of the senior-most Harding administration officials:** Hoyt, *Spectacular Rogue*, 188.

165   **"A man, to raise this amount":** Hoyt, 188.

165   **ran interference for Means:** Hoyt, 154.

166   **came forward with sworn affidavits:** Hoyt, *Spectacular Rogue*, 212. See also Daugherty to Mellon, May 4, 1923, DOJ Straight Numerical File 191307, NARA.

166   **the news became public:** "A Chicago Booze Scandal," *Kansas City Star*, April 23, 1923.

166   **nationwide manhunt:** "Searching Nation for Alleged Fixer," *Atlanta Constitution*, April 26, 1923.

166   **apprehended and indicted:** "Gaston B. Means Indicted as Leader of Huge Dry Plot," *Philadelphia Inquirer*, October 23, 1923.

166   **second federal indictment:** "Felder and Means Indicted for Plot," *New York Times*, March 8, 1924.

Chapter 22: "A Complete Master of Himself"

168   **looked so at ease:** Details about Means's casual comportment come from "Means, the 'Investigator,' Glories in Relating His Methods as a 'Snooper,'" *Brooklyn Daily Eagle*, March 15, 1924. Other setting details come from "Harding, Hughes, Daugherty Viewed Fight Films in Private Show at Ned McLean's—Means Says," *Atlanta Constitution*, March 15, 1924; "Smith, Daugherty's Friend, Accused by Means as Grafter," *Washington Post*, March 15, 1924; Arthur Sears Henning, "Master Spy's Boodle Tale," *Chicago Daily Tribune*, March 15, 1924; "Gaston B. Means Says He Paid It to Jess Smith," *St. Louis Star and Times*, March 14, 1924; "Means Says Smith Got $100,000 to Stop U.S. Aero Prosecutions," *Washington Evening Star*, March 14, 1924; Carter Field, "Means Charges Grafting to Daugherty's Friend; Calls Self 'Go-Between,'" *New York Tribune*, March 15, 1924; and "Declares Japanese Paid," *New York Times*, March 15, 1924.

168   **"let me ask you if you claim immunity":** Unless otherwise noted, all dialogue from Means's testimony comes from *Investigation*, 74–124.

168   **letter from Assistant Attorney General Earl Davis:** Davis replaced Crim as head of the department's criminal division after Daugherty appointed the latter as special counsel in charge of the Veterans Bureau investigation. Davis's letter appears at *Investigation*, 73.

168   **an implied grant of immunity:** "Self-Incrimination and the Concept of Immunity," Constitution Annotated, https://constitution.congress.gov/browse/essay/amdt5-3-1-3-1/ALDE_00000866/.

169   **impatient flick of the hand:** Edwin P. Hoyt, *Spectacular Rogue*, 229.

169   **smoke would be his plaything:** Hoyt, *Spectacular Rogue*, 231.

169   **shot it down through his two nostrils:** Hoyt, 229.

169   **erupted in laughter:** "Gaston B. Means Tells Lurid Story," *Huntington Herald*, March 14, 1924.

170   **never planned to take the witness stand:** "Means Repudiates Testimony He Gave Against Daugherty," *Washington Post*, September 22, 1924.

170   **spying for Harry Daugherty:** Means revealed in the fall of 1924 that he had been spying on the Senate committee's investigation. Accounts of Means's secret assignment and his eventual falling-out with Daugherty appear (almost certainly embellished) in the epilogue to his memoir at Gaston B. Means and May Dixon Thacker, *The Strange Death of President Harding*, 273–276; and Julie P. Means, "Amazing Intrigues of a Diabolic Grafter" [part of the syndicated series titled "My Life with Gaston Means"], *Philadelphia Inquirer*, September 24, 1939.

171   **"The attorney general says for you to go to hell":** Means and Thacker, *Strange Death of President Harding*, 275.

171   **face turned purple:** Julie P. Means, "Amazing Intrigues of a Diabolic Grafter" [part of the syndicated series titled "My Life with Gaston Means"], *Philadelphia Inquirer*, September 24, 1939.

171   **"I had crossed swords"**: Means and Thacker, *Strange Death of President Harding*, 276.

171   **"a complete master of himself"**: "Declares Japanese Paid," *New York Times*, March 15, 1924.

172   **"as though he were explaining a complicated and amusing game"**: Carter Field, "Means Charges Grafting to Daugherty's Friend; Calls Self 'Go-Between,'" *New York Tribune*, March 15, 1924

172   **"Nothing could be further from Sherlock Holmes"**: Arthur Ruhl, "At the Capitol's Vaudeville," *Collier's*, April 19, 1924.

172   **"What I could have done with that man"**: Hynd, "Gaston B. Means: Con Cum Laude," 392.

172   **Inside were copies of letters**: Henry Suydam, "Means, the 'Investigator,' Glories in Relating His Methods as a 'Snooper,'" *Brooklyn Daily Eagle*, March 15, 1924.

173   **roared in laughter**: "Gaston B. Means Says He Paid It to Jess Smith," *St. Louis Star and Times*, March 14, 1924.

173   **wrapped in yellow manila paper**: Philip Kinsley, "Means Charges Justice Graft Under Palmer," *Chicago Daily Tribune*, April 17, 1924.

174   **a $100,000 bribe**: Means's account appears at *Investigation*, 99–101.

174   **overcharged by some $6.59 million**: Morris Robert Werner, *Privileged Characters*, 288–289.

175   **"They knew the game"**: *Investigation*, 82–83.

Chapter 23: "Dope to Smear Wheeler"

176   **another line of testimony**: Means's admission that he spied on members of Congress appears in *Investigation*, 88–91, 117.

176   **"At whose direction"**: Unless otherwise noted, all dialogue from Means's testimony about congressional surveillance comes from *Investigation*, 88–91, 117.

177   **elaborate blackmail operation**: Little has been written about the operation against Senator Caraway, but the original investigative records can be found in Records of the Miller-Daugherty Trials, Box 9, NARA.

177   **publicly accused Daugherty of having him "shadowed"**: "Charges Daugherty Spies on Senators," *Boston Daily Globe*, May 25, 1922; and "Caraway Declares Spy Is Set on Him," *New York Times*, May 28, 1922.

177   **"malicious untruth"**: "Denies Caraway's Espionage Charge," *Boston Daily Globe*, May 26, 1922.

178   **"You have got them in Montana now"**: *Investigation*, 77.

178   **"One is out in Iowa"**: "'We Caught Sec Mellon' on Order from Harding," *Boston Daily Globe*, March 14, 1924.

178   **invaded the State of Montana**: The investigators included Special Agents Edwin W. Byrn Jr. and W. L. Buchanan; Expert Bank Accountant Robert M. Huston; Chief Accountant J. B. Cunningham; and attorneys Emmett Doherty and P. H. Marcum from the Office of the Attorney General. Notably, most of these investigators worked without the knowledge of the Bureau's special agent in charge in Montana, D. H. Dickason. The account of the Montana investigation is largely drawn from Wheeler's FBI file, 62-7903, and is also informed by *Investigation*, 723–733, 834–846; *Charges Against Senator Burton K. Wheeler of Montana: Hearings Before the Select Committee on Investigation*

of Charges Against Senator Burton K. Wheeler, of Montana, US Senate, 68th Cong. (hereafter cited as *Charges Against Wheeler*), 77–100, 123–131; and Richard T. Ruetten, "Burton K. Wheeler, 1905–1925," 112–133.

178 **"we must indict him and smear him":** "Plot to Smear Wheeler Laid to Harry and Burns," *Chicago Daily Tribune*, April 22, 1924.

178 **"the 'cop' who arrested Wheeler":** Coan to Burns, March 14, 1924, FBI file 62-7903-127.

179 **complaint from a disgruntled seasonal ranger:** FBI file 62-7903-108.

179 **movie producer moonlighting as an investigator:** I pieced together Coan's back story from multiple sources: "Three Give Lie to Helm Committee Testimony in Lorimer Hearing," *Inter-Ocean* (Chicago), June 28, 1911; "M. Blair Coan on the Job," *Day Book* (Chicago), March 19, 1913; "Woman Suicide Blames Her Love for Chicagoan," *Chicago Daily Tribune*, September 19, 1923; "G.O.P. Sleuth Welds Chain Tying Wheeler to Indictment," *Chicago Daily Tribune*, April 25, 1924; and Coan's FBI file, 62-534.

179 **reinvented himself as a producer:** "Expects New Lens Process to Aid Motion Pictures," *New York Tribune*, January 10, 1921.

179 **series of secret meetings:** *Investigation*, 1234–1236.

179 **joined by George Lockwood:** *Investigation*, 1234.

180 **already joined forces once before:** "William J. Burns in Lorimer Case Famous Sleuth," *Waukegan Daily Sun*, April 24, 1911.

180 **Burns worked his magic:** "Burns in the Lorimer Case," *Boston Daily Globe*, January 21, 1912.

180 **placed Coan on the payroll:** *Charges Against Wheeler*, 127.

180 **"dope to smear Wheeler":** Burns to Stone, May 8, 1924, FBI file 62-7824 -99X9.

180 **one particularly interesting attorney-client relationship:** Ruetten, "Burton K. Wheeler, 1905–1925," 112–133; "Sees Conspiracy to Oust Wheeler for GOP Senator," *Akron Beacon Journal*, January 27, 1925; and "Star Witness Tells of Free Ride Provided by Blair Coan," *Butte Miner*, April 19, 1925. See also *Charges Against Wheeler*, 77–101, 123–131.

181 **pecked away at his typewriter:** The hour was late, and they could not find a stenographer, so Coan typed himself. *Charges Against Wheeler*, 129.

181 **thence, without delay, to the Bureau of Investigation:** Riddick to Burns, March 17, 1924, FBI file 62-7903-48.

181 **come under Justice Department scrutiny:** The records of the department's internal investigation are preserved in DOJ file 23-44-42, NARA.

181 **two staff attorneys:** Their testimony appears in *Investigation*, 723–733, 834–846.

182 **Daugherty's hand-picked US attorney:** "Senator Slattery's Selection," *Butte Miner*, May 2, 1921.

182 **"a perfect specimen":** H. L. Mencken, "The Rewards of Virtue," *American Monthly*, August 1, 1925.

182 **long-simmering dispute:** "Slattery Held to Blame for Leak of Data Given to Him," *Butte Miner*, March 2, 1924.

182 **"We had so much on him":** *Investigation*, 834.

Chapter 24: "Victim of a Hostile Welcome"

183 **his mantra became "Follow the money":** Used here with apologies to William Goldman, screenwriter of *All the President's Men*. The catchphrase appeared in the film but not in the Bob Woodward and Carl Bernstein book on which it was based. See Garrett Graff, *Watergate: A New History* (New York: Avid Reader Press, 2022), 20, 676.

183 **appointed accountant John Phelon:** Wheeler and Healy, *Yankee*, 230–231.

183 **astounding discoveries:** The details of Phelon's inspection come from his testimony to the select committee at *Investigation*, 1425–1433. They are summarized at James N. Giglio, *H. M. Daugherty*, 176.

184 **"Mr. Phelon, sit down for a minute":** *Investigation*, 1429.

184 **"There had been no unfriendly discussion":** "Bank Inquiry Ban by Mal Daugherty," *New York Times*, March 21, 1924.

185 **issued a new subpoena:** *Investigation*, 376–378.

185 **served the subpoena:** *Investigation*, 645.

185 **"From advice of counsel":** "Mal Daugherty Won't Surrender Bank Records; Will Test Committee's Right to Demand Them," *New York Times*, March 23, 1924.

185 **"go the limit":** "Miss Stinson Faces Cross-Examination by Woman Lawyer," *Washington Post*, March 24, 1924.

185 **his findings ignored:** The agent was Hazel Scaife, whose initial testimony appears at *Investigation*, 638–664, 766–792.

185 **Another was fired:** The agent was B. C. Baldwin, whose testimony appears at *Investigation*, 162–190.

185 **"functioning as an aid to crooks":** *Investigation*, 780.

185 **slumped resigned in their chairs:** Bruce Bliven, "Wheeler's Way and Walsh's," *New Republic*, April 2, 1924.

186 **"swept from his moorings":** Bliven, "Wheeler's Way and Walsh's."

186 **more reckless in his accusations:** "What Wheeler Is After," *Chicago Daily Tribune*, April 7, 1924.

186 **"We demand . . . that no process of wholesale dishonoring":** "What Wheeler Is After."

186 **"It is quite true, of course":** Bliven, "Wheeler's Way and Walsh's."

186 **specialized in the legal gray areas:** Report of Special Agent Rudolph B. Seipel, FBI file 62-7903-334.

186 **"Mr. Hayes was your attorney?":** *Investigation*, 473.

187 **struggled to explain his actions:** Hayes's testimony appears at *Investigation*, 489–496.

187 **"He would kill his mother for five cents":** *Investigation*, 465.

187 **an enforcement mechanism did exist:** Todd Garvey, *Congress's Contempt Power and the Enforcement of Congressional Subpoenas*.

187 **resolved a dispute:** "Treat to Houston Opens Loan Data," *New York Times*, March 2, 1921.

187 **Its first major test:** The relevant facts in *Anderson v. Dunn* are narrated at Garvey, *Congress's Contempt Power*, 6–8.

188 **"be exposed to every indignity":** *Anderson v. Dunn*, 19 U.S. (6 Wheat.) 204 (1821).

188 **case of *Kilbourn v. Thompson*:** The relevant facts of the case are narrated at Garvey, *Congress's Contempt Power*, 8–10.

188 **"The general power of making inquiry":** *Kilbourn v. Thompson*, 103 U.S. 168, 189–190 (1881).

Chapter 25: "Rid of an Unfaithful Servant"

189   **"half-a-dozen trails of corruption":** Bruce Bliven, "Wheeler's Way and Walsh's," *New Republic*, April 2, 1924.

189   **defeated Coolidge in the South Dakota Republican primary:** "Coolidge and McAdoo Primary Victories in Last Week Significant of Strength," *Washington Evening Star*, March 23, 1924. Johnson's vote in the earlier North Dakota primary on March 18 was split with a massively popular write-in campaign on behalf of Sen. Robert La Follette. See also Louise Overacker, *The Presidential Primary* (New York: Macmillan, 1926), 209, 240.

190   **refused the select committee's request:** "Senate Refused Filibuster Data by Daugherty," *New York Tribune*, March 27, 1924.

190   **"are very confidential in their nature":** Harry Daugherty to Smith Brookhart, March 25, 1924, from FBI file 62-7824-102.

190   **"every facility":** 68th Cong., 1st sess., *Congressional Record*, 3307.

190   **asked President Coolidge to overrule his attorney general:** Richard T. Ruetten, "Burton K. Wheeler, 1905–1925," 98.

190   **summoned Daugherty to the White House:** "Daugherty Sees Coolidge Twice in a Day and Rumors Revive of His Speedy Resignation," *New York Times*, March 27, 1924.

190   **came prepared with a draft letter:** Harry M. Daugherty and Thomas Dixon, *The Inside Story of the Harding Tragedy*, 290.

190   **might be compelled to ask for Daugherty's resignation:** "Daugherty Lost as He Believed His Fight Won," *New York Tribune*, March 29, 1924.

190   **promised him he'd think it over:** Daugherty and Dixon, *Inside Story*, 290.

190   **a conspicuous vehicle parked outside:** Daugherty and Dixon, 290.

190   **"This probably means":** Daugherty and Dixon, 290, 291.

191   **"My dear Mr. Attorney General":** The letter is part of the Calvin Coolidge Papers, Subject File 26, Library of Congress. It is reprinted in full in Daugherty and Dixon, *Inside Story*, 311–313.

191   **ghostwritten by Secretary of State Charles Evans Hughes:** James N. Giglio, *H. M. Daugherty*, 173.

192   **sent shivers down their spines:** Ruetten, "Burton K. Wheeler, 1905–1925," 98–99.

192   **"rapidly approaching a definite decision":** "Coolidge Prepares Guillotine for Daugherty as Evidence of Unfitness for Office Piles," *Atlanta Constitution*, March 28, 1924.

192   **"case of the attorney general":** "Daugherty Will Be Ousted Soon Signs Indicate," *Philadelphia Inquirer*, March 28, 1924.

192   **"Coolidge Prepares Guillotine":** "Coolidge Prepares Guillotine for Daugherty."

192   **a terse follow-up note:** Calvin Coolidge Papers, Subject File 26, Library of Congress.

193   **Slemp remained in his office:** "Daugherty Will Be Ousted Soon Signs Indicate."

193   **a secret reason for the delay:** In fact, the reason has remained a secret for all these decades—or at least has escaped comment in all published accounts of Daugherty's resignation, where his delay is left unexplained. The account here is based on my discovery of telegrams between Daugherty and John S. Pratt in

the Department of Justice records at the National Archives—which presumably were not open for public research when earlier accounts were written.

193   **assuming his current post in August 1921:** *Charges Against Wheeler*, 133.

193   **"The charges made yesterday":** "'Hearsay and Gossip!,'" *Cincinnati Enquirer*, February 21, 1924.

193   **"Proceed to Washington immediately":** Daugherty to Pratt, March 26, 1924, DJF 226225-122, NARA.

193   **next morning at ten o'clock:** "Daugherty Jaunty, but Shows Strain," *New York Times*, March 29, 1924.

194   **a short, formal letter:** Daugherty and Dixon, *Inside Story*, 313.

194   **a second missive:** Daugherty and Dixon, 313–317.

195   **shouts of newsboys:** "Daugherty Lost as He Believed His Fight Won," *New York Tribune*, March 29, 1924.

195   **news reached the hearing room:** "Judgeship for Sale, Olcott Was Told," *New York Times*, March 29, 1924.

195   **visibly elated:** "Greet Retirement with Joy," *Kansas City Times*, March 29, 1924.

195   **"The country has gotten rid":** "Inquiry Will Not Halt with Daugherty Gone, Senators Brookhart and Wheeler Declare," *New York Times*, March 29, 1924.

195   **"in its work of uncovering crooks":** "Greet Retirement with Joy."

195   **"Senator Wheeler has been in Washington":** Julian Street, "Senator Wheeler Like a Tarkington Hero," *Binghamton Press*, April 7, 1924.

196   **talk that he might earn a place on a presidential ticket:** Arthur Sears Henning, "30 Democrats Yearn for Home in White House," *Chicago Daily Tribune*, April 13, 1924.

196   **an editorial celebrating "Senator Wheeler's Victory":** "Senator Wheeler's Victory," *Butte Miner*, March 29, 1924.

Chapter 26: "One of the Darkest Pages in American History"

198   **federal grand jury meeting in Great Falls:** Most details about the (secret) grand jury proceedings come from Pratt to Stone, April 8, 1924, DOJ Straight Numerical File 226469-2, NARA; and "U.S. Grand Jury Here Indicts Wheeler," *Great Falls Tribune*, April 9, 1924.

198   **courtroom decor:** H. J. "Jim" Kolva, "National Register of Historic Places Inventory/Nomination: Great Falls Post Office & Courthouse," National Park Service, September 1985.

198   **No court reporter:** Testimony of A. F. Sparling, *Charges Against Wheeler*, 101.

199   **pile of telegrams:** "Slattery Impounds Wheeler Evidence," *Billings Gazette*, April 12, 1924.

199   **taken out to lunch:** 68th Cong., 1st sess., *Congressional Record*, 9156.

199   **learned the news:** "Statements by Wheeler and Daugherty," *St. Louis Post Dispatch*, April 9, 1924.

199   **did not come as a complete surprise:** Burton K. Wheeler, "Reminiscences of Burton Kendall Wheeler, 1969" [transcript of oral history interview], Columbia Center for Oral History (hereafter cited as Wheeler oral history), 96.

200   **Ten days earlier:** 68th Cong., 1st sess., *Congressional Record*, 5947.

200   **"That's crazy":** Wheeler oral history, 96.

200 **"It was the first time in my life"**: Wheeler and Healy, *Yankee*, 235.

200 **ten-page indictment accused**: Records of the US District Court for the District of Montana, Great Falls Term, National Archives at Denver.

200 **"any service rendered"**: 68th Cong., 1st sess., *Congressional Record*, 9278.

200 **enacted in 1864**: Statement, Brief, and Argument for the Plaintiff in Error, *Burton v. United States*, 1905, 70–71.

200 **Only one member of Congress**: Anne M. Butler, Wendy Wolff, and Sheila P. Burke, *United States Senate Election, Expulsion, and Censure Cases, 1793–1990*, 275–276.

200 **innocently stumble into legal jeopardy**: "1925 indictment and trial," topical card file, Burton K. Wheeler Papers, 1922–1975, Montana State University Library, card 2.

201 **"some difficulties with oil lands"**: *Charges Against Wheeler*, 38.

201 **As Wheeler saw it**: Wheeler and Healy, *Yankee*, 237.

201 **"Who in the name of God"**: Wheeler oral history, 100.

201 **"nothing whatever to do"**: "Senator Wheeler Indicted as Taker of Fee to Sway Issuance of Oil Permits," *New York Tribune*, April 9, 1924.

201 **"That is palpably a frame-up"**: "Sole Purpose of Indictment to Turn Eyes from Inquiry," *Butte Miner*, April 9, 1924.

201 **"It is the culmination of a campaign"**: "Wheeler Calls It 'Frame-Up,'" *New York Times*, April 9, 1924.

202 **"I have never represented"**: "Wheeler Calls It 'Frame-Up.'"

202 **"one of the darkest pages"**: Alpheus Thomas Mason, *Harlan Fiske Stone*, 189.

Chapter 27: "The Most Damnable Conspiracy"

203 **longstanding dinner plans**: Details on Wheeler's dinner with Brandeis come from Burton K. Wheeler, "Reminiscences of Burton Kendall Wheeler, 1969" [transcript of oral history interview], Columbia Center for Oral History, 100; Wheeler and Healy, *Yankee*, 235–236; Brandeis to Frankfurter, May 28, 1924, Felix Frankfurter Papers, Box 27, Library of Congress; and "Daugherty investigation," topical card file, Burton K. Wheeler Papers, 1922–1975, Montana State University Library (topical card file subcollection hereafter cited as Wheeler card file), card 10.

203 **"a militant crusader"**: William O. Douglas, "Louis Brandeis: Dangerous Because Incorruptible," *New York Times Book Review*, July 5, 1964.

203 **"Are you worried"**: Wheeler and Healy, *Yankee*, 236.

204 **"They're trying to stop you"**: Wheeler and Healy, 236.

204 **"That's all they want to accomplish"**: "Daugherty investigation," Wheeler card file, card 10.

204 **steeled Wheeler's resolve**: Wheeler and Healy, *Yankee*, 236.

204 **"no man is above the law"**: The line comes from Roosevelt's third annual message to Congress, as quoted in *Forum* 35 (1904): 334.

204 **"This will all come out all right"**: "Daugherty investigation," Wheeler card file, card 10.

204 **"This indictment is merely"**: "Wheeler Calls It 'Frame-Up,'" *New York Times*, April 9, 1924.

205 **Eighty-two senators sat**: 68th Cong., 1st sess., *Congressional Record*, 5946.

205   galleries jammed with spectators: "Senate Orders Official Inquiry on Indict-
      ment of Wheeler," *Great Falls Tribune*, April 10, 1924.
205   only the sixth senator ever indicted: Anne M. Butler, Wendy Wolff, and Sheila
      P. Burke, *United States Senate Election, Expulsion, and Censure Cases, 1793–
      1990*.
205   "An atmosphere of intense interest": "Senate Will Inquire into the Indictment
      of Senator Wheeler," *New York Times*, April 10, 1924.
205   "Mr. President and members of the Senate": The text of Wheeler's speech
      comes from 68th Cong., 1st sess., *Congressional Record*, 5946–5948.
206   Emotion stirred: "Packed House Hears Senator Denounce Bill of Grand Jury,"
      Butte Miner, April 10, 1924.
206   never appeared so dignified: "'Frameup' Victim Wheeler Claims," *Boston
      Daily Globe*, April 10, 1924.
207   a risky proposal: Marc C. Johnson, *Political Hell-Raiser*, 59–60.
207   brushing tears from his eyes: "Packed House Hears Senator Denounce Bill of
      Grand Jury," *Butte Miner*, April 10, 1924.
208   "A serious charge": "Borah Will Sift Wheeler Attack on Every Angle," *Atlanta
      Constitution*, April 11, 1924.

Chapter 28: "The Straight Path of Justice"

209   "the shield of innocence": "Stone Sworn In; Promises Justice," *New York
      Times*, April 10, 1924.
209   "The nation . . . must be kept in the straight path of justice": "Stone Sworn In;
      Promises Justice."
209   "to get a $75,000 or $100,000 man": Howard H. Quint and Robert H. Fer-
      rell, *Talkative President*, 64.
210   ran into the six figures: Alpheus Thomas Mason, *Harlan Fiske Stone*, 134.
210   doubled as a job interview: According to Stone, several Republican senators
      were also present. Stone insisted that he wanted no government office but if
      drafted would accept. See Stone to Grace Coolidge, November 24, 1934, Har-
      lan Fiske Stone Papers, Box 8, Library of Congress.
210   "Well, I think you'll do": Kenneth D. Ackerman, *Young J. Edgar*, 374. Stone
      remembered the president's line as "Well, I think I will send in your name."
210   confirmed Stone's nomination: "Senate Confirms Stone," *New York Times*,
      April 8, 1924.
210   "in exceedingly bad odor": Curt Gentry, *J. Edgar Hoover*, 124.
211   "The key to [your] problem": Felix Frankfurter to Walter Lippman, ca. April
      9, 1924, Frankfurter Papers, Harvard Law Library. Frankfurter forwarded a
      copy of the letter to Stone.
211   Assistant Attorney General Rush Holland: Unknown author, "The Department
      of Justice Under Mr. Coolidge," Burton Kendall Wheeler papers, 1910–1972,
      Box 22, Montana Historical Society.
211   "a politician pure and simple": The colleague was Assistant Attorney General
      Mabel Walker Willebrandt. Mason, *Harlan Fiske Stone*, 165.
211   wanted such appointees out: FBI file 62-8782.
211   "doubted whether there was sufficient evidence": Stone to Pratt, May 29,
      1924, DOJ SNF 226469-27, NARA.
211   "part of a political fight": Mason, *Harlan Fiske Stone*, 189.

211   "an improper use of the federal process": Mason, 189.

211   in a safe deposit box: Burns to Stone, April 26, 1924, FBI file 62-7903-30.

211   "There is only one question presented": Stone to Frankfurter, May 22, 1924, Frankfurter Papers, Harvard Law Library.

211   "had been publicly charged": Mason, *Harlan Fiske Stone*, 190.

Chapter 29: "We Anticipate Contempt Proceedings"

212   face went ashen: "Burns Sent Agents to Help Build Case Against Wheeler," *New York Times*, April 11, 1924.

213   sent three men: All dialogue from Burns's testimony comes from *Investigation*, 1233–1236.

213   "nothing whatever to do": "Statements By Wheeler and Daugherty," *St. Louis Post Dispatch*, April 9, 1924.

214   visibly uncomfortable: William R. Hunt, *Front-Page Detective*, 183.

214   Not a soul believed him: Hunt, *Front-Page Detective*, 183.

214   share a Pullman car: Details about Wheeler's and Daugherty's shared trip come from "Daugherty Bank Gets Court Order Against Inquiry," *St. Louis Post-Dispatch*, April 11, 1924; "Go to 'Mal's' Banks," *Chicago Daily Tribune*, April 11, 1924; and Philip Kinsley, "Harry and Mal Defy Senators in Home Town," *Chicago Daily Tribune*, April 12, 1924.

214   "merely a coincidence": "Daugherty Bank Gets Court Order Against Inquiry."

214   burglarized: "Daugherty's Personal Files Are Burglarized," *Marion Star*, April 8, 1924.

214   a curious crowd: Kinsley, "Harry and Mal Defy Senators in Home Town."

215   thrilled to host the proceedings: B. E. Kelley, "2 Senators Here 40 Years Ago in Senate Quiz," *Washington Court House Record Herald*, April 11, 1964.

215   intercepted by Philip Kinsley: Details about Wheeler's conversation with Kinsey come from Burton K. Wheeler, "Reminiscences of Burton Kendall Wheeler, 1969" [transcript of oral history interview], Columbia Center for Oral History (hereafter cited as Wheeler oral history), 106–107; "Daugherty investigation," topical card file, Burton K. Wheeler Papers, 1922–1975, Montana State University Library (topical card file subcollection hereafter cited as Wheeler card file), cards 6–7; and Wheeler and Healy, *Yankee*, 231.

215   crowd pressed in at the doorway: Kinsley, "Harry and Mal Defy Senators in Home Town."

215   "May I interrupt": The dialogue between the committee and the four men comes from *Investigation*, 1426–1427; and "Senators Blocked on Daugherty Bank," *New York Times*, April 12, 1924.

216   Wheeler broke in: The *New York Times* ascribed the line to Wheeler, while the Senate transcript had Brookhart saying, "I guess that makes the issue clear, gentlemen." Both agree that Wheeler issued the contempt threat.

216   another man barged in: Details and dialogue from the committee's encounter with Sheriff Lewis come from Kinsley, "Harry and Mal Defy Senators in Home Town."

216   injunction barred Wheeler and Brookhart: Text of injunction from Mal Daugherty's petition for a writ of habeas corpus, quoted in "M.S. Daugherty Is Released on Writ of Habeas Corpus; Senate's Power Questioned," *Cincinnati Enquirer*, April 29, 1924.

216   **march the two senators to the local jail:** "Senators' Inquiry in Daugherty Bank Stopped by Court," *Washington Post*, April 12, 1924.

217   **sensational fact about Judge Gregg:** "Senators Blocked on Daugherty Bank."

217   **"good-looking bleached blonde":** Details about the attempted blackmail scheme come from Wheeler oral history, 106–107; "Daugherty investigation," Wheeler card file, cards 6–7; and Wheeler and Healy, *Yankee*, 231.

Chapter 30: "Young Man"

218   **an urgent summons:** This initial appointment as acting director is one of the most oft-repeated stories in Hoover biographies and histories of the FBI. For details about the events of May 10, 1924, and the dialogue between Hoover and Stone I consulted Curt Gentry, *J. Edgar Hoover*, 127; Don Whitehead, *The FBI Story*, 67; Alpheus Thomas Mason, *Harlan Fiske Stone*, 150–151; Kenneth D. Ackerman, *Young J. Edgar*, 378; and Fred J. Cook, *The FBI Nobody Knows*, 137–138. Additional context comes from Nichols to Mason, October 19, 1950, FBI file on Harlan Fiske Stone, 62-8782-40.

218   **meticulously polished desktop:** Ackerman, *Young J. Edgar*, 39.

218   **"Perhaps you'd better think that over":** Mason, *Harlan Fiske Stone*, 150.

219   **review of Eugene Debs's conviction:** Daugherty set the process in motion by inviting Debs, then imprisoned in Atlanta, to Washington, but he ultimately opposed Debs's release. James N. Giglio, *H. M. Daugherty*, 141–142.

220   **correct the new attorney general's thinking:** Ackerman, *Young J. Edgar*, 368.

220   **turn Justice Department intelligence over:** Hoover to Burns, March 27, 1924, FBI file 67-7903-20.

220   **"honest and informed":** Mason, *Harlan Fiske Stone*, 150.

221   **"The Bureau [at the time] was filled with men with bad records":** Mason, 149.

221   **"I am not much of a detective":** "Stone Abandons U.S. Spy System Daugherty Used," *Chicago Daily Tribune*, May 14, 1924.

221   **"the greatest detective force in the world":** "Stone Abandons U.S. Spy System Daugherty Used."

222   **"sweeping reforms":** Stone to Hoover, May 13, 1924, FBI file on Harlan Fiske Stone, 62-8782-36.

223   **"The Bureau of Investigation is not concerned":** "Attorney General Starts to Revamp Detective Bureau," *Akron Beacon Journal*, May 16, 1924.

223   **"There is always the possibility":** "Attorney General Starts to Revamp Detective Bureau."

223   **"The enormous expansion of federal legislation":** "Attorney General Starts to Revamp Detective Bureau."

223   **new piece of jewelry:** Anthony Summers, *Official and Confidential*, 43.

224   **fire Gaston Means, officially and finally:** Whitehead, *FBI Story*, 68.

224   **plunged headlong into Stone's more substantive reforms:** Hoover to Stone, May 16, 1924, Stone FBI file.

224   **"be neat in dress":** Whitehead, *FBI Story*, 70.

224   **strengthened the Bureau's chain of command:** Whitehead, 69.

225   **"this Mexican matter":** *Investigation*, 2449.

225   **"I want to say . . . that the new attorney general":** Dialogue from Hoover's appearance before the select committee comes from *Investigation*, 2447–2453.

225   **basic facts that Burns had refused to disclose:** "Plot to Bar Inquiry on Mexico, Charged," *New York Times*, May 18, 1924.

226   "very glad to note": Hoover to Stone, May 20, 1924, FBI file 62-7824-100X.
226   witnesses had been shadowed: Burton K. Wheeler, untitled manuscript about Harry Daugherty, Burton Kendall Wheeler papers, Box 23, 9.
226   testimony from Jessie Duckstein: *Investigation*, 2531–2559.
226   three female special agents: Federal Bureau of Investigation, *The FBI: A Centennial History, 1908–2008*, 8.
227   paperwork made the timing appear: FBI file 67-24617 on Jessie B. Duckstein.
227   "There, no doubt . . . new inspirations were advanced": "Treason Was Behind Move Seeking Justice Files, Daugherty Charges," *Cincinnati Enquirer*, April 24, 1924.
228   "Considerable discussion was carried on": Report of Special Agent E. B. Hazlett, August 23, 1924, FBI file 62-7903-117.

Chapter 31: "It Would Be Well to Suspend Judgement"

229   this committee of five senators: Besides Borah, the committee comprised Senators Thaddeus H. Caraway (D–Ark.), Charles L. McNary (R–Ore.), Thomas Sterling (R–S.D.), and Claude A. Swanson (D–Va.). See *Charges Against Wheeler*, unnumbered page preceding table of contents.
230   no gossip, no hearsay, no innuendo: Richard T. Ruetten, "Burton K. Wheeler, 1905–1925," 112.
230   three crucial affidavits: Ruetten, "Burton K. Wheeler, 1905–1925," 116–118.
230   a different lawyer: The attorney's name was William G. Feely. His testimony can be found at *Charges Against Wheeler*, 61–71.
230   Another of Campbell's attorneys: The attorney in question was Campbell's chief counsel, L. V. Beaulieu. His testimony can be found at *Charges Against Wheeler*, 43–60.
230   "I don't know a goddamned thing": *Charges Against Wheeler*, 47.
231   performed for citizens of Montana almost every day: 68th Cong., 1st sess., *Congressional Record*, 8975.
231   read Borah's report: 68th Cong., 1st sess., *Congressional Record*, 8524.
231   giddy as a schoolboy: "Senator Wheeler Is Exonerated on All Charges," *New York Times*, May 15, 1924.
231   "The committee wholly exonerates": 68th Cong., 1st sess., *Congressional Record*, 8524.
231   minority report: "Senator Wheeler Is Exonerated on All Charges."
231   four previous instances: They were the cases of John Smith, Charles H. Dietrich, Joseph R. Burton, Truman H. Newberry. In Smith's case, a Senate investigation led by John Quincy Adams recommended expulsion. During the subsequent proceedings before the full Senate, in which Smith's supporters and detractors heard testimony and introduced evidence, one of Smith's attorneys was Francis Scott Key, future author of "The Star Spangled Banner." See Anne M. Butler, Wendy Wolff, and and Sheila P. Burke, *United States Senate Election, Expulsion and Censure Cases, 1973–1990*.
232   editorial in the *St. Paul Dispatch*: As quoted in *Literary Digest*, May 31, 1924, 15.
232   vote of fifty-six to five: 68th Cong., 1st sess., *Congressional Record*, 9279.
232   "Today . . . there is a prevailing belief": As quoted in *Literary Digest*, May 31, 1924, 15.

233   "no reason for a change": "Stone to Press Case Against Wheeler," *New York Times*, May 16, 1924.

233   "The circumstances under which": Frankfurter to Stone, May 21, 1924, Felix Frankfurter Papers, Harvard Law School Library.

233   "I think it would be well": Stone to Frankfurter, May 19, 1924.

Chapter 32: "Take into Custody the Body of M. S. Daugherty"

235   last-minute change of allegiance: Before throwing his support behind Harding, Miller directed the effort to nominate the early front-runner, General Leonard Wood. "Two Delaware Men Given Big Posts by Harding," *Chambersburg Public Opinion*, March 14, 1921.

236   German industrialist named Richard Merton appeared: For a good summary of the case, see Don Whitehead, *The FBI Story*, 74–76.

236   "$7,000,000 Paid by Daugherty in 'Queer' Deal": *Louisville Courier-Journal*, May 27, 1922.

237   personally asked the Office of the Alien Property Custodian: Interview of Henry I. Foster, February 5, 1927, DOJ Straight Numerical File 228730, NARA.

237   "praiseworthy": James N. Giglio, *H. M. Daugherty*, 183.

237   "Did you attend a dinner": Miller's initial testimony on May 15, 1924, can be found at *Investigation*, 2354–2380. He later testified again on June 6, 1924.

238   "somebody or some group": "No Mention of Swiss," *Louisville Courier Journal*, October 9, 1922.

238   opened his own investigation: Stone to Hoover, June 7, 1924, DOJ Straight Numerical File 228730-X, NARA.

238   one of two paths: For an introduction to contempt of Congress, see Todd Garvey, *Congress's Contempt Power and the Enforcement of Congressional Subpoenas*.

239   more likely to compel compliance: Garvey, *Congress's Contempt Power*, 1.

239   no mood to resist: 68th Cong., 1st sess., *Congressional Record*, 7215–7217.

239   signed arrest warrant in hand: "Senate Asks Arrest of Mal Daugherty," *New York Times*, April 27, 1924.

239   fled Washington Court House for Cincinnati: "Out o' Town!" *Cincinnati Enquirer*, April 28, 1924.

239   placed Mal Daugherty under arrest: Details on Daugherty's arrest and subsequent release come from "M.S. Daugherty Is Released on Writ of Habeas Corpus; Senate's Power Questioned," *Cincinnati Enquirer*, April 29, 1924; "Mal Daugherty Released Under Habeas Writ," *New York Herald-Tribune*, April 29, 1924; and "Warrant Is Served on Mal Daugherty," *New York Times*, April 29, 1924.

240   "Whichever way I decide": "Authority of Senate Questioned in Arguments on Daugherty Habeas Corpus Writ," *Cincinnati Enquirer*, May 21, 1924.

240   "I am compelled to hold": "'Mal' Daugherty Freed by Court," *Baltimore Sun*, June 1, 1924.

241   vowed to appeal directly to the Supreme Court: "Committee to Take Appeal," *Baltimore Sun*, June 1, 1924.

241   authorized by a vote of seventy to two: 68th Cong., 1st sess., *Congressional Record*, 10647.

Chapter 33: "Double Crossed"

242   **stout, bald man, immaculately dressed in a tailored gray suit:** "Paid Jess Smith $250,000, Says Bootleg Chief," *New York Tribune*, May 17, 1924.

242   **with a white silk shirt, black bow tie, and tan shoes:** Ulric Bell, "Remus Rum Bribes Put at $300,000," *Louisville Courier-Journal*, May 15, 1924.

242   **flanked on either side:** "Paid Jess Smith $250,000, Says Bootleg Chief."

242   **largest supplier of bootleg liquor:** Daniel Okrent, *Last Call*, 198–199.

242   **reportedly inspired F. Scott Fitzgerald:** The case for Remus as Fitzgerald's model is by no means open and shut. See Bob Batchelor, *The Bourbon King*, 338–342.

243   **"Now, these permits":** Dialogue from Remus's testimony comes from *Investigation*, 2395–2428; and "$300,000 Protection Paid to Jess Smith, Says 'Bootleg King,'" *New York Times*, May 17, 1924.

243   **piercing blue eyes:** "Paid Jess Smith $250,000, Says Bootleg Chief."

243   **kept the liquor flowing:** Okrent, *Last Call*, 198–199.

244   **presented canceled checks:** "Get Bootleg Checks in Daugherty Case," *New York Times*, June 8, 1924.

244   **"got afraid":** *Investigation*, 67.

245   **"That there never would be any conviction":** *Investigation*, 2404.

245   **spending his days shelving books:** *Investigation*, 2396.

245   **"Remus has been betrayed by everyone he had trusted":** Karen Abbott, *The Ghosts of Eden Park*, 133.

246   **"black strap pumps of the very latest style":** "Woman Sees Prohibition as National Issue," *San Francisco Chronicle*, July 29, 1922.

246   **celebrated her appointment:** Bob Batchelor, *The Bourbon King*, 125.

246   **turned her hatchet on America's bootleg king:** For the fascinating story of Mabel Walker Willebrandt and her pursuit of Remus, see Karen Abbott, *The Ghosts of Eden Park*.

246   **advance warning in October 1921 from his "protection sources":** Mary Chenoweth, "Remus Opens Way to Whisky Throne," *Louisville Courier-Journal*, March 1, 1926.

246   **received the maximum statutory penalty:** "Whisky Ring Members Guilty; Penitentiary Terms Imposed," *Cincinnati Enquirer*, May 17, 1922.

Chapter 34: "He Did Not Dare"

247   **clamored for an opportunity to defend himself:** That was ostensibly the reason he requested a Senate investigation of the charges against him in his February 11, 1924, open letter to Senator Willis. See "Daugherty Seeks Hearing on Ouster," *Baltimore Sun*, February 12, 1924.

247   **remained a rallying cry:** See, for example, Senator Willis's remarks on March 28, wherein he complained that Daugherty's ouster was premature because he "had not yet had an opportunity to defend himself before his investigators." "Ousting of Daugherty Starts Senate Debate," *New York Times*, March 29, 1924.

247   **115 witnesses in all:** Wheeler and Healy, *Yankee*, 244.

248 **eyeing a summer recess:** "Daugherty Halts Probe by Refusal to Appear on Stand," *St. Louis Globe Democrat*, June 5, 1924.

248 **salivated over the prospect:** "Call Daugherty to Testify Friday," *New York Times*, June 1, 1924.

248 **"I wish to make the announcement":** All dialogue from the committee's announcement that it would call Daugherty as a witness comes from *Investigation*, 2963.

248 **lengthy letter from the former attorney general:** *Investigation*, 3017–3033.

250 **"Mr. Daugherty's legal position":** "Mr. Daugherty's Avoidance," *New York Times*, June 5, 1924.

250 **"He did not dare":** "Senator Wheeler, Exposing the Corruption in Government, Calls upon Voters to 'Turn the Rascals' Out,'" *St. Louis Post Dispatch*, June 5, 1924.

Chapter 35: "Look Elsewhere for Leadership"

252 **rejected the progressive spirit:** Walter Nugent, *Progressivism*, 122.

252 **"the kept woman of Wall Street":** Nathan Miller, *New World Coming*, 135.

252 **"the chief business of America is business":** Miller, 134.

252 **a marathon event:** Miller, 164–168.

253 **asked Wheeler if he would accept:** Wheeler and Healy, *Yankee*, 247–248.

253 **echoed this request:** "1924," topical card file, Burton K. Wheeler Papers, 1922–1975, Montana State University Library.

253 **"When the Democratic Party goes to Wall Street":** Wheeler and Healy, *Yankee*, 249.

253 **organize a third-party bid:** Kenneth Campbell MacKay, *The Progressive Movement of 1924*, 110–122.

253 **politely declined:** MacKay, *The Progressive Movement of 1924*, 134.

253 **appeared at Wheeler's doorstep:** Wheeler and Healy, *Yankee*, 250.

253 **enormous pompadour of white hair:** Henry L. Stoddard, *As I Knew Them*, 550.

254 **"Listen, I can get out and talk":** Burton K. Wheeler, "Reminiscences of Burton Kendall Wheeler, 1969" [transcript of oral history interview], Columbia Center for Oral History (hereafter cited as Wheeler oral history), 107–108.

254 **never once spoken from a script:** Wheeler oral history, 107–108.

254 **couldn't recite the same stump speech:** Wheeler and Healy, *Yankee*, 250.

254 **a riot of color:** Elizabeth Wheeler Colman, *Mrs. Wheeler Goes to Washington*, 64.

254 **preparing a second indictment:** Wheeler and Healy, *Yankee*, 250.

255 **"Is that so?":** Wheeler oral history, 15.

255 **infuriated:** Donald John Cameron, "Burton K. Wheeler as Public Campaigner, 54.

255 **marches straight to La Follette's office:** Burton K. Wheeler to John M. Wheeler, January 3, 1968, Burton K. Wheeler papers [2207], Box 3, Folder 18.

255 **"I've changed my mind":** Wheeler oral history, 15.

255 **"if the offer is still available":** Cameron, "Burton K. Wheeler as Public Campaigner," 54.

Chapter 36: "The Usual Silence"

256   **Thunderclaps:** Donald John Cameron, "Burton K. Wheeler as Public Campaigner, 1922–1942," 56.

256   **sea of straw hats:** See the photo accompanying "Wheeler Sharply Scores Coolidge," *Boston Daily Globe*, September 2, 1924.

256   **horrid weather:** "Wheeler Sharply Scores Coolidge."

256   **"this den of iniquity":** The text of Wheeler's speech was reprinted in "Corruption, Wheeler's Theme," *Boston Daily Globe*, September 2, 1924.

257   **"a strong, silent man, who never speaks unless speech is required":** "The Mystery of Coolidge," *Christian Century*, May 22, 1924, 653.

257   **whipped off his coat:** "Wheeler Sharply Scores Coolidge."

257   **carried off the stage:** Cameron, "Burton K. Wheeler as Public Campaigner," 57, footnote 5.

257   **entered a federal courtroom:** "Demurrer First Step in Trial of Senator," *Butte Miner*, September 2, 1924.

257   **"an attempt to prostitute":** "Nelson Scents Political Plot in Wheeler's Case," *Baltimore Sun*, August 28, 1924.

257   **scheduled Wheeler's arraignment to coincide:** "Call Wheeler to Court Sept. 1," *Boston Globe*, August 27, 1924.

257   **given his blessing:** "Trial Call Upsets Wheeler Campaign," *New York Times*, August 27, 1924.

258   **"Your honor, we demur":** "Demurrer First Step in Trial of Senator."

258   **rushed to Wheeler's defense:** "Wheeler's Slate Clear as U.S. Attorney, Says Bourquin to Montanans," *Great Falls Tribune*, November 3, 1922.

258   **"unable to preside":** "Long Delay Looms for Wheeler Trial," *Great Falls Tribune*, September 2, 1924.

258   **one-man comedy sketch:** The precise phrasing varied from day to day, but I aggregated Wheeler's empty-chair routine from several newspaper accounts: "Wheeler Queries Coolidge on Issues," *New York Times*, November 2, 1924; "Senator Wheeler Satirizes Silence of the President," *Washington Post*, November 2, 1924; "Puts Coolidge on 'Stand,'" *Kansas City Times*, October 23, 1924; "Wheeler Opens Up on Coolidge," *Oklahoma Democrat*, October 23, 1924; "Wheeler Cross-Examines Pres. Coolidge by Proxy About Many Scandals," *Sacramento Star*, October 10, 1924; and "Wheeler Assails Coolidge Here as Silent and Weak," *St. Louis Star and Times*, October 25, 1924.

258   **an empty chair:** If all this sounds familiar, you may be thinking of Clint Eastwood's performance at the 2012 Republican National Convention, during which he interrogated an empty chair that sat in for an absent "Mr. Obama." Eastwood borrowed the gimmick from Wheeler. See Eyder Peralta, "Debating an Empty Chair? 'Eastwooding' Was a Thing Back in 1924," NPR, August 31, 2012, https://www.npr.org/sections/thetwo-way/2012/08/31/160391513/debating-an-empty-chair-eastwooding-was-a-thing-back-in-1924.

259   **low voice with nervous intensity:** Cameron, "Burton K. Wheeler as Public Campaigner," 134.

259   **invited hecklers:** "P. P. Campaign," topical card file, Burton K. Wheeler Papers, 1922–1975, Montana State University Library, card 5; and Cameron, "Burton K. Wheeler as Public Campaigner," 80.

259 **a baseball game:** It was a *Cleveland Plain Dealer* reporter, writing on September 18, 1924, quoted in Cameron, "Burton K. Wheeler as Public Campaigner," 67.

259 **"There is the possibility":** "Weeks Scores La Follette," *Boston Daily Globe,* October 12, 1924.

259 **his private worries:** Cameron, "Burton K. Wheeler as Public Campaigner," 50.

259 **"I believe they came out":** Wheeler and Healy, *Yankee,* 265.

260 **in Minneapolis:** Wheeler and Healy, 258.

260 **In Puyallup:** Cameron, "Burton K. Wheeler as Public Campaigner," 81.

260 **in Southern California:** Donald J. Cameron, "Burton K. Wheeler, Spokesman for the Progressive Movement," 168–169.

260 **"No prima donna":** Cameron, "Burton K. Wheeler, Spokesman for the Progressive Movement," 169.

260 **optimism overcame him:** "Wheeler Predicts Election Deadlock," *New York Times,* August 22, 1924.

260 **symbolic protest:** Richard T. Ruetten, "Burton K. Wheeler, 1905–1925," 139.

260 **felt assured of victory:** "Wheeler Predicts Election Deadlock."

260 **poll showed them winning six to nine states:** "Hughes Sees Victory as Campaign Ends; Roosevelt Confident; Smith and Davis Make Final Plea; La Follette Hopeful," *New York Times,* November 2, 1924.

260 **deadlock and fail to elect a president:** "Coolidge or Deadlock," *New York Herald-Tribune,* October 19, 1924.

260 **"What will happen under the administration":** Gilson Gardner, "Our Next President: La Follette or Wheeler," *Nation,* September 17, 1924.

260 **took the stage at the Ohio state fairgrounds:** *Dayton Daily News,* September 19, 1924.

261 **Daugherty himself would be in the audience:** Cameron, "Burton K. Wheeler as Public Campaigner," 69.

261 **process server would mount the podium:** "Wheeler Predicts Suit," *New York Times,* September 18, 1924.

261 **"blackmail suits and framed indictments":** "Wheeler at Toledo Assails 'Ohio Gang,'" *New York Times,* September 19, 1924.

261 **"the Daugherty system":** "Thru Area of Enemies," *Lincoln Journal Star,* September 19, 1924.

261 **"Ohio gang":** "Thru Area of Enemies."

261 **shouted and cheered and roared in laughter:** "Wheeler Arouses Ohioans to Cheers by His Attacks on Republican Corruption," *Baltimore Sun,* September 19, 1924.

261 **"I expected to be run out":** "Wheeler Raps Daugherty in Ohio Speech," *Green Bay Press Gazette,* September 19, 1924.

261 **"I challenge Daugherty":** "Thru Area of Enemies," *Lincoln Journal Star,* September 19, 1924.

261 **"Wheeler has come and gone":** "Wheeler a 'Liar,' Says Daugherty," *New York Times,* September 20, 1924.

262 **failed to qualify for the ballot:** Marc C. Johnson, *Political Hell-Raiser,* 84.

262 **huge disparity in fundraising:** Johnson, *Political Hell-Raiser,* 95.

262 **disastrous last-minute change:** Cameron, "Burton K. Wheeler as Public Campaigner," 87–88, note 89.

262   **"The people voted"**: "'Not Surprised,' Says Wheeler," *New York Times*, November 6, 1924.

263   **long-delayed hunting trip**: "'Not Surprised,' Says Wheeler.'"

Chapter 37: "He Is Asking Justice"

264   **only the fifth in US history**: Anne M. Butler, Wendy Wolff, and Sheila P. Burke, *United States Senate Election, Expulsion, and Censure Cases, 1793–1990*.

265   **Crowds swarmed the entrance**: "Chief Figures in the Wheeler Case," *New York Times*, April 25, 1925.

265   **Newly strung telegraph wires**: "Trial Scribes Gain Numbers," *Great Falls Tribune*, April 15, 1925.

265   **seventy-five subpoenaed witnesses**: "Politics to Figure in Wheeler's Trial," *New York Times*, April 16, 1925.

265   **spiritualist minister**: "Rev. Cora Kincannon Lectures Wednesday," *Great Falls Tribune*, April 21, 1925.

265   **group of Blackfeet**: Elizabeth Wheeler Colman, *Mrs. Wheeler Goes to Washington*, 102.

265   **swarmed into town**: "Detectives Gather for Wheeler Case," *New York Times*, April 15, 1925.

265   **"Great Falls is busy"**: "Detectives Gather for Wheeler Case."

265   **"agents are always on hand"**: "Detectives Gather for Wheeler Case."

265   **orchestrated by John Edgar Hoover**: See, for instance, Hoover to Daly, date redacted, FBI file on Burton K. Wheeler, 62-7903-309.

265   **"checking hotel registers"**: Report of Special Agent W. W. Spain, April 15, 1925, FBI file on Burton K. Wheeler, 62-7903-330.

266   **"surveillance of persons"**: Report of Special Agent W. F. Scery, April 24, 1924, FBI file on Burton K. Wheeler, 62-7903-404.

266   **"engaged in under cover work"**: Report of C. C. Spears, April 23, 1925, FBI file on Burton K. Wheeler, 62-7903-409.

266   **"confidential matters"**: Report of W. A. Carroll, April 29, 1925, FBI file on Burton K. Wheeler, 62-7903-410.

266   **some twenty-five special agents**: Wheeler and Healy, *Yankee*, 239.

266   **"like a Justice Department convention"**: Wheeler and Healy, 239.

266   **nine months pregnant**: Wheeler and Healy, 241.

266   **he worried**: "1925 indictment and trial," topical card file, Burton K. Wheeler Papers, 1922–1975, Montana State University Library, card 3.

266   **legal dream team**: "Chief Figures in the Wheeler Case," *New York Times*, April 25, 1925.

267   **"any service rendered"**: 68th Cong., 1st sess., *Congressional Record*, 9278.

267   **twelve laymen**: "Surprise Evidence Due, Says Slattery," *Great Falls Tribune*, April 17, 1925.

267   **"answer all my critics"**: "Daugherty to Tell All," *New York Tribune*, March 31, 1925.

267   **sequestering the entire jury**: "Wheeler Goes on Trial; Coup Scored by U.S.," *Chicago Daily Tribune*, April 17, 1925.

268   **now under Stone's handpicked chief**: "Picturesque in Peace as Well as In War," *Boston Daily Globe*, April 5, 1925.

268   **obtained a long-threatened second indictment**: Richard Dunlop, *Donovan*, 154.

268 **announced a sensational development:** "Surprise Evidence Due, Says Slattery," *Great Falls Tribune*, April 17, 1925.

268 **"I won't divulge his name":** "Million Dollar Oil Plot Laid to Montana Solon," *Minneapolis Star*, April 17, 1925.

268 **"GEORGE B. HAYES!":** "Wheeler Offered Fee Split, Lawyer Testifies; Feely Served Campbell Interests, Says Booth," *Great Falls Tribune*, April 21, 1925.

268 **parade of prosecution witnesses:** Richard T. Ruetten, "Burton K. Wheeler, 1905–1925: An Independent Liberal Under Fire," 1957, 186.

269 **smiled broadly:** "G.B. Hayes Swears to Wheeler Deal for Oil Fee Split," *New York Times*, April 21, 1925.

269 **name didn't register:** Wheeler wrote that he didn't recognize Hayes at first. Wheeler and Healy, *Yankee*, 239.

269 **gray-haired man:** "G.B. Hayes Swears to Wheeler Deal for Oil Fee Split," *New York Times*, April 21, 1925.

269 **sharp, angular features:** Courtroom sketch by Don Stevens, "Surprise Witness," *Great Falls Tribune*, April 22, 1925.

269 **built like a middle-aged boxer:** "Chief Figures in the Wheeler Trial," *New York Times*, April 26, 1925.

269 **"would kill his mother for five cents":** "Witness Assailed Hayes During Daugherty Probe," *Boston Daily Globe*, April 23, 1925.

269 **"Do you know the defendant":** Unless otherwise noted, dialogue from Hayes's testimony comes from "G.B. Hayes Swears to Wheeler Deal for Oil Fee Split," *New York Times*, April 21, 1925; "Wheeler Offered Fee Split, Lawyer Testifies; Feely Served Campbell Interests, Says Booth," *Great Falls Tribune*, April 21, 1925; and Philip Kinsley, "Government's Side of Wheeler Case Is Finished," *Chicago Daily Tribune*, April 21, 1925.

269 **spoke at a machine-gun pace:** "Chief Figures in the Wheeler Trial," *New York Times*, April 26, 1925; and "G.B. Hayes Swears to Wheeler Deal for Oil Fee Split," *New York Times*, April 21, 1925.

270 **stared at the witness:** "Mr. Wheeler was facing the witness and his eyes never left him," the *New York Times* reported.

270 **damning it was:** The *Chicago Daily Tribune* commented that it immediately "changed the complexion of the case." Philip Kinsley, "U.S. Backs Up Phone Story in Wheeler Case," *Chicago Daily Tribune*, April 22, 1925.

271 **seized on the fact:** Dayton Stoddard, unpublished manuscript for Burton K. Wheeler biography, Burton Kendall Wheeler papers, 1910–1972 [MC 34], Montana Historical Society, E-9.

271 **hadn't been alone:** Wheeler and Healy, *Yankee*, 240.

272 **mountain of legal trouble:** Wheeler and Healy, *Yankee*, 243; and Basil Manly, *The Leading Facts in the Wheeler Case*, 18–19.

272 **"obtained under false pretenses":** Manly, *The Leading Facts in the Wheeler Case*, 19.

272 **lined up five witnesses:** "Booth Denies Asking Hayes Meet Wheeler," *Great Falls Tribune*, April 22, 1925.

272 **hear Eddie Booth:** "Booth Denies Asking Hayes Meet Wheeler."

272 **hear Arthur B. Melzner:** "Wheeler Defense Suddenly Closes; Argue Case Today," *New York Times*, April 24, 1925.

273 **hear William G. Feely:** "Hayes' Story of N.Y. Meeting Untrue, Says Senator on Stand," *Great Falls Tribune*, April 23, 1925.

273   **settled into the witness chair:** Unless otherwise noted, details and dialogue from Wheeler's testimony comes from "Hayes' Story of N.Y. Meeting Untrue, Says Senator on Stand," *Great Falls Tribune*, April 23, 1925; "Jurymen May Start Deliberation Today," *Great Falls Tribune*, April 24, 1925; "Wheeler Declares Fee Charge False," *New York Times*, April 23, 1925; "Wheeler Defense Suddenly Closes; Argue Case Today," *New York Times*, April 24, 1925; Philip Kinsley, "Senator Fights on Stand for Name and Toga," *Chicago Daily Tribune*, April 23, 1925; and Philip Kinsley, "Wheeler Sees Acquittal as Case Nears End," *Chicago Daily Tribune*, April 24, 1925.

276   **verdict was in:** Unless otherwise noted, details and dialogue from the announcement of the verdict come from several newspaper accounts: "Wheeler Free on 1st Ballot in Oil Trial," *New York Tribune*, April 25, 1925; "Wheeler Is Found Not Guilty," *Great Falls Tribune*, April 25, 1925; "Senator Wheeler Is Acquitted of Wrongfully Using Position as Stork Pays Visit to Home," *Indianapolis Star*; April 25, 1925; "Wheeler Freed, Doubly Happy," *Boston Daily Globe*, April 25, 1925; "Senator Wheeler Acquitted by Jury," *Butte Miner*, April 25, 1925; and "Wheeler Acquitted on a Single Ballot After Ten Minutes," *New York Times*, April 25, 1925.

276   **"A jury's duty":** "Wheeler Is Found Not Guilty," *Great Falls Tribune*, April 25, 1925.

276   **"The district attorney tells you":** "Wheeler Is Found Not Guilty."

277   **lit up his face:** "Wheeler Is Found Not Guilty."

277   **dine on the tab of the district court:** "Wheeler Free on 1st Ballot in Oil Trial," *New York Tribune*, April 25, 1925.

277   **crowded around a smiling Wheeler:** "Wheeler Free on 1st Ballot in Oil Trial."

277   **"It was just a case for me":** "Wheeler Free on 1st Ballot in Oil Trial."

277   **"I've got someone . . . who'll throw Hayes":** The story of the butcher's offer comes from Wheeler and Healy, *Yankee*, 241–242.

278   **delivered a baby girl:** "Wheeler Is Found Not Guilty," *Great Falls Tribune*, April 25, 1925.

Epilogue: "The Triumph of Justice"

279   **"one of the most contemptible":** Quoted at Don Whitehead, *The FBI Story*, 64.

279   **the benefit of the doubt:** Wheeler and Healy, *Yankee*, 243.

279   **interview George B. Hayes:** John Edgar Hoover was instrumental in tracking down Hayes, who had been working in Havana at the time, and delivering him to Pratt. FBI file 62-7903-247, -271, and -304.

279   **had every opportunity:** To be clear, there is no direct evidence that Pratt ever suborned perjury or otherwise doctored the evidence against Wheeler. Given his earlier denunciation of Wheeler and the circumstances behind his appointment, however, his complicity certainly seems more plausible than Donovan's.

279   **suspected Assistant Attorney General Donovan:** Wheeler and Healy, *Yankee*, 243. Donovan (with Slattery) also met with Hayes, although not before Pratt had met with him. Potentially exculpatory for Donovan is the fact that Pratt was already working up a second indictment against Wheeler before Donovan ever accepted a job at Justice Department headquarters.

280   **placed his own predecessor in his legal crosshairs:** The often-unacknowledged story of how Stone personally investigated his predecessor for criminal wrong-doing comes from Stone to Mack, October 22, 1926, Frankfurter Papers, Harvard Law Library; Whitehead, *FBI Story*, 76; and DOJ Straight Numerical File 228730, NARA.

280   **"As far as I know":** Stone to Mack, October 22, 1926, Frankfurter Papers, Harvard Law Library.

280   **$224,000 to the Midland National Bank:** Robert H. Ferrell, *The Strange Deaths of President Harding*, 49.

280   **hauled the former attorney general before a grand jury:** James N. Giglio, *H. M. Daugherty*, 183–184.

280   **"I refuse to testify":** Giglio, *H. M. Daugherty*, 184.

281   **burned them:** "Mal S. Daugherty Says His Brother Burned Records," *Washington Post*, February 16, 1927.

281   **stood trial in a New York courtroom:** Giglio, *H. M. Daugherty*, 187–189.

281   **would have convicted:** Giglio, 188–189.

281   **retried the case:** Giglio, 189–192.

281   **"the florist at the Hotel Astor":** Martin Mayer, *Emory Buckner*, 223.

281   **"I have never tried a case three times":** Transcript of second Miller-Daugherty trial, 2330-31, records of the Miller-Daugherty trial, Box 12, NARA.

281   **"May it please the court":** Transcript of second Miller-Daugherty trial, 2333-32, records of the Miller-Daugherty trial, Box 12, NARA. Daugherty was referring to President Grant's attorney general, George Henry Williams, who as mayor of Portland, Oregon, was tried and acquitted in 1905 for refusing to enforce laws against gambling.

281   **"The jury . . . in convicting Miller":** "'Miller Merely a Pawn,'" *News-Herald* (Franklin, PA), March 4, 1927.

282   **eleven-month stay:** "T. W. Miller Quits Penitentiary Today," *Washington Post*, May 7, 1929.

282   **convictions against five coconspirators:** "'Tex' Rickard Fined $7,000 in Fight Film Case," *New York Herald-Tribune*, March 31, 1925.

282   **only Fall was ever convicted:** M. R. Werner and John Starr, *The Teapot Dome Scandal*, 266–295.

282   **"a car as long as this block":** Bruce Bliven, "Tempest over Teapot," *American Heritage* 16, no. 5 (August 1965): 102.

282   **"made fraudulently":** *Mammoth Oil Co. v. United States*, 275 U.S. 13 (1927).

282   **"a faithless public officer":** *Mammoth Oil Co. v. United States*.

283   **"We conclude . . . that the investigation was ordered":** *McGrain v. Daugherty*, 273 U.S. 135 (1927).

283   **"We are of opinion . . . that the power of inquiry":** *McGrain v. Daugherty*.

283   **sustain generations of congressional investigators:** See, for instance, *Trump v. Mazars USA, LLP*, 140 S. Ct. 2019 (2020), which cites *McGrain* extensively (including a curious digression about the facts of the case in a dissent by Justice Clarence Thomas).

283   **April 15, 1926, testimonial dinner:** "Wheeler Asks Fund to Aid Brookhart," *Baltimore Sun*, April 15, 1926. Additional details about the "Civic Victory Dinner"—including the menu and printed invitation—can be found in Box 23, Folder 6, of the Burton Kendall Wheeler papers, Montana Historical Society.

283 **judge's recent dismissal:** "Conspiracy Case Against Wheeler Voided by Court," *New York Tribune*, December 30, 1925.

283 **"the triumph of justice":** "Wheeler Scores Brookhart Vote," *Washington Evening Star*, April 16, 1926.

284 **"The most hopeful thing":** "Wheeler Scores Brookhart Vote."

284 **few Americans remember him:** Wheeler's biographer considers his complicated legacy and the sometimes malicious slander of his memory in Marc C. Johnson, *Political Hell-Raiser*, 261–270.

285 **inspiration for 1939's *Mr. Smith Goes to Washington*:** Michael P. Rogin and Kathleen Moran, "Mr. Capra Goes to Washington," *Representations* 84, no. 1 (November 2003): 213–248.

285 **two episodes of *The Simpsons*:** "Mr. Smith Goes to Washington," Simpson Wiki, accessed July 4, 2022, https://simpsons.fandom.com/wiki/Mr._Smith _Goes_to_Washington.

286 **December 10, 1924:** This date has been misreported as December 19, but Hoover's official appointment letter is dated December 10, 1924. See Stone to Hoover, FBI file 67-561-2.

286 **"a man of exceptional intelligence":** Curt Gentry, *J. Edgar Hoover*, 142.

286 **"This Bureau cannot afford":** Quoted at Richard Gid Powers, *Secrecy and Power*, 144.

286 **now going by J. Edgar:** Kenneth D. Ackerman, *Young J. Edgar*, 380.

286 **"far greater promise":** Quoted at Alpheus Thomas Mason, *Harlan Fiske Stone*, 152.

287 **"Hoover has been zealous":** Stone to Frankfurter, January 19, 1925, Frankfurter papers, Harvard Law Library.

287 **"Hoover . . . might be a very effective":** Frankfurter to Stone, January 22, 1925, Frankfurter papers, Harvard Law Library.

287 **only a single column-inch:** "J. E. Hoover Succeeds W. J. Burns," *New York Times*, December 23, 1924.

287 **without any trace of a smile:** Gentry, *J. Edgar Hoover*, 142.

288 **"architect of the modern surveillance state":** Tim Weiner, *Enemies*, xvi.

Index